ARCHAEOLOGICAL INSTITUTE *of* AMERICA

118TH ANNUAL MEETING
ABSTRACTS

VOLUME 40

■ January 5–8, 2017 ■ Toronto, Ontario, Canada ■

Published by the Archaeological Institute of America
Located at Boston University
656 Beacon Street
Boston, Massachusetts 02215-2006
www.archaeological.org

Cover Illustration: View of CN Tower and Toronto waterfront from Lake Ontario. Image by Tom Moeres, Lifestyle-Pictures.de

Printed in Canada
ISBN-10: 1-931909-35-0
ISBN-13: 978-1931909358

Abstracts appear in the order of presentation and represent papers accepted by the Program Committee during its review process in the months of April and September 2016. Adjustments to the program or to individual abstracts made after November 30, 2016 are not reflected in this publication.

CONTENTS

Session 1

Session 2

Session 3

Session 4

Session 5

Session 6

Session 7

SESSION 1A: Colloquium
Transformative Movement

Sponsored by the Roman Provincial Archaeology Interest Group

ORGANIZERS: *Alexander Meyer*, University of Western Ontario, and *Kathryn McBride*, Brown University

Colloquium Overview Statement

In 2014, Miguel John Versluys argued that romanization studies should move toward globalization theory and the close study of material cultural per se in order to reinvigorate the romanization debate. Furthermore, he maintained that "objects in motion" are, or should be, primary to the study of Roman archaeology and our understanding of what constituted the Roman world. This session will accept Versluys' challenge by exploring objects in motion and the networks to which they belong. Specifically, it will investigate the ways in which the transgression of zones of interaction (be they borders, frontiers, or other conceptual boundaries) can change the meaning and value of objects, material, and practices in the eyes of those who import and export them. Understanding how and why these transformations take place can tell us about the cultures that received and used these objects and ideas; it also nuances the way we think about the relationship between the two cultures and how they were entangled with each other.

This colloquium will engage with the topic of transformative movement in a selection of papers that span the breadth of the Roman world, both chronologically and geographically. One of these papers will examine the meaning and significance of obelisks when they were removed from Egypt and found new homes in Rome and Constantinople. Another will examine the reuse and reinterpretation of imperial gold medallions in Scandinavia. A third will discuss the interpretation of payments of gold made by the Late Antique imperial administration to so-called barbarian tribes. The fourth paper will continue the theme of the use of precious metals but will focus on the use of Greek and Roman iconography prior to long-term and sustained contact with Rome and the abandonment of this iconography in the face of the threat of Roman conquest. The final paper will further expand the idea of transformation through movement by discussing the significance of the movement of an entire craft from the Continent to Britain during the period of Roman conquest and by discussing the significance of the glass bracelets it produced. As a whole, these papers will explore the various ways in which objects and ideas moved into and out of the empire's borders in order to highlight the connectivity that we believe should be more of a focus of current work in Roman archaeology.

Obelisks as Meaning in Motion

Grant Parker, Stanford University

A strong case can be made that the Roman fascination with obelisks had as much to do with movement as it did with the objects themselves. Indeed, movement is a paradox, given their enormous size. Both Pliny (*HN* 36.68 - 71) and Ammianus (*Res Gestae* 17.4.12 - 15), in their discussions of obelisks, focus at some length on the circumstances of their transportation. In such texts, the eventual arrival of the obelisks at Rome comes across as an engineering feat, the meaning of the object arguably encapsulated in its sheer bulk. The emperor Julian, writing to the Alexandrians, requests a collapsed obelisk and offers a colossal statue, presumably of himself, in exchange (Letter 48 [Wright], 363 C.E.). Once in its new location, argues Julian, this obelisk would impress any Alexandrian sailing into the harbor of Constantinople and thus bolster economic and diplomatic ties between the two cities: "It cannot but give you pleasure to have something that has belonged to you standing [in Constantinople], and as you sail towards that city you will delight in gazing at it." By the same token, many inscriptions also make reference to transportation, notably *CIL* 6 1163 (now lost, once inscribed below the obelisk Constantius had brought to Rome).

Such texts not only help us to consider Roman heavy transportation and the ideas associated with it; they also give us clues to the social meanings involved. To be sure, obelisks are charismatic objects rather than bulk commodities. The term "appropriation" seems relevant: here we have a chance to unpack it a little, tracing connections between physical and metaphorical movement. What role did the use of inscriptions play? Certainly the presence of hieroglyphics on obelisks was one of their distinctive features, a topic that engages Ammianus especially (17.4.17 - 23; cf. Plin. 36.64). Yet we ought also to consider how their sheer size, their charismatic and exotic nature, the cross-cultural encounter that they embodied, the distinctiveness of Egypt within the Roman thought-world, and the fact that for centuries Egyptians had fetishized elements of their own past invested the transportation of obelisks with special significance in the imperial Roman world.

All told, obelisks provide rich material by which to consider what meanings attended relocation, and even more tellingly how those meanings were created. While movement is a significant phenomenon in itself, subject to physical measurement, it is also a powerful metaphor for transformations of cultural context and meaning.

Networks and Entanglements from Rome to Scandinavia: Medallions on the Move

Nancy L. Wicker, University of Mississippi

Scandinavia lies far from the Roman empire, yet Roman objects, including fourth-century imperial medallions, are found in Denmark, Norway, and Sweden. The mechanisms by which they reached the north are uncertain; however, it seems that both eastern and western networks, through the Danubian region and also via the Rhine, may have been the transportation conduits. Northerners who had served in the Roman army most likely brought these medallions home to Scandinavia upon retirement after a military career. Although efforts to track specific northern soldiers have had little success, perhaps because Germanic names were often Romanized and thus are not identifiable, medallions discovered in Scandinavian graves and hoards betray evidence of long-distance contact between individuals. Furthermore, the movement of these artifacts was accompanied by transformations of their use and social significance. Once medallions reached Scandinavia, their function apparently changed in the new environment from male ornaments of military rank and favor to something else entirely.

In fact, display of a gold ornament of this type on the chest became so popular in Scandinavia and nearby areas that the original supply of imported Roman medallions was insufficient to meet the demand for them. Therefore, imitation medallions were produced; in addition, a new local type of object known as the Scandinavian bracteate emerged in the fifth century. These new objects were deposited exclusively in female burials, except for a few anomalous examples placed in the mouths of males and interpreted as Charon's coins. Furthermore, bracteate imagery undergoes a gradual transformation away from Roman imperial iconography, becoming "de-Romanized" into a Germanic, barbarian animal style. However, even in the fifth and sixth centuries, bracteates were made from melted-down Late Roman and Byzantine solidi, so even as their iconographic types and apparent meaning deviated from Roman motifs, these derivative objects were still entangled with the Roman world, at least through their gold content. This case study provides an elegant example of how artifacts of political and social significance could be reinterpreted, repurposed, and elaborated upon when transported into a new cultural milieu.

Power and Prestige: Late Roman Gold Outside the Empire
Peter Guest, Cardiff University

Late Roman gold solidi of the fifth and sixth centuries are found as often outside the boundaries of the empire as within, both as hoards and as single finds. These finds reveal the existence of formal links between the Roman imperial court and so-called barbarian peoples beyond the frontiers, though the nature of these connections is not necessarily as clear as it might at first appear. Modern scholarship has tended to focus on the mechanisms by which Roman gold arrived in the hands of barbarians-whether as war booty, tribute payments, or subsidies. This line of reasoning tends to assume that all parties, Romans and barbarians, perceived gold coins in the same ways, yet it is clear that solidi could perform a variety of roles and functions depending on the specific social context in which they were being used. This paper will explore the archaeological and historical evidence for Roman solidi as cultural as well as economic artifacts, proposing that a better appreciation of how these coins were perceived by the people that owned and exchanged them is needed if we are to understand what they tell us about the relationships between the later Roman empire and its barbarian neighbors.

Connectivity and Identity in Roman-Era South Arabia
Kathryn McBride, Brown University

The region of ancient South Arabia escaped conquest by the Assyrians, Persians, and Alexander the Great, although its valuable natural resources and lucrative trade routes remained remarkably tempting. The Roman annexation of Egypt in 31 B.C.E. and the (ultimately unsuccessful) invasion of South Arabia by the Roman prefect Aelius Gallus, in 26/5 B.C.E., however, shows that Rome had set its sights on becoming the dominant power in the southeast Mediterranean and the Arabian Peninsula. It is this interaction, between the geographically isolated southern tip of the Arabian Peninsula and the steamrolling power of Roman imperialism, that caused dramatic and dynamic changes in ancient South Arabia. This paper explores how South Arabia reacted to this increased level of connectivity with the wider Roman-controlled Mediterranean in the first century B.C.E. through the first century C.E. and how that reaction manifested itself within the material culture of the region, particularly in regard to changes within local coinage traditions.

This paper traces the development of coin types and iconography through this tumultuous period of South Arabian history to highlight how choices made regarding the forms, technology, and script of local coinage reflected local attitudes toward external forces. By doing so, I demonstrate how Greek, Roman, and local iconography, text, and traditions could be reinterpreted and revalued outside of Greek and Roman territory. While several of the earliest South Arabian coin types were silver imitations of Athenian tetradrachms (a common practice in the eastern Mediterranean, as Athenian coins were the most widely recognized and stable coinage of the time), the inclusion of South Arabian symbols and monograms had both economic and social implications. These coins evolved into a much more recognizably Roman style in the final years of the first millennium B.C.E. However, in a dramatic and sudden shift in the mid first century C.E., the coinage completely dropped any Mediterranean characteristics; its form was altered, and the technology of production changed substantially. Counterintuitively, this shift to a distinctly South Arabian style coincided with the advent of frequent and long-term contact between this region and the wider Roman world. The reimaging of the coinage of this region, I argue, reflects a larger process of solidifying a South Arabian identity that embodied the region's once great strength (the monopoly and trade of its rare natural resources) in the face of a growing Roman threat.

Romano-British Glass Bracelets: Transformation of La Tène Continental Technology to Fit Iron Age British Design

Tatiana Ivleva, Newcastle University

This paper presents a case study of the networks of interaction between craftspeople of various communities associated with the production and development of Romano-British glass bracelets. It argues that the British glass bracelets were a Roman-period British development of an existing Continental La Tène skill and as such represent the transfer and continuation of a pre-Roman tradition in the face of Roman conquest.

The European Northwest in the Late Iron Age and Roman period is conspicuous for the high occurrence of glass annular adornments, usually referred to as glass bracelets or armlets. The start of the production of glass annulars is dated to the second quarter of the third century B.C.E. It began in the heart of the La Tène cultural area, central Europe and spread farther west to Gaul and Germany in subsequent periods. With the arrival of Rome in the late first century B.C.E., the circulation of glass bracelets decreased, yet the craft reappeared in the periphery of the Roman empire, in Roman Britain, where it peaked in late first to mid second century C.E.

Earlier research into the distribution and typology of Romano-British glass bracelets suggested that British examples stand out in their decorative and production technique compared with bracelets made on the Continent. Moreover, Roman

Britain had no history of glass bracelet production prior to the Roman invasion in 43 C.E. This paper attempts to answer the question as to where the inspiration and skills for British glass bracelets came from by discussing their production technique. Experiments conducted by modern glassmakers and close inspection of the British glass bracelet fragments reveal that British annulars were most likely produced in a similar manner as some of the La Tène Continental bracelet types. However, the design of British bracelets is rather different from that of Continental ones. Most British annulars have either twisted cord decorations or trails with curved terminals. A convincing hypothesis was put forward by the earlier scholars that the design of some British bracelet types was probably closely related to, or may well have been developed from, the British insular Iron Age beads.

In the end, the paper emphasizes the transformative nature of craft and technology. By transferring La Tène glass bracelet technique to the British ground, craftspeople created unique regional variation of glass bracelets, the design of which became as popular among the native population as it was among newcomers, including the Roman army.

SESSION 1B: Workshop
Fresh in the Field: New Research and Resources in the Study of Ancient Surface Decoration

Sponsored by the Ancient Painting Studies Interest Group

MODERATOR: *Elizabeth M. Molacek*, Harvard University

Workshop Overview Statement

Bringing together archaeologists, conservators, curators, and others interested in ancient surface decoration, "Fresh in the Field: New Research and Resources in the Study of Ancient Surface Decoration" is a forum to share, discuss, and generate feedback regarding the newest research. While open sessions and colloquia provide access to finished or highly developed projects, this workshop intentionally highlights research in progress, often in the very early stages.

The workshop is sponsored by the Ancient Painting Studies Interest Group (APSIG), the North American correlative of the Association Internationale pour la Peinture Murale Antique, and is a forum for all individuals researching ancient painting and other forms of surface decoration. Like its European counterpart, APSIG aims to foster communication among scholars, and with this goal in mind the workshop draws on the diverse intellectual strengths of the APSIG community to increase conversation surrounding our shared interests.

Intentionally varied in chronologic, geographic, and cultural scope, the presentation topics offer a snapshot of current research in progress by scholars in varying stages of their careers. Egan, Rousseau, and Lucore each present new fieldwork to expand our understanding of well-known sites (Pylos, Sardis, and Morgantina, respectively); Berlin and Swetnam-Burland both offer new methods for the study of familiar material (domestic surface decoration); and Lakin uses a case study to demonstrate the possibilities of three-dimensional scanning to enhance the process of reassembling wall painting fragments. Finally, Cook expands our categorization of surface decoration, discussing a preliminary analysis of pigments on the surface of lapis basanites, the popular Egyptian stone.

Although structured around seven presentations, the session will rely equally on audience feedback and participation. It is meant as a productive environment in which to discuss new fieldwork and fresh approaches and even to raise questions or problems in hopes that others in the group might have insight. Through collegial conversation, this workshop hopes to move the field forward in new and interesting ways as well as to promote a community of intellectual collaboration.

PANELISTS: *Emily Egan*, University of Maryland, *Vanessa Rousseau*, Weisman Art Museum, *Sandra K. Lucore*, American Excavations at Morgantina, *Nicole Berlin*, Johns Hopkins University, *Molly Swetnam-Burland*, College of William and Mary, *Lara Lakin*, Radboud University, and *Emily Cook*, Columbia University

SESSION 1C: Colloquium
The Technological Revolution and Archaeology: New Ways of Understanding the Past

ORGANIZER: *Andrew M.T. Moore*, Rochester Institute of Technology

Colloquium Overview Statement

Technology has transformed our professional and personal lives. It has had an equally massive impact on archaeology. New technologies are fundamentally changing the way archaeology is practiced in the field and in the laboratory. Technological advances are leading to new ways of thinking about the past and are stimulating new interpretations of archaeological evidence for past human activities. This colloquium will explore these issues through a series of case studies that illuminate how technology is changing archaeology and consider the broader implications of its effects.

New imaging techniques allow us to see both the very small and the near invisible. Advances in remote sensing reveal whole landscapes from above with high precision, leading to the discovery of new sites. Related techniques expand our ability to detect subsurface structures on archaeological sites, thus bringing vastly greater accuracy to excavation strategies. Ever more refined radiometric dating enables us to detect synchronisms, and thus new possibilities for cause and effect, in past events. Advances in computing make it possible to generate and analyze vast data sets, opening up new ways of investigating the past. New modes of data presentation not only bring the past to life for broader audiences but also open up new possibilities for analysis. Genetic studies are bringing new insights and greater precision to our understanding of human relationships and past population movements from the earliest times. Molecular analyses are clarifying the interactions between humans, diet, and disease.

The participants in this colloquium argue that these and other advances do not simply enable us to do archaeology in new, more efficient ways. They are transforming the way that we think about human cultural development in the past.

Isotope Analysis of Neanderthal and Modern Human Diets

Michael Richards, Simon Fraser University

Isotope analysis of human remains is a powerful method for looking at past human diets and migrations. These isotope methods allow us to have direct measures of diet and mobility, as they use the human remains themselves. They can also be used to look at broad-scale dietary changes and migrations, but also at the scale of the individual to reconstruct the life history of that person.

In this presentation I briefly introduce isotope methods and will then focus on three case studies to illustrate the impact these methods have had in archaeology.

The first case study is on using isotopes to determine the diets of our closest relatives, the Neanderthals, and contrasting them with early modern humans in Europe. This research has shown that both were successful hunters, but there is evidence that modern humans had a broader dietary adaptation, which may have given them an advantage over Neanderthals.

For the other two case studies, I discuss the application of isotopic methods to much more recent time periods, where they can be particularly useful for identifying social and gender differences in diets within formal cemeteries. First I present data on isotope analysis for diet and migration in Bronze Age (Minoan) Crete, and then I discuss an on-going research project in southwest Turkey exploring diet and migration in the Roman and Byzantine periods.

The Younger Dryas Cosmic Impact Cataclysm 12,800 Years Ago: Extinction of Ice Age Giants, Disruption of Human Culture, and Abrupt Climate Change

James P. Kennett, University of California Santa Barbara, *Allen West*, Geosciences Consulting, and *Douglas J. Kennett*, Pennsylvania State University

We have discovered remarkable, widespread geological and archaeological evidence for a major cosmic collision (airbursts/impacts) with Earth 12,800 years ago (+/-150 years; 2σ). Massive energy release from this impact caused widespread biomass burning and other severe biotic and environmental changes, including broad disruption of continental vegetation. The event formed the widely distributed Younger Dryas Boundary (YDB) layer, containing peak abundances in multiple, impact-related proxies, including high-temperature, quenched spherules, melt-glass, nanodiamonds, carbon spherules, and anomalous concentrations of platinum, iridium, osmium, and nickel. The YDB cosmic impact hypothesis is consistent with explaining at least three major events that have long puzzled the scientific community: (1) the massive, abrupt extinction of large Late Pleistocene mammalian taxa (e.g., mammoths, camels, horses, sloths, saber-tooth cats) and large birds; (2) the abrupt disappearance of the widespread Clovis Technological Complex and associated human population decline; and (3) the triggering of abrupt cooling over broad areas of Earth and associated change in North American continental plumbing, outburst flooding into adjacent oceans, and major changes in oceanic meridional overturning.

The discovery of the YDB cosmic impact event, its effects, and implications has required a revision in thinking about the nature of past human cultural development and its causes. This, in turn, is the product of employing a wide array of modern scientific and technological approaches as follows.

A Space-Based Approach: The Future of Archaeology or Standard Practice?

Sarah H. Parcak, University of Alabama at Birmingham

Today, in archaeology, we face many opportunities and challenges. With rapid innovations in technology, we are able to see further and deeper into the past than ever before. New questions about our human origins, how and when we have evolved, and societal growth and collapse are being asked every day. At the same time, climate change, urbanization, war, and development are affecting thousands of archaeological sites. Site destruction in the Middle East has made near daily headlines for the past three years, affecting our colleagues and friends in many of the countries we have been fortunate to work and live in during fieldwork and sabbaticals. Many of us feel as though we are losing a battle. What, then, should our response be to all of these challenges and opportunities?

This paper discusses new approaches for archaeological exploration and discovery, from crowdsourcing (focusing on the 2016 TED Prize Platform, which will launch in early 2017), to social media (can discoveries be announced via Facebook Live?), to noninvasive forms of archaeological survey via remote sensing. Archaeologists have not considered best practices for these new approaches, and it is something we should do as a community (as different approaches will work per subfield).

These and other approaches offer exciting new avenues for research and have or will optimize fieldwork. What is even more exciting is how they are transforming our ability to ask better questions about past cultures. We have reliable country-wide archaeological site data, 3D scans of buildings and objects, and accessible and open-source online databases. Archaeologists are thus coming up with new questions relating to the scale of data availability. For example, by examining the size, type, and number of sites per time period out of a database of thousands, we can more reliably assess settlement pattern changes and ancient human environment interactions. We can also study patterns of modern site looting to assist recovery efforts. This scale of data will only increase as time passes. Thus, we need to think carefully about reframing our questions and asking new ones.

Drought-Induced Civil Conflict Among the Maya

Douglas J. Kennett, Pennsylvania State University

A growing number of archaeological and historical studies propose linkages between global climate change, violent conflict, and societal collapse in the deep past. With few exceptions, emphasis is placed on inter-group warfare rather than other forms of insidious civil conflict. This is a biased view because wars of conquest are more frequently glorified in the historical record, and civil conflicts are a far more common cause of political instability. However, the influence of climate change on civil conflict in the last century remains controversial. I am working with an interdisciplinary group of scientists to explore climate change, civil conflict, and societal collapse of Mayapán (1200 to 1450 C.E.), the last capital city in the Yucatan prior to first European contact in 1521 C.E. We have used high-precision AMS ^{14}C measurements and stable isotope analysis of human skeletal material (n=120), some mutilated and in mass graves (n=23), to explore these linkages.

These data are evaluated within a Bayesian chronological model for the development and collapse of this heavily fortified urban center. We compare these data with precisely dated subannual regional climate records and show an increase in interpersonal violence associated with drought between 1320 and 1450 C.E. Within this chronological framework we link four mass burials in the city to historical events recorded retrospectively using the cyclical Maya calendar. One of these mass burials corresponds to an ethnically charged uprising that resulted in the massacre of the paramount noble lineage and the dissolution of the Mayapán state. We conclude that preexisting ethnic tensions in the city made it vulnerable to fragmentation in the face of climate change. The interdisciplinary archaeological approach employed here is transforming our view of the inherent complexities of nature and society in the past with relevance to the present and future.

Spectral Imaging and the Future of the Past

Roger L. Easton, Jr., Rochester Institute of Technology

Spectral imaging is the term used for the practice of collecting imagery at a number of wavelength bands, often including bands outside the range of human vision, and subsequently applying various algorithms to combine those images with the goal of revealing or enhancing some feature(s) of interest. Spectral imaging has been used for a variety of purposes for more than a century, including military intelligence and environmental studies, but has become much more feasible and accessible since the pervasive deployment of digital imaging technologies and improvements in computing capabilities over the last two decades. Spectral imaging has become a useful and more widely available tool for recovering important details about the past. For example, it has been used to recover text from damaged documents, such as palimpsests (deliberately erased and overwritten manuscripts) and other important objects including historical maps, cave paintings, artwork, and writings on building walls. Such research has the potential to revise significantly our understanding of key episodes in the past.

This talk briefly introduces the current imaging system technologies available for collecting spectral imagery, including light sources created from light-emitting diodes (LEDs), lenses that retain focus over the broader range of wavelengths (350 nm–1,100 nm), and silicon sensors. Methods for processing these images are also outlined and examples of results are shown for a number of objects, including the Archimedes Palimpsest, the Syriac-Galen Palimpsest, the palimpsests from the "New Finds" collection at St. Catherine's Monastery, the world map (ca. 1491) by Henricus Martellus Germanus, and the Vercelli Mappamundi. The last section of the talk focuses on the Lazarus Project, which is a collaborative effort involving faculty and research staff of the Rochester Institute of Technology, the University of Rochester, the Early Manuscripts Electronic Library, and a number of independent scientists and scholars. The goal of the Lazarus Project is to provide imaging services to libraries and other repositories of important historical objects at little or no cost.

SESSION 1D
Cyprus

CHAIR: *Erin Walcek Averett*, Creighton University

Integrated Methodologies for Reconstructing the Materiality of the Cypriot Coastal Landscape

Georgia M. Andreou, Cornell University

Since the intensification and systematization of archaeological research on the coasts of the Mediterranean in the 1980s, it has become obvious that the material remains of maritime activities on the shoreline are obscure. This is related to the complex geodynamic nature of the coastline, which is described as the "living edge" between land and a body of water. In this respect, the coastal zone is affected by a variety of natural factors, as well as past and more recent anthropogenic ones, the "signatures" of which can be identified in geological, sedimentological, and geomorphological studies of coastal deposits. For the areas that have not been subjected to these scientific studies, however, the mapping, exploration, understanding, and subsequent protection of coastal archaeological sites remain a challenge.

It is hardly surprising that people have long used the coastlines of Cyprus for a series of activities to the extent that a significant part of the materiality of past maritime activities is obscured. While the present landscape of the south-central coast of Cyprus comprises industrial and touristic areas, coastal defense infrastructure, and permanent and temporary ports, the coastal structures and locations of previous chronological periods are not easily discernible in the material record. However, some maritime activity and evidence for imported artifacts are attested in the archaeological record of the area as early as the Bronze Age.

In this paper, I present a summary of the integrated historical and archaeological methodologies I employed to reconstruct the materiality of the south-central coast of Cyprus. These include terrestrial survey, aerial photography, photogrammetry, comparison of georeferenced aerial photographs, coastal erosion monitoring, a historical investigation of medieval cartography, and examination of ethnographic studies and the state archives of Cyprus from the British Colonial period. I conclude with a synthetic map displaying the location of the maritime activities on this part of the island between the Late Bronze Age and the early 20th century C.E.

Cyprus in Context: Researching and Reassessing the Cambridge Cypriot Collections

Anastasia Christofilopoulou, Fitzwilliam Museum, and *Jennifer Marchant*, Fitzwilliam Museum

The University of Cambridge is fortunate to hold one of three major collections of Cypriot antiquities in the United Kingdom, a collection comprising more than 1,000 artifacts spread across three university museums (the majority of objects currently located in the Fitzwilliam Museum). The collection was first studied in 1996-1997 by Vassos Karageorghis and the Fitzwilliam's then Keeper of Antiquities,

Eleni Vassilika, and resulted in the current display of Cypriot antiquities in the Fitzwilliam Museum.

However, the collection has not been holistically studied or published, despite it including some of the finest examples of ceramics, glass, bronzes, and marble sculpture from prominent sites such as Salamis, Palaepaphos, Marion, Tamassos, and Vounous. Moreover, both the Fitzwilliam's Egyptian and Greek and Roman collections have recently been the subject of extensive research projects, engaging current research approaches to classical and Egyptian archaeology, work that is heavily influencing the redisplay of both the Greek/Roman and the Egyptian galleries.

Given the intensification of theoretical advances in the fields of Aegean and Cypriot archaeology (paired with important developments in the field of island archaeology) and important new archaeological discoveries in Cyprus, the time is now ripe for a complete reassessment of the Cambridge Cypriot collections. A recently established, three-year research project on the Cambridge Cypriot material aims to address these advances and reframe the material both in its original archaeological context and in relation to Cyprus' wider identity as a "big island." Working collaboratively between conservation and curatorial staff, the project will build a body of research into the archaeological context, material and technology, and condition of the Cypriot material. This project will ultimately ensure that the collection reflects the fundamental role the island played in trade across the Mediterranean region and the way its insularity shaped a unique cultural identity, allowing indigenous cultural forms to be preserved and transmitted while new ideas and external influences were assimilated.

This paper presents the material culture categories currently under study (Early Bronze Age pottery from the Vounous excavations, archaic terracottas from Salamis, and Early Iron Age and archaic metalware in our collections) as well as the early research results of this project, while addressing the question of whether it is possible to integrate current theoretical debates and advances in archaeology into museum displays.

The God Who Speaks: Aphrodite's Consort in Palaepaphos, Cyprus

Georgia Bonny Bazemore, Eastern Washington University

The syllabic writing system of Cyprus was used exclusively by the inhabitants of this island and by Cypriots abroad, rather than the alphabet of the mainland Greeks. The Cypriot syllabary was employed from at least 1050 B.C.E. to 294 B.C.E., disappearing soon after the Ptolemaic conquest of the island. The archaeological remains of this script are not evenly distributed either chronologically or spatially. Of the almost 1,700 syllabic inscriptions found to date, at least 660 were placed in two sanctuaries immediately outside the walls of ancient Paphos. Both Homer and Hesiod identify ancient Paphos as the birthplace of the Greek goddess Aphrodite, the location of her home temple and fragrant altar. In sharp contrast with the extramural sanctuaries, the intramural sanctuary of Aphrodite did not receive written dedications as part of its cult rituals.

One of these great inscribing centers of ancient Paphos was located at the site of Lingrin tou Dhigeni, situated on a hilltop 6 km east of the city. The original site of the other sanctuary is not yet known, as its remains were ripped out in 498 B.C.E. by the Persians to anchor their siege mound. Most of these inscriptions consist of only an anthroponym. A single inscription from Lingrin tou Dhigeni is dedicated to the "God Who Speaks"; a single inscription from the siege mound gives a royal genealogy of the sixth century B.C.E. This paper will explore the relations between the two extramural temples of Paphos. Working from the evidence gathered by Tacitus from the Paphian priests themselves, I will compare the artifact assemblages of these sites, including the types of votives and the media on which the syllabic inscriptions were inscribed. The temple remains at Lingrin tou Dhigeni paint a vivid portrait of the internecine warfare between the legendary Kinyrad kings of Paphos and their Tamyrad counterparts. The material evidence for this conflict will be presented.

Limestone Votive Dancing Groups from the Sanctuary at Athienou-Malloura, Cyprus

Katherine A.P. Iselin, University of Missouri - Columbia

The representation of dance in ancient Cypriot art, which is featured on a variety of media with both male and female participants, is common. Although it is impossible to recreate the music or movements associated with dancing rituals, visual representations provide crucial information about the participants and allow us to consider the significance of such performances. In 2015, excavations by the Athienou Archaeological Project unearthed a substantial number of limestone draped statuette fragments at the Late Geometric - Roman rural sanctuary at Athienou-Malloura, located on the edges of the Mesaoria in southeastern Cyprus. Sculpted, veiled female figures link together to form circular dancing groups attached to a limestone disk. More than 30 fragments have been found, all wearing the same veiled drapery and carved in a relatively schematic fashion. The differences in size, style, and relationship to the limestone base suggest at least three different groups. Although the majority of the fragments were found in looter pits, they are concentrated in one area of the sanctuary.

Only a few dancing groups of this type carved in limestone have been found on Cyprus. The majority of representations are handmade or molded in terracotta. The large number of dancing-group fragments found at Malloura indicates this votive type had a significant presence at the sanctuary. Although representations of dancing groups are found from other sites on Cyprus, the Malloura dancers differ greatly in style. This paper examines the dancing groups with a particular focus on garments, comparanda, and the importance of dance within sacred spaces in order to understand how these objects fit into the broader ritual context of the site. Additionally, this study will incorporate broader comparative material from both Greek and Near Eastern traditions in recognition of Cyprus' unique position as a crossroads within the ancient Mediterranean.

Woes and Wealth of Votive Deposits on Cyprus: An Investigation into Attitudes Towards Dedications and Their Treatment

Mackenzie Heglar, Bryn Mawr College

Votive deposits and the objects contained within the features are interpreted as a conscious reflection of the values, attitudes, and practices that create social and religious infrastructure. While votive deposits and sacred spaces cannot/should not be studied in isolation, an explicit methodology for the systematic study of votive deposits is necessary. This paper takes a fresh look at votive deposits from the Sanctuary of Herakles-Melqart at Kition and the sanctuary at Mersinaki on Cyprus. These deposits reflect transition of space from sacred to secular. My depositional analysis consists of three steps: I start by reconstructing basic aspects of the deposits by relying on the stratigraphic, topographic, and photographic documentation of the excavators. I recontextualize statues by linking the levels and squares noted for each object in the object register to the deposits. Then I explore the orientation and grouping of fragments, highlighting the intentional subdivision of space within deposits. Analyzing the structure of these depositions enables me to discuss the manner in which votives were deposited, which ranged from carelessly discarded to carefully buried. I argue that these practices and processes are not mutually exclusive. Finally, I consider joins between fragments with a view to reconstructing depositional episodes. My analysis provides insight into how the nature of a votive deposit informs our understanding of social motivation and sacred space and allows for a better understanding of the management and operation of sanctuary centers as reflected through disposal practices. In this way, I demonstrate that thorough depositional analysis may shed new light on attitudes toward dedications at the end of their use life and practices deemed necessary to prepare sacred spaces for new uses.

Royal Consumption in the Amathus Palace Through the Cypro-Classical I - II Periods: Exploring Local Pottery Productions

Sarah Lambert, Laval University

The main purpose of this paper is to identify the diversity of local pottery workshops evolving in and for the Amathusian palace elite. As pottery production is closely intertwined with the development of customs and their social settings, the paper aims to explore in what forms and under which variations we perceive royal consumption related to preparation and consumption of food and drinks, in the setting of either storage or cult. Rooms II and XVIII are two rare contexts that were sealed off after a reorganization of the palace, protecting a specific material culture dated between two different phases of destruction. The first took place at the beginning of the fifth century with the king Onesilos' revolt; the second followed the devastation in 312 B.C.E. associated with the Antigonides' attack, which marked the end of the Cypriot kingdom polities. Local pottery production in such a palatial context is unknown elsewhere in Cyprus, and the numerous Amathusian examples show a richness still unpublished for the Classical Periods I and II. Those two rooms present an overview of the opulent productions (the regular tableware, festivities ware, or cultural ware) relating to consumption in a specific aristocratic setting. Moreover, those contexts underline the developments that occurred at the end of the Archaic period and throughout the Classical one, illuminating the various processes of exchange and influence through the choices made between regular imitation, adaptation, and importation in a matter of common and daily goods, allowing a previously unknown portrait of the elite's everyday life.

Late Classical/Hellenistic Idalion, Cyprus: A Report on Some Recent Excavations

Rebecca Bartusewich, University of Massachusetts Amherst

In 2012, the team at Idalion, Cyprus, began to excavate in the northeast section of Lower City South, an area within a large Iron Age city-kingdom. There, we found architecture on a straight north - south, east - west orientation. Previous excavations had uncovered angled northwest - southeast and northeast - southwest oriented structures. These two architectural sequences have been uncovered together in two excavation units, but they are on different elevations and belong to different phases. The architectural design in the northeast is also different from other structures, using a large amount of sandstone and fewer river cobbles. The Lower City South has been interpreted as a sanctuary, but interestingly there is no ritual element associated with this new building phase. There is some evidence that this area was used in a more domestic fashion, but it has not been exposed enough to know for sure. The pottery suggests a Late Classical, Early Hellenistic date. It may be a new addition after the arrival of people from Kition in the mid fifth century B.C.E. and a change in the administration of the city. While previous work has shown that there may not be a cultural change in the Lower City, there is now evidence of some kind of change, at least as represented through the orientation of the architecture and the way it is constructed. This paper will discuss the archaeological finds in this area, the possible interpretation of the structure, and what this new area of the site suggests about the overall interpretation of Lower City South.

SESSION 1E: Colloquium
New Studies on Vase Painting in the Royal Ontario Museum's Greek Collection

ORGANIZERS: *SeungJung Kim*, University of Toronto, and *Jacquelyn H. Clements*, University of Toronto

Colloquium Overview Statement

Toronto's Royal Ontario Museum (ROM) possesses a strong collection of black- and red-figure vase painting, a large part of which was accessioned before the 1930s and published in the 1934 catalogue by Robinson and Harcum. A *CVA* volume only for the black-figure vases, authored by Hayes, was published in 1981 and remains the sole fascicule in the Canada series. This panel brings together a series of papers that explore the diverse nature of the ROM's vase-painting collection—many of them drawing on the relatively understudied corpus of Athenian red-figure vases—to spark a much-needed conversation around its rich range of material.

At the core of this panel is an interest in iconography and recent issues regarding social, gender, and sexual interpretations. Two papers consider the rituals and gestures of nuptial iconography, using very different approaches. The first presents newly restored, unpublished fragments of a lebes gamikos that adds to the distinctiveness of the Washing Painter's iconographic repertoire. The artist's penchant for treating many of his subjects in an unusual fashion extends here to his nuptial iconography, which will heighten the understanding of this relatively overlooked late fifth-century painter. The second paper, in contrast, takes a gendered approach and analyzes how the female viewer relates to the imagery on a self-referential nuptial loutrophoros, using the framework of information theory and structuralist narratology and exploring how visual markers act as gender-specific signals.

The third paper looks at a mid fifth-century pelike by the Pig Painter and reinterprets the vase in light of recent systematic studies of pederastic iconography. This study not only adds something new to the discourse on homoerotic relationships in mid fifth-century Athens but also provides a significant contribution toward the growing tendency in scholarship to regard Greek vases in their entirety, rather than viewing their scenes in isolation. It is complemented by the fourth paper, which looks thematically at a range of vases in the ROM collection featuring satyrs and puts them into the context of the mythological creature's upbringing, a new perspective that sheds further light on the educational structure of *paideia* in Athenian society.

A final paper turns from Athens to Hellenistic Etruria for a contextual study of the Group of Toronto 495's pottery and its link to earlier Tarquinian traditions. This paper further situates the conspicuous Group of Toronto 495 in its rightful historical context by examining recent archaeological discoveries in the necropolis of Tarquinia-Fondo Scataglini.

The presenters selected for this panel represent a diverse mix of international scholars in various stages of their careers, providing a setting for which productive conversations can be initiated about current scholarly issues around the ROM collection. The panel is currently being envisioned as taking place at the Royal Ontario Museum, with an additional 45-minute "study session" in the galleries proper, where scholars, curators, and students will have a rare opportunity to exchange further conversations with the objects at hand.

The Royal Ontario Museum's Fragments from a Lebes Gamikos

Paul Denis, Royal Ontario Museum

Attributed to the Washing Painter, ca. 425 B.C.E., the marriage scenes preserved on unpublished fragments from a large red-figure lebes gamikos are interpreted here in light of the recent restoration of the vase at the Royal Ontario Museum. The vase painter conflates nuptial and prenuptial scenes and innovatively transforms them into his own original vocabulary. The main scene shows a seated bride making a wreath, and one attendant offering her a plate of food. According to traditional customs, she must eat when she enters her husband's home following her wedding. This act signifies her acceptance of his sovereignty over her and inclusion into his household, as the matron of the *oikos*.

In another section, a woman presents a second seated bride with a jewelry box and a larnax with a male infant perched on the lid. He represents the ultimate gift from an Athenian marriage, alluding to the bride's most important social role of bearing legitimate male children. The adornment of the bride symbolizes her transition to womanhood through marriage, and the male child represents her transition form virgin to motherhood. Eros, flying above the bride, offers her a necklace. He has been dispatched by his mother, Aphrodite, who stands behind her. Peitho, her frequent attendant and the personification of persuasion, embraces the goddess of love while staring at the bride. The bride is infused with Aphrodite's sexual attractiveness, Eros' eroticism, and Peitho's power of persuasion to captivate her husband and release her from any apprehension.

These images demonstrate the inventiveness of the Washing Painter. The gifting of the male infant resting on a chest is unique to Attic red-figure vase painting. Instead of following the usual formula of having a single bride as the focus, the painter improvises by placing two brides within the same panel and positioning one on either side of the male infant, who becomes the center of the composition. The young Athenian bride-to-be would have seen her future life unfold before her eyes as an allegory: her transition from virgin to bride to mother, and to matron of the *oikos*. The feminine intimacy of the picture with women adorning, grooming, caressing, and exchanging gifts would have resonated with her present communal experience of a passage to a new life. The iconography as such will be discussed in the context of Washing Painter's other oeuvres and related imagery used by other vase painters.

Girl Talk: Female-Directed Communication About Marriage on Attic Loutrophoroi

Danielle Smotherman Bennett, Bryn Mawr College

The iconography of marriage on ancient Greek vases has been traditionally understood as reinforcing the social institution of matrimony and primarily directed at female viewers. The well-preserved loutrophoros attributed to Polygnotos in the collection of the Royal Ontario Museum (929.22.3, 635) belongs to a group of wedding vases that have self-referential imagery- that is, vases depicting representations of marriage that were given to a woman on the occasion of, or her death before, marriage. Side A presents the groom—the sole male figure—grasping the wrist of his bride in his right hand and leading her forward as he gazes back at her. This gesture of grabbing the wrist *cheir' epi karpo* is known in both marriage and abduction scenes, but the accompanying women holding torches, and the other women that appear on the neck and Side B, identify the occasion as a celebratory wedding. Other self-referential marriage images include depictions of the bride bathing or being adorned, and other such known stages of the ceremony.

Through examining the Royal Ontario Museum loutrophoros and other self-referential classical loutrophoroi, I argue that these vases are active agents of communication for the intended viewer as much as sources of information about marriage. By surveying the types of visual markers used, such as body language, gaze, gesture, and objects held, which are both recognizable and relatable to female viewers, I examine how the imagery actively transmits information to the viewer. These visual markers function on two levels: within the images as part of the narrative conversation among the figures, and as the key components of the signal that is transmitted to the viewer. These types of images invite the female viewer to look for herself in the images, encouraging her to identify and interact with figures in the scenes through such signals. This deeper engagement requires that the viewer relate to the images on an instinctive level; therefore, the forms of communication must resonate with activities and behaviors familiar to the intended viewer. Unlike self-referential scenes directed at male viewers on sympotic vases, these scenes rarely depict women interacting directly with the viewer. This study thus forms a key part in a larger exploration of how visual markers directed at female receivers differ from their counterparts directed at a male audience, and examining the role of gender on the transmission of visual information.

Pederasty and Male Love on a Red-Figure Pelike by the Pig Painter in the Royal Ontario Museum

Anthony F. Mangieri, Salve Regina University

The Pig Painter is an Attic red-figure vase painter, mostly of column-kraters and pelikai, who was active during the second quarter of the fifth century B.C.E. While scholars today do not praise the draftsmanship of this Early Mannerist painter, he has left us an intriguing scene on a pelike in the Royal Ontario Museum (inv. no. 365). Two draped youths, one holding a lyre and the other a piece of fruit, flank a flaming altar. What are they doing? This paper examines the iconography of this scene to recover its narrative and meaning.

By studying the youths on inventory number 365 within the contexts of the Pig Painter's work and of pederastic iconography on Athenian pots, I propose that our vase painter depicts a romantic couple. On the other side of the Toronto pelike, the Pig Painter depicts a pederastic courtship scene with an older bearded man holding out the gift of a ribbon toward a draped youth. This pederastic subject, in part, provides a framework and prompt for interpreting the scene related to male love on the other side, since the Pig Painter often connects the images on both sides of his pelikai thematically and visually. At the same time, the lyre and fruit appear on other vases by the Pig Painter as love gifts.

The Pig Painter's portrayal of the two unbearded youths brings to mind numerous representations of young *erastai* and *eromenoi* in Attic vase painting, a familiar artistic convention toward the middle of the fifth century B.C.E. Furthermore, the lyre that the one youth holds may signify the location as the gymnasium, where music lessons took place. If so, the altar might be the altar of Eros attached to the Academy in Athens that appears in some pederastic vase paintings.

My argument is that the Pig Painter compares different kinds of male love on this vase, a practice that we see also in the work of Late Archaic vase painters. Our artist juxtaposes the pederastic man/youth couple on one side with the youth/youth pair on the other. The youth holding the fruit gestures and turns his head in a way that implies a thwarted liaison that perhaps comments on the nature of love between youths compared with the relationship between men and boys. The Pig Painter's vase thus speaks to the vexed place occupied by pederasty and other forms of male love in fifth-century Athens with the burgeoning of democracy.

When Does a Satyr Become a Satyr?

Hollister N. Pritchett, Bryn Mawr College

As part of the collections of the Royal Ontario Museum (ROM) there are a particularly abundant number of Athenian vases that depict satyrs–the ribald mythological creatures who are represented in Greek vase painting as human figures with equine ears and tails–acting in situations that are usually connected to the god Dionysus. These companions of Dionysus are often shown in processions, carrying wine sacks or sympotic drinking vessels, and also are depicted cavorting with or chasing women. The ROM's more than two dozen vases with representations of satyrs form a well-defined corpus of satyr imagery that illustrates the types of iconographic behavior known to us. In a similar fashion to their mortal counterparts, as well as to several of their divine brethren, satyrs also had childhoods. There exists a small corpus of Athenian vases that depict satyr children at various ages and developmental stages.

This paper looks at the images of satyr children depicted on archaic and classical vases that are held in various collections and world museums and examines the settings in which we see the satyr babies and children, the activities in which they are occupied, and who accompanies them in these scenes. I examine the satyr child's parentage as well as determining how, and possibly when, the satyr children were taught their adult behavior. Some Athenian vases depict mortal children being taught various skills, either at home or at school, but as far as we know there were no such schools for satyr children. It is of additional interest that several representations of satyr families show similarities to illustrations of human families, including depictions of satyr children playing with toys similar to those of their mortal equivalents, which I argue is an artistic parody of proper Athenian citizenship.

The complete corpus of satyr vases in Toronto's ROM sets the stage for such examinations into the childhood of satyrs, as the end product of their educational and developmental process. As part of a larger, ongoing study of the representations of children on Athenian vases, these ROM vases, together with the depiction of satyrs as children, are examined to ponder the question, when does a satyr become a satyr? With this new approach of comparing the educational development of satyrs with that of their human counterparts, I show that satyr imagery as a whole provides a complex mirror to the societal construct of the Athenian *paideia*.

The Toronto 495 Group Reconsidered: Early Hellenistic Pottery Production at Tarquinia

Bice Peruzzi, Grand Valley State University

Within the class of Etruscan vases decorated with floral pattern only, Beazley recognized the conspicuous Group of Toronto 495, named after an oinochoe in the Royal Ontario Museum. Vases belonging to this group present a large preserved band on the body, which was covered in a thin layer of miltos and decorated with a frieze of palmettes. The similarities between these vases and those by the better-known Turmuca and Geneva Groups convinced Beazley that the production of the Group of Toronto 495 should be dated to the second half of the fourth century B.C.E. and possibly located in Vulci.

However, the presence of more than 100 vases belonging to this group in the National Archaeological Museum in Tarquinia, as well as the discovery of more examples in the necropolis of Tarquinia-Fondo Scataglini in the last 30 years, calls for a reexamination of this class of materials. This paper analyzes these vases in the broader context of contemporary South Etruscan pottery production, offering new hypotheses for these vessels' production centers, chronology, and destination.

While the Group of Toronto 495's vases in the Tarquinia Museum have no recorded findspots, those recovered in the last few decades come largely from late fourth- to early third-century B.C.E. funerary contexts. The limited circulation of these objects and the characteristics of their clay indicate that Tarquinia was probably the main center of production, with at least three active workshops. Moreover, despite their repetitive decoration, the shapes in the Group of Toronto 495's repertoire show that these vessels constitute an important link between the last red-figure vases at Tarquinia and later Hellenistic productions. Some shapes–such as the calyx craters–are very close in profile to those previously attested in red-figure pottery in the second part of the fourth century B.C.E. Others (e.g., situlai, paterai, askoi) seem to be inspired by metal prototypes and find closer parallels among vases in so-called *argentata* ware, a class of pottery produced in several Etruscan centers until the mid third century B.C.E.

The Group of Toronto 495 has been largely ignored by scholars. Yet with the help of data recovered in recent archaeological excavations it is possible to place these vessels into their rightful historical context; thus, we can finally shed light on an important and lesser known chapter of Tarquinia's ceramic production.

SESSION 1F
The Eastern Roman Empire: Recent Fieldwork

CHAIR: *Michael C. Hoff*, University of Nebraska-Lincoln

Recent Results from the Graeco-Roman Village of Qarah el-Hamra in Fayum, Egypt

Emily C.C. Cole, Institute for the Study of the Ancient World, New York University, and *Bethany Simpson*, Getty Research Institute

In this paper, I present the results of the 2016 field season at the Graeco-Roman Village of Qarah el-Hamra. Discovered in 2004 by the University of California, Los Angeles, Fayum Project, the site lies on the north shore of Lake Qarun in the Fayum region of Egypt. The small settlement was briefly explored at that time, and a magnetometry survey was performed. Based on the results of that work, a new project was begun in 2016 under the direction of the author and Bethany Simpson. Our goal is to explore the relationship between this smaller site and larger neighboring towns, most importantly Soknopaiou Nesos and Karanis. In this field season, traditional excavation methods were employed in relevant areas of the site. These allow us to address important questions regarding the chronology of Qarah el-Hamra, its place in the network of new foundations of the Ptolemaic administration, and the subsistence strategies used by the inhabitants.

Omrit Settlement Excavations Project: Report on the 2014 - 2016 Seasons

Daniel Schowalter, Carthage College, *Jennifer Gates-Foster*, University of North Carolina, Chapel Hill, *Michael Nelson*, Queens College, City University of New York, *Jason Schlude*, College of St. Benedict, and *Benjamin Rubin*, AIA Member at Large

The Omrit Settlement Excavations Project (OSEP) nears the end of a five-year research program investigating the area to the north of the Roman-period temple complex at Omrit in northern Israel. Previous excavations in the temenos identified Roman, Late Roman, Early Byzantine, and Mamluk ceramic and architectural phases. OSEP's current excavations significantly refine our understanding of all periods in the site's history and offer a nuanced picture of the site's development, particularly in the Roman and Late Roman eras.

The 2016 excavation season clarified three distinct phases of the settlement. Prior to the late second and early third centuries C.E., the settlement consisted of well-appointed domestic structures, including a building adorned with frescoes and outfitted with a fountain or small shrine that likely dates no earlier than the late first century C.E. In the next phase, a large, public, stoa-like building was erected along the settlement's cardo that led to the temple temenos. Such monumental street architecture gave Omrit an urban character that was common to larger cities in the Roman East. In the third phase, dating to the mid third to fifth century, formerly public places and spaces were repurposed. For example, the stoa-like building was partitioned into individual shops and homes, and new structures were built on the cardo itself. During this phase, perhaps when occupation at Omrit reached its peak, the settlement engaged in various types of agricultural production. The scale of some of these activities suggests regional distribution.

This paper presents the preliminary results of the last three seasons of excavations at Omrit, updates the history of the site, and contextualizes its archaeology and material remains within the broader region.

The 2015 - 2016 Excavations at Huqoq in Israel's Galilee

Jodi Magness, University of North Carolina at Chapel Hill, *Shua Kisilevitz*, Israel Antiquities Authority, *Matthew J. Grey*, Brigham Young University, and *Dennis Mizzi*, University of Malta

Since 2011, excavations at Huqoq in Israel's Eastern Lower Galilee have brought to light parts of the Jewish village of the fifth to sixth century and the Ottoman-period Muslim village of Yakuk. In this paper, we report on the results of the 2015–2016 excavation seasons, which focused on a monumental, Late Roman (fifth-century) synagogue paved with extraordinary mosaics. The mosaics uncovered in these two seasons include a Hebrew inscription surrounded by Dionysiac imagery; the first historical scene ever discovered decorating an ancient synagogue (perhaps a depiction of the legendary meeting between Alexander the Great and the Jewish high priest); and the first scene from everyday life ever discovered decorating an ancient synagogue (a date-harvesting scene). The synagogue was expanded and reused as a public building in the Middle Ages (12th to 13th century), when the stylobates and pedestals were lifted one meter, and the aisles were paved with mosaics. Column drums from the synagogue that were used in the medieval building to support the lifted stylobates still preserve their original painted decoration. This paper provides an overview of these discoveries.

The Town of Nebo Archaeological Project: Results of the First Two Seasons of Excavation at Khirbat al-Mukhayyat, Jordan

Debra Foran, Wilfrid Laurier University

The site of Khirbat al-Mukhayyat has been identified as the ancient town of Nebo. Material culture from a wide range of periods has been documented at the site; however, previous work at the site focused primarily on its Byzantine remains. The Town of Nebo Archaeological Project (TNAP) was established in 2012, under the auspices of the University of Toronto, to investigate the site's sacred landscape and explore the economic impact of pilgrimage across multiple cultural and historical periods. This paper presents the results of TNAP's first two seasons of excavation, which exposed remains dating to the Late Hellenistic period (first century B.C.E.) and the Iron Age (ninth to eighth century B.C.E.). This work was made possible through the support of Wilfrid Laurier University and the Department of Antiquities of Jordan.

Three fields of excavation were opened in 2014. Field A extended along the southern slope of the site's acropolis and produced a series of retaining walls associated with the Byzantine Church of St. George located on the summit. Work in field B, to the south of the acropolis, exposed a portion of the site's fortification system and numerous complete Late Hellenistic cooking pots. Excavations in field C, to the north of the acropolis, yielded a number of artifacts, including coins, and bedrock-cut features that suggest that Mukhayyat was under Hasmonean control during the first century B.C.E. The discovery of a Late Hellenistic *miqveh*, or Jewish ritual bath, in this area is of particular importance.

In 2016, excavations in field B enabled us to determine an Iron Age foundation date for the defensive architecture in this area. This fortification system had gone out of use by the Hellenistic period, at which time field B was used for ritual activities that involved the deposit and subsequent burying of cooking vessels. Excavation in the area surrounding the *miqveh*, field C West, produced several plaster and bedrock installations, which may support the hypothesis that, during the Late Hellenistic period, the site was used primarily for agricultural and ritual purposes.

Although further excavations are being planned for Mukhayyat, the results of the first two seasons have greatly contributed to our knowledge of the socio political and religious landscape of the site and the region during a period, the Late Hellenistic, for which only scant evidence exists.

New Archaeological Research in Ancient Gerasa (Jerash): The Danish-German Northwest Quarter Project

Rubina Raja, Aarhus University, Denmark, and *Achim Lichtenberger*, Ruhr Universität Bochum, Germany

Since 2011, a Danish-German team headed jointly by Achim Lichtenberger (Ruhr-Universität Bochum, Germany) and Rubina Raja (Aarhus University, Denmark) has been working in the Northwest Quarter in Gerasa. This area of approximately 4 ha, is the highest point within the walled city and lies in close proximity to the Roman-period Artemision. The area has remained largely unexplored, apart from two test trenches, which were laid out in the 1980s and did not give any conclusive results. The work carried out by the Danish-German team has revealed dense settlement in the Late Antique and Early Islamic periods and furthermore has given indications for earlier Roman-period structures in the area.

Among other things, our research has brought to light evidence for an earlier sanctuary as well as Roman-period water-management installations and traces of extensive quarry activities. For the Late Antique period, dense settlement and production complexes have been uncovered and give insight into the flourishing period, which the fourth to sixth centuries were in this region. Furthermore, a new ecclesiastic complex from the sixth century has come to light, which gives new information about the Roman army in the Near East. Last but not least, knowledge about Early Islamic domestic housing has been gathered. This comes from the so-called Eastern Terrace, which was destroyed during the earthquake of 749 C.E. and since then has remained untouched. The houses excavated here present quasi-Pompeii situations and have revealed intact houses with complete inventories, which tell us about the nature of life in the transitional period between late antiquity and the Early Islamic period.

This paper will present the work undertaken from 2011 to 2015 and focus on the periods from the first century C.E. until the middle of the eighth century C.E.

Petroglyphs Associated with the Roman Fort and *Vicus* at Humayma, Jordan

M. Barbara Reeves, Queen's University

The archaeological site of Humayma, in southern Jordan's Hisma Desert, retains traces of human occupation spanning thousands of years. Excavations and surveys over the past three decades have focused on many aspects of the site's occupation, revealing a great deal about its Upper Paleolithic, Paleolithic, Nabataean, Roman, Byzantine, Early Islamic, and later phases. One category of Humayma's archaeological remains that has, however, received only passing scholarly attention is the petroglyphs that exist on sandstone landmasses adjacent to the ruins of the ancient town and fort. Interest in these petroglyphs increased in 2012 after members of the Humayma Excavation Project, conducting research on the character of the Roman garrisoned town, discovered an elaborate petroglyph that, as analyzed by M.B. Reeves (*JRA* 28 [2015], 451 - 60), seems to show a Roman officer conducting a religious ceremony in the presence of a regimental and a local deity. During its 2014 field season, the Humayma Excavation Project returned to the sandstone ridge on which this petroglyph was found with the goal of documenting all petroglyphs and other signs of human activity in its vicinity. Over four days, more than 150 petroglyphs were found both on the same ridge as the Roman officer's petroglyph and on two adjacent landmasses. The petroglyphs show humans worshiping and hunting, riders on horses and camels, wild and domesticated animals, human footprints, and abstract symbols. Although the corpus as a whole was carved over thousands of years, some petroglyphs existed at the same time as the Roman garrisoned town and were either carved or seen by the Roman soldiers and civilians. After the survey results and the evidence for dating the petroglyphs are introduced, particular groups of petroglyphs that may be associated with the fort and *vicus* are presented. The rationale for producing these petroglyphs is discussed in relation to Roman graffiti and religious practices.

SESSION 1G
Maritime Archaeology

CHAIR: To be announced

Three-Dimensional Modeling for Research, Heritage Management, and Outreach at Marzamemi, Sicily

Justin Leidwanger, Stanford University, *Leopoldo Repola*, Suor Orsola Benincasa University of Naples, *Elizabeth S. Greene*, Brock University, and *Sebastiano Tusa*, Soprintendenza del Mare

Three-dimensional models derived from digital survey techniques have increasingly become a mainstay of archaeological research and cultural heritage management. The high precision and accuracy of such modeling lends itself to a wide range of purposes from site recording and interpretation to object analysis and reconstruction. This contribution focuses on two allied aspects of digital survey undertaken—both underwater and on dry land—as part of the investigation of a shipwreck off the southeast coast of Sicily at Marzamemi. This sixth-century C.E. vessel sank while carrying a massive cargo of largely prefabricated architectural elements intended for the construction and decoration of a church somewhere in the Late Antique west. The dynamic shallow (7 - 8 m) environment presents significant challenges to the interpretation of depositional and post depositional activities as well the reconstruction of the cargo and individual architectural elements. At the object level, the cargo offers two simultaneous puzzles: how to reconstruct the broken marble pieces into the quarry state in which they would have been transported, and how to assemble semifinished pieces into their intended architectural forms. To this end, three-dimensional documentation underwater has centered on new stereoscopic scanning that allows rapid and precise mapping of the site, seabed topography, and finds. On land, structured light scanning and photogrammetry have facilitated recording for multiple uses: conservation, study, reconstruction, and public presentation. Together these methods offer innovative solutions not only for research and preservation but also for heritage management and public outreach. With the newly established Museum of the Sea in Marzamemi and archaeological dive trails as regional centerpieces of heritage tourism and public outreach, such collaborative digital initiatives offer a powerful vehicle for innovative engagement—augmented reality, immersive environments, and the like—using a mix of real objects, virtual and physical copies, and reconstructions.

Harbors and the Hellenistic Polis: Miletos and the Lion Harbor

Lana J. Radloff, University at Buffalo, State University of New York

Often considered in terms of trade, transportation, and technology, harbors also served as important mediators within settlements and between settlements and larger Mediterranean culture. Through the appropriation of natural topography and its elaboration with man-made structures, patterns of integration and separation were created between maritime and terrestrial urban space. In this paper, I examine the spatial and functional relationship between harbors and urban planning at Hellenistic Miletos to explore the complex dynamics between city and sea and the role of harbors in the polis. Taking a holistic approach to the maritime environment that emphasizes the interaction of sea, coast, land, and islands, I argue that harbors were similar in form and function to agoras in defining urban space, particularly during the Hellenistic period, when stoas became increasingly common. Their use, as well as lines of sight and spatial access, served to integrate harbors more fully into the urban grid and, thereby, the polis.

Sacked by the Persians in 494 B.C.E., Miletos was rebuilt on a Hippodamian plan and slowly regained much of its former glory throughout the fourth century B.C.E. and Hellenistic period, when extensive building took place around the North and South Agoras and the Lion Harbor. The Lion Harbor was framed by monumental architecture and equipped with facilities to accommodate its military and commercial uses, mirroring the form and function of the North and South Agoras and demonstrating the importance of harbor space within Miletos. Such an arrangement allowed access to be controlled from the sea but provided greater permeability between harbor and urban interior. Nevertheless, connectivity with the larger maritime environment was maintained through monuments lining the southern sea route into the Lion Harbor. Dedicated to important maritime deities, figures, and events from Miletos' myth-historical past, the structures linked coast, land, islands, and sea, creating a maritime *chora*. Meanwhile, lines of sight and the Sacred Road increased connectivity between the Lion Harbor and urban interior, where major public buildings, such as the Delphinion and agoras, were located. As a result, the Lion Harbor was integrated into the Milesian polis as part of the *asty*. By serving as a transitional space between the larger maritime seascape and interior urban space, Miletos' intra-urban land- and seascapes, disparate maritime and terrestrial regions, and topographical features were tied together, bringing the maritime sphere into the polis.

The Delos Underwater Survey Project (2014 - 2016)

Mantha Zarmakoupi, University of Birmingham, and *Magdalini Athanasoula*, Ephorate of Underwater Antiquities, Hellenic Ministry of Culture and Sports

This paper presents the results of the three-year Delos Underwater Survey Project (2014 - 2016), a synergasia between the Ephorate of Underwater Antiquities of the Hellenic Ministry of Culture and Sports and the Institute of Historical Research of the National Hellenic Research Foundation under the direction of the Head of the Ephorate of Underwater Antiquities Dr. Aggeliki Simosi. The survey focused on the submerged areas of two Hellenistic neighborhoods that were created at the height of Delos' urbanization period, the Stadion District and the Skardana District. The Cyclades have seen a relative rise in sea level of about 2 m over the last 2,000 years. Water has engulfed many areas of the once heavily urbanized island. By examining the submerged areas of these two neighborhoods, the project aimed to define their use and role in the commercial activity of the island in the Late Hellenistic period.

Over the course of three seasons, the survey project identified structures providing evidence for commercial activities in the submerged area of the Stadion District, changing the predominant assumption that this neighborhood did not have an instrumental role in the operation of the Delian emporion. The project also identified remains of harbor installations in the submerged area of the Skardana District, indicating that the bay of the Skardana was an anchorage. These finds are significant, as they clarify the function of the bays that were located next to the newly formed neighborhoods on the island. It seems that commercial harbors operated both in the bay of the Stadion District and in the bay of the Skardana District, complementing the activities of the central harbor. Whereas previous research focused on the main harbor area, assuming that the emporion of Delos depended solely on a single harbor, the Delos Underwater Survey Project—the first underwater survey to be conducted around Delos—provides a different picture of the ways in which the port city functioned. Although the mechanisms of trade were weighted toward direct preferential links between emporion ports, rather than toward random coastal tramping or cabotage, an emporion has several harbors, which could be used according to the weather conditions. The results of the survey project show that the bays of the Stadion District and the Skardana District served as anchorages around the island, allowing skippers to avoid crossings in difficult weather conditions, thus facilitating the busy emporion of Delos in the Late Hellenistic period.

The Life and Afterlife of a Hellenistic Flagship: The "Sixteen" of Demetrius Poliorcetes Revisited

Thomas C. Rose, University of Tennessee, Knoxville

In this paper, I present new evidence to support the theory that the ship Lucius Aemilius Paullus sailed up the Tiber in 167 B.C.E. was in fact the "sixteen" built more than a century earlier by Demetrius Poliorcetes.

Plutarch (*Demetr*. 20, 43) reports that Demetrius' naval building program culminated in the early third century B.C.E. with the construction of a "sixteen," the largest single-hulled warship constructed in antiquity. There is no evidence that any of Demetrius' Antigonid successors ever built or deployed ships approaching the size of this vessel: Antigonus Gonatas dedicated a "nine" at Delos (Paus. 1.29), while the "ten" of Philip V was destroyed in the Battle of Chios in 201 (Polyb. 16.3). It is well established that by the end of the third century, the "big ship phenomenon" had largely run its course.

The Antigonid kings were participants in a larger Greek tradition of dedicating ships at sanctuaries, beginning with Demetrius' construction of the Neorion at Delos, an elaborate gallery for the display of a votive ship. I suggest that his "sixteen" remained intact for so long because it, too, was housed in a *neorion*. The most likely location would be Demetrias, Demetrius' eponymous foundation, most important port, and final resting place (Plut., *Demetr.* 53). Furthermore, there is evidence of the later reuse of just such a dedicated ship. Philipoemon, in 192 B.C.E., reused an Antigonid ship that had been dedicated at Aegium by the Achaeans 80 years earlier (Livy 35.26; Plut., *Phil.* 14).

Paullus demonstrated a sustained interest in appropriating Antigonid commemorative practices for his own purposes, most famously at Delphi, where he repurposed Perseus' dedicatory column to celebrate his own victories in Greece. After he defeated Perseus at Pydna, Paullus made two visits to Demetrias separated by an interval of several months (Livy 45.28)—more than enough time to have the old flagship restored and refitted for the journey to Rome. In a final act of Antigonid emulation, Paullus installed the "sixteen" in a custom *neorion* near the Tiber (Polyb. 36.5).

Demetrius' most famous ship was constructed and displayed as a symbol of Macedonian power; the repurposing of this ship by Lucius Aemilius Paullus was thus a potent demonstration of Roman dominance over the Greek world.

Antikythera Shipwreck Excavation Results

Brendan Foley, Woods Hole Oceanographic Institution, and *Theotokis Theodoulou*, Hellenic Ephorate of Underwater Antiquities

We present results from our ongoing excavation (2014-2016) of the Antikythera Shipwreck and analysis of artifacts recovered during the 1901 and 1976 interventions. We propose that the wreck provides a first look at what has been until now an elusive quarry for maritime archaeology: an ancient grain carrier. These huge ships were a crucially important enabling technology for urbanization in the Hellenistic and Roman eras. On a practical seafaring level, a cargo of grain would have provided an excellent packing material and paying dunnage for the ship's 36 life-sized and colossal marble sculptures and at least eight life-sized bronze statues. The close study of this wreck and its artifacts offers a bounty of new insights into the literal mechanisms of trade feeding the appetites of a nascent imperial Rome.

The recent excavations have produced extraordinary artifacts such as a human skeleton, the first recovered from an ancient shipwreck since the advent of DNA studies. Artwork includes two bronze spears from statues, and fragments of marble sculptures, luxury goods such as unguentaria and lagynoi, several varieties of glass bowls, bone flute sections, bronze furniture components, and gold jewelry. Some of the most enlightening artifacts are massive ship's equipment: the largest lead (Pb) salvage ring ever found; a lead pipe 10 cm in diameter; and an assortment of medium (6 – 9 kg), heavy (14 kg), and extremely heavy (45 – 47 kg) lead weights. Some of these are depth sounding weights, the only examples reported from the Aegean. They are similar to those found off the Levantine coast and associated with Alexandrian grain ships. The Antikythera ship was very large and robustly built as demonstrated by hull planks 10-11 cm thick, far outsizing planks from every other ancient vessel yet discovered. The Antikythera site yielded in 2016 an archaeologically unique "war dolphin", a 100 kg lead and iron defensive maritime weapon. Dolphins are known from ancient written sources, where they are described as equipping large merchant vessels. A comprehensive program of isotopic analysis of this wreck's lead artifacts uniformly points to sources in Chalkidiki, northern Greece.

Taking all evidence into account, we hypothesize that the Antikythera ship was an enormous and well-defended Greek-built grain carrier plying a route from the Black Sea through the Aegean and into the Mediterranean, perhaps toward Rome itself.

The Survey of the *Flash* in Satchell Marsh of River Hamble, in Hampshire, England

Aikaterini Velentza, University of Southampton

This paper presents the results of the 2016 survey project that was conducted on the hulk of the boat *Flash*, found in Satchell Marsh of the River Hamble, in Hampshire, England. The project was conducted by the author and four other postgraduate students during spring 2016 and was part of the assessment of the 2015 - 2016 master's degree in Maritime Archaeology at the Center of Maritime Archaeology in the University of Southampton. The boat *Flash*, which now lies in the intertidal zone of the River Hamble, is a 19th-century fishing boat, possibly a cutter or a dry-smack, which was transformed into a hospital boat for the naval training school T.S. Mercury during the last decade of the 19th century. The intertidal site of Satchell Marsh and the archaeological remains of the *Flash* have been previously surveyed and partially recorded in 2008 and in 2013/2014. The 2016 survey project revisited the site with the objective to record thoroughly the remains of the *Flash*, understand the form and the construction techniques of the vessel, find archaeological evidence proving the exact dates of its second use as a hospital boat for T.S. Mercury, and comprehend the site-formation processes as well as the rate of degradation of the boat, which has been abandoned and unprotected on the River Hamble since the 1930s. The *Flash* survey project included archival research but also an on-site archaeological survey for the collection of data that enabled the creation of digital maps, reconstructions of the site, and three-dimensional models and drawings of the boat and important structural parts of it. Additionally, a variety of artifacts (glass medical vessels, thermometers, coins, stamped china plates) were recorded in situ and studied in the lab to establish the dates of use of the boat as a hospital. Finally, the pictures, the plans, and the three-dimensional models of the 2016 project were compared with the 2008 and 2013/2014 survey data to spot several changes that have occurred on the hulk of the *Flash* in the course of eight years. Therefore, it has been highlighted that the *Flash* has been subject to heavy erosion and degradation due to the fluvial environment of the site and is in need of constant monitoring and recording to avoid further loss of archaeological material.

SESSION 1H: Colloquium
"Satis sit una aliqua gemma": Collecting Classical Gems from Antiquity Through the 19th Century

ORGANIZERS: *Maya Muratov*, Adelphi University, and *Tiziana D'Angelo*, University of Cambridge

Colloquium Overview Statement

This colloquium combines four papers that seek to identify elements of change and continuity in the strategies and trends of collecting Greek and Roman engraved gems from antiquity to the modern era. To the ancient Romans, it was sufficient "to have a single gem before the eyes" (Plin., *HN* 37.1) to be able to grasp the perfection of Nature. However, owning "una aliqua gemma" turned out to be not enough, and the role of gems changed deeply as they became part of proper collections. While earlier scholarship has concentrated primarily on the study of individual collections or specific historical contexts, we adopt a broader diachronic and cross-cultural approach. We aim to analyze the different ways in which collections of gems were assembled, used, and shared, and we are interested in reconstructing the private and public identity of gem collectors in Europe and North America.

"Dactyliothecae Romanae: Collecting Gems in Ancient Rome" investigates the earliest stages of the phenomenon. By focusing on the dichotomy between Roman private and public collections, this paper approaches gem collecting from the perspective of its social, cultural, and political implications. "Collecting Magic: Graeco-Roman Gems in the Early Modern Period" offers a psychoanalytic approach that allows us to see such objects as talismans and fetishes used to navigate the social transformations and anxieties of the gem collectors in Renaissance Italy. "Collecting at Alnwick Castle: Engraved Gems in the Collection of the Duke of Northumberland" features a case study of a quintessential 18th-century British collection (still in private hands) and follows its formation and the developing tastes of the owners. The last paper, "'Fraudulent Ingenuity': Charles W. King and 19th-Century Collections of Antique Gems," focuses on the problem of the increased demand and supply of copies, fakes, and forgeries of classical engraved gems in the latter half of the 19th century and re-assesses the value and impact of modern forgeries and interpolations in the history of gem collecting.

By gathering academic and museum scholars with a variety of innovative and thought-provoking approaches to ancient glyptic and its reception, this colloquium explores the impact that classical engraved gems had on the history of collecting in the Western world.

DISCUSSANT: *Kenneth Lapatin*, J. Paul Getty Museum

Dactyliothecae Romanae: Collecting Gems in Ancient Rome

Roberta Casagrande-Kim, The Onassis Cultural Center New York

In his 37th book, which is dedicated to the history of precious stones, Pliny the Elder, records the introduction of the practice of collecting gems in Rome. He attributes the first of such collections to Marcus Aemilius Scaurus, elected praetor in 56 B.C.E. (*HN* 37.5 - 6). As the term "dactyliotheca" suggests, Pliny perceived this tradition as a "mos peregrinus" cultivated by the affluent non-Roman elite that lived in the newly acquired provinces of the growing empire.

This paper investigates the phenomenon of Roman collecting from the Late Republic to the reign of Constantine from the perspective of its social, cultural, and political implications. Pliny himself alludes to the multifaceted nature of collecting: whereas Scaurus is mentioned for his private collection, Pompey, Caesar, and Marcellus dedicated precious gems and finger rings to the main temples of Rome. Using this passage as the underlying theme for my case studies, I will focus on the dichotomy between private and public collections, their respective meanings and functions, and their reception by elected audiences of invited guests, in the first instance, vs. the populace at large, in the case of public collections. The contrast between private and public will also highlight the symbolic meaning of gems as one of the means through which the Roman elite could assert cultural superiority and social status, and as invaluable tools in the policy of largesse, often disguised under the pretense of religious and civil *pietas* that defined much of the Roman imperial political strategy.

Collecting Magic: Graeco-Roman Gems in the Early Modern Period

Liliana Leopardi, Hobart and William Smith Colleges

Collecting antique gems and cameos was a passion shared by a number of elite class patrons in the 15th and 16th centuries. Cyriacus of Ancona, Niccolò Niccoli, Cardinal Pietro Barbo, who became pope Paul II in 1464, Lorenzo de' Medici, and Cesare Borgia, also known as Il Valentino, are only a few of a great number of collectors of that period. Such collectors engaged in collecting gems not only because they represented the hallowed past or because they were a sign of wealth and power but also because the gems were believed to have magical power. Plain and engraved gems were not seen as inert matter that could be categorized, classified, and disposed of; rather, they were thought to be living entities in direct relationship with man and most importantly in direct relationship with those occult energies that pervaded the universe. A psychoanalytic approach allows us to see such objects as talismans and fetishes used to navigate social transformations and anxieties: a transitional object used to mediate the relationship of the Self (unmediated experience of body and mind) to the Other (external world). This analysis will evidence the period's concerns and fears that body and mind could be transformed by images as matter was transformed by the divine energies it absorbed. Furthermore, it will conceptualize the use of such magic objects as engraved rings–a category often dismissed in the art historical literature as a mere curiosity–as an early modern's attempt to provide a path to psychological integrity for a Self that was understood not as an autonomous and self-contained entity but as porous and fragmented.

Collecting at Alnwick Castle: Engraved Gems in the Collection of the Duke of Northumberland

Claudia Wagner, University of Oxford

The Duke of Northumberland's collection of gems is one of the most important in Britain still in private hands. The most prolific collector of the family was without doubt Algernon Percy, 1st Earl of Beverley (1749 - 1830). However, he was not the only member of the family with an eye for engraved gems.

Enthused by Greek and Roman art, his father had arranged the services of Louis Dutens as Algernon's tutor. The classical scholar and his pupil embarked on the Grand Tour, and it was not marble sculpture but engraved intaglios and cameos they identified as desirable antiquities to collect and bring home. Even after his return, Algernon continued to enlarge the significant collection, which at one time comprised more than 300 items, enough for any connoisseur. Some of his gems had a renowned collection history before they were added to the Duke's collection, such as the gems that had belonged to Cardinal Grimani, whose collection had been published in the early 16th century by Enea Vico, perhaps the earliest publication of gems in drawing.

Many of the collection's ancient gems are important pieces and reveal their influence on other arts of the Renaissance. The subjects where copied, and gems with classical themes emerged. In the 18th and 19th centuries neo-classical artists followed their activities enthusiastically. In the Duke's collection, all of these are represented: classical gems, copies of famous gems, copies of the gems Algernon already owned and must have commissioned himself, new designs of artists of the Renaissance and neoclassical creations. Old gems are found to have been reset into practical settings, such as snuff boxes, so that they could be shown off to friends of the Duke's. Particularly coveted were ancient gems with signatures, and Percy managed to acquire works by Pharnakes and Boethos. Famous engravers of the Renaissance, such as Nassaro, are represented, as are the leading English contemporary engravers of the 18th century, Nathaniel Marchant and Edward Burch, with particularly important pieces. In the 19th century, these are joined by family commissions, cameos commemorating the lives of women of the household, such as the cameo of a poignant Eros with an upturned torch. This colorful and rich collection of gems is a tribute to the acumen of what became a family of collectors with taste and the right connections.

"Fraudulent Ingenuity": Charles W. King and 19th-Century Collections of Antique Gems

Tiziana D'Angelo, University of Cambridge, and *Maya Muratov*, Adelphi University

In his 1866 *Handbook of Engraved Gems*, the British scholar, collector, and connoisseur Charles W. King stated that "it may be asserted with confidence that for every antique gem of note fully a dozen of its counterfeits are now in circulation." A classicist with particular interests in Pliny the Elder, Pausanias, and minerals, King became a Fellow of Trinity College at the University of Cambridge in 1842 and devoted the rest of his life to the study and collecting of antique gems.

This paper examines King's gem collection, correspondence, notes, and publications to shed light on the development of a new concept and meaning of artistic authenticity in the latter half of the 19th century. King was especially concerned with the increase in the demand and supply of copies, fakes, and forgeries of classical engraved gems. While for other collectibles forgeries were in part responsible for the growing appreciation of the original objects, King condemned this "fraudulent ingenuity" and identified it as one of the main causes of the crisis of gem collecting in his time. This paper discusses how his approach marked an active and mature response against this trend. Not only did King collect classical gems through the last years of his life, but his erudite approach made him an international authority in the field, so that collectors, connoisseurs, amateurs, dealers, and museum curators from Europe, the United States, and Asia relied on his expertise to evaluate the quality and originality of engraved gems they owned or wished to purchase. His papers, bequeathed to Trinity College at Cambridge upon his death, offer valuable insights into the nature and characteristics of 19th-century gem forgeries and signature interpolations and allow us to reconstruct the strategies implemented by King and his circle to recognize them. In spite of his knowledge and experience, King's collection of Greek and Roman engraved gems, acquired by the Metropolitan Museum of Art in 1881, counts a number of forgeries, which we use as unique case studies to explore the criteria and methodology he adopted in the evaluation of antique gems.

By focusing on Charles W. King, this paper aims to reassess the value and impact of modern forgeries and interpolations of classical engraved gems in the 19th century, thus reaching a better understanding of a transitional and critical phase in the history of gem collecting.

SESSION 1I: Colloquium
Interwoven Lives: The Eastern Mediterranean in the 13th to 17th Centuries

Sponsored by the Medieval and Post-Medieval Archaeology in Greece Interest Group

ORGANIZERS: *Rebecca M. Seifried*, University of Chicago, and *Lucie Wall Stylianopoulos*, University of Virginia

Colloquium Overview Statement

This colloquium, sponsored by the Medieval and Post-Medieval Archaeology in Greece Interest Group, focuses on patterns of interaction in a variety of spheres in the Late Medieval and post-Medieval periods (ca. 13th to 17th centuries C.E.). Beginning with the Fourth Crusade in 1204 C.E., the authors in this panel trace the effects of cross-cultural exchange using local case studies from Greece, Turkey, Lebanon, and the Balkans. Uniting all these papers is the theme of "Interwoven Lives"—the idea that culture is complex, richly layered, and above all else deeply influenced by the patterns of trade, migration, and warfare that characterized the eastern Mediterranean at this time. The panel has two overarching goals: first, to challenge traditional characterizations of these periods by demonstrating the intensity and vibrancy of the cultural exchange taking place at this time; and second, to use local-scale archaeological data sets to provide a long-term perspective on the process of interaction as it played out in specific locations within the region. The multiscalar approach, first developed by the Annales School, has become a common tool in archaeological studies for tracing cultural change over time. One of the recent advances in this field is the acknowledgement of local agency and decision-making processes, even in remote areas that are typically framed as passive receivers of "culture." Applying these paradigms to the Medieval and post-Medieval periods can provide more nuanced perspectives on a stretch of time that has, historically, received less archaeological attention. As the papers in this panel demonstrate, new advances in archaeological research are bringing to light evidence of the complex interplay between local individuals and foreign representatives, whether in the form of crusaders and soldiers, sea pirates, priests and missionaries, administrative officials, or everyday people and citizens.

Embedded Networks in World Systems: A Case Study from Late Medieval and Early Modern Cyprus

P. Nick Kardulias, College of Wooster

Over the past three decades, scholars with interests in long-term social change have increasingly turned to archaeological and historical data to build and test models concerning the nature of culture contact. This exploration of "deep history" developed out of the realization that a clear understanding of contemporary trends required a long-range perspective, so some have mined the archaeological record to build databases. A fruitful dialogue has opened between these scholars and archaeologists on such topics as how best to characterize the cultural interaction on frontiers or border areas, how information and goods flow between societies, the degree of social/political/economic integration (i.e., incorporation), and similar issues. Among the questions that such research pursues are the following: Do the data support a model of cyclical activity, and if so over what lengths of time? Under what conditions do we see expansion and contraction of interaction spheres? Which models or approaches provide the best opportunities for exploring the nature of culture contact? This paper argues that world-systems analysis (WSA) provides a robust approach to address such questions. Among the key arguments of WSA is that four types of networks govern interactions between social units and define the nature of world systems: bulk goods, prestige goods, political/military, and information. The degree to which a particular system emphasizes one of these networks reflects its complexity, but the four types tend to be nested. This approach provides a useful way to assess the nature of incorporation, also referred to as globalization. Using data from the Athienou Archaeological Project, I explore the nature of interaction within this region of central Cyprus, the island as a whole, and the broader area of the eastern Mediterranean. Settlement function and distribution were subject to both internal and external pressures throughout this period (roughly the 13th to 19th century) as revealed in material retrieved from excavation and survey since the origin of the project in 1990.

Colonization in Frankish Greece: An Archaeological Reassessment

Grant Schrama, Queen's University

The focus of this paper is on the existence of a colonial Frankish society in Greece from 1204 to 1261 C.E. as revealed through archaeological remains. In 1204 C.E., Latin crusaders en route to Egypt sacked the city of Constantinople in what is now known as the Fourth Crusade. As a result of this conquest, western European migrants settled in Constantinople and Greece, establishing a colonial society within these regions. This paper argues that a colonial society was established in Constantinople and Greece from 1204 to 1261 C.E. by the Latin crusaders, and evidence of this colonialism is most prevalent in the archaeological remains left behind by the conquerors.

When the Latin crusaders conquered Constantinople in 1204 C.E. and then Greece in 1204 - 1205 C.E., they created a colonial society based on the western European feudal model, with the indigenous Byzantines subservient to their new Latin masters. Scholars of Frankish Greece have hesitated to properly label this new establishment as "colonial" despite the many characteristics that support such a description. One of the best ways to identify the colonial nature of Frankish Greece is through the archaeological remains of churches, castles, and other secular and religious buildings constructed by the conquerors. I analyze these remains throughout this paper, arguing that they were built as a display of conquest and power for the western European crusaders and were meant to be symbols of Latin imperialism and colonialism. I examine the presence of Byzantine architectural techniques and styles within these "western" structures, attempting to establish whether any cultural interaction occurred between the colonizers and colonized. This analysis thus brings to light any cultural symbiosis that may have occurred during this period between the Latin settlers and the indigenous Byzantines. Although the study of Frankish Greece has increased to a certain degree over the past few years, no scholar has labeled the conquest of Constantinople and subsequent settlement of the Aegean region as an act of colonialism. In sum, my paper brings forth a new way to describe the events of 1204 - 1261 C.E. and a way to analyze them through archaeology.

Kythera: Churches and Pirates on a Small Greek Island

Lita Tzortzopoulou-Gregory, Australian Archaeological Institute in Athens, and
Timothy E. Gregory, Ohio State University

Interaction among peoples in the Mediterranean during the later Middle Ages/ early modern period was heavily impacted by the Crusades and the competition between the growing power of the western states and that of the Ottoman empire. The analysis of this phenomenon has been broadly investigated, at both the larger and the local scale. This presentation seeks to focus primarily on the latter, with analysis of how one small area was affected by outside influence.

The island of Kythera is an ideal "focus" for such an analysis, in part because its location, astride the most important sea lanes in the Mediterranean, made it a place that was necessarily "caught" between East and West and where recent archaeological and archival research provides good information about the larger phenomenon of interaction there. Of course, as a result of its relatively small size and few natural resources, Kythera would normally have been on the "receiving end" of interaction from others, but our research argues that this was not always the case. Much of the research we will discuss is based on evidence connected with the Australian-Kythera Archaeological Survey, which carried out fieldwork from 1999 to 2003 and which plans to conduct further fieldwork and analysis from 2016 to 2018.

In the interest of time, our paper for this session will investigate two case studies. The first of these will look at the impact of external forces on the architecture and the decoration of churches on Kythera. Scholarship on this issue has generally argued that these phenomena on Kythera were, in fact, heavily influenced by "foreign" traditions, and we will question this conclusion with specific examples. Our second case study will investigate how piracy in the waters around Kythera had a significant impact on the island itself, both in terms of settlements and defenses, but also on local culture and the Venetian rulers themselves.

The Polychrome Sgraffito Ware of Thrapsano and the Regional Markets of Venetian Crete (15th to 17th Centuries)

Mark D. Hammond, The Pennsylvania State University

Ethnographic studies conducted during the 20th century documented the early modern ceramic traditions of Thrapsano in central Crete, but until recently the history of ceramic manufacture in the village before the 19th century remained vague. The finds collected during the Galatas Survey Project (2005–2007), concentrated to the south of the Venetian capital city of Candia (modern Herakleion), offer an opportunity to reconstruct part of this lost history. In this paper, I present evidence attesting to a previously unknown center of 15th- to 17th-century sgraffito production at Thrapsano and explore its relationship to the highly regionalized patterns of production and distribution that marked rural, Venetian Crete.

Despite the lack of imported pottery, the production of polychrome sgraffito ware at Thrapsano during these centuries developed within the context of a period of relative peace and cultural flourishing. These fine wares appear to have employed a refined version of the ceramic fabric used by the pithos makers of the early modern period and are characterized by a standard decorative motif resembling a four-armed star that appears on most examples. The additional find of countless kiln separators whose shape agrees with scars on the bowls confirms that they were manufactured in the area surrounding Thrapsano.

Additional finds from the survey indicate that Thrapsano was not alone in its production of polychrome sgraffito ware with this decorative motif. The recovery of similar products manufactured in different fabrics reveals that the survey zone was supplied by different centers of production. Furthermore, the publication of similar vessels from other parts of the island may suggest that such workshops were not limited to central Crete alone. The evidence therefore suggests that Thrapsano was one of numerous manufacturers of polychrome sgraffito ware with a limited geographic distribution to local or immediately neighboring markets. While market competition or artistic influences might account for such a widespread production of similar products, the practices of itinerant potters should also be considered. The latter may have an ethnographic parallel in the 19th- and 20th-century practice of the *vendema*, in which itinerant potters from Thrapsano traveled to other markets and used local resources to manufacture their pithoi. In the near-total absence of imported pottery collected during the survey dated to the Venetian period, the 15th- to 17th-century sgraffito from Thrapsano offers insight into the dynamic market activities that were practiced within rural Crete.

The Social-Spatial Dynamics of Hydraulic Landscapes: Water in Village and Inter-Village Life in Ottoman Lebanon

Stephen McPhillips, University of Copenhagen

Water is the most significant element for human life, and in the Middle East it has been carefully harnessed over millennia in often highly adaptive and socially complex ways. Recent archaeological work has begun to document the history of a rural landscape in the Batroun region of northern Lebanon, with a particular focus on how it changed through the Ottoman period (between 1500 C.E. and 1918 C.E.), combining methodologies developed in landscape archaeology, architectural analysis, and historical and ethnographic investigation. The river valleys and hillsides of northern Jabal Lubnan (Mount Lebanon) preserve an unusually high number of hydraulic remains from premodern periods. Among the best examples is the Nahr al-Jawz (the Jawz Valley). It represents an ideal case study for investigating the lived spaces within and between villages, which in Jabal Lubnan, as elsewhere in the Middle East, turn around the construction, maintenance, and production activities associated with water and hydraulic infrastructure. Archaeological evidence of these activities survives in many forms (water channels, watermills, roads, bridges, threshing floors, domestic architecture, village fountains, and cisterns), while archival and other historical sources make the link with local monastic houses, urban society, and the state, and ethnographic data provide insights into how the landscape is viewed now and in oral traditions by its inhabitants. The study area corresponds to the lower watershed of this river, within which a detailed analysis of distribution hierarchies and collective approaches to water networks offers new perspectives on intervillage and regional social structures.

SESSION 1J
Discerning Food, Health, and Mobility in the Past

CHAIR: *Calla McNamee*, Wiener Laboratory

Paleomobility and Paleodiet Through Biogeochemistry in Early Bronze Age Attica

Eleni-Anna Prevedorou, Wiener Laboratory of the American School of Classical Studies at Athens, *Jane E. Buikstra*, Arizona State University, *Gwyneth W. Gordon*, Arizona State University, and *Kelly J. Knudson*, Arizona State University

This study addresses the role of paleomobility and maritime connections during the formation of late Final Neolithic and Early Helladic I Attica (ca. 3500–2650 B.C.E.), characterized by intensified interregional networks, metal ore exploitation, and organized cemeteries. We focus on the Early Helladic cemetery of Tsepi at Marathon, which constitutes the earliest formalized cemetery in Attica and presents both mainland and island features. We adopt a biogeochemical approach and use the Tsepi skeletal assemblage to examine archaeological hypotheses regarding the degree of residential relocation, the nature of the interaction between the Attic coast and the Cycladic Islands, the traditional hypothesis of Cycladic colonies, and the identity of the cemetery groups.

Radiogenic strontium isotope ($^{87}Sr/^{86}Sr$) and elemental concentration analyses were performed on archaeological human enamel samples (N=100) from the Tsepi cemetery following established methodologies in order to investigate individual origins and possible migration to the site. Archaeological faunal specimens from Tsepi, comparative archaeological human assemblages, and modern environmental samples were used to characterize the locally bioavailable strontium in the region. Most individuals (96%) from Tsepi showed biochemical values well within the local range, suggesting a local character for the cemetery sample. Of the 75 individuals analyzed, only three clearly showed "nonlocal" biochemical values indicating that, as long as local strontium food and water sources were consumed, they spent their infancy in a region geochemically distinct from Tsepi and the northeastern Attic coast. The biochemical values of the three "nonlocals" might suggest a common provenance reflecting a link between Tsepi and a single locale. Burial location did not depend on geographic origins, suggesting that the "non local" individuals were fully integrated into the community. To examine possible geochemical origins, an extensive database of radiogenic strontium values was generated. Furthermore, we applied stable strontium isotope ($\delta^{88/86}Sr$) analysis, a recently developed analytical technique, to reconstruct paleodiet and strontium dietary intake. The results showed a wide variation in dietary practices, including marine resource consumption associated with male individuals. The observed sex-based difference may reflect a maritime association for the community. Overall, this study exemplifies the use of biogeochemistry in identifying residential mobility and marine diet in the area. The results point to more nuanced interpretations of human mobility and interregional contacts in the prehistoric Aegean and support recent scholarship on the integrative nature of coastal zones.

This study was funded by the National Science Foundation and the Wiener Laboratory of the American School of Classical Studies at Athens.

Soup's On! Expanding the Picture of Minoan Meals Through Functional Analysis of Cooking Pots and Tablewares

Micaela Carignano, Cornell University

The topic of feasting has been widely discussed in the field of Minoan archaeology, especially as it pertains to the palaces and villas of the Proto- and Neopalatial periods. The primary objects of study have been ceramic drinking sets, which lead scholars to suggest wine-drinking rituals as key arenas for expressions of power relations and legitimization of status. However, these discussions of feasting do not take into account the importance of other foods or of other dining contexts. My paper aims to expand our conception of Neopalatial dining and food culture. I achieve this through a comparative examination of food-preparation and consumption contexts from elite and nonelite houses as well as palaces. Using a functional analysis of cooking ceramics and tablewares, I argue that besides wine, Minoan meals were based around the consumption of liquid-like foods such as soups, stews, and porridges. The ingredients and seasonings could be altered to create a near-infinite variety of dishes, but the basic structure of the meal was similar in elite and nonelite contexts, as well as across feasts and everyday meals. This similarity is significant because while wine drinking may have served to distinguish ruling elites as a separate class, homogeneity of diet would have lessened this distance, especially as expressed in public banqueting practices. In summary, by examining a broader context of food consumption, my paper expands our understanding of Neopalatial feasting and food culture and its role in creating and maintaining Minoan sociopolitical structures.

The More Things Change, the More They Stay the Same: Using Microbotanical Evidence to Examine Bronze Age Subsistence

Calla McNamee, Malcolm H. Wiener Laboratory for Archaeological Science, American School of Classical Studies at Athens

Reconstructions of prehistoric plant-based subsistence strategies typically occur at the site level, making it difficult to examine how these strategies are culturally influenced on a wider scale. This paper takes a broader perspective by examining microbotanical evidence from several sites across mainland Greece to explore similarities and differences through space and time in subsistence practices from the Final Neolithic to the Early Iron Age. The investigation focuses primarily on starch grains and phytoliths extracted from ground-stone tools from the sites of Mitrou and Tsoungiza, which, although spatially separated, share similarities in occupation span and history. Results from the sites of Tiryns, Eleon, and Kontopigado at Alimos provide supporting data. In total, this research draws on the results from microbotanical analysis of more than 200 ground-stone artifacts.

In this paper, I suggest that the grinding of food resources on stone tools can be considered as an indicator of multiple factors impacting the subsistence spectrum from agricultural production to consumption. The nature of the analysis, as well as the spatial and temporal span of the samples analyzed, allows for an examination of cultural patterns at different scales, including the broad regional scale, affected by the wider socioeconomic system, and the local household and domestic scale, influenced by cultural transmission and social learning.

Within this framework, the results from this study indicate two significant trends: (1) the occurrence of differential resource utilization across space and through time, and (2) the existence of a long-standing practice of heat treating grains prior to processing. I propose that the first trend reflects variation in production between sites and through time, with more diverse starch assemblages on ground-stone tools being associated with localized agricultural production and household allocation of resources, whereas more uniform assemblages are indicative of intensive agricultural production and increased resource commodification. Emergent and expanding trade networks, increased social stratification, and increased resource control are also considered as causal factors that contribute to this decrease in variation. The persistence of heat treating, in contrast, is interpreted as indicative of consistency in domestic practice through time at the household level. It is considered a reflection of a "community of practice," which functions to solidify social relationships. Despite the major sociopolitical changes across the region through this extended time period, I argue that the transmission and maintenance of grain preprocessing testifies to intergenerational social learning and underlying cultural continuity.

Geographic Origins and Mobility in Pre-Roman and Roman Apulia Through Stable Isotope Analysis

Tracy Prowse, McMaster University

Archaeological survey in the environs of Gravina in Puglia, southern Italy, indicates a decrease in settlement size and density after the end of the Iron Age (ca. fifth century B.C.E.). Historical evidence from the early Roman republic (ca. fourth to third centuries B.C.E.) suggests significant political and social upheaval in the region of Apulia associated with conflicts between the expanding Roman republic, and indigenous Italian groups, as well as Greece and Carthage. The apparent outcome for many locations in southern Italy after the Samnite, Pyrrhic, and Punic Wars was the subjugation of local residents, a decline in settlements, and the confiscation of land by the expanding Roman empire. There is further archaeological evidence for a resurgence of occupation in the region by the first century C.E., including the presence of at least one large imperial estate.

The site of Vagnari is one of these imperial estates, and archaeological excavations at the site since 2001 have revealed a large site (3.5 ha) with both residential and industrial areas, along with a necropolis dating between the second and fourth centuries C.E. Given the history of the region, the question is whether the people who lived and worked on this estate were local to the area or whether they moved to the region (or were brought there) by the owner(s) of the estate. This paper explores the changing patterns of migration between the Iron Age and Roman periods in this region of Apulia through oxygen isotope analysis ($\delta^{18}O$) of teeth from the Iron Age (seventh to fourth centuries B.C.E.) sites of Botromagno and Parco San Stefano (n=20) and the Roman site of Vagnari (n=45). Results of this analysis indicate that there was, in fact, lower mobility in the Roman period, with only a small percentage (9%) of the sample displaying $\delta^{18}O$ values indicative of nonlocal origins. In contrast, approximately 30% of the Iron Age sample appears to have been born outside the region. The results of this study indicate that mobility did not increase with the social upheaval caused by Roman expansion in southern Italy and further suggest that the people who lived and worked at Vagnari were likely local inhabitants, not foreign workers or slaves.

Vitamin D in the Roman Population

Megan Brickley, McMaster University, *Michele George*, McMaster University, *Simon Mays*, English Heritage, and *Tracy Prowse*, McMaster University

Symptoms of vitamin D deficiency in the Roman era are identified in the medical writings of Soranus of Ephesus and Galen (both second century C.E.), but the extent of the problem has never before been pursued. We present initial data from the first large-scale study of vitamin D deficiency in diverse Roman populations throughout Europe. In healthy humans, vitamin D is synthesized in the skin when it is exposed to natural light, with higher levels available at lower latitudes, but it can also be acquired from a small number of dietary sources. Adequate levels are required for the formation and maintenance of healthy bones, and severe vitamin D deficiency results in skeletal deformity; the term rickets is often used for changes in juveniles and osteomalacia in adults. An assessment of vitamin D deficiency can provide information about a number of important aspects of Roman life, such as attitudes about health, child-care practices, and inequalities based on gender, status, and age. Through the integration of skeletal and funerary evidence, this project offers new insights into the health of Roman populations from diverse geographic contexts and contributes to emerging debates about the causes and consequences of vitamin D deficiency.

Thus far, data from 2,853 skeletons of all ages from a range of latitudes (between 37°N and 53°N) and from predominantly larger settlements in the United Kingdom, France, Italy, and Spain have been recorded. In the final field season (summer 2016), data collection has focused on small towns and rural sites. Initial results show that there is no simple correlation between levels of vitamin D deficiency and latitude. While latitude clearly plays a role, with the highest levels found in the most northern site (Ancaster in the United Kingdom), settlement size and levels of social complexity are clearly also important. Relatively high levels of vitamin D deficiency were found at Isola Sacra (Italy) and Barcino (Spain), both midsized port cities with a southern location. However, the only site that has as yet not produced skeletal evidence of vitamin D deficiency in juveniles (who provide a more sensitive indicator of deficiency than adults) is Vagnari, a rural site in southern Italy. Our results thus indicate that vitamin D deficiency was far more widespread than anticipated and would have affected many Roman communities across the empire.

A Stable Isotope Investigation of Diet at the Roman Imperial Site of Vagnari, South Italy

Lisa Semchuk, McMaster University, and *Tracy Prowse*, McMaster University

Studies of Roman diet typically draw from historical sources, which may be biased toward urban elite perspectives and leave the dietary practices of rural inhabitants underrepresented. The cemetery at Vagnari, an imperial estate in southern Italy (first to fourth century C.E.), provides an opportunity to investigate the foods eaten by estate laborers and learn more about the lives of rural Romans. This paper presents analysis of diet using stable carbon ($\delta^{13}C$) and nitrogen ($\delta^{1?}N$) isotopes from human bone. Isotopic composition of bone collagen and carbonate from individuals in the Vagnari cemetery indicates a diet largely composed of C? plants, such as wheat, with the incorporation of some animal-based proteins and C? foods (e.g., millet). These isotopic results align with suggestions from historical sources of ordinary Roman diet as a "Mediterranean triad" of cereals, olives, and wine.

Individual isotopic variation in diet at Vagnari stems mainly from age-related differences, with nitrogen values and total diet changing with increased age-at-death.

No sex-based differences in stable isotope ratios are apparent. Isotope ratios from Vagnari are also compared with those from other imperial Italian sites to situate the diet within a broader Roman context. The Vagnari diet is isotopically similar to the diets at other inland and rural sites and differs from those at coastal urban sites, where marine resources were regularly consumed. These results indicate the diversity of foods eaten in Roman Italy and provide further details on the diets of rural Roman populations.

SESSION 2A: Colloquium
Insulae Coniunctae: Mediterranean Archaeologies of Insularity in the Age of Globalization

ORGANIZERS: *Jody Michael Gordon*, Wentworth Institute of Technology, and *Anna Kouremenos*, Independent Researcher

Colloquium Overview Statement

Recently, complex interpretations of sociocultural change in the ancient Mediterranean world have emerged that challenge earlier models. Influenced by today's hyperconnected age, scholars no longer perceive the Mediterranean as a static place where "Graeco-Roman" culture was dominant but rather see it as a dynamic and connected sea where fragmentation and uncertainty, along with mobility and networking, were the norm. Hence, a current theoretical approach to studying ancient culture has been that of globalization, which Pitts and Versluys (*Globalisation in the Roman World* [Oxford 2014] 11) have defined as "processes by which localities and people become increasingly interconnected and interdependent." Globalization approaches redefine "global" as any place and time where interregional interaction and connectivity intensified, and "globalization" as a process of change that accrued via increased social interactions. Certain eras of Mediterranean history (e.g., the Roman empire) known for their increased connectivity have thus been analyzed from a globalized perspective that examines rhizomal networking, cultural diversity, and multiple processes of social change. Archaeology has proven a useful discipline for investigating ancient "globalization" because of its recent focus on how identity—or one's sense of belonging based on socially recognized differences (e.g., language, religion, or ethnicity)—is expressed through material culture negotiated between both local and global influences when levels of connectivity are altered.

One form of identity that has been inadequately explored in relation to globalization theory is insularity. Insularity, or the socially recognized differences expressed by people living on islands, is a form of self-identification created within a particular space and time. The omission of insularity from many globalization studies is problematic since islands are often some of the most hyperconnected places. Moreover, islanders often produce archaeologically legible material culture(s) that expresses identities affected by levels of connectivity. Insularity, then, as a social identity affected by "global" forces, should be viewed as an important research paradigm for archaeologies concerned with reexamining cultural change.

This colloquium explores how comparative archaeologies of insularity can contribute to discourse on ancient Mediterranean "globalization." It brings together archaeologists working on different islands and a range of material culture types to examine how Mediterranean insularities changed during eras when connectivity increased. Through a diachronic analysis of how insular identities were constructed, the colloquium provides insights on how levels of connectivity change, the nature of "glocal" (i.e., hybrid global and local) identities, and the social ruptures fostered by increased cross-cultural interaction.

Acting (G)locally: Monumental Place-Making and Identity on Late Bronze Age Cyprus

Kevin Fisher, University of British Columbia

The Late Bronze Age (ca. 1650–1100 B.C.E.) in the eastern Mediterranean saw the growing economic and political interconnection of various empires and polities stretching from Mesopotamia to Greece. Indeed, some have argued that it was one of the earliest examples of globalization. Cyprus' insularity, which had during some prehistoric periods facilitated an isolation from the sociopolitical and economic developments of the surrounding littoral, made it an important node in Late Bronze Age maritime networks. It is no coincidence that during this period Cyprus transformed from a relatively insular, egalitarian, and village-based society to one characterized by economic intensification and specialization and hierarchical and heterarchical social structures as emerging elites took advantage of external demand for the island's rich copper resources. These elites materialized their status through various media that referenced an "international style," combining elements of Egyptian, Levantine, and Aegean iconography and used to express elite identity throughout the region. While drawing on the globalized nature of this style as means of legitimacy, its use was adapted for local consumption through a process of reinterpretation and synthesis best described as glocalization. This process extended beyond portable luxury items to include architectural elements employed in the construction of the island's first large-scale monumental buildings.

This paper examines the place-making activities of Late Bronze Age Cypriot elites, who drew on architectural elements of the wider eastern Mediterranean koiné but adapted them to facilitate new local modes of social interaction centered on feasting, through which social statuses, roles, and identities were negotiated and reproduced. While monumental court-centered buildings were used throughout the region, a local Cypriot style was materialized through the purposeful configuration of space to encourage (or discourage) particular types of interaction, as well as through the strategic placement of ashlar masonry and other symbolically charged architectural elements as a means of reifying social boundaries. These monumental buildings and the urban landscapes in which they were situated were socially constructed and meaningful places of action and interaction that became a central component of Cypriot elite identities.

Insularity, Connectivity, and Identity: Sardinia and the Western Mediterranean in the Iron Age

Andrea Roppa, University of Leicester

Increased interaction has been recently proposed as the distinctive common feature of the Iron Age Mediterranean (ninth–sixth centuries B.C.E.). In the western Mediterranean, the development of Greek and Phoenician colonial networks resulted in sustained movements of goods and people, which connected in unprecedented ways both local communities and newcomers. Recent scholarship has drawn on insights provided by the discourse on contemporary globalization to gain insights into the entangled materiality of the archaic Mediterranean. Consumerism perspectives have been adopted to grasp the archaeological complexity of this "protoglobal" world. On the other hand, the focus on "hybrid objects" has shown in great detail the complex interplay between local meanings and new social practices. The discourse on Iron Age protoglobalization acquires a particular significance on the island of Sardinia, where a strongly defined local culture flourished in the course of the Bronze Age. While in traditional reconstructions the local civilization came to an end in the Iron Age, when it was replaced by Phoenician colonial culture, recent perspectives have pointed to the vitality of Nuragic culture well into the Iron Age.

In this paper, I discuss the themes of insularity and identity in the context of increasingly sustained Iron Age connectivity by focusing on Sardinia's ceramic material culture, particularly on two specific aspects: first, the distribution of Nuragic ceramic material in the western Mediterranean at colonial and indigenous sites, which were connected by the Phoenician network; and second, the appearance of the so-called Sant'Imbenia type amphoras in the Nuragic ceramic repertoire, a type of transport vessel derived from Phoenician transport amphoras but produced according to traditional techniques. By focusing on ceramic distribution patterns and "hybrid objects" I aim to explore, on the one hand, the vitality of the island's identity in the context of the protoglobal Iron Age Mediterranean. On the other hand, I show how the appearance of new types of material culture responded to the needs of Sardinian communities to actively participate in the opportunities provided by increased connectivity.

Religious Activity as an Index for Globalization and Insularity in Archaic and Classical Sicily

Justin St. P. Walsh, Chapman University, and *Tamar Hodos*, University of Bristol

Evidence of shared practices and localized differences—the balance within globalization processes—are often more pronounced in island contexts. Sicily, as a discrete, bounded landmass that required collaboration and cohabitation among its residents, had an island character that played a critical role in shaping the interplay between common and divergent behaviors between its diverse cultural groups. This is exemplified in developments in religious practices during the Archaic and Classical periods. Demeter's and especially Kore's mythologies were widely recognized to be linked with Sicily. Most famously, the shores of Lake Pergusa, at the island's center, served as the setting for many versions of Kore's kidnapping to the underworld by Hades. The discovery of numerous, and often highly visible, shrines to the mother-and-daughter pair at Greek sites across Sicily (e.g., Selinous, Gela) have been seen as physical indicators of the goddesses' particular significance to the colonizers in this context. Moreover, the appearance of worship of Demeter and Kore in some indigenous and mixed-population towns has suggested the conflation or syncretism of these goddesses with local fertility cults. At Morgantina, an extramural sanctuary founded in the Archaic period seems to have persisted through the destruction of the town and its refoundation, which may have been up to three decades later. This sanctuary featured multiple private shrines, adorned with images of the deities (including acrolithic sculptures made partly in imported Greek marble). In the new, Classical-era Morgantina—a city which appears to have had both Greek and indigenous settlers—Demeter and Kore also received their own apportionment of individual house-sized lots within multiple neighborhoods. At Sabucina, an indigenous settlement, Demeter may have been the recipient of private worship in the form of terracotta votives, or else a local divinity for whom Demeter's attributes were deemed appropriate was being revered. We explore the material evidence for Demeter and Kore's worship in Sicily as an element that both fostered common understanding, creating a point of mutual recognition for both Sikels and Sikeliotes, while also respecting divergent traditions. These practices also highlight the respective roles of women, often overlooked in globalization discussions.

Globalization and Insularity in (Dis)Connected Crete

Jane Francis, Concordia University

The position of Crete on the intersection of cultural and trade routes provided the island with numerous economic advantages throughout its history, but its incorporation into the Roman province of Creta et Cyrenaica in the 30s B.C.E. introduced prospects for enhanced levels of global participation. Scholarship is now recognizing that the central government at Rome and even its assignees resident in Crete did not interfere dramatically or regularly in the day-to-day life of the Cretans. Many factors indicate the rise of a cultural hybridity on Crete that cuts across social classes and site location but did not affect all Crete equally. With Crete, it is possible instead to envision multiple insularities, given the island's bitter regional divisions and demonstrated topographical segregation. There is no uniform reaction or accommodation to Roman rule, which on the contrary had polyvalent outcomes depending on whether one looks at the question of globalization from an intra-island or extra-island perspective. Some sites can be considered "globalized" to a certain degree, but many other parts of Crete barely seem to have noticed the Romans at all. Furthermore, Crete in the Early Roman period, which tended to look west, is quite unlike the island of the Late Roman era, when its emphasis shifts east. The degree to which Cretans wanted to be Roman—or even had an option of doing so—cannot be known, but the material remains on the island indicate the degree to which they joined the Roman world and how this was manifest, both on the island and beyond.

This paper addresses the question of what it meant to be a "Cretan" during the Roman Empire and explores the degree of engagement of Crete within the broader Roman world that can be articulated through its material remains.

SESSION 2B
Numismatic Evidence for the Republican Period

CHAIR: To be announced

Cross-Cultural Currencies: The Litra and Sicilian Fractional Silver

Giuseppe C. Castellano, University of Texas at Austin

The indigenous inhabitants of Bronze and Iron Age Sicily exchanged bronze objects as a protomonetary currency. Ingots, tools, and scrap were hoarded as wealth and traded by weight, eventually coming to be reckoned against a variety of regional libral standards that included the Sicilian litra. Greeks and indigenous Italic peoples in Sicily had been in contact for centuries before the advent of coinage, and so would have become accustomed to one another's protomonetary practice. The hybridized currencies and standards that emerged from this intercourse speak to the strong cultural and economic links between Italy, Sicily, and the Greek homeland.

I argue that the indigenous tradition exerted a strong influence on the monetization of Sicily, and that the litra standard for Greek-style silver coinage was derived from a long-standing native bronze standard. With the introduction of Greek-style coinage in the sixth century B.C.E. the litra took on new significance as a small silver coin equivalent in value to the native bronze weight measure. These coins were minted alongside the obol, the traditional Greek fraction. Despite variations in weight among obols—the expected result of differing Greek regional standards—the silver litrai remain fairly consistent. This suggests that they were at least initially tied to another standard, the native bronze, unaffected by the variability among traditional Greek systems. The silver litra and its fractions formed a neat solution to the problem of exchange, allowing for direct conversion between the native bronze system and the Greek silver system, which would have greatly facilitated trade between Greeks and the indigenous peoples of Sicily. Colonial encounters of this kind often engender complex rearticulations of economic and cultural practice, and it is clear from literary, archaeological, and numismatic evidence that the Greeks were receptive to foreign standards and were willing to modify their own systems or assimilate elements of others in response to social, political, and economic exigencies.

This overlap of diverse currencies led to the creation of hybrid monetary systems that bore elements of both the imported Greek and native Italic traditions. These parallel standards show a greater entanglement between the Greek notion of coinage and existing local practices than has usually been assumed. What emerges is a more nuanced view of Greek colonization than the historical narratives suggest: this is not merely a story of the colonizers and the colonized, but of complex colonial and postcolonial populations attempting to coexist, cooperate, and prosper.

Wheels, Keels, and Coins: A Landscape of Human Movement at Roman Vicarello in the Third Century B.C.E.

Rabun Taylor, University of Texas at Austin, *Edward O'Neill*, University of Leicester, *Michael O'Neill*, Independent Scholar, and *Giovanni Isidori*, Independent Scholar

One of the most famous votive treasures of the ancient world comes directly from the scalding waters of Vicarello, near the ancient town of Forum Clodii on Lake Bracciano northwest of Rome. In antiquity this spa, one of a pair of therapeutic sanctuaries called Aquae Apollinares, lay in a semirural district served by an extensive road system. It was a popular destination, as demonstrated by the famous votive deposit recovered from the spring in 1852 dating as far back as the Neolithic but especially well represented from the Archaic period through late antiquity. More than 5,200 coins were recovered from this deposit, most of which date to the third century B.C.E. Their provenance and distribution point to a significant demographic phenomenon centered on the First Punic War: first, more than 700 coins of one type probably minted at Cosa just before 269 (*Roman Republican Coinage* [*RRC*] 17); second, more than 1,100 examples of a single aes grave series from Rome (*RRC* 14); and third, an unusually high representation of coins minted in South Italy, especially Campania, crowned by 1,160 examples of a single issue probably minted at Naples (*RRC* 18).

In light of recent reassessments of Roman naval power in the years before and during the First Punic War, this deposit—along with another one at Carsoli, east of Rome—argue for the mass movement of people between Campania, Rome, Cosa, and other important nodes of transport and defense in the first decades of the third century. The impetus for this movement—and for the founding of the colonies of Cosa and Paestum in 273 B.C.E.—may have been to build up a Roman navy, partly auxiliary and partly home-grown. An inscribed rostrum recently recovered from the Battle of the Aegates (241 B.C.E.) suggests that the ship's construction was overseen at Cosa; it has also been proposed that the Minerva coin was issued there to support a naval training base. Allies from the south, lending their maritime expertise, would thus have been traveling northward and back, as would their agents requisitioning ship materials from various parts of Italy. Along the way, Vicarello's Sanctuary of Apollo, a god revered by coastal Campanians, drew crowds of southern travelers to its therapeutic waters.

All this benefited nearby Forum Clodii, which lay along the Rome-Cosa highway and probably administered the Vicarello sanctuary. We briefly report on a preliminary analysis of the town's known remains from the Republican period.

Novel Identifications of some Early Roman Moneyers

John D. Morgan, University of Delaware

Unlike Roman moneyers in the last century of the free republic, who usually spelled out their names on their coinages with sufficient fullness that modern scholars can easily identify them, between ca. 210 and ca. 150 B.C.E. Roman moneyers usually indicated their names, if at all, in a very abbreviated form, or by canting symbols, which are much harder for modern scholars to decipher, though their meaning must have been recognizable by contemporary Romans. In this talk I propose several novel identifications of some of these moneyers.

Michael Crawford (*Roman Republican Coinage* [RCC] 75) has assigned to a Sicilian mint and dated to 209–208 B.C.E. a moneyer who abbreviated his name as C·AL, which modern scholars have implausibly expanded to yield an otherwise unattested C. Al(lius) or C.A(i)l(ius), assuming that AL is the abbreviation of a *nomen gentilicium*. Since the contemporary Sicilian coinage (*RRC* 74) of C·VAR(ro) presents the moneyer's cognomen, I propose that C·AL was C. Cincius Alimentus, a younger relative of L. Cincius Alimentus, the praetor and propraetor in Sicily in 210–209 B.C.E.

Two slightly later issues (*RRC* 130 and 131) dated by Crawford to 206–200 B.C.E. feature on the obverse a staff (*scipio*) and on the reverse a feather or wing (*penna*). I suggest that these symbols refer to the famous P. Cornelius Scipio (consul in 205 B.C.E.) and to M. Iunius Pennus, a plebeian aedile in 205 B.C.E. and the *praetor urbanus* in 201 B.C.E. One generation later the feather reappears on the reverse of *RRC* 163, dated by Crawford to 179–170 B.C.E. This later moneyer can be identified with M. Iunius M.f. M.n. Pennus, a praetor in 172 B.C.E. and consul in 167 B.C.E., who was the earlier moneyer's son.

Also dated 179–170 B.C.E. is *RRC* 159, which features on its reverse a fly (*musca*). This moneyer can be identified with Ti. Sempronius Musca, who in 168 B.C.E. was a member of a five-man commission that decided a boundary dispute between Pisa and Luna in Etruria (Livy 45.13.10–11).

Yet another issue dated 179–170 B.C.E. is *RRC* 156, which features on its reverse a prawn (*squilla*). I suggest that this moneyer should be identified with the tribune of the plebs in 172 B.C.E. whose name appears as "M. Marcius Scylla" (Livy 42.21.3) in the frequently corrupt unique manuscript of Livy's fifth decade. "Scylla," an unlikely cognomen for a man, could well be a corruption of "Squilla."

RRC 195, dated 169–158 B.C.E, depicts on its reverse a little male ass (*asellus*). I suggest that this moneyer was Ti. Claudius Asellus, a son of the Ti. Claudius Asellus who was a praetor in 206 B.C.E. and plebeian aedile in 205 B.C.E., and the father of the Ti. Claudius Asellus who was a tribune of the plebs in 140 B.C.E.

The possibility of making these identifications suggests that further progress can be made in identifying more early Roman moneyers who indicated their names in very abbreviated forms, or only as canting symbols.

A Reassessment of the Narbo Warrior Denarius Serratus (*RRC* 282)

Ellen M.H. MacDougall, University of St Andrews

This paper provides a reassessment of the significance of the Narbo warrior denarius serratus (*RRC* 282) when it comes to considering how foreign peoples were represented on Roman coinage in the late Roman republic. This denarius serratus depicts a nude male Gallic charioteer who is armed and in the process of hurling a spear toward an unseen enemy. With a minting date of ca. 118 B.C.E., this denarius serratus marks the earliest extant appearance of a foreign people on Roman republican coinage. In spite of this, it has attracted very little attention in scholarship that considers how foreign peoples were represented on Roman republican coinage. Standard scholarship has identified the image of the shackled and defeated captive, submissive to triumphing Roman power as the standard, even defining, image of a foreign people in Roman republican numismatics. However, the composition of the Narbo warrior denarius serratus presents a vastly different picture. Rather than being shown bound and submissive, he is shown active, armed and aggressive, with the outcome of his struggle as yet unclear. By placing the coin type as far as possible within its contemporary context, this paper considers how an ancient viewer might have understood this image. The paper offers two potential avenues for interpretation. Firstly, the coin is considered against the contemporary backdrop of ongoing conflicts and uncertainty in what was a far from settled region surrounding Narbo. Secondly, the coin is interpreted in the light of contemporary or near contemporary attitudes toward Gauls reflected elsewhere in Roman artwork and literature. There is a clear second-century B.C.E. literary and artistic focus on Gallic warriors at moments of combative action. In this tradition, while the threat of the Gauls is acknowledged in the form of the armed and active warrior, a contemporary ancient viewer might nevertheless have also understood this scene as anticipating a Roman victory through superior military strength. A thorough investigation of this coin type in the light of its contemporary historical, literary, and artistic context provides a more nuanced picture of foreign peoples in late Roman republican numismatics than just the image of the captive.

SESSION 2C: Colloquium
Small Finds; Writ Large

ORGANIZERS: *Catherine K. Baker*, Bowdoin College and *Leigh Anne Lieberman*, Princeton University

Colloquium Overview Statement

The study of small finds is experiencing a revolution. New and exciting tools and approaches to artifacts now complement more traditional analyses based primarily on qualification and quantification. These fresh perspectives have given new life to objects that would once have been neglected in busy storerooms or appreciated mainly for their aesthetic qualities. New digital technologies offer flexible and dynamic means for organizing, categorizing, and examining artifactual data on large and small scales. Furthermore, recent approaches demonstrate the importance of a contextual and spatial understanding of finds and their distribution. The study of artifact assemblages is ideally situated now more than ever to contribute in significant ways to our understanding of the ancient world.

This colloquium takes advantage of this moment to highlight these developments, bringing together scholars who utilize artifactual data in new and groundbreaking ways across a wide chronological and geographical range. These papers thus offer innovative approaches to the study of object use, artifact deposition, and the contextualization and organization of small finds data. Papers in this colloquium review the changing priorities of excavators in recording artifactual data, examine the utility of microdebris analysis to identify ancient activities in the archaeological record, consider the life histories of various classes of artifacts, and employ varied statistical methods to illustrate patterns in the spatial, chronological, and contextual distribution of small finds. By highlighting in this panel the myriad possibilities for studying small finds, we demonstrate that artifacts have the potential to shed light on new and exciting aspects of ancient behaviors and interactions.

DISCUSSANT: *Elizabeth Fentress,* International Association for Classical Archaeology

Rural Culture in Roman Tuscany: Small Finds from the Roman Peasant Project
Stephen A. Collins-Elliott, University of Tennessee, Knoxville

Roman archaeology has long made use of an urban-rural dichotomy to conceptualize and frame questions about the material record, carrying over values of urbanism and rusticity explicit in ancient textual sources. The construction of the "rural"; however, deserves articulation not as a received idea, but through comparison of actual assemblages recovered from archaeological contexts in the countryside. Accordingly, this paper seeks to examine the small finds—the metal, glass, and miscellaneous artifacts from the Roman Peasant Project (2009–2014)—for what they reveal about the material manifestations of past practices in the ancient Tuscan countryside, toward addressing the category of rusticity.

I approach the study of finds through correspondence analysis, a standard multivariate statistical technique whose use is closely allied with practice theory, to show the way in which the small finds from the Roman Peasant Project run against a monolithic construction of rural culture. Whether examining past assemblages on an artifact-by-artifact basis or on a site-by-site basis, it is difficult to generalize across the Roman Peasant Project study area regarding the varieties of practices that took place at each site, the cultural resonance of those practices, and what precisely separates those behaviors from ones evidenced in other non-rural assemblages. For example, artifacts attesting to agricultural practices are rare, with equal evidence of finds that have been associated with military or urban lifestyles. The result is a rural landscape that is not uniform or monotone, but rather diversified in the rhythms of its *habitus*—where the lines between what is precisely urban or rural cannot be effectively drawn, since the cultural expectations created by those categories do not happily accord with the material reality of the past.

The Pompeii Artifact Life History Project: New Methodological Approaches and Illustrative Results
J. Theodore Peña, University of California, Berkeley, and *Caroline Cheung*, University of California, Berkeley

In this presentation we report on some of the innovative methods being employed by the Pompeii Artifact Life History Project (PALHIP), illustrating these by presenting some of our results. PALHIP is a long-term research initiative being carried out by the University of California, Berkeley, with the authorization of the Soprintendenza Speciale per i Beni Archeologici di Pompei, Ercolano e Stabia. The project's aim is to elucidate aspects of the life history (manufacture, acquisition, use, storage, maintenance, reuse/recycling, discard) of portable material culture at Pompeii and its environs through the detailed characterization of selected sets of materials recovered in various past excavations.

During its first four seasons (2012–2015) PALHIP has completed studies of the artifact assemblage recovered at the Villa Regina a Boscoreale, the artifact assemblage recovered in refuse deposits on the surface of the street between Insulae IX.12 and IX.13, the artifact assemblage recovered in four refuse middens deposited against the outer face of the fortification wall between Tower VIII and the Nola Gate, and a group of nine dolia recovered in the urban garden in Insula I.22. In the 2016 season the team will initiate a study of the approximately 1,200 amphoras recovered at Oplontis Villa B, in large measure used Dressel 2-4s found stacked in inverted position, presumably for refilling with wine.

Our work has involved the development and application of methods for the systematic characterization of the different kinds of use alteration attested on various classes of artifacts, including abrasion, chipping, bending/denting, cracking/breakage, and the deposition of residues (including vessel content and soot), as well as episodes of repair and other kinds of maintenance/modification. This generally involves the careful inspection of artifact surfaces by naked eye under natural light, ultraviolet light, and concentrated artificial light, aided by macro- and micro-photography.

We have also mobilized for our work various digital technologies, including an AutoCAD routine that calculates vessel volume and capacity from profile drawings and the documentation of artifact manufacturing sequences by means of flow charts produced using Harris matrix software.

In our 2016 season we plan to employ several new methods to study the Oplontis Villa B amphoras, including ultraviolet photography to document fugitive *tituli picti*, gas chromatography-mass spectrometry (GC-MS) analysis of absorbed residues to determine vessel content, and the use of a three-dimensional scanner to make direct measurements of vessel volume and capacity.

This Quintessence of Dust: Microdebris Analysis in Olynthos, Northern Greece

Elina Salminen, University of Michigan

This paper serves two purposes. It first introduces microdebris analysis as a method, since its use has been limited especially within classical archaeology, and then discusses the methodology used at the Olynthos Project, an excavation in northern Greece of domestic buildings dating to the late fifth and fourth century B.C.E.

Microdebris analysis, the study of small archaeological materials retrieved from soil samples, has been most popular within New World and Near Eastern archaeology, and shows promise in identifying activity areas, providing a more balanced picture of the range of artifact types, and quantifying and comparing densities of cultural materials across deposits. Ethnographic studies back up the principles underlying the method. Results have varied greatly depending on the type of site the method has been applied to, with some sites showing distinct activity areas and others not.

Since the method has not been used in a classical Greek context, the Olynthos Project's microdebris study is something of a pilot study. Excavations are ongoing and results are not yet available; however, the paper introduces the methodology used at the site and discusses the surprising perks and problems with the method the project has encountered. Our work suggests that microdebris study can be useful in identifying the formation processes of ambiguous deposits, such as very decomposed mudbrick or bioturbation. On the other hand, sorting ceramics into functional classes has proven very difficult because of the inherently small size of the fragments, complicating the identification of activity areas and comparison of ceramics types represented in the excavated versus the microdebris samples. Some of these issues are specific to classical archaeology, and the paper concludes by evaluating the promise and challenges of microdebris analysis on long-studied sites such as Olynthos in comparison to, for example, the Savè area of precolonial Bénin.

Artifacts in Contexts: Beyond Time and Space

Christopher Motz, University of Cincinnati, *Catherine K. Baker*, Bowdoin College, and *Leigh Anne Lieberman*, Princeton University

In recent years, the study of small finds has moved beyond straightforward typologies, descriptions, and quantifications. New approaches to artifact analysis have drawn attention to the myriad ways in which objects could be used and reused, deposited and redeposited in the ancient world. As part of the ongoing study and publication of the substantial assemblage of nonceramic artifacts recovered by the Pompeii Archaeological Research Project: Porta Stabia (PARP:PS), we have developed an innovative organizational scheme that allows us to contextualize and prioritize artifacts in terms of their taphonomic formation, chronological period, and spatial provenience.

In this paper, we demonstrate that by simultaneously employing traditional typologies based on artifact types and broader classifications based on functional groupings, our analysis sheds light on the broad range of processes by which artifacts came to be deposited in our insulae. We illustrate our methodological contribution by means of a case study that draws on multiple artifact categories to explore the life histories of the materials contained in our deposits. We argue that while dumping and reuse rather than primary-use activities brought most of the artifacts to our insulae, a more nuanced consideration of certain groupings can shed light on the ancient choices and practices that shaped specific spaces.

SESSION 2D
Digital Approaches to the Study of the Ancient World

CHAIR: To be announced

From Scanner to Scholar: Artifact Catalogues in the Age of Digital 3D Modeling

Derek B. Counts, University of Wisconsin-Milwaukee, *Kevin Garstki*, University of Wisconsin-Milwaukee, *Erin Walcek Averett*, Creighton University, and *Michael K. Toumazou*, Davidson College

The publication of archaeological material recovered from excavations has been at the core of the discipline since its inception in the 19th century. From lavish, monumental folio collections produced by antiquarians and early modern collectors to contemporary scientific investigations published by archaeologists and cultural heritage professionals, the catalogue has remained a primary vehicle to document and publish artifacts. In the past, such publications were expensive and space limitations meant that only a selection of objects were illustrated. Changes in both imaging technologies and publication models, however, have necessitated a reevaluation of how archaeological catalogues are prepared and disseminated. Today, publications are increasingly becoming digital, online, and freely available through Creative Commons licenses.

Since 2014, the Athienou Archaeological Project (AAP) has produced a corpus of digital three-dimensional models of limestone and terracotta votive sculpture excavated from the Athienou-Malloura rural sanctuary in central Cyprus using a structured light scanner. This paper discusses the Malloura eCatalogue, AAP's dynamic, open access digital publication that will allow us to advance current trends in three-dimensional artifact publishing, which often relegate three-dimensional models to Web-based galleries and online supplements, divorcing them from their complementary archaeological narrative. Our innovative publication, produced in collaboration with the University of Wisconsin-Milwaukee's Digital Commons (a virtual repository for the storage and publication of research data), incorporates standard contextual information and brief analyses with three-dimensional digital models of each artifact within a dynamic platform that allows user-friendly manipulation and study. By integrating the digital three-dimensional artifact models within the traditional artifact catalogue, we are developing an enhanced publication that allows user discovery not otherwise possible through traditional publications with two-dimensional illustrations. For example, three-dimensional models can be (1) measured digitally, (2) viewed with different lighting or surface conditions to accentuate details like tool marks or fingerprints, and (3) manipulated with 100% access through rotation and zoom at any scale, allowing for more dynamic and accurate investigation than traditional photographs.

The application of three-dimensional visualization technologies has transformed the way we "see" material culture from site to object, compelling us to consider new publication models that exploit fully the potential of three-dimensional models to enhance documentation and analysis, as well as address the difficulties in publishing these data in an integrated and reproducible way.

The Sounds of Ancient Rome: Expanding the Use of Digital Reconstruction in Museums

Alison K. Rittershaus, University of Michigan

Digital reconstructions have become one of the most promising ways of communicating archaeological discoveries to the public, and they play an increasingly prominent role in museums. For the most part, however, they continue to provide strictly visual access to the ancient world, maintaining the museum's traditional focus on sight to the exclusion of other sensory experiences. This paper discusses the creation of "soundscapes" as another means of connecting the results of academic research with a broader audience. "Soundscapes" are site-specific, brief auditory vignettes designed both to minimize the intrusive sounds specific to contemporary society (such as lighting and air systems or passing cars) and to immerse a gallery visitor more fully in the experience of the ancient world.

I begin by describing the development of a methodology for creating a sound program for the Kelsey Museum of Archaeology's spring 2016 installation of the traveling exhibition *Leisure and Luxury in the Age of Nero: The Villas of Oplontis near Pompeii*, curated by Elaine Gazda. Drawing upon a combination of literary and artistic primary sources, as well as archaeological material and scholarship on the natural history of the region around the Bay of Naples, I developed a range of potential auditory experiences that might have occurred at a seaside luxury villa like Villa A at Oplontis. A combination of field and audio recordings designed to approximate selections from this range were then edited into a one-minute, ambient soundscape designed to play when gallery visitors entered a near-life-sized reconstruction of Villa A's Room 11.

While the installation at the Kelsey Museum proved largely successful, it also illuminated areas of possible improvement and expansion in sound design in relation to the ancient world. Reconstructing the sensory ephemera of antiquity is a task that straddles the border between academia and art. I argue that further exploration along this boundary, by increasing the specificity of the scenes represented and by making the listening experience a focus rather than an ambient addition to the gallery space, would result in improved visitor experience. Sound is a viable medium for communicating academic knowledge about the ancient world as well as the emotional impact of connecting with the past.

Mediated Heritage: Digital Humanities Practices at Italian Archaeological Sites

Hunter Vaughan, Oakland University

Archaeology and heritage studies are in the midst of a transformation triggered by the embrace of recent innovations in media technology, and in Italy in particular this combines an archaeological richness with a strong national screen tradition. This forces us to assess problems regarding the direction of the field at large: how have recent heritage sites and archaeological practices integrated new media to preserve and even to redefine local and national identity for the 21st century? How does this process change in relation to the role of media technology and screen traditions in different regions? In this paper, I use methods of field work, textual analysis, and archaeological and art theory to raise questions of how site-specific media installations are being used to reveal, disseminate, and redefine the significance of ancient ruins, religious sites, and material culture in relation to collective identity. In particular, I connect digital humanities with heritage studies to present an analysis of how and why contemporary media practices in Italy are being used to reveal, connect to, and educate the public. As a media scholar, I have long been interested in the relationship between cultural practice, collective memory, and identity, and my current work looks at the interaction between new media and archaeological sites, and how this impacts cultural heritage. My presentation outlines how my larger project explores Italian image-cultural practices in archaeology and heritage studies—including multimedia projections in archaeological sites such as Cerveteri, open-air film projections on Renaissance city-center walls such as the summer program in Siena—and, in the process, bridges screen studies, environmental humanities, heritage studies, archaeology, and urban studies in a way that has not yet been done. Researchers and scholars often loosely use the term "media archaeology," a methodological problem I raise and offer an alternative to through a study of what I call "virtual excavation": in one example, at the Basilica di Santa Maria Antiqua, the oldest Christian monument in the Roman Forum, digital projectors provide a three-dimensional educational tool for narrating and visualizing the history and significance of what the site calls a "palimpsest wall." There is a critical need to analyze these media practices due to the fact that contemporary visitors to sites are now highly screen- and media-oriented as never before, and thus media installations are one of the most effective ways in which to engage with such an audience.

The Uffizi Gallery: Digitizing an Ancient Sculpture Collection

Kelly E. McClinton, Indiana University at Bloomington

The Uffizi Gallery houses one of the most extensive collections of Greek and Roman sculpture in Italy. Despite its size and importance, the collection has not been catalogued in more than 50 years, and online photography exists for only a fraction of the statues. In May of 2016, the Virtual World Heritage Lab at Indiana University was granted permission to digitize the Uffizi's collection in three dimensions using photogrammetry. This project aims to preserve a digital record of the museum's collection, increase visibility of the material to the public, and stimulate new studies with the potential to produce new insights about the current state of the statues as well as how their original condition should be visualized.

This paper explores several methodological issues that arose in the first summer of the project. For example, several team members gathered data on the same artifact, and afterwards it was not uncommon for several people to work on creating the three-dimensional model. How can we ensure consistency in photogrammetric data and metadata collection during the modeling process? As part of this question, we explore the best practices for transferring data, postprocessing, and presenting the final results to scholars and the general public. Presentation methods that this paper explores include other museum installations, mobile applications, virtual reality, and websites. Through exploring these questions, this paper aims to open a dialogue between art historians, archaeologists, museum professionals, and computer scientists about the best practices for three-dimensional modeling sculpture, digital database creation, and how three-dimensional modeling technology can be used to further research in the field of archaeology.

SESSION 2E
Ancient Sicily

CHAIR: To be announced

Prehistoric Obsidian Trade to Ustica (Sicily): Analyses of the Abundant Artifacts from Multiple Neolithic, Chalcolithic, and Bronze Age Sites

Robert H. Tykot, University of South Florida, and *Franco Foresta Martin*, Laboratorio Museo di Scienze della Terra Isola di Ustica, Italy

The small island of Ustica, 67 km north of Palermo (Sicily) in the Tyrrhenian Sea and just 8.6 km^2 in area, was inhabited starting in the Neolithic and continued through the Chalcolithic and Bronze Ages, with several distinctive sites identified. Surprising is the extremely large number of obsidian artifacts found at these sites, with formal excavation conducted at Faraglioni. An early analysis of a dozen obsidian artifacts, as part of the fieldwork conducted by R. Ross Holloway and Susan S. Lukesh (R. Tykot, in *Ustica I* [Providence, R.I. 1995] 87–90]), indicated the obsidian came from the Lipari (150 km eastward) and Pantelleria (220 km southward) island sources.

That small study has now been intensively expanded, first with analysis of a now-mixed surface collection of 170 artifacts from several sites using the electron microprobe and LA-ICP-MS (Foresta Martin et al., *Archaeometry*, forthcoming), and most recently using a portable X-ray fluorescence (pXRF) to nondestructively analyze more than 550 additional artifacts from several different sites on Ustica. The use of pXRF analysis to determine obsidian sources and subsources in the Mediterranean and Near East is well established and used by an ever-increasing number of archaeologists to rapidly analyze complete obsidian assemblages in museums rather than a potentially biased subset made available for analysis in laboratories elsewhere.

Overall, about 85% of the obsidian artifacts tested in this study come from Lipari, and 15% from Pantelleria. For the Lipari obsidian all but a few come from the major Gabellotto geological source, while for Pantelleria most are from Balata dei Turchi, but some are from the Lago di Venere geological sources. The use of Pantelleria obsidian on Ustica appears to have been proportionally far less than at the Early Neolithic Grotta dell'Uzzo site (near Trapani); while one hypothesis is this could be due to chronological differences, Pantelleria obsidian was widely used during the Late Neolithic through the Early Bronze Age on Malta, which is about the same distance as Ustica from both Pantelleria and the Sicilian coast. Little difference is also observed between the Neolithic, Chalcolithic, and Bronze Age sites on Ustica. One variable to consider is the direction and frequency of long-distance open-water maritime transport routes in antiquity. An alternative hypothesis to obsidian reaching Ustica primarily from the Palermo area of northwestern Sicily (and more likely having a similar proportion of sources as Uzzo) is that there was also significant transport more directly from Lipari.

Beyond Typology: Archaeometric Characterization of Sicilian Middle Bronze Age Ceramics

Gianpiero Caso, University of South Florida, *Davide Tanasi*, University of South Florida, and *Robert H. Tykot*, University of South Florida

The excavations at Sant'Ippolito Hill (Caltagirone, Catania, Sicily) led to the discovery of a prehistoric site that still represents the most important evidence of Middle and Late Bronze Age settlement in this area. During the excavations, archaeologists located a hut, a store for ceramic storage vessels, and a pottery workshop, all of which provided a large quantity of heterogeneous ceramics with apparent typological parallels in other areas of Sicily, such as Syracuse, Augusta, and Messina. A large number of specimens were selected in order to cover all the macroscopic types and the main classes. The results identified five petrographic fabrics. Most of the ceramics are characterized by abundant tempers consisting of volcanic rock fragments and occasionally of grog. Only a few samples contained common fine-grained quartz. The groundmass ranges from nonmicaceous to very micaceous.

The aim of this contribution is to present the preliminary data about the non-destructive analysis of 30 samples chosen from the above-mentioned classes via a portable X-ray fluorescence spectrometer to characterize the Middle Bronze Age pottery and compare it with the data already available for other Middle Bronze Age sites in the Catania territory. Pieces were tested using a Bruker III-SD and samples were analyzed for 120 seconds on both inner and outer surfaces, and on broken edges, using a filter that provides highly precise data for trace elements Rb, Sr, Y, Zr, and Nb. Quantitative values in ppm were produced using widely shared calibration software for these elements. The second step was to analyze microscopically the same group of samples, in order to visually assess differences and similarities in tempers and fabrics to be compared with previous data. 18 were studied through the use of an optical microscope, whereas the remaining 12 have been sent to the Florida Center for Analytical Electron Microscopy at FIU to be analyzed via SEM.

Analysis of the chemical composition of the ceramics revealed the existence of two groups with low and high calcium contents. The high iron content (more than 8.7 wt%) is probably due to the use of temper from altered pyroclastic rocks, which are of local provenance as SEM data suggest, even if petrographic and chemical results suggest that different raw materials may have been used. The data provided by these archaeometric analyses have made a significant contribution to the study of Middle and Late Bronze Age pottery from the Catania area.

Butera: A Case of Adaptivity and Continuity in Southern Sicily

Emma Buckingham, The University of North Carolina at Chapel Hill

Butera, a Sikanian hill settlement approximately 16 km from Gela, was first extensively populated around the ninth century B.C.E.; its location provided access to trade routes both along the coast and into the interior along nearby rivers and valleys.

The site's occupation, including its necropolis, evidences two periods. Period I, through the early seventh century, is characterized by remarkable cultural receptivity, with ceramics from several different cultural traditions rooted in Early Iron Age predecessors from many areas of Sicily. In Period 2, from the early-seventh to early-sixth century B.C.E., the site redirects its outlook locally and towards nearby coastal zones, with more locally made goods and vases imported from Greece or the nearby Greek colony of Gela. Burial assemblages tend to be more standardized, although with increased richness of burials and variety of funerary practices.

In the conventional view, Butera was the ancient Omphake, sacked, according to Pausanias, by Gela, and changes in grave goods and burial practices reflect large-scale settlement by Geloans. This argument rests especially on two unusual burials evidencing akephalia, removing the skull and burying it in a pottery vessel, separate from or with cremated remains; the vessels are placed in stone enclosures not encountered elsewhere in the cemetery. The burial practice has been interpreted as Cretan, brought with Gela's initial settlers. However, this overlooks the pottery types in these burials, largely local items and goods traditionally associated with Geloan production but rooted in long-established indigenous traditions.

Since the initial 1958 excavations were published there has been little reevaluation in light of newer Sicilian excavations. I argue that viewing the Greeks' arrival as the defining event in the site's history obscures the true significance of the archaeological record of a community's successful interaction with many cultures. The site is a chronicle of cultural receptivity from the Iron Age, in contrast with several inland sites showing limited integration of new artifactual typologies and practices. Contextual analysis of the burials in each necropolis reveals that intensification of relations with Gela led to reorientation towards the coast and reception of yet another culture (i.e., Greek). No sharp change occurred; instead, persistence of the settlement's receptivity towards different cultural groups and maintenance of already-established trade networks enabled the site to continue and even flourish in the succeeding century. This, and the site's continuous occupation until two centuries after Pausanias's date for the sack of Omphake, make the association with Omphake questionable.

The Elymian Sanctuary at Contrada Mango, Segesta

Margaret M. Miles, University of California, Irvine, *Jessica Paga*, College of William & Mary, *Thomas C. Rose*, University of Tennessee, Knoxville, and *Morgan Condell*, University of Pennsylvania

Segesta is best known for its famous Unfinished Temple (ca. 420 B.C.E.), studied by Mertens (1984). Not as well known is a Doric temple of similar size, but built some 50 years earlier, in the sanctuary at Contrada Mango on the south side of Segesta's acropolis. Pieces of its superstructure lie scattered on the ground. With the permission of the Archaeological Park of Segesta and the Soprintendenza of Trapani, we conducted surface fieldwork on the accessible remains of this mostly unstudied temple in the summer of 2016. We thoroughly documented 188 diagnostic architectural blocks with GPS, measurements, and photographs. We also explored the countryside around the temenos to see how the sanctuary was set within Segesta's landscape and the larger Elymian territories. This new documentation and exploration forms the basis for new reconstructions and a new plan of the sanctuary, and a fresh evaluation of its setting and historical significance.

The temple is enclosed by a finely built, monumental temenos wall, of double thickness on the west and south, where the wall supports the terrace-like setting of the temple. The temenos wall was excavated by Tusa in the 1950s, along with test trenches within the sanctuary. The large peripteral temple, with a likely 6 x 14 plan (ca. 28 x 56 m), is built of limestone quarried at Alcamo, some 15 km distant. It was finished, stuccoed, and painted. The construction techniques resemble those of contemporary temples at Greek Selinous.

What makes this temple and sanctuary particularly interesting is the constantly asserted ethnic identity of Elymian Segesta, detailed by Thucydides (6.2.3). Refugees from Troy called themselves Elymians, founded Segesta and Eryx, and were later joined by some storm-driven Phokians. The Trojan ethnic component may reflect a Sicilian tradition at least as early as the late sixth century B.C.E. (Stesichoros), and it strengthened through time, so that by the Roman period Segesta won tax relief on the basis of "kinship diplomacy." Sorting out what is Elymian about Segesta is a challenge (already undertaken in two international congresses, Pisa 1997, 2000). This early fifth-century sanctuary and its handsome temple provide further insight. Whereas Mertens was able to document Athenian influence in the Unfinished Temple, other influence, and originality, are evident here. The tantalizing remains of this sanctuary help to illustrate the religious history, variegated ethnic identities, and engineering capabilities of fifth-century B.C.E. Segesta.

Life and Death of Greeks of Sicily: New Archaeological and Archaeometric Data from the Necropolis of Viale Scala Greca, Siracusa

Davide Tanasi, University of South Florida, *Robert H. Tykot*, University of South Florida, *Stephan Hassam*, University of Wisconsin, Milwaukee, and *Andrea Vianello*, Independent Researcher

One of the most fascinating aspects of the research of archaeology of death is to compare funerary practices with the biological information provided by laboratory analyses. The aim of this contribution is to shed light on some aspects of life and death of Greeks of Sicily through the evidence produced by new archaeological excavations and archaeometric analyses. In 2011, during infrastructural work on a plot of land along Viale Scala Greca, the Superintendence of Cultural Heritage of Siracusa discovered portions of a large archaic cemetery mainly composed of rock-cut fossa graves. The exploration led to the identification of 135 burials. Seventy-two untouched tombs produced skeletal remains and grave goods including ceramic vessels, bronze jewels, iron weapons, clay figurines, coins, and alabaster vases. On the basis of the funerary assemblages and of some tomb features, a preliminary distinction has been made between rich/average/poor tombs on a subsample of 15 tombs. In order to further test this hypothesis, both elemental and stable isotope analyses have been conducted at the University of South Florida on samples of cranial and postcranial bones and on teeth in order to ascertain if there were differences in the dietary habits of individuals believed to belong to different social and economic levels. Elemental analysis was conducted nondestructively using a Bruker III-SD X-ray fluorescence spectrometer, specifically measuring calcium, barium, strontium, and other elements to measure the importance of aquatic food in the diet. Carbon and nitrogen isotope analyses were conducted on bone collagen, which represents primarily dietary protein, and bone apatite, which represents the whole diet. The stable isotope results obtained were quite consistent among the individuals tested, with no differences based on status. The highly negative collagen carbon isotope values indicate little if any seafood in the diet, and this is supported by the nitrogen isotope data, which with modest values consistent with terrestrial foods does not suggest higher trophic level fish. The apatite carbon isotope values, however, were noticeably elevated from those that represent a baseline C3-plant diet. Since the collagen values are negative, this suggests perhaps some C4 plants such as millet in the diet. The dietary results obtained through archaeometric analyses, for the first time in the history of research about Greek Sicily, together with the important new archaeological data about funerary practices of the ancient Syracusans, makes the necropolis of Viale Scala Greca an emblematic case study.

SESSION 2F
Neo-Assyrian and Achaemenid Imperial Art and Archaeology

CHAIR: To be announced

Power and Plants in Neo-Assyrian Palace Decoration

Rachael Dodd, University of Colorado, Boulder

The Assyrian Sacred Tree is pervasive throughout the reliefs of the Northwest Palace at Nimrud, appearing 96 times alone in Room I. Despite the Assyrian Sacred Tree's appearance in the numerous carved reliefs of Nimrud as well as in later Assyrian palaces, the symbolism of the Assyrian Sacred Tree is not fully known and has been thoroughly debated. Most recently, scholars have convincingly argued for the Assyrian Sacred Tree being a stylized date palm probably representing Ishtar, the goddess of fertility and warfare, but few scholars discuss the tree within the larger context of the narrative panel reliefs that line the walls of Assurnasirpal II's throne room. Those that discuss both the narrative relief panels and the Assyrian Sacred Tree suggest that the presence of the Assyrian Sacred Tree overshadows that of the narrative relief panels in the room.

Instead, by considering the iconography of the Assyrian Sacred Tree in conjunction with the bas-relief panels depicting scenes of warfare, this paper shows how it is possible to read the entire room as a message of Assyrian abundance. While the Assyrian Sacred Tree is a stylized date palm representing the abundance granted to the Assyrian empire by Ishtar, the scenes of historic battles include details of naturalistic date palms representing Ishtar aiding the Assyrian conquests in her role as goddess of warfare. Thus, visitors are presented with symbolic and historic representations of divine abundance granted to the Assyrian empire through their conduit, the king Assurnasirpal II. The entire room is an illustration of the gods' role in Assurnasirpal II's military successes, as well as a way to thank the gods and insure their continued gifts of abundance through war and the fertility of the Assyrian land and its people.

Furthermore, by adapting the unique iconography implemented by Assurnasirpal II in the Northwest Palace at Nimrud, each successive king chose a new way to illustrate how his close relationship to the gods brought abundance to the empire. By looking at three successors of Assurnasirpal II—Shalmaneser III, Sargon II, and Sennacherib—this paper shows three different adaptations, all of which influenced the famous "Garden Party" scene of Assurbanipal at Nineveh. Though the "Garden Party" reliefs are stylistically and iconographically different from the reliefs at Nimrud, they present the same ideological message as the innovative narrative reliefs of Assurnasirpal II carried down to Assurbanipal through generations of palace decoration.

Introducing Hama: The Discovery of a Lost Neo-Assyrian Queen Laid to Rest Amongst a Curious Cache of Bronze Coffins in the Nimrud Tombs

Tracy L. Spurrier, University of Toronto

In 1988, while clearing debris from rooms in the Northwest Palace at the ancient Assyrian capital Kalhu (modern day Nimrud), the Iraqi Department of Antiquities discovered a vaulted tomb chamber under one of the floors. Over the next few years, further excavations revealed the existence of several tombs belonging to the Queens of the Neo-Assyrian empire. These tombs contained massive stone sarcophagi, luxurious elite goods, and an unparalleled wealth of gold and jewelry. As the excavators began work on Tomb III, which belonged to Mullissu-mukannišat-Ninua, the wife of Assurnasirpal II (883–859 B.C.E.) who built the Northwest Palace, they encountered a curious cache of three bronze coffins piled in the antechamber. When first discovered, it was thought all of the coffins contained the fragmentary remains of numerous individuals with lavish grave goods all found in secondary burial contexts. This is clearly the case for Coffin 3, which contained the partial remains of at least six individuals. However, the context for the other coffins is more difficult to establish. The paleopathological evidence for Coffin 2 shows that the sole occupant, a young woman found wearing a delicately crafted gold crown, was initially interred in this bronze coffin. By taking a multidisciplinary approach, examining the archaeological, skeletal, and textual data from these tombs in tandem, in this paper I identify the remains of a young queen previously known in name only: Hama, wife of Shalmaneser III. This paper also discusses the context of the bronze coffins, as well as attempts to reconstruct the postmortem history of the occupants. I suggest the coffins' placement in the Tomb III antechamber dates approximately 50 years after Hama's death, and nearly 150 years after the tomb owner's death, to the mid eighth century B.C.E. during the reign of Tiglath-Pileser III—a usurper king who increased his own power by reestablishing territorial expansion and in turn intensifying the hegemonic control of the Assyrian empire over much of the ancient Near East.

In March 2015, ISIS blew up the remains of the Northwest Palace at Nimrud and it is highly likely the queens' tombs below were damaged during the blast, if not completely destroyed. Last documented, the skeletal remains were being stored in the Mosul Museum, which was also attacked by ISIS. It is unknown what condition the bones or the tombs are in today, making it more important than ever to commemorate the Neo-Assyrian queens.

All That Glitters is Gold: A Retelling of the Tell Ta'yinat Roundel

Kiersten Neumann, Oriental Institute, University of Chicago

During the Iron Age, luxurious works of art were produced under the command of the wealthy independent kingdom of the Amuq Valley, objects of prestige and grandeur that stand as testament to the skilled artisans and craftsmen at whose hands they were fashioned, the local customs and traditions of the time, and the broad international contacts that stretched across the region. Embedded within this powerful matrix was the site of Tell Ta'yinat in southwestern Turkey, the Syro-Hittite royal city of Kunulua and later administrative capital of the Assyrian province, following the Assyrian conquest of 738 B.C.E.

This paper reconstructs the cultural and sociopolitical dynamics within which Tell Ta'yinat was situated through the enduring power and prestige of one object—a copper roundel (T-3264). Unearthed during the Oriental Institute's Amuq Expedition in the year 1937 near the monumental temples and palace of the West Central Area of the Tell Ta'yinat citadel, this visually impressive work of art now hangs in the Syro-Anatolia Gallery of the Oriental Institute Museum in Chicago, where it is in the company of an equally masterful work—the watercolor painting of the roundel rendered by the expedition archaeologist Robert Braidwood. While regularly admired by scholars and museum visitors alike, the engaging history and significance of this work of art has yet to be fully appreciated. Comparisons to material culture from the Iron Age Amuq Valley and Assyria to the east situate it within the stream of artistic traditions and technological achievements of the period; a study of its raw materials and sensory attributes articulates its culturally grounded value and affect; while an investigation of the original excavation documents helps shed light on both its performative role in antiquity—as a dedicatory foundation deposit—and its archaeological resting place, from whence it was recovered in the early 20th century.

Dedicated to the mighty god Adad by the high official Aššur-rēmanni on behalf of the king Tiglath-Pileser III (744–27 B.C.E.), this roundel epitomizes conceptions of the efficacy and potency of prestigious raw materials—copper, gold, and precious stones—and their import in acts of deposition and the consecration of ritualized space within a first-millennium Assyrian elite context. The interment of the roundel served to animate the very foundations of the city with the solidity and sacred purity that was necessary in order to ensure the prosperity of the Assyrians' monumental building program and of their newly established administrative capital as a whole.

Early Imperial Imagery in Achaemenid Glyptic as Found in the Persepolis Fortification Archive

Christina L. Chandler, Bryn Mawr College

This paper analyzes an unpublished seal (hereafter PFUTS 305*) known from its numerous impressions on administrative tablets from the Persepolis Fortification Archive. The archive, consisting of thousands of clay tablets, documents state payment of food rations to a wide variety of agricultural workers and administrative personnel in the period 509–493 B.C.E. in the reign of Darius I. The archive preserves one of the largest glyptic corpora surviving from ancient western Asia; some 3,400 different seals have been identified to date (surviving only as impressions on the clay tablets).

Such a dense concentration of glyptic imagery coming from one place and dating to a short span of time offers myriad avenues of study. The seal in question, PFUTS 305*, exhibits a particularly sophisticated scene with a wealth of iconographic detail: in front of the seated king, who holds a lotus blossom, there is a standing captive. Behind the captive an attendant bows at the waist and places a hand over his mouth; behind the king a second attendant stands with a bowcase. An Aramaic inscription runs vertically in the terminal field. The whole of the scene is elevated on a series of inverted floral devices.

The scene of the seated king receiving captives is unique within the known imperial arts of the Achaemenid period. In many ways, the scene bridges several of the most famous monuments of the Achaemenid imperial repertoire: the rock-cut reliefs at Bisotun and Naqš-e Rostam; the central panels of the eastern and northern stairways of the Apadana; and the statue of Darius from Susa.

This paper explores the complex ideological connections that PFUTS 305* has with these famous monuments as well as lesser known and new examples of glyptic scenes with court-centric iconography coming from the Persepolis Fortification Archive. A few of the most intriguing thematic issues that the scene raises include narrative/emblematic tension, implied royal violence, the "king on high," and the role of subject peoples in Achaemenid imperial propaganda. PFUTS 305* thus provides a particularly focused portal into the emergence of a visual rhetoric of empire in the early years of the reign of Darius I.

Imperial Itineracy in the Achaemenid Persian Empire

Emily Wilson, University of Chicago, and *Shannon O'Donovan*, AIA Member at Large

This paper uses machine learning data mining and network analysis techniques to examine the interplay between text and seal image in the Persepolis Fortification Archive (PFA). This archive comprises a part of the burgeoning imperial bureaucracy implemented under the reign of Darius the Great to administer his new palace at and the greater surrounding area of Persepolis. The archive contains thousands of tablets—written in both Elamite and Aramaic—that recorded the storage, taxation, and disbursements of food, livestock, grain, and other commodities to people authorized to stop at various official way stations around the region of Persepolis in the years 509–494 B.C.E. In addition to the extensive inscribed transactional information, almost every tablet is also impressed with multiple seals—both the seals of the individual and the seals of the various offices working under the royal aegis. The vast amount of information contained within the archive has restricted the breadth of analysis possible via more traditional academic methods. However, the application of modern data management technological solutions allows for the quick processing of information, unveiling relationships not otherwise apparent or yet examined.

Leveraging this technology, this paper looks at the medium of travel in the archive. In particular, we identify the people undertaking travel, including their roles, their companions, their purpose for travel, and the glyptic iconography of the seals they used. We also look at travel in a greater geographical context, including the destinations and origins of itinerants, the seasonality of movement, and the use of this greater spatial network. Finally, we examine the imperial bureaucratic support network for travel within the Persepolis region by focusing on the disbursements available to itinerants, inclusive of their type and amount, as well as the individual officers and offices that made these disbursements.

By tracking and considering these seal impressions and texts together through the application of modern data mining approaches, we populate the area around Persepolis with people, the time of year they traveled, their destinations, their purposes, and the people and offices with which they interacted on their journeys to provide a holistic understanding of itinerant individuals and groups in the Achaemenid Persian empire in the late sixth and early fifth centuries B.C.E.

SESSION 2G
Iberia

CHAIR: *John Hale*, University of Louisville

Beyond the Emporion: Seaborne Traders and Their Local Partners in the North West of the Mediterranean (Sixth–Third Centuries B.C.E).

Alexis Gorgues, University of Bordeaux Montaigne

Most of the studies about cross-culture trade on the ancient western Mediterranean, from the beginning of the Greek colonization until the Roman period, tacitly assume that exchange activity was held in an institutional framework that was structured according to the seaborne traders, own habits and interests. Since the moment of the foundation of the Greek colonies of Massalia and Emporion, the local cultures would have been involved in a process of progressive modification of their traditional structures, and would have developed new institutions allowing a swift practice of trade with their Greek, Italic, or Punic counterparts. One, probably the most significant, of these institutions would have been the emporion. This Greek word, referring to spaces devoted to seaborne and international trade, has been used, in the context of modern-days western Mediterranean Iron Age archaeology, to coin a model designating a neutral site, that function was specifically to host cross-culture trading activity. The development of such an institution would have come alongside the spreading of monetary economy, the formalization of metrology, etc.

In this paper, I propose an alternative point of view, through a reexamination of the evidence for the Languedoc and northern Catalonia, the area at the center of which were settled two Greek colonies, Emporion and Rhodè. I firstly discuss the local, native, institutions of trade and their rhythm of development. I specifically analyze aspects linked with metrology and standardization of potential commercial containers, and show that their apparent homogeneity was a consequence of broadly homogeneous production patterns (learning through watching) rather than one of the existence of state-enforced trading norms. I then try to define who the local partners of the seaborne traders were, and what resources they could bring in the negotiation process, and to assert their own exchange practices. I therefore focus on the commercial encounter itself, with a particular emphasis on its temporality. Last, I build on what was previously said to offer a reinterpretation of an epigraphic document, the "Pech Maho lead," dated from the fifth century B.C.E., and to show how this document enlightens the specificities and the difficulties, for a Greek trader, to operate in such a peripheral, liminal area as the northern part of the Iberian world.

Resistance and Assimilation in the Northwest of the Iberian Peninsula

Lucia Pinheiro Afonso, University of Toronto

The conquest and transformation of the Iberian Peninsula took place within a period of almost 200 years (208–19 B.C.E.). The Romans moved from the southern coast of Spain all the way to the south coast of Portugal, further into inland, and all the way to the north of the Iberian Peninsula. Through war and treaties, the Romans encountered a great diversity of peoples. In the northwest the Romans came across people living in hillforts, known as castros, which are set on hills, lowlands, or near water courses. Castros have been identified in Portugal along the Douro River all the way to the east, bordering at the river Pinhao and to the frontier with Spain, continuing through the northwest region of Spain called Galicia. It was the Romans, who gave the name Gallaecia to the northwest of the Iberian Peninsula. In 137 B.C.E., the Romans claimed victory over the various peoples of this region.

As the Romans implemented themselves in the conquered territory of the northwest of the Iberian Peninsula, they faced a protourban culture—the castros culture. These castros are walled. Inside the walls, most have rounded houses of similar size, but others have squared houses. All of these castros have a system of streets. Most of them also have one large single building. There are a few castros that have not only one large building, but also a very unique building defined as thermae.

Not only the architectural layout of the many castros contributed to their protourban arrangement; the presence of thermae in the vicinity of some of those hill-forts emphasizes also their protourban character. I present the archaeological remains of three hillforts: Santa Maria de Galegos (Barcelos), Citania de Briteiros (Guimaraes), and Citania de Sanfins (Pacos de Ferreira) to demonstrate that the protourban stage of the castro communities facilitated the embracing, emulation, and assimilation of the Roman culture to a certain extent. Moreover, I also look at the Roman town of Tongobriga (Marco de Canaveses) in the region of the castro culture, which has archaeological remains of a pre-Roman castro and thermae to further support my argument. The particular presence of a public building such as thermae in some of the northwest castros demonstrates the presence of a defined public building, but it also denotes increasing social changes.

Epigraphic Evidence for an Indigenous Bear Cult in Roman Spain

David Wallace-Hare, University of Toronto

Honey and the bear are highly linked in indigenous Celtiberian religious thought during the Roman republic and empire. This connection has gone unnoticed despite being present among the most important documents of Celtiberian-Roman relations, namely the third Botorrita Tablet and the deditio of the Seanoci found at Alcántara.

The idea that bears love honey is not a modern fantasy. Children's books like *Winnie the Pooh*, by A.A. Milne, caricature this very real behavior. I show that bears acted as patronal figures over honey and honey production in Spanish ursine cults, not as hunting deities, as many scholars attempt to classify such animal deities. In this role bears may have originally led nearby tribes to new honey sources. The reverence for the bear and its close association with honey is found in toponyms, personal names, clan names featuring the Celtiberian roots Arc-/Mat-("bear") and Medu-("honey"), hospitality tablets, Greek and Latin sources, and can be shown through a variety of zoologic- and bioarchaeological studies.

The epigraphic evidence connecting bears and honey in Spain is often concentrated in specific geographic settings, primarily mountainous areas, many of the very areas we find bears distributed even today in Spain. Here we find collections of indigenous bear and honey cognonomina, toponyms (as Arcobriga and Medubriga), and clan names all featuring the roots for bear and honey in Celtiberian. In these same areas, as the empire progresses, around the second–third centuries C.E., we see a translation of these names into the less expressive Latin cognomen Ursus and variants thereon, a phenomenon seen elsewhere in Celtic-speaking regions of the Roman empire where bear-deities have been discovered, as Artio at the aptly named Bern in Germania Superior and in a plurality of areas in Narbonese Gaul and Aquitania.

Through a collection of archaeological and epigraphic sources I show that the Celtiberian personal names in Medu- and Art-/Mat- are connected with one another and suggest that the bearers have received the name primarily for its cultural/religious aspects and not fashion. Secondly, I show that many of the individuals with Latin names meaning "bear" in Spain are the product of this native onomastic/religious habit. It is revealed that the high concentrations of Ursi in Celtic-speaking areas of the Roman empire are often indicative of indigenous theophoric tendencies of piety rather than fashion.

SESSION 2H
Greek and Roman Sculpture

CHAIR: To be announced

The Kritios Boy. On the Difference between the Subjects of Public and Private Offerings

Makoto Komatsu, The University of Tsukuba

The Kritios Boy is deemed to be one of the most important figures of the Greek Severe Style, and scholars have proposed two interpretations of it—as depicting either an athletic victor in the Panathenaia, or Theseus. Neils (1984), for example, points out the similarity of the hairstyle to that in depictions of Theseus on red-figure vase paintings (Louvre G 195; New York 53.11.4), and that kouroi were rarely dedicated on the Athenian Acropolis.

The latter interpretation, however, seems difficult to corroborate. Representations of Theseus in architectural decoration, wall painting, and in vase painting since ca. 510 appear to have been connected to the public policies of the Peisistratids, the Alcmeonids, and Kimon. In both literary and archaeological evidence, Theseus appears to have been represented only in narrative subjects on the Acropolis, which would urge us to reflect on the difference between the subjects of official and private offerings.

We can confirm five monuments on the Acropolis that include a representation of Theseus. The marble statue group of Theseus and Prokrustes (Acropolis Museum 145; 370) has been interpreted as referring to the battle against the Megarians. The statue of Theseus and the Marathonian Bull, dated ca. 490, was erected by the public body, by the citizens of the deme of Marathon (Paus. 1.27.8–9), representing the legendary offering of the bull by Theseus to Athena on the hill of the Acropolis. Pausanias states that the statue group of Theseus and the Minotaur was dedicated there (1.24.1). Androgeos was a victor at the Panathenaic games. In two monuments the hero is also represented with Aegeus (Paus. 1.27.8), who is said to have committed suicide on the Acropolis.

These examples thus demonstrate the following points: (1) the subject of Theseus appears only in narrative representations and probably only in the public context of the contemporary Acropolis; (2) by means of the subject depicted in a monument, the viewer could perceive in general the difference between a public and a private cult; and (3) no statues of Theseus as a single monument appear to have been set up on the hill.

New Observations on the "Archilochos Relief" in Paros

Rebecca Sinos, Amherst College

The Totenmahl relief discovered in 1960 (Paros Museum, inv. no. 758) remains our earliest complete example of this type of hero relief, as well as the largest. Once a fine example of the skill for which Parian sculptors were known, its surface has suffered such damage as to make some of its more spectacular features difficult to reconstruct. My aim in this paper is to call attention to some of the relief's features that deserve more attention than they have received so far. Visual inspection in June 2016 revealed details that suggest real technical daring, such as a delicate marble leg standing free from the background in order to reveal the relief sculpture behind it. In some cases the remains of marble contours indicate the presence of marble objects where previous descriptions had assumed metal attachments were used. Finally, some of the holes on the table, where the remains of metal clearly indicate the presence of metal attachments, are oriented in a pattern that allows us to reconstruct an additional object once attached in metal, which inspires new ideas about the reconstruction of the most damaged part of the relief, and its connection to the Parian hero Archilochos.

One Hundred Years of Change: Greek Mainland Comic Actor Figurines

Heather Elaine Bowyer, Arizona State University

The fourth century B.C.E. was rife with change due to the Athenian loss of the Peloponnesian War and the fluctuating political, economic, social, and military supremacy by Sparta, Thebes, and Macedonia. Uncertainty during this period was the catalyst for cultural changes within religion, philosophy, theater, and art. The creation of small scale theater figurines during the Late Classical and Hellenistic periods and the depiction of specific theater character types as seen on stage became a popular motif. The figurines were produced throughout the mainland therefore, due to prevalence in the corpus, the figurines from Attica and Boeotia will be examined.

This paper demonstrates how culmination of Old, the entirety of Middle, and the commencement of New Comedy was used as a foundation for the evolution of grotesque character figurine types and play narrative. Nicholas Himmelmann in his book, Realistische Themen in der griechischen Kunst der archaischen und klassischen Zeit (New York, 1994), defined grotesques as, "figures characterized by laughable and monstrous distortions" (98). His definition will be used in reference to slaves, hetaerae, and old men that will be evaluated for shifts in physiognomy and, in certain cases, clothing. This evaluation integrates with the turbulent political, social, and economic contexts to provide critical inquiry into the division of Greek Comedy into Old, Middle and New Comedy based solely on storyline.

The Mahdia and J. Paul Getty Museum Bronze Herms of Dionysos: New Observations

Beryl Barr-Sharrar, New York University

The relationship of the bronze herm of Dionysos purchased in 1979 by the J. Paul Getty Museum to the similar herm signed by Boethos found in 1907 in the Mahdia shipwreck, now in the Bardo Museum in Tunis, remains unresolved. A recent response by this author in the *Bryn Mawr Classical Review* (2016.02.29) to a review of the catalogue of the *Power and Pathos* exhibition of bronzes during its final viewing at the National Gallery of Art in Washington, D.C., questioned both the reviewer's and the catalogue editors' assumption that Greek bronzes were cast in multiple editions, and that the two herms represent that practice.

In rejecting this notion, the author suggested that the indirectly cast Getty herm had every appearance of having been produced as an overcast copy of the Hellenistic Mahdia herm, of which the head, with its complex headdress with deep undercutting and penetrations though the bronze forms, was manifestly cast directly. She tentatively suggested that an overcast could conceivably have been made in Tunis in the 1940s, when scholars were attempting to create a group sculpture of the herm together with the Mahdia bronze Eros, and plaster casts were made.

The only area of the Mahdia herm exactly replicated by the Getty herm is the face. Differences in the two headdresses are obvious to the eye and verified by measurements made of plaster casts of both herms by the Getty conservation laboratory. These variations are a direct result of the dependence of the Getty herm on the Mahdia herm and the different methods of casting the two herms. It can be demonstrated that the space of every undercut area and every void circumscribed by directly cast draped folds in the Mahdia herm headdress, importantly including one that is now broken, are repeated, in effect matched, by closed volumes with continuous surfaces in the Getty herm's indirectly cast headdress. This is further indicated by analyzing overlaid slices of two-dimensional tomography of the two herm heads.

New focus on a detail of the Mahdia herm, the significance of which was not fully diagnosed by the author earlier, plus correspondence with David Scott, former Getty conservator, and Jeffrey Maish, current conservator, has led the author to conclude that the Getty herm is very likely a Roman Republican overcast of the Mahdia herm.

SESSION 2I
Fieldwork in Greece

CHAIR: *Kevin Daly*, ASCSA and Bucknell University

New Epigraphic Evidence from the Sanctuary of Zeus on Mount Lykaion

Kyle W. Mahoney, University of Pennsylvania

Current excavation at the Sanctuary of Zeus on Mount Lykaion is further clarifying our understanding of religion in ancient Arcadia. Work is focused on both the Ash Altar and the Lower Sanctuary, which afforded the venue for the Lykaian Games. An important component of the project has been the reassessment of all inscriptions discovered on the mountain. The present paper reports on new findings from two inscribed texts.

IG 5 2 548 is a bronze plaque discovered outside the northeast corner of the large (38 x 20 m) building characterized by Kourouniotis as the Xenon (1909). The document—until now only partially published—mentions a damiorgos of the Arcadian League and proceeds to list men labeled with Arcadian ethnic adjectives. One obscure sequence, OYPIO, can only be restored as Kynourios, the ethnic of an Arcadian tribal group that ceased to exist during the 360s B.C.E. The plaque, which was probably affixed to the exterior of the building, thus provides a terminus ante quem for the beginning of construction in the Lower Sanctuary. Other data from the inscription indicate that it belongs to the period of Arcadian domination over Olympia (365/4), which may suggest that control over the riches of Olympia helped to facilitate the monumentalization of Lykaion.

IG 5 2 550 was discovered inside Kourouniotis' Xenon and includes two victory lists from the Lykaian Games, the first of which can be dated to 308 B.C.E. Preceding this list is a catalogue of political officers. Prosopographical analysis shows that this catalogue lists men from different Arcadian communities and thus must emanate from a federal organization. This conclusion is significant both for Arcadian political history and the life of the sanctuary, for it indicates that the latter was administered by a federal organization for more than half a century. Current scholarship does not acknowledge the existence of an Arcadian federal state after 362, and this text thus takes on added historical significance. Study of the stone has even revealed two previously unknown offices of the Arcadian League, the Hipparchos and Toxarchos.

Accordingly, these documents enhance our knowledge of the dating, architectural program, and historical significance of the Sanctuary of Zeus Lykaios in Late Classical and Early Hellenistic times. Taken together, the political and administrative nature of the records support the conclusion of the excavators that the Xenon was in fact an administrative building and headquarters of the federal officers known as the damiorgoi, who I suggest organized the festival.

The 2016 Mazi Archaeological Project: Regional Survey and Settlement Investigations in Northwest Attica

Alex R. Knodell, Carleton College, *Sylvian Fachard*, University of Geneva, and *Kalliopi Papangeli*, Ephorate of Antiquities of West Attica, Piraeus, and the Islands

The third field season of the Mazi Archaeological Project (MAP) continued regional survey activities (begun in 2014) as a collaboration between the Ephorate of Antiquities of West Attica, Piraeus, and the Islands and the Swiss School of Archaeology in Greece. The project is a diachronic archaeological study of the Mazi Plain. Located in the often contested borderlands on the fringes of Attica, Boeotia, and the Megarid, the study area occupies a critical crossroads on the main land route between Eleusis and Thebes and ultimately links central Greece to the Isthmus and the Peloponnese. Stemming from these geographical factors and the rich history of borderlands and border studies, the Mazi Archaeological Project is a diachronic regional survey that aims to address questions of territoriality, regionality, and connectivity in the very long term.

In 2016 an international team continued intensive and extensive pedestrian archaeological survey in and around the Mazi Plain. In this final season of large-scale fieldwork, we completed the intensive survey by covering—through systematic fieldwalking—all "walkable" territory in the survey area. The side-by-side survey in total covered some 12 km^2 of territory in 2,968 survey units, accompanied by documentation of 552 archaeological features through intensive and extensive exploration. Site-based investigations were a major component of MAP's work in 2016. Architectural cleaning was done at the expansive, multiperiod site of Kato

Kastanava (discovered in 2015 and notable for its prehistoric remains) and at the fortress and settlement of Eleutherai, in order to clarify the architectural plan and phasing of several structures. Cleaning was accompanied by detailed documentation through mapping, photogrammetry, and traditional architectural drawing. Investigations at Eleutherai were particularly illuminating, clarifying an earlier phase of the circuit wall first noted in 2015, as well as the plan and function of the two main gates, the course of a road running between them, and the inscription that adorns one of them. Gridded collection was undertaken in several locations at Kato Kastanava, as well as at a newly discovered Byzantine settlement at Aghios Dimitrios, and geophysical survey was conducted at and around Oinoe. Finally, in addition to field operations, preliminary studies of all pottery and lithics were completed, supplemented by a detailed study of architectural tiles. This paper discusses the aspects of the project noted above in the context of our broader results and provides a set of preliminary interpretations concerning the long-term settlement pattern and history of the Mazi Plain.

The Olynthos Project: A Report on the Fieldwork Carried Out in 2016

Lisa Nevett, University of Michigan, *Bettina Tsigarida*, Greek Archaeological Service, *Zosia Archibald*, University of Liverpool, *David Stone*, University of Michigan, *Bradley Ault*, SUNY Buffalo, *Anna Panti*, Greek Archaeological Service, *Timothy Horsley*, Northern Illinois University, and *Christopher Gaffney*, University of Bradford

The Olynthos Project is a multidisciplinary collaboration between the Greek Archaeological Service and the British School at Athens, centered on an investigation of the classical city of Olynthos, Chalkidiki. The aim of the project is to explore the history of urbanization at Olynthos and to understand the construction of identity by the community's inhabitants at the household, neighborhood, community, and regional scales. These questions are being addressed using geophysical and field survey techniques together with targeted excavation.

The present report outlines the results of the third year of field research by the Olynthos Project. This includes the continued excavation of House Bix6 on the North Hill, revealing much of the central section of the building as well as parts of the neighboring buildings and a street to the south. Field survey of the area surrounding the fenced archaeological site also continued to the north, east, and west of the North Hill, revealing a variable halo of material that is largely contemporary with the main phase of occupation of the city itself. This year work was also begun on the South Hill, where geophysical survey using earth resistance and electromagnetism has for the first time revealed the layout of the streets and building blocks over the central and southern parts of the hill. Comprehensive surface collection across the whole of the South Hill has provided a range of material, including local ceramics, suggesting that the first-millennium settlement here originated in the Early Iron Age to Archaic periods, as defined by the local ceramic chronology. Trial trenches located within the area of the geophysical survey are beginning to provide stratified evidence for the history and character of that occupation.

Paximadi's Past: Work on Early Canadian Excavations near Karystos in Euboia

Elizabeth Langridge-Noti, Deree, The American College of Greece, *Rachel DeGraaf*, University of Alberta, and *Patrik Klingborg*, Uppsala University

The Southern Euboia Exploration Project began exploring the area surrounding the modern town of Karystos in southern Euboia in the 1980s under the auspices of the Canadian School of Archaeology and with permission from the Greek Archaeological Service. While the long-term goal of the project has been a full understanding of the archaeologically little-known territory of southern Euboia, a primary area of concentration has been the Paximadi peninsula on the west side of the bay. Early archaeological research consisted of a detailed survey of the area in order to map the pattern of settlement on the peninsula from the prehistoric period to the present day. Supplementary to the survey was a series of excavations that addressed questions pertaining to both the prehistoric and historic periods in southern Euboia and that was meant to serve as a series of site-based stratified deposits. The two historical-period sites chosen for excavation were a cistern within a small settlement at Cape Mnima (C27) and a farmhouse closer to modern Karystos that is a 15-minute walk to the shore (C38).

While the ceramic material found at both sites serves the original purpose of the excavations in creating a chronological scaffolding for this part of southern Euboia, these excavations serve a broader purpose as well. By focusing on the spatial organization and architecture of site C38 and its artifacts and artifact distribution, the current investigation of the farmhouse explores the types of domestic and agricultural activities carried out on farmsteads on the Paximadi peninsula. The study of the cistern site, C27, although differing radically from the farmhouse in terms of preservation and available material, as only the cistern was excavated, aims to establish a chronological and functional framework for the water-supply system at the site in order to gain a better understanding of the area's development.

This paper examines the factors responsible for the formation of the material assemblages of architecture and pottery associated with these excavations and how they may affect our assessment of date and function for the two sites. It also places the two sites within the context of what is known archaeologically about southern Euboia, expanding our understanding of the diachronic development of this area. Finally, we compare these sites and assemblages to similar ones elsewhere in order to explore the changing dynamics of usage and interaction with the broader Aegean for the area of Karystos and the Paximadi peninsula.

SESSION 2J: Joint AIA/SCS Workshop Classics, Classical Archaeology, and Cultural Heritage: Toward a Common Understanding of Professional Responsibilities for the Study of "Exceptional Objects"

MODERATORS: *Elizabeth S. Greene*, Brock University, and *Brian I. Daniels*, University of Pennsylvania Museum Heritage Center

Colloquium Overview Statement

Despite holding a joint annual meeting and an assortment of joint panels, the Archaeological Institute of America (AIA) and the Society for Classical Studies (SCS) along with their associated *American Journal of Archaeology (AJA)* and *Transactions of the American Philological Association (TAPA)* promote somewhat different approaches to the treatment of cultural heritage. With respect to its Annual Meeting, the AIA's code of ethics states: "...the Annual Meeting may not serve for the announcement or initial scholarly publication of any object in a public or private collection acquired after December 30, 1973, unless its existence can be documented prior to that date, or it was legally exported form the country of origin. An exception may be made...if the presentation emphasizes the loss of archaeological context."

AJA's editorial policy presents similar guidelines, designed to preserve archaeological context as a critical factor in an object's meaning (*AJA* 109 [2005] 135-36). The standards presented as part of the SCS's statement of professional responsibilities are somewhat less transparent:

"Members of the profession should abide by the 1970 UNESCO convention . . . At the same time, however, the objective of advancing knowledge about classical antiquity demands that scholars challenge unnecessary restrictions on research and publication."

Respect for the 1970 Convention falls within the spirit of the AIA's guidelines, but the SCS's statement leaves open the possibility that unprovenanced objects can be presented at the Annual Meeting and within publications of the society. In light of the close connection between the two societies and ongoing current threats to heritage as a result of current world affairs, it would seem timely to reflect on the mandates of the two societies with regard to the stewardship of heritage by professionals in the field.

This workshop aims to consider how archaeologists and classicists might reach a similar understanding of best practices in the ethical study of physical artifacts that drive research on classical antiquity. A frequent topic in recent discussions about archaeological provenance is the treatment of "exceptional objects," including papyri, inscriptions, coins, and other artifacts for which arguments have been made (1) that an object's content can provide information independent of archaeological provenience; (2) that archaeological provenance is less meaningful for objects produced for the purpose of circulation; and (3) that looting in zones of conflict over the past 25 years has resulted in the discovery of new archaeological material, some of which is too important to be ignored. In addressing such issues from a Near Eastern perspective, the American Schools of Oriental Research recently added a "cuneiform exception" to its Policy on Professional Conduct, allowing limited exceptions to its publication and presentation policy for cuneiform texts. Through a series of open discussion groups about a variety of contested objects, we hope to determine whether particular categories of objects warrant exceptional treatment in AIA and SCS venues and what factors might be considered in creating policy that balances research interests with a responsibility to combat the looting of cultural heritage and the illicit trafficking of antiquities. This public workshop is designed to include participation of scholars who work on various categories of "contested objects" from philological, historical, and archaeological perspectives, as well as those involved in the creation of professional policy. We envision the workshop as a mix of guided small-group discussion and debate rather than a series of formal papers.

PANELISTS: *Jane Carter,* Tulane University, *Nathan Elkins,* Baylor University, *Jane DeRose Evans,* Temple University, *Todd Hickey,* University of California, Berkeley, *Laetitia La Follette,* University of Massachusetts, *Justin Leidwanger,* Stanford University, *Richard Leventhal,* Penn Cultural Heritage Center, *John Miller,* University of Virginia, and *Dirk Obbink,* University of Oxford

SESSION 2K
Poster Session

Haffjarðarey: Differential Diagnosis of Dental Pathology in Western Iceland

Sarah E. Hoffman, University at Buffalo

This study aims to understand the causal factors that contributed to a severe and complex pattern of dental pathology present within the medieval Icelandic population at Haffjarðarey between 1200 and 1556 C.E. Within these 400 years, the Haffjarðarey church cemetery served as a burial site for the larger surrounding region. A paleopathological analysis of the population reveals a high rate of antemortem tooth loss, severe tooth wear, alveolar bone resorption, and a mosaic of nonspecific stress indicators including linear enamel hypoplasia and cribra orbitalia. Despite the church and its surrounding communities being situated within one of the most prosperous coastal fishing areas of western Iceland, the human skeletal remains from Haffjarðarey suggest dietary or nutritional stress. Throughout the 13th–16th centuries Iceland endured dramatic social, political, and economic restructuring as a result of Norwegian, and later Danish, authority. I argue that political changes impacting the medieval fishing industry, as well as a lack of nutritional supplements necessary for the maintenance of healthy dental tissue, and perhaps occupational stress, resulted in widespread periodontal disease.

Triclinium C, Villa Farnesina: An Egyptian Narrative Cycle in Roman Wall Painting?

Steven L. Tuck, Miami University

The Villa della Farnesina, believed to have belonged to Marcus Agrippa, ca. 20 B.C.E., was excavated along the banks of the Tiber in Rome. Triclinium C in the villa is one of the oldest black-ground painted rooms that survives in Roman wall painting. The triclinium walls are painted with a flat dado; the columns that subdivide the walls into panels are exaggerated slender candelabra crowned with statuesque figures, and the entablature is painted in narrow bands in blue and yellow. Spread over the fields in the middle of the wall are delicate landscapes, while a figural frieze runs immediately below the entablature, divided by slender columns into 28 episodes: nine on each of the long walls, and five on each of the short walls. The subject of the figural frieze has thus far defied identification; it is variously described as everyday life scenes, popular stories, playful or adventure stories, or scenes of justice.

I argue that the evidence from the panels themselves supports the conclusion that the figural frieze illustrates stories from ancient Egyptian popular tales, possibly supplied in this post-Actium decoration by its Alexandrian painters. The evidence starts with the color scheme. Late Second and early Third Style paintings regularly feature the use of black-ground painting and Egyptian figures, for example in the tablinum of the Villa of the Mysteries, cubiculum in the House of the Orchard, and the Black Room in the villa at Boscotrecase.

The subdivision of each of the long walls into nine scenes corresponds to a common Egyptian narrative division (e.g., Complaint of the Peasant with the nine speeches that form the core of the story and the nine days of the Voyage of Unamun). The best-preserved panels feature an enthroned figure in each panel observing or commenting on the actions undertaken by the figures that fill the panel, a motif in Egyptian stories in which the pharaoh is never the main protagonist, but serves to resolve the conflict. Other details reflect Egyptian culture as well. The figures seeming to undertake various forms of divination in several of the panels are bald, a standard feature of Egyptian priests. The central panel on the left wall shows the circumcision of an adult male, while other panels show elements known from Egyptian stories including a wild ass, shepherds in a boat (Story of the Herdsman), and a young man with a ladder (The Enchanted Prince).

Pilot Osterøy Field Project (PILOST): Report for the 2016 Field Season

Erika Ruhl, University at Buffalo, *Sarah E. Hoffman*, University at Buffalo, *Christopher B. Troskosky*, University at Buffalo, *Torill Christine Lindstrøm*, University of Bergen, and *E.B.W. Zubrow*, University at Buffalo

Southwestern Norway has been described as an upside-down and inside-out world with regard to the majority of archaeological landscapes due to the incredible topographical variability of the local terrain. On this glacial and post-glacial depositional landscape agricultural lands lie not on alluvial plains, but on terraced shelves and plateaus carved into the steep topography. On this landscape human use of space has taken different forms than those observed elsewhere in Scandinavia.

The PILOST Field Project is an archaeological survey of southwestern parts of the Island of Osterøy, Norway, as a joint project of the University of Bergen's Department of Archaeology, History, Cultural Studies and Religion and the University at Buffalo's Department of Anthropology. The focus of the project addresses the changes in patterns of enclosure of the landscape as well as settlement and burial patterns from the Neolithic through the historic periods in southwestern Norway.

The first field season of PILOST (summer 2016) initiated extensive field survey, with subsequent seasons in the planning stages in summer 2017 and beyond. GPS units were utilized to both track survey progress and create GIS maps of the surveyed areas. PILOST serves to further inform wider archaeological understandings and discussions regarding not only land use through time, but the interpretation of and attachment of fishing-farming communities to the archaeological landscape.

The 2016 field season data records more than 145 distinct landscape features, consisting primarily of walls, fences, and other boundary markers. These features were identified based on their potential utility to document and inform a wider archaeological discussion of the evolving nature of boundaries, in/outfield usage, and land ownership within farming communities.

The Dolia of Regio I, Insula 22: Evidence for the Production and Repair of Dolia

Caroline Cheung, University of California, Berkeley, and *Gina Tibbott*, Temple University

Dolia form an interesting and unusual component of Roman (semi-)portable material culture that appears throughout the Mediterranean world. They constitute a class of large-scale, and expensive, ceramic vessels that were probably produced alongside brick and tile products in workshops that supplied Roman building industries; they functioned primarily in agricultural contexts, such as farms, warehouses, and ports, and generally stored foodstuffs such as wine, olive oil, grain, and fish sauce. However, despite their ubiquity and importance no systematic study of dolium production, use, or maintenance has been conducted.

In this poster presentation, we discuss the methodology and results of a dolium research project, in connection with Pompeii Artifact Life History Project (PALHIP), directed by J. Theodore Peña, from University of California, Berkeley. The dolium research project studied the nine, mostly intact, dolia and dolium fragments from Regio I, Insula 22 in Pompeii, a property that was excavated in various stages between the 1950s and 1980s. Although none of the dolia have been entirely excavated, and most are still buried in lapilli, their placement and position allowed detailed autopsy and measurement of dimensions that are otherwise difficult or impossible to note, such as wall thickness and base diameter. Overall, these dolia provided an opportunity to study evidence of manufacture, use alteration, damage, and modifications, such as repairs.

This poster presents evidence suggesting some dolia were coil built on a slow-turning wheel, and that their rims were constructed in at least two steps. In addition, the poster presents evidence for use alteration and calculations of several dolia's capacities. Furthermore the repairs found on several dolia differed, suggesting that there were different techniques and materials utilized in repairing dolia. We hypothesize that different repairs corresponded with the stage during which the dolium was repaired (pre- or post-cocturum), the type of damage people attempted to rectify, and/or the skill and expertise of the person(s) executing the repair. Our poster thus sheds light on the (intricate) production processes for dolia, an important, unique, and understudied class of pottery that was essential for various agricultural activities in antiquity.

Ceramic Kitchenwares at 14th-Century Thebes, Boeotia: Exploring Diversity in a Latin-occupied city of Medieval Greece

Florence Liard, Université libre de Bruxelles, and *Fotini Kondyli*, University of Virginia

We present the results of a combined petrographic and typological analysis of 30 cooking pots discovered in a closed context at the medieval city of Thebes, Boeotia, during joint excavation at Ismenion Hill run by Bucknell University and Ephorate of Antiquities at Boeotia. These pots were part of a larger assemblage of several hundred tablewares, kitchenwares and transport jars, numerous coins and minor objects, that were found in a waste discard pit (bothros) and are currently dated in the first half of the 14th century C.E.

The aim is to characterize local strategies of cookingware production and supply at Thebes during a period of extraordinary political turmoil when Thebes passed from Byzantine to Frankish (1204) then Catalan (1311) control. Comparisons are proposed with our current research on 12th-century pottery from Thebes, and with recent scholarship on Late Medieval kitchenwares from Corinth, Liguria, Provence, and Spain. Attention is drawn to fabric mineralogy, clay processing, and tempering methods; rim profile, body forms, wall thickness, and overall pot proportions. These technical choices were, at least in part, driven by the aim to make a pot suitable for certain foodstuffs and cooking conditions. They are expected to provide insights into potting practices and culinary habits at Thebes, both of which are usually bound up with issues of lifestyles and sociocultural backgrounds of the populations.

Fabrics mineralogy, combined with typological elements of the pots, indicate that a cookingware production activity was distributed among several workshops at Thebes. Pots were also imported from the area of Venetian Chalkida, 40 km to the east. This moderates the resilient hypothesis in medieval archaeology that ceramic kitchenwares were invariably locally made. It also provides insights into Thebes' commercial networks and economic relations within central Greece, particularly with Euboea.

Our results moderate the theory of "Frankish" long-necked cooking pots in a silicate-tempered red fabric, that were allegedly elaborated in Provence or Liguria, then gradually introduced and finally routinely fashioned in some Frankish-controlled cities of Greece such as Corinth. Indeed, a quartz tempering practice is attested as early as the 12th century at Thebes and is developed after 1204 with the use of crushed chert; in parallel, Byzantine shapes are perpetuated. Chalkidian imports are made of a standardized, petrographically different fabric, and they display distinctive typological features. This suggests a distinct organization of cookingware production in this Venetian-ruled city, and specific needs of the Theban population that it supplied.

Post-Occupation Burials at the Villa Romana di Vacone (Lazio, Italy)

Devin L. Ward, University of Toronto, *Dylan M. Bloy*, Rutgers University, *Gary D. Farney*, Rutgers University, *Tyler Franconi*, University of Oxford, and *Candace Rice*, University of Edinburgh

Post-occupation burials in Roman villas are common in central Italy. The style and location of these burials evolve considerably from Late Imperial Rome through the Medieval period. In the first two centuries C.E., tombs were often constructed close to and sometimes even attached to habitation quarters. But following the abandonment of many villas beginning in the early 300s C.E., several styles of burials have been identified within the walls of villas. According to site-specific publications, these interments seem to diversify into other styles through the Late Antique period; these are usually less elaborate, but they often incorporate material from the ruined villa itself. It is not unusual for medieval churches and cemeteries, some functioning today, to be built on the foundations of villa cemeteries.

Previous research has proposed that this trend is related to reoccupation and reuse of villa structures after the collapse of the Roman empire, or alternately it is related to more general economic and religious changes. While some authors promote one of these two causes as the primary factor leading to burials in villa ruins, this trend is most likely connected to both.

We apply findings from ongoing excavation in the Sabina Tiberina as a case study of burials inside villa structures after abandonment, to elucidate potential chronology of different burial styles after the fourth century. To date, excavations in the Roman villa at Vacone have uncovered a minimum of six individuals in four graves, including four adult males, one subadult, and one infant. All adult individuals exhibit signs of poor dental health, developmental stress, and possible infection. No grave goods have been recovered. All individuals, excluding the infant, were buried with knowledge of the villa's physical structure; material from the roof and walls is incorporated into each burial. We expect forthcoming radiocarbon dates to solidify the chronology of these burials.

Though previous research has used the presence of human remains to indicate the end of villa function, burials in fact provide evidence of continued importance of Roman structures beyond their ruin. Burial style may reveal changes in religion and relationships with the dead, whereas skeletal remains themselves reveal changes in the health, mobility, and demography of local populations. It also has the potential to elucidate local attitudes toward Roman remains in the early Medieval period.

"Not Much of a Cheese Shop is it?" An Examination of Cheese Production at Poggio Civitate (Murlo)

Andrew Carroll, Regis Jesuit

The industrial center of Poggio Civitate's 7th century B.C.E. complex yields copious amounts of evidence for different forms of manufacturing including such diverse items as bronze working, ivory carving, textile production, production of ceramics, tiles, and more. Moreover, in addition to the more durable markers of manufacturing, grape seeds, carbonized wheat, and olive pits preserve aspects of Etruscan daily life that are often absent in the archaeological record. However, cheese, like many food items, is lacking in the archaeological record and therefore any examination of it needs to occur from the products used in its production instead of the final product itself. It is clear from the preponderance of sheep bones recovered during the past 50 years of excavations, that the inhabitants were exploiting sheep for both meat consumption and textile production. It would follow that since they were keeping sheep for many years for their wool, that they would make use of other secondary products, such as their milk. The Etruscans would need to overcome the obvious lack of refrigeration by transforming the milk into an item that can be kept for months. While producing cheese seems like the obvious choice for stabilizing milk, the production of it requires specialized equipment. Without the aid of modern instruments to more precisely control temperatures, the Etruscans would have needed specialized equipment for this process. In recent years of excavation several types of ceramic fragments were recovered that puzzle excavators. When taken collectively, and in conjunction with the zooarchaeological evidence, the ceramics appear to be different specialized items for the production of cheese. I argue that ceramic fragments with large fenestrations, or piercings through the side of the vessel, are used for helping control the temperature of the milk during the boil, while those with small fenestrations would have been used in connection with a coarse linen cloth in the process of separating the curds and whey from one another. The joining together of the ceramic evidence with the faunal analysis allows for a more secure understanding of the use of these fenestrated ceramics that until now has eluded excavators. For the first time, this poster joins together the evidence of cheese production that provides a more nuanced understanding of food production at this important Etruscan site of habitation.

Levelling up: The Results of the 2015–2016 Excavations of the Gabii Project's Area C

Sheira Cohen, University of Michigan, *J. Troy Samuels*, University of Michigan, *Giulia Peresso*, Roma Tre University, and *Katherine Beydler*, University of Michigan

This poster presents the results of the Gabii Project's 2015–2016 excavations of the archaic and Early Republican levels of one city block, so-called Area C, in the ancient Latin city of Gabii. The Gabii Project, under the auspices of the University of Michigan and directed by Nicola Terrenato, has excavated at Gabii since 2009. Eight city blocks have been intensively explored, revealing both private and public architecture, spanning the Early Iron Age to Medieval periods. Area C, in particular, is a multiphase complex delimited on two sides by the late fifth-century orthogonal grid; the first phase of excavations of the Area C block, initiated in 2009 and completed in 2011, revealed an early Imperial industrial complex and Late Republican House. In 2015, excavation of the earliest phases of the Area C house was reopened, allowing further clarification of the construction phases of the republican domus and providing insight into the archaeological transition from the Archaic to Republican periods. These recent excavations have uncovered the earliest remains of the atrium-style domus, dating to the fourth century B.C.E. Through careful stratigraphic excavation of the construction layers associated with this earliest phase, it has been possible to better understand the process of repetitive leveling, occupation, and abandonment throughout the Area C house, an element of architectural construction that has been overlooked in previous excavations that concentrate solely on large-scale remodeling and stone structures. Archaic pre-house features have also been discovered, providing the first glimpse into the nature of continual habitation at Gabii during the crucial transition from the Archaic into the Republican periods. The discovery of different occupation zones and hut features along variable orientations within the Area C complex provides further insight into the imposition of an orthogonal street plan on preexisting structures and complexes. This poster serves as a preliminary presentation of the stratigraphy and material remains of the Early Republican and archaic phases of the Area C house and provides an epistemological study of the archaeology of leveling fills, an oft-ignored yet rich archaeological resource for understanding the everyday activities and minutiae of repeated actions in the Gabine past.

I Can't Believe It's Not Bronze! Mycenoan Metallurgy During the Late Bronze Age "Collapse"

Alison M. Crandall, University of California Los Angeles, *B. Lee Drake*, University of New Mexico, *Miriam G. Clinton*, Rhodes College, *Georgia Flouda*, Heraklion Archaeological Museum, and *Andrew J. Koh*, Brandeis University

In June 2016, a collaboration of the ARCHEM team, Mouliana Project, and Heraklion Archaeological Museum, scientifically analyzed artifacts from the Late Minoan (LM) IIIC (12th century B.C.E.) tholos tombs at Mouliana Sellades in the western Siteia foothills of Crete. These funerary objects are attributed to a people who moved inland in response to the Late Bronze Age (LBA) "collapse" and threats from the sea. Though a settlement has yet to be studied, its tomb artifacts suggest that the previously achieved technological sophistication was not lost despite the population's retreat from the coast and its maritime trade routes.

The assemblage was examined, documented, and analyzed. Using two portable X-ray fluorescence (pXRF) spectrometers, more than 700 sample points were taken from 36 artifacts and subsequently interpreted for the elemental composition. Alongside the research plan devised for the artifacts, pXRF allows researchers to determine the composition of alloys, reconstruct details about production, and gather data to provide an accurate interpretation of the ancient materials despite variations in bulk or surface topography, as well as any other conditions that may have altered the chemistry of the objects.

Most metals from the Bronze Age are loosely classified as bronze, correlated to either arsenical copper or copper-tin alloy by visual examination or elemental analysis. This investigation has shown the qualitative and quantitative presence of a range of metals including some unexpected discoveries (e.g., zinc) that may be the result of materials experimentation in LM IIIC due to lack of traditional resources (e.g., tin). Regardless, bronze, red brass, and iron were found together in the Sellades tombs, physically representing the metallurgical transition into the Iron Age.

These alloys do not adhere to analogous modern alloys or the preconceptions of LBA alloys, particularly those containing a higher zinc-tin ratio than is commonly attributed to LBA bronzes. Possible catalysts for change include a lack of tin on the island necessitating substitution, evolving trade routes, technological innovation, or some combination thereof. While it is possible that these changes were internal attempts at innovation irrespective of external conditions, the gold objects contain higher concentrations of silver, similar to electrum, and when compared with earlier objects this suggests a practical solution to diminishing resources post-"collapse."

Further studies need to be performed on archaeological metals from Greece to understand the larger metallurgical picture. However, the available evidence from this initial study suggests continued and sophisticated metallurgical production during this period, perhaps to replicate familiar materials despite changing times.

Examining Diet using Stable Isotopes Throughout Prehistoric Greece

Stephanie M. Fuehr, Mississippi State University, *Nicholas P. Herrmann*, Texas State University, *Michael L. Galaty*, Mississippi State University, and *Aleydis Van de Moortel*, University of Tennessee

Carbon and nitrogen stable isotopes from 18 bone collagen and 51 dental enamel samples from various burial contexts at the Bronze and Iron Age sites of Mitrou and Tragana Agia Triada (TAT) are examined to understand diet in prehistoric central Greece. In addition, isotopic data from across Greece is compared with the Mitrou and TAT assays to examine regional dietary patterns from the Neolithic to Iron Age. While isotopic studies are performed in Greece, few combine the results from multiple sites within a regional framework. This research aims to analyze new data from central Greece, as well as previously published data, in an attempt to determine if diet across regions of prehistoric Greece varied geographically or temporally. The sample consists of more than 400 recently published isotopic assessments as well as the Mitrou and TAT values. One-way ANOVAs and scatterplots are run through the statistical program JMP to analyze the isotopic data. The results of the Mitrou-TAT study indicate that there is no change in diet through time or between the two sites. The broader study supports the results from the Mitrou-TAT study, with the exception of the southern Neolithic. This suggests that the southern Neolithic had access to a greater variety of plants, thus indicating the difference between the other regions and time periods. When applied to the broader aspect of societal change, these results suggest that, even with a significant societal change, diet is not significantly influenced.

Archaeological Aspects of the Kelsey Museum's Collection of Decorative Stone

Leah Long, Virginia Commonwealth University in Qatar

At the turn of the 20th century, Francis W. Kelsey began to amass a large collection of artifacts from archaeological sites across the Mediterranean to broaden the teaching of ancient studies at the University of Michigan. Among the objects now housed in the museum bearing his name is a collection of colorful stone objects that date to the Roman period. While Kelsey acquired most of the pieces, he also energetically solicited donations from other leading classical archaeologists and wealthy Detroit industrialists. The resulting collection, numbering some

700 samples, is probably the largest corpus of Roman decorative stone outside Europe and is one of the richest and most varied anywhere. In contrast to European collections of decorative stone, such as the Corsi collection in Oxford, ours is composed of objects, gathered largely as architectural fragments that derived from well-known ancient buildings, such as the Baths of Diocletian in Rome. The well-preserved fragments include floor paving and wall veneer, figural and geometric-shaped *opus sectile*, architectural revetment, reworked architecture, labra, candelabra, sarcophagi and sculpture recut into revetment, and debris from ancient quarries.

In keeping with the nature of the collection, this study's thrust is archaeological. This paper presents each constituent class of material as a single entity, while addressing aspects of production, distribution, display, and materiality. Because the collection had never been subject to systematic investigation, each piece was carefully examined and entered into a Filemaker database that included classification fields for object identification, history of use and reuse, provenance, measurements, material and variety, and surface treatment. The collection is remarkable in that it showcases the breadth and quantity of colorful marbles used for decorative display and the full range of marbles quarried in the Roman period. Particularly impressive are illusionistic marble revetment, cut to imitate three-dimensional architecture, and individual pieces of *opus sectile*. Fragments of fluted pilasters, intarsiated capitals, cornice moldings, and *opus sectile* with vegetal motifs were made of expensive imported marbles and rival the decorative programs of the imperial Horti Lamiani villa in Rome and the late Roman aristocratic residence at Porta Marina in Ostia. This paper highlights the unique pieces in the collection, places them in the wider context of the Roman world, and underscores how a great deal of archaeological information can be gathered from objects in a museum collection that do not always have secure provenience.

Low-Cost First Aid for Mosaics: A Method for Temporary Field Conservation

Elizabeth Bevis, Johns Hopkins University

In each of its first four seasons (2013–2016) the Santa Susana Archaeological Project has uncovered fragmentary Late Roman mosaics on the site of a Roman villa in the central Alentejo, Portugal. The fragile condition of the mosaic fragments required the staff to develop a process to document, consolidate, and rebury these features until such time as they can be treated by a professional conservator. Due to the small size of this project and its mission as a field school, the mosaic conservation process had to meet two very specific criteria: (1) the conservation methods must be simple enough to be performed by student volunteers and staff with no previous experience in object conservation; (2) the materials used must be obtainable in rural Portugal and within the project's operating budget. During the 2016 excavation season the mosaic fragments were uncovered to check their condition, consolidated where necessary, and reburied with updated methods. This poster presents the process of documentation, consolidation, and reburial of in situ mosaics developed at the Santa Susana villa site in consultation with archaeological conservator Sanchita Balachandran (Johns Hopkins University).

Documentation of the mosaics was accomplished through standard photography and technical drawing at a 1:20 scale. If the condition of the mosaic fragments allowed, they were then gently cleaned with scalpels followed by wet cleaning with water and cotton pads in a way that disturbed the tesserae as little as possible. After cleaning, mosaic fragments were directly traced with colored permanent markers on translucent paper to record the design and colors at a 1:1 scale. Mosaic fragments were consolidated at any visible areas of instability (cracks, holes, loose tesserae) by the application of a 4:1 solution of water and gum arabic. After consolidation, the mosaics were photographed again and reburied under approximately 8 cm of sand and 15 cm of sifted excavation dirt, with the layers separated by sheets of Tyvek. The entire workflow was managed through the use of a comprehensive checklist and recording sheet.

The good condition of the majority of the mosaic fragments at their 2016 check-up attests to the effectiveness of this process. It is hoped that this experience and the resources presented in this poster will help archaeologists facing similar challenges preserve mosaic pavements in situ until a professional conservator's assistance can be secured.

New Data on Copper Age Metallurgy in Northern Italy

Kyle P. Freund, Indian River State College, *Claudio Cavazzuti*, Museo Nazionale Preistorico Etnografico Luigi Pigorini, *Alessandra Serges*, Museo Nazionale Preistorico Etnografico Luigi Pigorini, and *Robert H. Tykot*, University of South Florida

This paper presents data on early copper-based metallurgy from 16 Copper Age sites in northern and north-central Italy (ca. fourth–third millennia B.C.E.). As early as the mid fifth millennium B.C.E. Neolithic communities of the region began to experiment with metal technology. In these early phases, metal use appears to have been highly restricted and is only represented by a small number of total artifacts, the products including items for personal adornment, weaponry, and simple tools such as awls, points, and axes. By the time of the Copper Age, however, we began to see the widespread adoption of metalworking as well as broader social and symbolic transformations represented by new forms of interpersonal violence (e.g., daggers, halberds) and funerary practices. In certain instances these changes are viewed as part of an interrelated cultural whole, referred to as the Beaker Culture.

While there have been numerous studies on the "origins" and spread of metallurgy in the central Mediterranean, there is a comparative lack of data on how particular production practices varied through time and space. To address this research bias, 21 metal artifacts from 16 Copper Age sites were analyzed at the Museo Nazionale Preistorico Etnografico Luigi Pigorini in Rome, Italy, with the goal of exploring the local factors that informed early metal use at these sites and how these practices varied across space. This included combining typological classification with compositional analyses to reveal sets of choices made at multiple stages of the production process. This type of integrated approach is producing high-quality data that allows for the comparison of differences in the form and function of various objects across space as well as differences in the raw materials being used to create them. Compositional analysis using portable X-ray fluorescence (pXRF) spectrometry has revealed a combination of pure copper and arsenical copper-based metallurgy, while typological analysis has identified nine axes, eight daggers, and four halberds. When contextualized within the broader circumstances of their occurrence, these results have important implications as it relates to debates about the technological, socioeconomic, and symbolic relevance of these products in wider cultural processes.

Our Storied Past: Using Story Maps to Teach Geography, History, and Archaeology

Erin Warford, Hilbert College

Geography, history, and archaeology are inextricably linked. However, it can be difficult for instructors to effectively demonstrate these links to students through readings, powerpoint slides, or static printed maps. When instructors hand out a blank map and a list of 20 places for students to find and label, how much are students really learning?

One of the recent trends in education has been towards active learning, in which students engage in activities that promote analysis, synthesis, and evaluation of the course material. In this poster I suggest a new tool that instructors can use to promote active learning: story maps. These maps, which can be created online using open-source applications provided by ESRI, allow the mapmaker to combine geographic data with text, images, and other multimedia in order to tell a story—an ideal approach for an interdisciplinary field such as classics. In addition, the maps can be accessed through any browser and do not require any special software to view.

In my World History and Geography course, I have created story maps to supplement the textbook reading for topics such as the first cities (Old Kingdom Egypt, Sumeria, and the Indus River Valley civilization) and Alexander the Great's conquests. I have embedded in the map relevant textual excerpts, background information, and images, which students can explore by clicking through the map and investigating pop-ups. I provided my students with one or two short essay questions to think about as they explored the map; they then brought their answers to class, where we discussed their observations and conclusions. My poster presents one of these story maps, as well as student responses and feedback gathered via in-class surveys about the effectiveness of story maps as a learning tool. I will also offer handouts with instructions for creating story maps using ESRI's online resources.

Story maps are a powerful new tool for instructors in classics courses, no matter the subject matter. Courses on ancient texts could use story maps to provide valuable geographic context—or students could create the maps themselves. History and archaeology courses could also benefit from the ability to link texts, artifacts, and buildings to geographic locations and demonstrate the connections and networks that were so vital to the ancient Mediterranean. Story maps need not be solely a pedagogical tool, either—they are also an interactive, visually impressive method for presenting research to the public, particularly for historians and archaeologists.

Rethinking Abandonment at Imperial Gabii: Results of the 2016 Excavations of the Gabii Project's Area I

Jason Farr, University of Michigan, and *Sabian Hasani*, University of Michigan

In this poster we present the initial results of the Gabii Project's 2016 excavations in Area I, a zone occupying the southern end of a city block near the center of the ancient Latin city of Gabii, 20 km east of Rome. The imperial phases in this area have great potential to shed light on the economic processes and material consequences of urban abandonment in the hinterland of the capital. The Gabii Project, an archaeological initiative under the auspices of the University of Michigan and directed by Nicola Terrenato, has conducted open-area excavations at Gabii since 2009. The city, an early rival to nearby Rome, had already declined significantly by the first century B.C.E., and the relative lack of later construction permits investigation of the entire lifecycle of the city—from urbanization in the Early Iron Age and Archaic periods to gradual abandonment over the course of the first few centuries C.E. Our work in the 2016 season featured the opening of a new zone of excavation, Area I, and the discovery of an Imperial-period structure situated along one of the major roads of the city. The building itself is relatively small (ca. 14 m on a side) but complex, with eight separate rooms and multiple phases of construction and reorganization. In the latest phase, before abandonment sometime in the third century C.E., the structure was adapted for the production of oil or wine, indicated by the presence of features associated with pressing, collection, and storage. At the same time, several of the rooms seem to have been highly decorated, with painted plaster preserved on several walls and large amounts of similar plaster and colored marble found in associated collapse and abandonment deposits. Such finds may be relics of an earlier domestic function—in places, our excavations revealed hints of earlier floors and other features that may belong to a house—but also may have resulted from dumping activities as nearby properties were demolished or altered. In either case, our results speak to the kind of specific material changes that take place as settlements shrink and urban space is repurposed. In particular, the presence of pressing facilities, usually associated with rural villas, near the center of a town in decline raises interesting questions regarding the role of agricultural production in processes of urban abandonment and economic change in the suburbs of Imperial Rome.

A New Online Database of Roman Temples

John D. Muccigrosso, Drew University

This poster describes recent work in creating an on-line database of Roman temples for research and teaching. The database builds on information already available in existing gazetteers such as the Pleiades Project, Vici.org, and DARE, by including features specific to temples (and other buildings related to religious activity), such as the divinity to whom the temple is dedicated and its foundation date. These data are derived from existing publications on temples in the ancient world, and the database thus serves as a convenient central place for discovery and exploration of information from disparate sources that are currently difficult to assemble. As the project progresses, we aim to provide the capability for users to interact with the data visually, mapping various queries, or more directly by downloading it in a convenient format. For example, users could show the distribution of temples to a particular divinity, or the changing placement of temples in the city of Rome over time. We also plan to link to other relevant projects, allowing users to discover, for example, depictions of a particular temple on coinage (e.g., http://numismatics.org/collection/1953.171.1288). The data will be freely available under an appropriate Creative Commons license and we hope to have currently unforeseen, but valuable, uses of it by others. The project also aims to contribute back to the existing databases by sharing relevant data with them (e.g., by adding the locations of currently unlisted temples to Pleiades).

The project is connected with several others already ongoing at Drew University, including a database of shrines ("edicole") in the city of Rome, to which we plan to connect more closely in the future.

The project began as a teaching exercise in class on classical archaeology, based on previous research into the locations of temples in the Roman republic. It has been aided this summer by a grant from the Mellon Foundation in support of a growing digital humanities effort at my home institution, which allowed for a research project by an undergraduate student. It will hopefully serve as a valuable addition to the existing—and growing—number of digital projects on the classical world.

Building a Digital Site Plan at Isthmia

Jon M. Frey, Michigan State University, *Timothy E. Gregory*, Ohio State University, and *James Herbst*, ASCSA Excavations at Corinth

While electronic three-dimensional modeling has been commonly used in industrial applications for quite some time now, the lower costs and improved usability of this technology has brought it within the reach of most archaeological projects. In particular, the technique known as structure from motion (SfM) allows for the creation of remarkably accurate virtual models of both objects and landscapes from a series of digital still images. Yet, as "lifelike" as the resulting models may appear, in many ways archaeologists have not moved beyond their initial fascination with the technology to an examination of what these new tools can do to improve our understanding of the past.

This poster presents one such practical application of SfM technology at the site of Isthmia in Greece. Up to this point, Isthmia has not enjoyed the benefit of a single, scalable, digital plan. Thus, while traditional state plans exist for many of the areas of interest around the site, the three-dimensional locations and relationships of all excavated (and unexcavated) monuments and features are much less certain. To remedy this problem affordably, archaeologists from the Ohio State University Excavations, in collaboration with the University of Chicago, Michigan State University, and the ASCSA Excavations at Corinth, engaged in a week-long aerial drone survey, followed by the creation of a three-dimensional model, orthophotomosaic, and topographic plan. As is shown in this poster, the resulting digital models serve as a highly detailed backdrop and spatial control against which one may test important hypotheses concerning the organization of structures at the site as well as the locations of roadways through the area in antiquity. What is more, these models offer a low-cost alternative to satellite/LiDAR imagery or time-consuming traditional cartographic surveys.

Itea Panaghia/Profitis Ilias: An Important Multi-period Site from Grevena, Greece

Nancy C. Wilkie, Carleton College, *Mary E. Savina*, Carleton College, *Jayne Pasternak*, Carleton College, *Suzanne Hansen*, Macalester College, *Mary Pyott Freeman*, Independent Scholar, *Jeff Bartlett*, Independent Scholar, and *Thomas Upshaw*, Independent Scholar

Itea Panaghia/Profitis Ilias, a multiperiod archaeological site in the Grevena prefecture, western Macedonia, Greece, is a prominent landmark on a ridge end near the confluence of several streams. As part of the Grevena Project, a multidisciplinary archaeological survey of the 2,500 km^2 prefecture, magnetometry surveys of the site took place in 1988 and 1989. Field-based evidence supports a complex history of the site, suggesting its function as the location of a settlement, convent, and church across time. Judging from pottery fragments found on the surface, the site was occupied in the Bronze Age, Early Iron Age, Geometric, Archaic, Classical, Hellenistic, Late Roman, Early Medieval, and post-Byzantine periods. This chronology represents a longer and more complex archaeological history than most of the 300+ sites identified by the Grevena Project in the nomos. A road cut at the site exposes a pebble floor consistent with an archaic building of some kind, as suggested by a radiocarbon date and associated potsherds. A rich oral history revolves around an 18th-century church (severely damaged by a 1995 earthquake) and a convent (demolished 1912).

Magnetometry results were reanalyzed in 2014–2016 with the goal of determining whether the uniform upper surface of the site conceals any now-buried structures. The surveys, covering 8,500 m^2, were conducted at four meter intervals with a single proton-precession magnetometer. When compiled and interpreted, two datasets reveal a linear anomaly of two parallel magnetic lows 12 m apart stretching east-west for at least 100 m, possibly representing a buried building foundation east of the 18th-century church. Several discrete dipolar anomalies were also noted, which may be caused by discarded debris. The geophysical data do not seem to show an extension of the pebble floor exposed in the road cut at the southeast end of the site, perhaps because there is little magnetic contrast between the pebble layer and the enclosing material.

Although there have been many advances in the technology and methods of remote sensing in archaeological contexts over the last three decades, revisiting legacy data with modern processing techniques and the subsequent interpretation of these results proves to be valuable in the interpretation of buried archaeological remains.

Decoding Ritual: Investigating the Neolithic Rhyton

Carolin Fine, Florida State University

The term "ritual" is common in ceramic studies when more traditional explanations founded on vessel function elude the archaeologist. In the case of so-called rhyta of Neolithic Greece, their unusual shape has led to such a classification, marginalizing this class of vessel in general discourse on contemporary pottery. As yet, no comprehensive study has been undertaken to define the function and significance of this unique shape in Greece. My dissertation takes as its focus the rhyta with the specific aim of investigating its meaning within the broader social and economic contexts of Neolithic Greece. This poster presents preliminary research on a corpus of more than 150 fragments of rhyta excavated from Corinth—a collection of rhyta more than three times the size of any other known site—and compares this material to contemporary rhyta found at a number of other sites on the Greek mainland, the Adriatic coast, and the Balkans. While still in an early stage, these results open a dialogue not only about ceramic analysis of specialized shapes but also about religious and ritual practices that took place during the Neolithic. Given the wide geographic distribution of the Neolithic rhyta, further investigation may in fact indicate a vast area of mutually intelligible practice during the Late and Final Neolithic across the Mediterranean and southeastern Europe.

A Thousand Years of Transformation in the City Center of Gabii: New Evidence from the 2016 Excavations in Areas G and H

Arianna Zapelloni Pavia, University of Michigan, *Parrish Wright*, University of Michigan, *Zoe Jenkins*, University of Michigan, and *Andrew C. Johnston*, Yale University

Previous seasons of excavation by the Gabii Project at the Latin city of Gabii (2009–present) have illuminated developments in central Italian urbanism and architecture in the archaic and Republican periods. During the 2016 field season, two new areas of excavation were opened—Areas G and H—that promise to contribute further to our knowledge of the mid republican city, as well as the hitherto mostly unknown Late Antique and Early Medieval phases of occupation. This poster reviews these early results and preliminary hypotheses.

Excavation in Area H—a wide city block south of the main trunk road (Via Gabina), at the central intersection—has revealed several phases of occupation and construction, the earliest of which appears to relate to a building complex of mid republican date, which may have been connected to a large open space to the south. Its rooms were paved in tufo slabs, with walls in massive ashlar blocks, several courses of which are preserved. During the Imperial period, this building underwent a spatial and functional reorganization into an industrial or productive zone. Although the complete plan of the complex and the details of its phasing remain to be uncovered, it is already clear that this building will provide important information regarding the layout of the city and transformations in urban space.

Excavation in Area G, immediately to the north across the Via Gabina, revealed remains of a large building dated to the Imperial period, the construction of which reorganized the earlier Republican-era portico that ran along the north side of the main road. Within the rooms of this building, as well as running across the Via Gabina itself, the latest phase of occupation was represented by a labyrinthine network of irregular walls composed of tiles and reused architectural elements. The present hypothesis is that these walls were part of an extensive land reclamation, dated to the Early Medieval period, which entailed the clearing of the collapse debris of this part of the city and the raising of the ground level by several meters in order to enable agricultural activities, likely associated with the monastery and church of S. Primus located only a few hundred meters to the south. This clear evidence for large-scale, labor-intensive projects, and for the obsolescence of the Via Gabina in the direction of Tibur, dramatically impacts our current understanding of the economy and mobility in Latium after the abandonment of the city in late antiquity.

Excavations at a Wadi Rabah Late Neolithic Site in Wadi Quseiba, Northern Jordan

E. B. Banning, University of Toronto, *Isaac Ullah*, San Diego State University, *Philip Hitchings*, University of Toronto, *Khaled Abu Jayyab*, University of Toronto, *Stephen Rhodes*, University of Toronto, and *Emma Yasui*, University of Toronto

In August 2014, a team from the University of Toronto conducted excavations at a "candidate site" that the Wadi Quseiba Survey had recently discovered in Wâdî al-Bîr, one of Wadi Quseiba's main tributaries, in its 2013 test of Bayesian survey methods in northern Jordan. The excavations resulted in good evidence for occupation during the Late Neolithic, including abundant pottery and lithics, some ground stone, and associated surfaces, pits, and possible traces of architecture. It appears to have been a camp or farmstead of the late sixth millennium cal B.C.E., contemporary with Tabaqat al-Bûma in Wadi Ziqlab to its south and sites in northern Israel that archaeologists assign to the "Wadi Rabah culture." The finds at this site, in conjunction with the unorthodox methods used to discover it, have broader implications for our understanding of the extensiveness of Neolithic settlement in the southern Levant during the sixth millennium B.C.E. and the nature of Neolithic social landscapes.

The Battle of the Crocian Plain: A Topographical Perspective

Andrew G. Nichols, University of Florida, and *Robert S. Wagman*, University of Florida

The battle fought by Philip II of Macedon and Onomarchus of Phocis during the second phase of the Third Sacred War (352 B.C.E.) was one of the largest and bloodiest military confrontations in Greek history. Yet much of what we know about this important event is clouded in uncertainty, starting from the very location where the battle took place. Based on the vague indications of the sources, modern scholars believe that the two armies engaged somewhere southwest of Pagasae, in the mountain-bound plain adjacent to the gulf by the same name (Dio. 16, 35, 4–6). Known as the Crocus or Crocian Plain (Strabo 9, 5, 8, 14; Steph. Byz., s.v. "Dēmētrion"), in antiquity this region was accessed through a number of mountain routes that are no longer in use today, having been superseded in later times by a new national road running along the coast. Despite the relevance of the ancient communications network to our understanding of the battle's topographical and strategical details, no in-depth study has ever been done on the topic.

Based on two years of field research, this poster offers a detailed topographical discussion of the district where the battle took place and of all the routes and passes leading to it, including previously ignored remains of a road running through one of the main mountain saddles. Through a new examination of the terrain's characteristics that are likely to have affected the movements and composition of the troops in each force, the authors present a fresh perspective on the Crocian Plain that challenges many of the accepted views on the famous battle of 352 B.C.E. The poster is thoroughly illustrated with maps and images of key land features, many photographed for the first time, from this area of eastern Thessaly.

Cosa Excavations 2016

Christina Cha, Florida State University, *Allison Smith*, Florida State University, *Anastasia Belinskaya*, Florida State Univerisity, *Nora K. Donoghue*, Florida State University, and *Ann Glennie*, Florida State University

In the summer of 2016, Cosa Excavations, an international archaeological collaboration between Florida State University, Bryn Mawr College, and Universität Tübingen, returned to its investigation of the bath complex at the Roman colony of Cosa. The project began in 2013 to better our understanding of Roman bathing culture at the site, with inquiries primarily focused on the question of water supply and the precise layout of the bath structure. Previous seasons revealed exciting information about the building's design and usage, and various artifacts, including inscriptions, brick stamps, and pottery, have been used to date the initial construction of the bath, as well as to attest to its longevity.

Excavations of the bath between 2013 and 2016 have revealed building techniques and artifacts consistently dateable to the Hadrianic period, as well as a number of rooms that can be identified as pertaining to distinct, Roman bathing activities. In order to further understand the function of these various spaces in the bath, four new areas were opened for exploration in the most recent campaign, primarily in the northern and western sectors within the bathing block. The 2016 season saw the investigation of a large room directly to the north of a circular laconicum, as well as a previously unexcavated area in the northwest corner of the complex. One of the most exciting discoveries of the season was a small apsidal pool with the remains of a hypocaust preserved underneath. Two other areas were opened this season, one to examine the northern limits of the complex, and another to explore the space just outside the hydraulic rooms in the southwest sector.

This poster presents a summary of our ongoing research of the bath at Cosa. It includes information pertaining mainly to the 2015 and 2016 excavation seasons—particularly on those areas intimately connected with the functional spaces used to run this bath—in order to present our most recent findings. Through future campaigns, the project seeks to fully understand the chronology and organization of the bath at Cosa.

Sequencing of Chloroplast Genomes from Medieval Millet Grains Excavated in Armenia

Stephen M. Richards, The University of Adelaide

Millets are a group of grasses from the family Poaceae that include some of the first domesticated cereals. The major millet crops were domesticated in arid areas of Africa and China and then spread to other regions of the world. Currently little is known about the routes by which millets dispersed from their origins of domestication. In the current study, we describe the sequencing and analysis of chloroplast genomes (sans inverted repeat regions) generated from millet grains excavated from the Areni-1 cave in southern Armenia and carbon dated to Medieval times (873 ±36 and 1118 ±35 years BP). A phylogeny of the chloroplast matK gene identifies the Armenian millet as *Panicum miliaceum* or broomcorn millet, a cereal domesticated in northern China approximately 10,000 years ago. This study is noteworthy because it demonstrates that millet grains can preserve significant levels of DNA for hundreds of years and that grains recovered from excavations can be used to trace the spread of domesticated millet.

Further Research on the Roman Republican Cult-Place under Sant'Omobono

Daniel P. Diffendale, University of Michigan

The temples of Fortuna and Mater Matuta in Rome's Forum Boarium underwent numerous modifications during the Roman republic, from the initial construction of the twin temples on a large square podium in the years ca. 500 B.C.E. to the reconstruction of the sanctuary following a fire in 213 B.C.E., before a site-wide restructuring perhaps in the Late Republic or Early Imperial period. The Sant'Omobono Project, a collaboration between the Sovrintendenza Capitolina, the Università della Calabria, and the University of Michigan, aims at a full reconsideration of the archival, monumental and artifactual evidence from the site. Based on my work with the project since 2011, and especially on work undertaken during the summer of 2016, I present new conclusions and new questions about the architectural development of the site during the republic, including results of further chemical analysis of tuff types used in the construction of the sanctuary structures and advances in understanding the republican architectural terracottas.

Identifying Obsidian Procurement Habits During the Pre-Pottery Neolithic in the Levant Using Network Analysis

Zack Batist, University of Toronto

Due to obsidian's unique geochemical properties, whereby each geological source has its own chemical signature, artifacts made from this material may be chemically characterized and linked to the geological source from which they derive. This helps to determine the extent of regional interaction throughout prehistory, and reflects participation within socioeconomic systems that contributed to the material's distribution. Through direct comparison of the range of raw materials used at a site, as well as techno-typological readings of chipped-stone assemblages, a more nuanced understanding of shared habits pertaining to the procurement of obsidian may be attained. Using network analysis methods, obsidian sourcing data pertaining to the Pre-Pottery Neolithic in the Levant have been compared in order to identify clusters representing such diversity. The results of this analysis are then compared against techno-typological analyses in order to derive an alternative model of heterogeneity pertaining to this archaeological setting.

Textile Artifacts from Karanis: A New Interpretation

Shannon Ness, University of Michigan

The University of Michigan's Kelsey Museum of Archaeology currently displays a variety of toys from Karanis, a Graeco-Roman agricultural town located in the Fayum. Playthings such a rattle, a horse-shaped pull-toy, and a wooden sword readily recall modern toys and allow visitors to envision a childhood in antiquity. Included among these objects are several "rag dolls." These small textile artifacts consists of one or more pieces of cloth bounded together to form a head or knot with the remaining fabric hanging loosely below. A few examples have additional features interpreted as anthropomorphic details: one object has a braid of hair attached to the knot, while another has decoration that resembles a pair of eyes. These features, however, are not shared by all of the rag dolls, and of the 16 examples held by the Kelsey Museum, only one object features more than one anthropomorphic detail. Thus these rag dolls are strikingly different in scale and form from play-dolls known from Egypt and the wider Roman empire.

The Kelsey rag dolls lack the articulated limbs and detailed anatomical features that are characteristic of cloth dolls, Coptic bone dolls, or jointed dolls. The Kelsey examples range from 3–10 cm in height and are therefore consistently smaller than other known play-dolls dating to the Roman Imperial period. Furthermore, it is difficult to reconcile these textile objects with modern theories on toy-play that suggest playtime with toys allows children to be socialized into their society. A child with a toy horse and a wooden sword may pretend to be a soldier without the real world consequences of warfare. Similarly, dolls allow young children to act out motherhood or domestic situations in meaningful ways that prepare them for their future lives.

The Kelsey rag dolls are inconsistent with current theories on dolls and should no longer be identified as such. Instead, working with cross-cultural practices in infant care, I offer a new interpretation for these artifacts as soothers, objects intended to comfort infants and younger children. In scale and form, these objects closely resemble ragbags, scraps of cloth tied around foodstuffs or other objects, which were given to children to suck on. Such cloth soothers were widely used in agricultural communities until the introduction of the modern dummy nipple or pacifier. Such an interpretation can allow for a more detailed image of infancy in Roman Egypt.

The Management of Water at the Etrusco-Romano site of Coriglia, Caster Viscardo, Italy

Darlene Forst, Institute for Mediterranean Archaeology, and *Will Ramundt*, University of Arizona

This poster examines the diachronic management of water on the site of Coriglia, an Etrusco-Roman site that was occupied from the beginning of the eighth century B.C.E. until the 15th century C.E. The site had a hot spring that rose in antiquity as well as a freshwater spring (that still rises). There are a series of large vascae to the south of the site, a large bath complex and nymphaeum at the north of it, as well as a drainage system that runs in the current state of excavation 200 m.

The drainage system was in use from at least the Hellenistic Etruscan phase until the fifth century C.E. There are also a series of drains and sewers that are associated with a road system that persists for 1,000 years. Much of the last few years' work at the site has resulted in a better understanding of how Romans engineered the movement of water both in service of a bath complex and in an attempt to keep roads serviceable from the Republican period until the fifth century. This poster presents the drainage and sewer system as well as freshwater systems that served the site and their development over time to accommodate changes in use of the site and adapt to environmental and geomorphological developments as well.

Gardens of the Hesperides: The Rural Archaeology of the Loukkos Valley. Preliminary Results of the 2016 Pilot Season

Aomar Akerraz, Institut National des Sciences de l'Archéologie et du Patrimoine, and *Stephen A. Collins-Elliott*, University of Tennessee

The ancient city of Lixus (Larache, Morocco) was one of the oldest cities in northwestern Africa, founded on the Atlantic coast by Phoenician traders in the eighth century B.C.E. While the city of Lixus has received attention in its capacity as a center of maritime commerce, the aim of the newly formed joint Moroccan-American project, "Gardens of the Hesperides: The Rural Archaeology of the Loukkos Valley" (INSAP-University of Tennessee), is to investigate the ancient agricultural economy of the hinterland of the city. In order to assess the contribution of regional economic systems for the city's development from the Early Iron Age to late antiquity, a multivariate model is employed that can measure the degree to which Lixus was integrated with its hinterland, and, more broadly, how its agricultural economy, both in its production and consumption of goods, changed throughout its occupation by the Roman empire.

This poster presents the preliminary results of the 2016 pilot season, which consisted of an archaeological field survey that combined both systematic fieldwalking and extensive methodologies. Ceramic vessel finds were quantified by sherd count, weight, and EVE (estimated vessel equivalent) to mitigate the influence of post-use depositional processes on their quantification. The spatial distribution of finds was then obtained using a Bayesian approach to data analysis, which could incorporate materials recovered both through systematic and nonsystematic means, in order to present a "profile" of ceramic vessel use for each topographic unit, here to illustrate the degree to which commodities imported via amphoras were consumed in the countryside. Thus, even with preliminary finds data while in search of sites of agricultural production, a picture of the changing habits of consumption in the countryside can be constructed for the region of the Oued Loukkos.

The Taphonomy of the Human Skeletal Remains from the Philistine Cemetery at Ashkelon, Israel

Sherry C. Fox, Arizona State University, *Kathryn Marklein*, Ohio State University, *Rachel Kalisher*, New York University, *Marina Faerman*, Hebrew University, *Patricia Smith*, Hebrew University, *Adam Aja*, Harvard University, and *Daniel Master*, Wheaton College

Following the fourth and final field season of excavations in 2016 by the Leon Levy Expedition at the Philistine cemetery at Ashkelon, a better understanding of the taphonomy of the human skeletal remains, representing more than 200 individuals, is presented. Taphonomy can inhibit the study of human skeletal remains, limit the types of analytical tests undertaken, and it can lead to misinterpretations of results. Located outside the city walls of the ancient city, the Philistine cemetery is situated not far from the Mediterranean Sea, in soil that is mostly composed of sand with some clay, under a few meters of soil. Due to the weight of the soil, some of the crania are deformed taphonomically. Additionally, some of the bones are concreted in a salt from the burial environment. The outer cortex of the bone has exfoliated in other individuals, as well, due to taphonomic conditions. Although the bone was not recovered in an excellent state of preservation, ^{14}C results have been obtained from some of the human remains. The burial environment has also allowed for the preservation of calcified tissues, including calcified sternal rib cartilage. By far, one of the more intriguing finds has been circular holes found in some of the bones, including long bones and crania, among others, that were produced in the burial environment by land snails. The most likely candidate is the land snail, *Theba pisana*. These holes simulate pathology and should not be confused with pathology. Despite taphonomic conditions that impede scientific interpretations of the human remains, a great deal has been gained already from the study of the human remains at the Philistine cemetery of Ashkelon.

Radiocarbon (AMS) Dates of Early Helladic III and Early Prepalatial Child Burials from Mitrou

Aleydis Van de Moortel, University of Tennessee, *Nicholas P. Herrmann*, Texas State University at San Marcos, *Eleni Zahou*, Greek Archaeological Service, *Salvatore Vitale*, Italian School of Archaeology at Athens, and *Christopher Hale*, British School of Archaeology, Knossos

The 2004–2008 excavations conducted by the Greek Archaeological Service and the University of Tennessee at the prehistoric settlement of Mitrou, in central Greece, have uncovered some 57 stratified occupation levels ranging from the Early Helladic IIB to the Late Protogeometric phase. Pottery studies have established the existence of 37 ceramic phases at the site. This long and well-dated sequence offers good opportunities for addressing issues of absolute chronology in the Bronze Age Aegean.

In this paper we discuss ^{14}C (AMS) dates of bone (collagen) samples from three child burials, carried out by Beta Analytic, Inc. One sample was taken from an infant burial dated by its stratigraphic position to the end of the Early Helladic III phase at Mitrou. Its AMS date, calibrated with OxCal v4.2.3 Bronk Ramsey (2013) and r:5 IntCal13 atmospheric curve is cal B.C.E. 2039–1894 with 91.7% probability. This date supports the widely accepted 2050/2000 B.C.E. end date for the Early Helladic III phase.

The second sample was taken from a three–five-year-old juvenile burial dated stratigraphically to Late Helladic I phase 2. Its calibrated B.C.E. AMS date is 1747–1615 (95.4% probability), with most dates (55.7%) falling within the cal B.C.E. 1694–1630 range. These results invalidate the traditional 17th-century date for the Middle Helladic III phase and support the high chronology of the Theran eruption, but do not entirely rule out the lower chronology.

The third sample came from a disturbed infant burial dated originally to Late Helladic I phase 4. Its AMS date is cal. 1497–1389 cal BC (89.7% probability). Such date is younger than would be expected for Late Helladic I phase 4. Closer examination of the grave's stratigraphy suggests that a Late Helladic II date cannot be ruled out. If the grave dates to Late Helladic II, our AMS date would be in line with that obtained for a grave at Saqqara containing a Late Helladic IIA alabastron. Other factors affecting ^{14}C dates of Mitrou's human samples will be considered, such as the diet of the site's inhabitants and the fact that two of the samples were taken from infant bones.

Documenting Cultural Resources in the Caves of the Cumberland Gap National Historical Park

Charles E.A. Finney, Cave Research Foundation, *C. Stuart Daw*, Cave Research Foundation, and *Joe Settles*, Cave Research Foundation

Cumberland Gap in the southeast United States is a natural passage through the Cumberland Mountains and was used extensively by prehistoric animals and humans. First documented by European visitors in 1750 and later traversed by Daniel Boone as part of the Wilderness Road, it was originally called Cave Gap because of the prominent cave located just south of the saddle of the gap. This area was not heavily occupied by Native Americans, so little if any apparent visitation evidence remains, but the advent of European transients and settlers starting in the late 18th century saw increasingly diverse visitation to and utilization of the cave resources. From saltpeter mining during the War of 1812 to extensive visitation by Civil War soldiers to a century as a highly regarded tourist cave, the story of Gap Cave is one of interwoven demographics reflecting the sensibilities of the periods.

In 2003, in collaboration with the National Park Service, the CRF initiated an ongoing project of cartographic, geological, and biological documentation of the many caves in the Cumberland Gap National Historical Park (CUGA), and a dedicated Cultural Resources Survey began in 2006. While some physical artifacts of previous human visitation still are present in the cave, graffiti primarily of personal signatures forms the vast majority of evidence of visitation. Here, we report on our efforts to document cultural resources in CUGA caves using a variety of recording techniques. Of special value is ancillary research to link signatures with historical records of their creators to produce a more nuanced view of the caves' multifaceted role in the local history, culture, and economy.

We highlight the development of our recording and research techniques as well as significant examples of how cave artifacts exclusively fill in gaps about the history of the Cumberland Gap area. Further, we demonstrate the use of advanced photographic techniques such as Reflectance Transformation Imaging and photogrammetry to document features and even reproduce replicas of artifacts for public educational purposes. This work helps to document the rich history of the Cumberland Gap cave system and fulfill the National Park Service's mission of documenting the history of the park and preserving cultural heritage resources for future generations.

The Wall is in Your Court: A Hellenistic Etruscan Settlement at Vescovado di Murlo

Eoin M. O'Donoghue, National University of Ireland, Galway, and *Nora K. Donoghue*, Florida State University

The Etruscan settlement on the hill of Poggio Civitate has long provided fascinating insights into early Italy. The discovery, and continued excavation, of a series of monumental complexes dating to the seventh and sixth centuries B.C.E., along with their subsequent sudden and deliberate destruction, continues to inform and challenge our understanding of central Italy during this period. Nonetheless, our understanding of Poggio Civitate and its hinterlands has been largely confined to the excavation of the area of the main complex and its comparatively brief existence. In this poster we continue the process of situating the site in its broader physical and temporal landscape, through an examination of an area of industrial activity previously uncovered, but that has also been the focus of more recent excavations in 2015 and 2016 in Vescovado di Murlo, a small hamlet some 3 km north of Poggio Civitate.

Specifically we present the discovery in the recent excavations of a large retaining wall and pathway that appears to have been associated with an atrium building nearby, and dating to the late fourth/early third century B.C.E., based on the evidence of black-gloss and Greek imported ceramics. The pathway itself was formed through the construction of a large ditch that was deliberately filled over with roofing tile, an abundance of pottery, and other materials—including human remains—that appear to be associated with the destruction and abandonment of Vescovado di Murlo at this time. Furthermore, we detail the results of ongoing GPR survey in the hinterlands surrounding this site in order to show the possible extent of the ancient settlement in the area.

Zaldapa (Southern Dobruja, Bulgaria): Archaeological Perspectives on a Late Antique Fortress of the Lower Danube's Hinterland

Nicolas Beaudry, Université du Québec à Rimouski, *Dominic Moreau*, Université de Lille 3 – Sciences humaines et sociales, *Pascale Chevalier*, Université Blaise-Pascal, Clermont-Ferrand, *Brahim M'Barek*, Eveha, Strasbourg, and *Elio Hobdari*, Instituti i Arkeologjisë, Tirana

With its fortifications defending 25 ha of a densely built plateau, Zaldapa (Krushari, Bulgaria) is the largest known Romano-Byzantine stronghold of the hinterland of Scythia and Moesia Secunda. The site is mentioned as an episcopal see in the sixth century and is the birthplace of general Flavius Vitalianus († 520), who rebelled against Anastasius and contributed to the rise of the Justinianic dynasty. The city is thought to have been abandoned towards the end of the sixth century in the context of the Avar and Slavic migrations, and was never reoccupied.

The site offers a remarkable archaeological potential, but exploration has remained relatively limited to this day. Between 1889 and 1910, Karel and Herman Škorpil, the "fathers of Bulgarian archeology", planned the fortifications and a large intramuros structure (granary?), excavated a basilical church, and identified a second one. Romanian archaeologists conducted limited excavation between 1913 and 1915, and a large vaulted cistern was exposed in 1949 before a dam was built to create an artificial lake at the foot of the hill. In 2014, G. Atanasov and V. Yotov found a third, larger church at the crossing of the main thoroughfares, and they have since focused on excavating what is thought to be the city's cathedral.

Invited by the Bulgarian team, a French and Canadian team joined in from 2015 to contribute to the investigation of Late Antique Zaldapa. This poster presents its preliminary results after two short seasons in the field, and the perspectives they open. Results include an updated plan of the city and its defensive system based on satellite imagery and field investigation, as well as contributions to the record and study of the churches and cistern. Fieldwork also allowed an assessment of the archaeological interest of the site, as well as the design of a forthcoming project to investigate Zaldapa's urban fabric.

iGraffiti: Digital Recording of Ancient Graffiti from Herculaneum, Italy

Jacqueline F. DiBiasie Sammons, Sewanee: The University of the South, and *Holly M. Sypniewski*, Millsaps College

More than 320 ancient graffiti were once inscribed on the walls of Herculaneum. This poster explores the application of mobile tablets (iPad Pro) in the documentation and study of ancient graffiti during the 2016 field season of the Herculaneum Graffiti Project. The goals of the Herculaneum Graffiti Project are to record, photograph and digitize the graffiti from the site. The use of iPads for field documentation has advanced in several years, notably through the work of the Pompeii Archaeological Research Project: Porta Stabia (PARP:PS) and the Sangro Valley Project (SVP), but the unique nature of graffiti as an artifact necessitates a slightly different application of this technology. We show that iPads both streamline the process of recording ancient graffiti and provide better means to record these inscriptions than traditional methods alone.

iPads were used in three sectors of the project: data management, access to bibliography, and photography. Through the use of FileMaker Go software, team members were able to access information from prior field seasons about each graffito and record new data. In addition, these devices made it possible to obtain reference materials in the field.

Unexpectedly, iPads also proved useful in photographing graffiti, especially inscriptions in challenging or inaccessible locations. Finally, several apps have proved useful in digitally reproducing graffiti. We discuss the challenges encountered in implementing iPads at Herculaneum as well as plans for future development.

Exploring Genetic Diversity in Iron Age Cemeteries in Southern Italy

Matthew V. Emery, McMaster University, *Ana T. Duggan*, McMaster University, *Tracy Prowse*, McMaster University, and *Hendrik N. Poinar*, McMaster University

Population diversity in pre-Roman southern Italy has traditionally relied on archaeological and historic evidence to reconstruct its rich past. However important, these lines of information fail to capture the deep biological heritage and unique story these inhabitants carry within their biology. While the DNA we carry in our cells starts to degrade immediately following death, new methodological techniques developed over the last 10 years have greatly improved our ability to obtain authentic genetic information from highly degraded human remains. In this study we present whole-mitochondrial genomes from a pre-Roman Iron Age skeletal assemblage (seventh–fourth centuries B.C.E.) from Gravina in Puglia, southern Italy, sampled from teeth. Our analysis suggests that despite drastic fluctuations in burial and postexcavation storage environments, it was possible to capture, sequence, and assemble authentic mitochondrial genomes. Our preliminary data from 19 individuals indicate that maternal genetic diversity in Iron Age southern Italy comprises the major Eurasian haplogroups (U, T, V, J, and H). This evidence points to low maternal gene flow from disparate geographic regions, such as North Africa and the Near East, a trend presumed to have changed with the increase in biogeographic diversity ushered in subsequent centuries by the Romans. In addition, our results remain consistent with the current idea that Italy, along with Iberia, the Balkans, and Near East, acted as a postglacial refuge before the reexpansion of human populations into continental Europe after the last ice age. This research is the first to generate whole-mitochondrial DNA sequences from Iron Age Italian cemeteries, and demonstrates the ability to gain valuable genetic information from ancient human remains stored in less than optimal conditions.

Buried Cooking Pots: Late Hellenistic Ritual Practices at the Ancient Town of Nebo

Lauren Mason, Wilfrid Laurier University

The site Khirbat al-Mukhayyat, located approximately 9 km northwest of Madaba in central Jordan, has been identified as the ancient town of Nebo. The Town of Nebo Archaeological Project (TNAP) was established in order to investigate the site's sacred landscape and explore the importance of religious pilgrimage across multiple cultural and historical periods. The two excavation seasons conducted to date have revealed a number of Late Hellenistic (first-century B.C.E.) artifacts and features, including a large collection of intact cooking pots. These vessels have emerged exclusively from the southern end of the site.

All of the vessels were found sitting upright on a series of superimposed surfaces not associated with any other living activities. The cooking pots appear to have been intentionally concealed after having been placed on the exposed ground. The fill that surrounds the cooking pots contains significant amounts of Iron Age ceramics, suggesting that the inhabitants used the surrounding soil, which contained earlier cultural material, to bury the cooking pots. The stratigraphy indicates that this activity took place at regular intervals, possibly once a year, over a period of time. Analysis of the soil surrounding the cooking pots reveals that although some of the vessels show signs of use, no cooking-related activities were taking place in this location. There is no evidence of burning in or around the vessels.

To date, 38 complete Late Hellenistic cooking vessels, in addition to a multitude of fragments, have been uncovered. Analysis of the form and style of these vessels has enabled us to establish a date in the first century B.C.E. for this deposition activity. The closest parallels for these cooking pots are found at sites to the north and west, including Hesban, Jericho, and Jerusalem, indicating Mukhayyat's inclusion within the Hasmonean-controlled region.

Given the complete lack of any associated architecture or evidence for domestic activity coupled with the singular nature of the ceramic collection, these deposits of cooking pots must be the result of a local religious or cultural tradition. Although ritual feasting was a popular activity throughout antiquity, these cooking vessels are not associated with food preparation or consumption. Instead, they were placed in this obscure area of the site and subsequently buried so as to be hidden from view. The exact nature of this ritual activity remains unclear; however, it is a testament to the importance and continuity of Mukhayyat's sacred landscape.

Ceramics and the Socioeconomic Significance of La Biagiola Through Etruscan, Roman, and Lombard, and Modern Settlement

Letitia C. Mumford, St. Olaf College

The central question that drives my inquiry is: "Why do spaces persist in their economic significance when populations change?" I am drawing on past research from La Biagiola Field School in Sovana, Italy, in association with the Associazione "Cultura e Territorio" under the direction of Luca Nejrotti. La Biagiola is an Etruscan villa that changed hands over time as Romans, Lombards, and medieval Italians settled and transformed the space to suit their different cultural needs. I investigate the history of Roman settlement in the Sovana territory, where La Biagiola is located, the relationship between the Langobards and the Byzantines in the Early Middle Ages, and the Aldobrandeschi medieval rule. La Biagiola offers insight into economic culture because it changed hands so many times between multiple groups, each of which left behind significant architectural and ceramic remains. Through study of the site, I can understand the importance of this particular area in relation to its economic significance.

My primary interest in understanding the persistence of the particular area rests in pottery analysis. Using pottery classification and ceramic fabric techniques, I compare the types of ceramics to aggregate and identify Etruscan, Roman, and Medieval pottery to understand the intensity of use of the site. Through study of the amounts of coarse ware, fine ware, and semi-fineware, we can understand the socioeconomic significance of the site. Though many fragments of coarse ware were discovered, there were also many decorated fine ware sherds from each phase of the site, including painted decoration from the Etruscan period, sigillata from the Roman and Late Antique period, and glazed fine ware from the Lombard and following Medieval period. The amount of fine ware ceramic indicates the level of significance of the area, showing not only the high status of the users but also the centrality of the area to said users. At La Biagiola, the same area was in use from the Etruscan period through the modern era, so the site is considered a significant area and today is still used as a local winery.

SESSION 3A
Tombs and More in Etruria

CHAIR: *Gregory Warden*, Franklin University Switzerland

Liminal Bodies: Gender and Sex and the Etruscan Demon

Jacqueline K. Ortoleva, University of Birmingham

Male and female demons, as seen in fourth- through second-century B.C.E. Etruscan funerary iconography, are often depicted in a manner that emphasizes their physical sex characteristics while destabilizing the social construction of the gendered body. For example, the figure of Vanth is often portrayed with bare breasts or with genitalia exposed. She appears female, yet the revelation of her body in this manner undermines broader cultural expectations of feminine behavior. Conversely, the physical sex of seemingly male demons, including Charun, is not as overt. Though Charun is shown in many tomb paintings with bluish or gray-green flesh, other depictions represent him with light, pinkish skin—a convention adopted in both Greek and Etruscan art for the representation of women. Because of this, and the fact that he is sometimes shown with a clean-shaven face, some scholars have suggested that Charun is either female, part female, part male, or perhaps asexual.

A similar debate also surrounds the gender and sex of the figure of Tuchulca, as seen in the Tomb of Orcus II, in Tarquinia. Illustrated wearing a simple chiton associated with female attire, this depiction also possesses various theriomorphic attributes, such as the beak of a large bird, the ears of a wolf or donkey, and writhing snakes representing hair. Tuchulca also seems to be depicted with the suggestion of breasts, which has led many scholars to label it as a "female" figure. However, I argue that Tuchulca exhibits both male and female characteristics, and thus is intentionally more sexually ambiguous.

This paper does not venture to designate the perhaps impossible task of assigning a sex or gender to all demons in Etruria. Rather, I suggest that by paying attention to the articulation of each figure's sex and gender, or lack thereof, along with their explicit function in the funerary setting, a clearer picture of the religious role of the Etruscan demon may thus emerge. In this paper, I offer a chronologically ordered assessment of demon figures from two specific forms of media: sarcophagi and tomb paintings. I focus on attributes often linked to sex and gender, such as clothing, skin color, and the inclusion of sexual organs. This analysis enhances our understanding of the function that each type of figure (male, female, asexual) assumes in the funerary narrative. In sum, I suggest that the sexualized and gendered nuances seen in the depiction of demon figures in Etruria served to enhance each figure's function.

'Reading the Ritual': Representation and Meaning on an Etruscan Funerary Monument in Perugia

Laurel Taylor, University of North Carolina Asheville

An unusual circular funerary monument in the National Archaeological Museum in Perugia (inv. no. 634) depicts a remarkable, multifigured narrative combining generic and unique scenes of Etruscan funerary ritual. Despite its singular character, this Archaic-period monument has never been the focus of an in-depth study. Measuring 70 cm in diameter and 30 cm in height, the monument features a frieze with two distinct scenes, each composed around a central focal point. On one side appears a prothesis scene in which a corpse occupies the central space with figures aligned on each side of the funerary bed. On the opposite side, figures are arranged on both sides of an altar featuring a burning fire, a scene without comparison in Etruscan funerary iconography. Though many of the figures have parallels within Etruscan imagery in both gesture and in attribute, much about this monument—from its morphology to its pendant scenes—is exceptional. Prothesis scenes, which appear almost exclusively in the Chiusi area and only during the Archaic period, are typically combined with images of funerary banqueting, dancing, and/or lamentation scenes. The pairing here with the altar/fire image raises interesting interpretive questions about the constitutive effect of these two events and how these may have been read and comprehended by the ancient viewer. Formally, the scenes seem constructed to invite connection and comparison, perhaps even to convey a symbolic and/or temporal relationship between these two events. The prothesis may have preceded and necessitated some sort of ritual purification by fire. Alternatively, the fire may reference a type of sacrifice part of funerary ritual. Neither, however, was part of the iconographic tradition. In attempting to "read" these scenes, this paper uses a proxemics-based approach (a model used frequently in New World archaeology), to understand how the formal and physical characteristics of the monument reflect aspects of ancient visuality—that is, the interplay between viewer, perception, and space. The figuration, composition, and morphology of this monument suggest that these scenes were intended less as narratives to be read and more as evocations of a ritual landscape whose broad contours could be perceived and understood with even a cursory engagement. These scenes are the visual evocation of ritual performance and, as such, are largely totemic in their articulation, encapsulating in perpetuity ritual acts and environments. Though unusual in many aspects, the Perugia monument has broad implications for understanding ancient viewership.

Exploration of Two Tombs in the Necropolis of Crocifisso del Tufa (Orvieto, Italy)
Claudio Bizzarri, PAAO, and *David B. George*, Saint Anselm College

The year 2015 marked the commencement of new excavations at Crocifisso del Tufo after almost two decades. The last two seasons have resulted in a number of interesting results. In 2015 a *tomba a casseta* (Tomb 200) was explored. The tomb was high on the landscape, and the assumption was that it would have been previously "tampered" with. At the outset of the excavations it became clear that the tomb had been untouched. Bronze and black bucchero objects were found in it along with disarticulated human remains set in a corner of the tomb. The tomb appears to be a late sixth-century B.C.E. redeposition of a somewhat earlier sixth-century burial. The bronzes have been cleaned and restored. These and the black bucchero are presented. This season, a chamber tomb (Tomb 203) was explored. It had clearly been "tampered" with, but because of interesting aspects of the geomorphology of the site some of the grave goods had not been seen. These include an interesting mid sixth B.C.E. Attic vase as well as jewelry. The female remains from the round seventh-century B.C.E. tomb that was previously excavated were subject to osteological analysis. The intriguing findings are presented.

Vulci 3000: Fieldwork Season 2016
Maurizio Forte, Duke University

The study of Etruscan cities and urbanism is very much related to the concept of city-state and its organization, a very complex and independent socioeconomic unit, self-organized but very open to trading and connections in and outside the influence of Etruscan territory. The study of Vulci (Viterbo, Italy) can open new research perspectives on the dawning development, and transformation of Etruscan cities and their surrounding landscape. "Transformation" is the key word for a correct contextualization of the site and a new understanding of urban identity: this analysis is focused on dynamic processes rather than the study of static phenomenon in chronological cages. In other words, this project analyzes and tracks the transformation and development of Vulci into a city and city-state and finally into a Roman city.

More specifically, this paper reports the preliminary results of the first campaign of archaeological excavations in the Western Forum of the site, and it is the first stratigraphic excavation in the urban area in this millennium. The site was firstly mapped by georadar prospections and drone's multispectral photography (RGB, infrared, red edge), then excavated and documented by digital technologies (the documentation is totally paperless). The first results of the excavations show a series of iso-oriented (north–south) walls in tuff blocks, *opus reticulatum*, and *opus incertum*, dating back to the second-first centuries B.C.E and very large retrieval pits (ca. 350 C.E.). The monumental foundations and its decorations (marble from northern Africa and Asia Minor) suggest a public destination of the building with the main entrance identifiable in front of the decumanus.

Recent Research on the Late Etruscan and Early Roman Phases of Corglia, CV (Umbria, Italy)

David B. George, Saint Anselm College, and *Claudio Bizzarri*, PAAO

This paper presents the results of the 2015 and 2016 site excavations, which revealed many new and suggestive data about the nature of site as well as the relationship between the end of the Etruscan phase and development of the Early Roman phases. The excavations have been ongoing for the last 12 years. The site has a long life, beginning in eighth century B.C.E. and persisting until the end of at least the 15th century C.E., when there is evidence for its destruction by earthquake and mudslide. We can date the planting of an olive grove over the northern part of the site from shards found in the drainage pits under the root balls to the 15th century. From its origins the site has been tied to water, both hot springs and sweet springs, as well as a large bath complex from the first century C.E. that was still in use at least in the fourth century C.E. The last two seasons have recovered a quantity of interesting architectural terracotta fragments with Dionysiac and related scenes in relatively good condition deposited in trenches that were part of a third–fourth century C.E. renovation of the site. Most of the redeposited material is datable stylistically to the first century B.C.E./first century C.E. A number of the loci that were excavated this season recovered evidence as well of republican/Early Imperial construction in areas of the site that had had Etruscan structures. This season the excavation of a first-century C.E. staircase and vault (likely Tiberian) yielded Etruscan and Early Imperial material with implications for the Roman transformation of the use of the site.

This paper reviews the evidence for the late Etruscan phase of the site and discusses the evidence for Roman adaptation of parts of the Etruscan structures and transformation of others with suggestions of reasons for both largely drawn from evolving social functions of the spaces.

Radical Modifications of the Stage Design Archetype in the First-Century B.C.E. Roman Theater in Volterra

Wladyslaw Fuchs, University of Detroit Mercy School of Architecture, and *Andrew Findley*, Ivy Tech Community College

The first-century B.C.E. Roman theater in Volterra, Italy, is recognized in literature for its exceptionally large regia niche. This study proposes that the size of the regia niche was a manifestation of an innovative functional and aesthetic vision of the greater scenae frons design. A new approach to the archaeological material, paired with a digital three-dimensional analysis of the theater building form, render three principal features of the scenae frons identifiable. First, the columnatio of the stage was divided into three sections that simulated individual building facades. Second, the spaces between the buildings created by the oversized regia niche were designed to look and function like streets between the buildings. Finally, an additional set of doors on each side of the regia allowed actors to enter and exit the stage through this mock urban space. Each of the above features is unique relative to the archetype of the Roman theater; together these features composed a well-harmonized new concept of the stage form and its related function.

In this study, the rationale for the distinct design of the Volterra theater is traced to the various aspects of the Roman culture of the period. Using the scenae frons to emulate urban space was perfectly suited for the setting and social interactions often on display in Roman comedies. The Volterra design also makes extensive use of the perspective correction found in the architectural frescoes of the period, adding to the illusory quality of the performance. In Volterra, the cultural context was clearly used to reinterpret the classical paradigm of the continuous scenae frons facade and create a spacious, complex design of the theater stage.

To understand more fully the nature of this design innovation, and perhaps the motivations behind its creation, this study looks at the social context of the Volterra theater and compares it with other Roman structures of the same kind and period. In light of these internal and external factors, the design of the scenae frons is both an architectural and a functional achievement, which provides more insight into the creativity that abounded among first-century B.C.E. architects, builders, and patrons.

The Cult of Mithra in Etruria: The Case of Veii (Rome)

Ugo Fusco, Sapienza, University of Rome

This paper examines a newly discovered marble relief composed of two pieces found on the plateau of the city of Veii. The relief provides new and significant evidence of the Cult of Mithras in Veii in Etruria. The paper is organised in three parts in order to provide the most comprehensive historical archaeological context in which to consider the new find. The first part is a brief introduction to the cult of Mithras with particular focus on its presence and spread in Etruria based on previous studies and the most recent archaeological discoveries. The second part concentrates on the discovery itself and deals with the problems linked to the area in which it was found, with the analysis and interpretation of the subjects depicted, and with the chronology. Although it features the typical bull-slaying scene (tauroctony), the high stylistic quality of the piece and the presence of an iconographic feature uncommon among other existing Mithraic reliefs, are what distinguish it from other similar finds. Finally, the third part provides the historical background of the site of Veii during the Roman age, including an overview of the main cults that existed during the Imperial age.

The dating of the find, late Hadrianic/early Antonine period, can only be estimated by basing it on the stylistic qualities of the piece, as the original archaeological context is unknown and any other evidence such as inscriptions which would allow for a more precise chronology is absent. The total number of Mithraic reliefs documented in Etruria (Regio VII), including this discovery in Veii, is seven. The relief from Veii emerges as unique in terms of its size (lgth. 2 m; ht. 1.54 m; wdth. 0.16–0.33 m) and stylistic qualities compared with the others. Furthermore, the proposed chronology makes it the most ancient of the Mithraic reliefs in Etruria, and it could also be considered as one of the earliest testimonies of the cult of Mithras in Regio VII. The high artistic quality and size of the relief suggest that the person who commissioned it was of notable wealth and was part of the elite of the town of Veii. The question of the shrine the relief comes from remains unanswered, and no shrine has been located to date. The most probable hypothesis is that the location of the shrine is in the area closest to where the relief was found.

SESSION 3B: Colloquium
Shaping Cities: New Ways of Examining North African Urbanism

ORGANIZER: *Elizabeth Fentress*, Independent Scholar

Colloquium Overview Statement

If Roman North Africa was a quintessentially urban landscape, little of what we study there would be acceptable under any modern analysis of urbanism. Examining cities today, one looks at the reflexive interaction of people and space; the tentacular reach of the city into the countryside and the wider patterns of circulation; interaction, and investment. Archaeologists are left, at best, with the plan of the city, but far more often with a few major monuments, a rough estimate of size, the arrangement of the urban furniture, and its date. Timgad remained for many years the only fully developed model of a Roman North African town, and it remains the city everyone lectures on. All of this is now changing, thanks to new ways of investigating city structure, particularly through geophysics. Geophysical survey on a grand scale has now been applied to such diverse cities as Meninx, Utica, and Chemtou, giving us new plans whose details rival those of Timgad. From these, we can finally comment on urban histories through more than monumental buildings and their inscriptions. Divergent grids give an idea of the chronology of their development, while the relationship between monuments and urban structure becomes more transparent. Geophysics have also shown that various cities are far larger than was previously believed.

This colloquium investigates the North African city in the light of the new knowledge that these investigations have produced. The presenters will discuss the shape of the city: was it planned (clearly the case of Utica and Timgad) or the result of a relatively random urban development? What was the relationship between the monumental centers and the areas occupied by housing? Is it possible to read any zoning, or clustering, within the confines of the cities—do industrial or artisanal areas stand out? And what was their relationship to the monumental and domestic spaces? To the three papers based on geophysical survey are added three more traditional investigations—of the monumental center of Utica, of the Numidian evidence from Bulla Regia, and of the evidence for the tiny cities in the pertica of Carthage—and one completely new question, that of traffic patterns within cities, based on the evidence for the trajectories of wheeled vehicles within Timgad, providing an answer to the question "did the Romans drive on the right, and how does it matter in terms of the interaction between individuals and the city?"

DISCUSSANT: *Steven Ellis*, University of Cincinnati

The Making of a Provincial Capital: Utica 100 B.C.E.–200 C.E.

Elizabeth Fentress, Independent Scholar, *Imed Ben Jerbania*, Institut National du Patrimoine, Tunisia, *Faouzi Ghozzi*, Institut National du Patrimoine, Tunisia, *Ben Russell*, Edinburgh University, and *Andrew Wilson*, Oxford University

A Phoenician foundation of the mid ninth century, and very much the second city of Punic Africa, at the end of the third Punic War Utica was the obvious choice for the provincial capital and seat of the governor. The INP-Oxford Utica Project has carried out a citywide investigation, with several specific areas of concentration. One of these was the monumental center at the northeastern end of the peninsula. Sadly, its monuments were systematically robbed for lime kilns during the French occupation of the site. However, the giant robber trenches they left behind reveal not only the plans of the buildings—the basilica, a large quadriporticus with a temple in the center, and a wide street with a two-level portico that presented a monumental facade for the whole complex—but also the previous history of the site of the complex, with Punic buildings, industrial areas, and, most strikingly, a defensive ensemble comprising a rampart and massive defensive ditch. The relationship between the two cities provides a compelling interplay, with the defensive ditch morphing into the two-story portico, resulting in a monumental center that recalls such imperial complexes as Tarragona and Augusta Emerita. The fate of the city in the later empire is reflected in the history of this complex, whose early abandonment reflects the disappearance of the city's port. Utica is thus unusual in many ways, in terms of African cities, and much of this can be read in the history of this giant set piece.

The Urban Development of Utica, Tunisia: Taking Stock of the Latest Geophysical Survey Results

Sophie Hay, Southampton University, *Andrew Dufton*, Brown University, *Eleanor Maw*, British School at Rome, and *Stephen Kay*, British School at Rome

The overall plan of the ancient city of Utica, Tunisia, has been a constant focus of study since the first western investigations of the site. While the earliest 19th-century accounts often bear little resemblance to reality, excavations in the early and mid 20th century provided more detailed recording of the monumental core and a few adjacent city blocks. It is these works that form the basis for our current understanding of the development of the site from a Punic city to the first provincial capital of Roman Africa. Yet in the absence of systematic survey, the full extent of the city and its structure away from the earliest Punic settlement remain largely speculative.

This paper discusses the results of an extensive program of geophysical and topographic survey undertaken as part of the INP–Oxford Utica Project with the support of the Portus Limen, Rome's Mediterranean Ports project. Covering both excavated and unexcavated areas of the site, these works confirm some basic understandings of the city's layout established by the fundamental research of Alexandre Lézine in the 1950s: the alignment of the urban plan, the size of individual blocks, and the proposed locations of key monuments. However, this latest survey work demonstrates the city is notably larger than Lézine's estimate, and we now have a far clearer picture of the variation in grids, suggesting an original (republican?) layout and a later extension to the north. The high-resolution details provided in these results offer further new insights into the full extent of the city and the nature of its settlement, including regular subdivisions of blocks and the layouts of individual houses and production centers.

Around the Marble Mountain: New Research on the Urbanism of Simitthus

Philipp von Rummel, German Archaeological Institute, and *Moheddine Chaouali*, Institut National du Patrimoine

Simitthus (Chimtou), in northern Tunisia, is a very particular, if not a unique case of a Roman site. Built around a hill of yellow marble, it combines the imperial quarries of the marmor Numidicum (giallo antico), the camp for the administration of the quarries, and a large town surrounding the marble hill on three sides. A geophysical survey of the site between 2011 and 2015 (undertaken by a team of the Tunisian Institut National du Patrimoine, the German Archaeological Institute, and the University of Cologne) gives many new insights into the ancient site and allows us to draw a new plan of Simitthus that covers about 80 hectares. Ancient Simitthus was thus a quite large town compared with other, more famous, cities such as Thugga, with 25 hectares or Thuburbo Maius, with 30 hectares. The survey shows at least five different rectangular patterns of street orientation, and many hitherto unknown details of the urban fabric, including domestic and artisan spaces. It helps to understand the urbanistic evolution of the town, where excavations have shown occupation from the Iron Age well into the Medieval period. New information has also emerged on a monumental temple complex, later transformed into a massive basilica.

Think Global, Act Local? Microregional Urbanism in the Hinterland of Roman Carthage

Paul Scheding, University of Munich

Publications on architecture in Roman North Africa have tended to focus on one type of building, such as temples or theaters. These studies have expanded our knowledge about the development of architecture in this part of the Roman empire. But it is difficult to distinguish what constitutes a general "North African" development and what is in fact part of a specific regional process, when looking at one building type in a city.

In this paper, I suggest another approach that examines specific urban and architectural characteristics in their microregional context. Several authors have argued that Africa experienced significant economic growth, especially during the second century C.E. From the mid second century onward, African communities, presumably represented by extremely wealthy elites, erected all kinds of monumental buildings in their cities. We know that the local elite was highly involved in agricultural production in the territory of their cities. But we also know that there was a considerable degree of variation in the conditions of land use, organization of production, and administration in different regions of North Africa. The question is: what is the impact of the "local ecosystems" on public benefaction and elite ostentation that visibly altered townscapes? Furthermore, did the architecture and urbanism reflect the needs of the elites in these local conditions? What were the important factors influencing the imagination of architecture and urbanism in a particular region?

The focus of this paper is on the large numbers of small cities in the territory of Roman Carthage and their relationship to different estates. Using the example of the pertica of Carthage and the "boom" of the late second century C.E. I will discuss how agricultural organization and socioeconomic development influenced the cityscapes in this microregion.

Circling the Square: Traffic and Urbanism in Roman North Africa

Eric Poehler, University of Massachusetts

In 1986 William MacDonald observed in his landmark book, *The Architecture of the Roman Empire: An Urban Appraisal*, that in 100 C.E. the strict, rectilinear grid of Timgad "was almost an anachronism." In the context of Roman urbanism of the second century in North Africa, the city's urban form was at very least an anomaly. This landscape, however, was unusually well designed and well equipped for the free movement of people, animals, and wheeled traffic. It was also particularly well suited to both receive and preserve the evidence of each of those forms of movement. In fact, Timgad has fivefold more evidence of traffic than any other site in the Roman world outside of Pompeii, Italy. The present paper takes this remarkable concentration of evidence at Timgad as the starting point for a fuller exploration of movement in a North African Roman city, including the patterns of wear from cart wheels found inscribed on the architecture of the street, the expansion and elaboration of pedestrian spaces, and the penetration of domestic space by movement infrastructures, such as ramps and stables. For wheeled traffic more specifically, the evidence from Timgad is used to test the wider Roman preference for driving on the right side of the road, the restriction of streets to a single direction, and the ability of such directional restrictions to be controlled, inverted, or subverted. In the end, it is argued that the "anachronism" of Timgad's network of streets offers a way to understand its exceptional concentration of evidence of urban movement.

Bulla Regia: A Showcase Site for Urban Studies in Pre-Roman North Africa

Stefan Ardeleanu, SFB 933 Materiale Textkulturen, University of Heidelberg, and *Moheddine Chaouali*, INP Tunis

Bulla Regia is one of Tunisia's best-studied Roman towns. Although the site has been continuously providing pre-Roman finds, a synthesis of the city's earliest phases is still lacking. This paper therefore gives an overview of the town's pre-Roman urbanism. The core goals are (1) to systematize and reassess the published evidence and (2) to present new field survey work conducted during the last few years. The overall picture allows us to draw a new town plan of one of Numidia's capitals that had at least three orthogonal grids, paved streets, a developed system of water channels, an enormous rampart, monumental sanctuaries, a possible square, several living quarters, and at least four necropoleis with varying tomb types. According to the latest surface finds and to the distribution of dated remains, we can assume that Bulla Regia was one of North Africa's largest towns during the last two centuries B.C.E. with a size of about 30 ha. The city undoubtedly played a predominant role in the densely settled Medjerda Valley. That it was perfectly integrated in the political and economical circuits of the Late Hellenistic world, is confirmed by domestic layouts, masonry techniques, architectural decoration and ceramic imports. In contrast to what has been assumed to be an underdeveloped settlement structure in North Africa's pre-Roman interior regions, Bulla Regia is one of the best examples proving a complex urbanism in that period.

Geophysics and Urbanism at Meninx

Stefan Ritter, University of Munich, and *Sami Ben Tahar*, Institut National du Patrimoine

This paper presents the first results of a Tunisian-German project in Meninx, the largest ancient city on the island of Jerba and one of the main production centers of murex dye in the Mediterranean. In contrast to other important Roman seaports such as Leptiminus, Sabratha, or Leptis Magna, the urban structure of the spacious port town is characterized by the fact that it did not extend towards its immediate hinterland, being covered by infertile mudflats, but expanded instead along the coast of the Gulf of Bou Grara for more than a kilometer.

The impetus for our ongoing investigation was the results of a geophysical prospection conducted in 2015, during which we surveyed a broad coastal strip, up to 600 m long and 200 m wide and making up the core of the Roman city, by means of magnetometry. As these investigations have revealed, the city was not organized within an orthogonal grid. The irregular layout of the Roman town indicates that it is the result of a long-term urban development. The central area of the city is crossed by two slightly converging main roads that, running roughly parallel to the coast towards the forum, divide the city into several urban zones of different character. Whereas the area between the two main roads, between 65 and 90 m wide, has a very irregular design and seems to be dominated by habitations, the coastal zone, extending from the huge Horrea and the Macellum in the south to the enormous theater in the north, is occupied by monumental building complexes, among them several storage buildings, all of which were probably constructed in the second and third centuries C.E., so at about the same time when the trapezoidal forum was redesigned by the erection of new temples and other edifices. The row of public, mainly commercial buildings along the coastline must have given Meninx a most impressive appearance from the sea side and demonstrates the unusual extent to which the port city, whose economy was based on purple dye and fish industries, was oriented towards the Mediterranean trade.

SESSION 3C
Ostia: Houses, Infrastructure, and Cult

CHAIR: To be announced

Ideology or Archaeology? Ostia, Italo Gismondi, and the Plastico di Roma

Anne Hrychuk Kontokosta, New York University

It is difficult to deny the influence of the so-called Plastico di Roma—the largest and most historically accurate model of ancient Rome—as today its image can be found in almost every basic Roman art, architecture, or archaeology textbook. The Plastico was initially created in 1937 by Italo Gismondi for display at the Mostra Augustea della Romanità show and was permanently installed at the Museo della Civilità in Rome in 1955. Constructed of plaster, the 2,000-square-foot model documented fourth-century C.E. Rome in minute detail, incorporating famous monuments (the Colosseum, Pantheon, Fora, and Imperial Thermae) with more generic-looking buildings that reproduced a largely lost urban fabric. While the scale and some details of the Plastico were based on fragments of the Forma Urbis Romae and additional elements reflected the findings of contemporary large-scale excavations instigated for Mussolini's 1932 Piano Regolatore, it was up to Gismondi to fabricate the remainder of the city, particularly the suburbs of ancient Rome. The tracts of seemingly nondescript housing that he created for the periphery of the Plastico have been influentially interpreted as signaling a movement towards Roman modernism and a reflection of a new functionalist mentality promoted by Fascist urban propaganda. This paper argues, however, that such a view ignores the actual archaeological evidence for domestic architecture in the ancient Roman world. It suggests that critical to the creation of the Plastico was not Mussolini's urban dogma, but Gismondi's more than forty years of experience as an archaeologist and architect at Ostia Antica, where the best-preserved examples of concrete, multistory housing (insulae) still stand today. Upon close scrutiny, a number of compelling connections are apparent between the archaeological remains of Ostia and the Plastico. Chief among these are the model's apartment blocks, which Gismondi divided into three basic plans mirroring the threefold typological division of Ostia's insulae. The significance of the Plastico and Gismondi's contributions to Roman archaeology and architecture have only very recently begun to be recognized and so the time is right to also reconsider the archaeological (as opposed to the ideological) foundations of his famous model. This paper reassesses Gismondi's extensive fieldwork, particularly in the context of Ostia, in an attempt to identify anew the archaeological fundamentals of the Plastico di Roma and reframe its ultimate—and immensely influential—manipulation of the urban landscape of ancient Rome.

The Facade of Frontages at Ostia

Claire J. Weiss, University of Virginia

Ostia presents one of the largest areas of exposed ruins in Italy, making available an extensive, contiguous expanse of Roman urban construction. The city is often lumped together with Pompeii and Herculaneum as one of the handful of well-preserved Roman cities to which scholarship has returned time and again as a source of incomparably complete data. This is a misperception. The example set by the Vesuvian cities, their appearance very similar to that at the moment of their destruction in 79 C.E., has distorted the conceptualization of, approach to, and resulting discussion surrounding Ostia. The 20th-century excavators of Ostia looked toward Pompeii especially, since they were interested in creating a site that evoked the same sense of completeness but in closer proximity to Rome. The resulting reconstruction was often more a fabrication of the urban structures expected to appear in such a city than a presentation of the true nature of Ostia's features. Unsurprisingly, the public is unaware of the magnitude of reconstruction, but so are many scholars of Roman urbanism not well versed in Ostia's excavation history, who fall victim to the same assumption of unproblematic completeness upon which the reconstructions capitalized. The interventions extend to the very streets and sidewalks of the city, often uncritically assumed to have suffered little disturbance.

During the excavation campaigns of the early 20th century lead by Vaglieri and those promoted by Mussolini leading into World War II, most of the streets in the city were dug through in an effort to find the underlying, earlier structures. The streets were repaved at an arbitrary level, in order to present a semblance of their original aspect. Additionally, modern excavators left unpaved strips of ground between the building frontages and the (re)pavement of most streets, likely for the convenience of laying modern utility lines. Because of their placement, these spaces appear to be ancient sidewalks to the untrained eye and create a false sense of sidewalk pervasiveness across the site. This paper presents the results of a city-wide frontage and street survey conducted at Ostia in 2014 and 2016, proposing an identification of the portions of the streets that have been disturbed and relaid, as well as the portions of the streets and sidewalks that are preserved in their original aspect. Without accounting for the degree of reconstruction, conclusions about urban activity at Ostia will remain as fanciful as the structures on which they are based.

Water Water Everywhere: Sustainability and Ostia

Mark A. Locicero, Leiden University

This paper applies sustainable resource models to the evidence of Roman urbanism to illustrate what forces shaped Roman water use. Both in archaeological research and in the modern globalizing world there has been a dramatic shift in the past several decades in understanding the connection between landscape and human actions. By adapting methodologies used to investigate water usage in modern cities, a more nuanced view is provided of Roman water usage. This integrative approach combines archaeological, paleoenvironmental, and cultural data to create a contextualized snapshot of urban water usage, and builds upon previous studies focussing on individual aqueducts or bath buildings.

The city of Ostia acted as an early harbour for Rome on the Mediterranean, and has received archaeological attention since the mid 19th century. In terms of its potential hydraulic resources, the city benefitted from easy access to its ground water, the Tiber River, and rainwater, and it was connected to multiple aqueduct lines over its lifetime. A little researched sewer system is thought to run under a significant number of Ostia's streets. The abundance of archaeological and literary evidence makes Ostia the ideal case study for this project.

This paper discusses the archaeological evidence from three city blocks (insulae), which have been systematically documented to clarify how and why the urban water system changed over time. Each of the blocks (Regio III.i, IV.ii, and V.ii) contain more than a dozen diverse structures, and they offer a chronology stretching from the Republican to the Late Antique period. By dividing the archaeological evidence into periods based on major changes to the hydraulic infrastructure, four distinct snapshots of the acquisition, distribution, and drainage of water are visible.

The preliminary results of this study present a micro and macro picture of the distribution of water on a city-block level: usage at this scale is dictated not only by the available technological infrastructure, but on the dynamic interaction between technology and cultural patterns of water usage. When the hydraulic histories, or water "footprints," of the city blocks are compared, it is clear that multiple sources of water are organized in different combinations over time.

It is hoped that this dialogue between ancient and modern urbanism can provide valuable insights into the forces that shaped and continue to influence how cities utilize their limited water resources.

Beyond the Temple: Urban Integration of Ostia's Serapeum

Katherine A. Crawford, University of Southampton

The Roman city was a landscape of religious activity, consisting of a complex map of sacred spaces that intersected with all aspects of society. Statues, reliefs, inscriptions, temples, and ritual activities are just a few examples of the ways in which religion punctuated the urban fabric. Various religious activities, including festivals, sacrifices, and processions, were grounded and articulated within specific religious spaces, the most discernible of which contained monumental temples. Beyond serving as a center for religious practices, temples served a larger physical context in which associated cults could be understood. Ritual actions of processional movement were one way in which religion was spread across urban space, constructing a multifaceted web of interactivity. This paper considers Ostia's Serapeum as a case study, presenting new insight into the construction of a religious landscape through the examination of possible processional routes. Development of a computer-based methodology is employed to examine the ways in which processions at Ostia can be modeled to create a human-based approach to the study of ritual movement in the past urban landscape. Moving focus beyond the Temple of Serapis, critical analysis of how the Egyptian cult was integrated into the wider cityscape through the practice of processions provides new insight into understanding the ways urban space was structured and offers new perspectives on ritual experiences within Ostia.

A New Date for the Foundations of the Ostia Synagogue

Mary Jane Cuyler, University of Sydney, and *Jaimie Gunderson*, University of Texas at Austin

Ostia's ancient synagogue was discovered in 1961. Excavations were carried out from 1961 to 1964, and again in 1977. Although final reports were never published, director Maria Floriani Squarciapino revealed some of her principal conclusions in a number of short articles. She assigned the current state of the building to the third or fourth century C.E. but maintained that the *opus reticulatum* walls of the structure dated to the first century C.E. These conclusions were based mainly on masonry typology.

The Ostia-Synagogue Masonry Analysis Project (OSMAP) is funded by the Institute for the Study of Antiquity and Christian Origins at the University of Texas at Austin and works under the auspices of the Ministero dei Beni e delle Attività Culturali del Turismo of Rome. OSMAP has carried out masonry analysis of the synagogue (2001–2004), new excavations at the synagogue complex (2005, 2007, 2009, 2011, 2012, and 2015), and archival research of the documents pertaining to Squarciapino's excavations as well as extensive analysis of the previously excavated archaeological material. The project's goal is to understand the chronology of the synagogue through the study of artifacts collected during stratigraphic excavation and through the study of the archival materials.

This presentation examines the earliest phases of the structure. Excavations along the walls of the synagogue building have revealed that the foundations of the earliest reticulate walls were poured into trenches that were dug into the sandy soil. This subsoil apparently represents a major ground-raising fill deposited sometime before the construction of the earliest walls. Analysis of finds from 19 trenches exploring this subsoil has shown that the latest material from the ground-raising fill dates to the mid second century C.E. This provides a terminus post quem for the first foundations of the structure; contrary to Squarciapino's conclusions, the reticulate walls could not have been built in the first century but must belong to the mid second century at the earliest. This provides stratigraphic confirmation for the use of reticulate masonry in later periods.

What can now be said with certainty is that there is no archaeological evidence for a first-century monumental synagogue at Ostia. Whether the building functioned as a synagogue in its earliest phases remains an open question. The new date for the foundations allows for a reexamination of Jewish religious practice in Ostia and Rome, and facilitates a more nuanced discussion of construction practices in this area of the ancient city.

SESSION 3D: Colloquium
Objects in Focus: Recent Research into the Royal Ontario Museum's Collections

ORGANIZER: *Sascha Priewe*, Royal Ontario Museum

Colloquium Overview Statement

When it was formally established in 1912, the Royal Ontario Museum (ROM) sought to develop a collection of international scope within the city of Toronto that explored the intersections between art, culture, and nature. The diverse ancient cultures represented in the collections of the ROM today continue to afford many opportunities for study and exploration. While the collection as a whole represents a wide range of cultural heritage, showcasing the breadth of human experience and artistic endeavors, each subcollection also displays substantial depth with representative works of art and material culture.

This session highlights the current research of scholars who employ the collections of the ROM. Beginning with two papers examining the ROM's Nubian and Islamic ceramic collections, these papers highlight the potential for insights gained from collections built up through archaeological fieldwork as well as from the scientific analysis of existing collections. Moving from large groups of objects to individual pieces, two papers focus on sculpture in the museum's ancient Mediterranean collection. Both probe questions of authenticity, representation, and provenance. The final paper examines the educational tools of models and murals of the Parthenon created for the ROM's Gallery of Greece. Together these papers demonstrate the bandwidth of potential inquiries into museum practices, happening both in the collections not currently on display and in the galleries and exhibitions.

Potters of the Nile: Meroitic Ceramic Culture, Typological Analysis, and the Nubian Ceramic Collection at the Royal Ontario Museum

Annissa Malvoisin, University of Toronto

The Kingdom of Meroe of ancient Nubia produced a specialized ceramic culture out of which appeared extraordinary artistry. This paper presents a brief study of A-Group and C-Group culture pottery as an introduction to Meroitic pottery specialization and production with an incisive focus on domestic ware, fine ware, and the Academic School style as specified by Steffen Wenig. Further, this paper emphasizes that although its focus is on the emergence of a specific type of pottery during a particular time period, the production techniques have survived contemporarily, and in many instances continued to be practiced among the present potters along the Nile. Relevant comparisons to Egyptian ceramic production during the same time period are also addressed.

This report is an overview of Meroitic ceramic culture and production. I have used artifacts from of the Nubian ceramic collection at the Royal Ontario Museum as a guide, although I mention further cultural institutions that hold remarkable relevant collections as well. Meroitic ceramics succeeded its A-Group and C-Group predecessors through technology, technique, and decoration; becoming an example of ancient and contemporary artisanal accomplishment. This report began as a difficult journey towards determining what it meant to be Nubian with a territory located between two countries, displacement due to irrigation advances, and sovereignty in the face of cultural and religious assimilation. Today, Nubians are among both Egypt and North Sudan's indigenous communities that continue to celebrate the successes of their ancient kingdoms, of which one method is through clay.

Pottery from the Mediaeval Middle East: Collections Research at the Royal Ontario Museum

Robert Mason, Royal Ontario Museum

A comprehensive multidisciplinary study on the technically and artistically most elite ceramics of the central Islamic lands has been ongoing at the Royal Ontario Museum (ROM) since the late 1980s. The collections include objects from current-day Egypt, Syria, Iran, and Iraq. The approach of this study has been to combine the standard typological methodologies of archaeologists, that of drawing of profiles, seriation of attributes, and so on, with archaeometric techniques. Petrographic microscopy is used to examine ceramic bodies primarily for attribution to production centers. Scanning electron microscopy with attached micro-XRF analysis is deployed to examine the nature of ceramic technologies. Both techniques provide complimentary data sets that improve the resolution of findings and further our interpretations.

The results of these investigations show that the pottery of the Islamic world represents high technology, exhibiting a synthesis of earlier knowledge coupled with an innovative development of those techniques. They represent a significant industry, with massive productions that spread across the full extent of the Old World. But they are also illustrative of stability and prosperity, as it is an enterprise encouraged by strong governments that invest in infrastructure and industry.

These investigations have relied heavily on the collections of the ROM and other museums across the world. The project has highlighted the importance of collections-based research, incorporating objects that have been in museums since before they were scrupulous about provenance. The study has also involved destructive sampling, in a time when the destruction of collections in the Middle East is troubling.

Secrets of the Goddess: The ROM's "Minoan" Ivory Figurine and Collecting Antiquity

Catherine Cooper, Royal Ontario Museum

Suspected forgeries of ancient material are a common problem, particularly for museums where many antiquities lack known archaeological contexts. Although rarely discussed, the investigation into these problematic objects—why they were originally created and acquired, and how they have affected the modern perception of the past—is an important area of study. In this paper I focus on an object from the Royal Ontario Museum (ROM) to consider issues of museum collecting habits, archaeological provenience and the creation of forgeries.

In 1931 the ROM bought a small ivory figurine thought to have come from Minoan Crete. The figurine had no attested archaeological findspot and was authenticated by Sir Arthur Evans, who named it "Our Lady of Sports," believing it represented the goddess of those bull leapers depicted in the frescoes of Knossos. The "goddess" became an icon of the ROM's collection for more than 70 years and was featured in many publications on the Aegean Bronze Age. However, the figurine is now generally believed to be a fake, created by Cretan craftsmen in the early 20th century to meet the demand for Bronze Age objects, and modeled on Evans' preconceived notions of Minoan society. The authenticity of the ROM "goddess," and that of several ivory Minoan figurines in other museums, had been suspected for decades, but it was publications by Kenneth Lapatin, culminating in *The Mysteries of the Snake Goddess* (Boston 2002), that finally made those suspicions public. Several museums were prompted to address the presentation of these "Minoan" artifacts, and by 2005 the ROM "goddess" was relegated to the museum storeroom.

Lapatin's work demonstrated that there are many reasons to doubt the authenticity of these ivory figurines, based on their style, collection history, and particularly on the "happy coincidence" that these figurines supported theories already espoused by Evans. However, despite the several suspicious factors, it is clear that there is little conclusive evidence to definitively date the figurines. My recent investigation into the ROM "goddess" through the archival records and material investigations has reconsidered the figurine in detail. It reveals what stylistic comparisons, documentation studies, and scientific analysis can (and cannot) resolve about the issue of authenticity. The ROM figurine is also used as a case study to consider the broader issues of how the loss of archaeological context, and the creation of modern forgeries, have each affected our understanding of the ancient world.

The ROM's Aphrodite in the So-Called Venus Genetrix Type

Bjoern C. Ewald, University of Toronto

The Royal Ontario Museum's (ROM) Aphrodite of the Louvre/Naples type (so-called Aphrodite Fréjus/Venus Genetrix) is a highlight of the sculpture collection that stands out for its extraordinary quality of execution; it is arguably the most sophisticated of the few copies and variations of the type in North American collections.

Nearly everything about the statue type and the Toronto replica, published in 1927 by C. Harcum, is problematic. The type has been variously linked to the "Aphrodite in the gardens" by Alkamenes, or to the sculptor Callimachos, or the Temple of Aphrodite Nymphia in Troizen, as well as to Arkesilaos' cult image for Caesar's Temple of Venus Genetrix on the Forum Iulium (or to the latter's Trajanic restoration). Most of these (and many more) suggestions have been plausibly rejected, with good arguments, in the most recent scholarship. M. Brinke, for example, deems an attribution to the school of Polykleitos most likely, based on the statue's formal characteristics; the attribute held by the goddess was an apple that may (or may not) connect her to the judgment of Paris. It appears that we have to accept that the statue type remains without a reasonably secure attribution, and that the fame of the original statue may not have matched the extraordinary popularity of the type in the Hellenistic and Roman periods: There are about 100 replicas and variations of the Venus Genetrix type, more than any other female statue type, if one leaves aside the more popular Herculaneum women and "Ceres" types. While we are left without attribution, some inferences can nonetheless be made regarding the role of Aphrodite and the judgment of Paris in art and culture of late fifth-century B.C.E. Athens.

This paper also clears up the conflicting accounts about the statue's provenance and makes a new suggestion regarding the possible context of the ROM's replica. Upon closer inspection, the statue is a variation that differs from the majority of copies in the rendering of the folds over the upper body, as well as the covering of the left breast. The latter feature, often found in adaptations of the type for portrait statues, as well as the likely provenance from Rome or Italy make it distinctly possible that we are looking at the portrait statue of a young female in the guise of Venus, from a funerary, domestic, or public context.

From Athens to Toronto: Sylvia Hahn at the Royal Ontario Museum

Jacquelyn H. Clements, University of Toronto

The Toronto artist Sylvia Hahn (1911–2001) was an important figure in the development and display of the Graeco-Roman antiquities collection in the Royal Ontario Museum (ROM). Born into a family of prominent artists, Hahn was employed in the ROM's art department beginning in 1937. In her decades working for the museum, she created a number of large-scale paintings and models of the ancient world for the museum's antiquities galleries, from an elaborate scene of everyday life on a street in Pompeii to a lengthy Ionic frieze-like illustration of scenes from Greek vase painting. This paper considers Sylvia Hahn's contributions to the ROM and the place of Greek archaeology and historical models in the context of mid 20th-century Canadian history and museums.

Besides her work in the creation of a number of the ROM's murals, Hahn was also talented in the three-dimensional arts. Under the direction of Neda Leipen, she created an intricate scale model of the Athena Parthenos, which was built on carefully considered available evidence and scholarship. She also made significant enhancements to a model of the Athenian Acropolis, a copy of an original created under the direction of G.P. Stevens in Athens in the 1940s. The ROM's Acropolis model included additions by Hahn of architectural ornamentation and many of the votive statues that adorned the Acropolis, in addition to added realistic landscape elements. These addenda to the Stevens' original model illustrate not only Hahn's observations of Greek architecture and Athenian topography, but also her knowledge of Pausanias as well as current scholarship.

In this study, I explore how these modern objects serve as pedagogical tools that illuminate the ancient world. Constituting a gallery on Athenian Public Life that was planned specifically for the ROM, the addition of models of the Parthenon's metopes and the shield of Athena Parthenos along with the Acropolis model and the Parthenos itself collectively emphasize the elaborate and careful attention to accuracy that was core to Hahn's method. Even today, with the advent of digital technologies to represent the past, the models and murals created by Hahn still serve an educational purpose and are of great teaching value within the museum environment. Furthermore, they also accentuate the budding interests in classical archaeology in Toronto, especially in the years surrounding and following World War II.

SESSION 3E: Joint AIA/APA Colloquium
God the Anthropologist: Text, Material, and Theory in the Study of Ancient Religion

ORGANIZERS: *Megan Johanna Daniels*, University of Puget Sound, and *Sandra Blakely*, Emory University

Colloquium Overview Statement

Anthropological approaches to ancient religion encompass a tantalizing spectrum of possibilities, from studies focused on foodways and economic exchange to quantitative modeling of social interactions. Their application to the ancient religions of Greece and Rome creates, at its best, innovative conversations with textual, archaeological, and art historical approaches. These conversations offer productive contributions to ongoing analyses by highlighting the agency and materiality inherent in ancient religious systems and allow for integration of local and global conceptions of the divine in a perpetually globalizing Mediterranean. Such approaches suggest the heuristic potential in moving beyond the polis/state as the dominant heuristic concept for religion in the Graeco-Roman world and offer frameworks for examining a much broader array of lived experiences, practices, and relationships to the divine embodied by individuals and groups.

This panel brings together scholars using anthropological methods and models to create productive, innovative bridges between the textual and material evidence specific to Greek and Roman religions. Papers provide methodological reflection through the context of specific case studies: "Economic Anthropology, Economic Theory, and the Study of Ancient Religions" examines the merits and limitations of approaches from economic anthropology and economic theory to the study of ancient Mediterranean religions, particularly religion's role in economic decision making and the lowering of transaction costs in precarious ecological environments. "Magical Power, Cognition, and the Religion of the Intellectual" explores intellectual attitudes towards magic in two imperial Roman texts through cognitive and contextual analyses, thus illustrating often-ignored modes of epistemic and ritualistic communication with the divine in the Roman world. "Divining Data" examines the virtues and vices of quantitative modeling of both monumental religious construction projects and votive deposition in Middle Republican Rome and Latium, and calls for explicit methodologies in quantitative and statistical analyses to pave the way for comparative and theoretical frameworks of religion in the ancient world. "Greek Libations from a Visual Perspective" problematizes the tendency of scholarship to subordinate visual media to the primacy of texts, and shows how images played key roles in shaping religious experience in the ancient world. "Cult Dynamics and Information Technologies" explores how communities of Mithraists maintained a striking level of coherence across the Roman world over several centuries through the mediation of information transfer networks and practices, and argues for a shift from general models of social embeddedness of religion to more dynamic models of knowledge transfer.

DISCUSSANT: *Ian Rutherford*, University of Reading

Economic Anthropology, Economic Theory, and the Study of Ancient Religions

Barbara Kowalzig, New York University

This paper discusses the effectiveness and limitations of approaches from economic anthropology and economic theory for the study of ancient Mediterranean religions, distinguishing three broad directions. Ancient historians of religion are familiar with, firstly, approaches from classic economic anthropology from Marcel Mauss' ritualized gift-giving to Mark Granovetter's social embeddedness of economic actions; but there are a number of contemporary approaches in economic anthropology, developed e.g. on the basis of Mesoamerican religions, that have escaped the notice of classicists. The paper, secondly, examines the usefulness of New Institutional Economics (NIE), popular with ancient historians, for an understanding of the interrelations between religion and economy in the ancient world. NIE broadly understands institutions, especially state institutions, as counteracting uncertainty in economic decision making; they reduce transaction costs by providing information and establishing trust, and thus affect economic outcomes. An often-repeated tenet is that religious and cultural beliefs generate people's knowledge and influence their economic choices, but this is rarely explored beyond religious affiliation functioning as an informal, private-order enforcement mechanism within a trading diaspora (e.g., A. Greif, *Institutions and the Path to the Modern Economy*). This section, then, examines, "religious and cultural beliefs" in the ancient world as knowledge systems underlying economic choices and explores the possibilities of understanding myth, ritual, and cult as "institutions" in the NIE sense. Ancient examples suggest that religious practice and imagination can be seen to affect outcomes under persistent conditions of uncertainty, such as ecological precariousness, while sanctuaries emerge as privileged institutional environments for the lowering of transaction costs through the aggregation of information and production of economic knowledge. Economic choices thus often fall squarely between social and religious imperatives and profit maximization. The third section of the paper briefly introduces the recent "economics of religion," which attempts to relate religion to economic growth through applying free-market dynamics to religious choices. While problematic, some of the mechanisms developed in this school open up ways of thinking about the relationship between state and religious practice, of festival competition and renewal, and of the economic role of festivals at large.

Magical Power, Cognition, and the Religion of the Intellectual in the Roman Imperial West

Andreas Bendlin, University of Toronto

Exploring the relationship between religion and social identity, my paper discusses cognitive aspects and reconsiders the socioreligious context of two texts concerning "magic": the recently discovered invocation of *omnipotentia numina* by their self-styled "guardian," Verius Sedatus, and Apuleius' *Apology*.

First, cognition: I sketch—through the lens of cognitive studies—Sedatus's invocation ritual and Apuleius' recognition of the ritual power of "magical acts" (e.g., Apol. 26.6), whereby in a cognitive perspective ascriptions of non-ordinary power are made to achieve non-ordinary goals. Scholars of ancient "magic" have traditionally considered anthropological approaches but rarely engage with recent critical thinking that applies cognitive or attributional theories to "magical rituals." I engage these approaches to explore Sedatus' ritual and Apuleius' exegesis.

Second, socioreligious context: scholarship has highlighted the Imperial-period mobility of the ritual expert, the textualization of Egyptian magical knowledge, and its dissemination through the medium of the book outside of Egypt. The reception—by way of migrant experts, ritual texts or objects—of the Graeco-Egyptian magical tradition in the Latin West since roughly the second century C.E. appears confined to a small number of data (e.g., gems and a few curse inscriptions). That tradition may have been attractive primarily to an affluent, educated audience, who conceptualized Egypt as one of the places of origin of magic. I outline how Sedatus, who rudimentarily applies techniques (the use of *voces magicae*) from that tradition as early as the late first/early second century, and Apuleius, who is familiar with the concept of *nomina magica* (Apol. 38.7), also illustrate this process of reception.

Merging cognitive analysis and socioreligious contextualization, I illustrate how communication with the divine world operates at two interrelated levels, epistemic and ritualistic. Apuleius—in a rhetorical performance of "high intellectualism"—defends *magia* as an epistemic endeavor whereby the philosopher acquires privileged access to the divine. As recognized by Apuleian scholarship, his argumentation foregrounds the philosopher's epistemic control of *magia*. However, Sedatus's invocation ritual and the ritualistic competence that emerges from Apuleius' *Apology* also demonstrate the bricoleur's innovative ritual agency. Both individuals have been claimed as "magicians" or quasiprofessional ritualists. I suggest that findspot (Sedatus) and literary context (Apuleius) rather suggest learned domestic appropriation of the magical tradition by nonprofessional bricoleurs. Their respective religious portfolios thereby included elements of what I label "the religion of the intellectual"—one facet of ancient religious identities historians often ignore.

In conclusion, I propose that we read Apuleius' *Apology* as conceding the precarious position of the intellectual in a contemporary field of social practice that increasingly criminalized the notion and any alleged acts of *magia*. Scholars sometimes misapprehend the reasons for the *Apology*'s marginalization of the magical tradition's ritual potential, whereas in reality Apuleius' pillorying of the persona of the magus, as a societal "other," may aim primarily at averting suspicion of his own ritualistic expertise. Sedatus' recently discovered invocation ritual should warn against concluding too rashly that Apuleius did not experiment with some learned ritual himself.

Divining Data: Temples, Votives, and Quantitative Sensibilities

Dan-el Padilla Peralta, Princeton University

Ancient history's recent quantitative and social-scientific turn reflects a renewed and rising interest in adapting models from the "soft"—and occasionally the "hard"—sciences for the study of Graeco-Roman antiquity. The turn is on full display in ancient religion, where interpretations of the material evidence for cultic observance and ritual practice have of late grappled with quantifying models and techniques. Informed by this turn but conscious of the need to critique it, this paper puts forward a series of quantitative and statistical procedures for recreating the religious world of Middle Republican Rome (ca. 400–200 B.C.E.). Although the application of these procedures helps clarify Rome's evolving religious dynamics in the course of its ascent to Mediterranean empire, I argue that one of the most important takeaways from the application of these procedures is the possibility of ranging beyond Rome (or any discrete case study) so as to situate the conclusions derived from the application of these procedures within a comparative framework. Perhaps the core virtue of quantitatively focused work on religious practice is that it facilitates certain forms of regional and supraregional comparison—indispensable to the project of identifying and tracking patterns of globalization and "glocalization" in the ancient Mediterranean.

The paper's argument proceeds in two steps. Opening with a section on temple building in the Middle Republic, I outline and explain how a model of the labor parameters of monumental religious construction can yield a more richly textured understanding of the rhythms of cultic and social life in fourth- and third-century B.C.E. Rome. To the end of demonstrating how such an understanding becomes possible through the praxis of model building itself, I document and justify why my specific framework for Middle Republican temple building exploits not only classical and Hellenistic Greek comparanda for public construction but evidence for pre-modern monumental activity taken from well outside the Graeco-Roman Mediterranean (e.g., Mesoamerican economic specialization, architectural energetics, and urbanization). Without presupposing some transhistorical constant in the human experience of building sacred structures, this section contends that it is not sufficient to formulate a local model of temple construction: a conceptual framework erected on the bedrock of comparative praxis is most fruitful when retested through systematic comparison. In an effort to illustrate some of the heuristic rewards of calibrated contrast, I briefly sketch how Middle Republican construction patterns stack up against those of its Hellenistic contemporaries and how they measure up against monumental activity during other periods of Rome's history—comparisons that in themselves spawn new models.

The second (and shorter) part of this paper moves away from monumental construction to model a different kind of religious activity: the deposition of votives at Rome and throughout Latium during the fourth and third centuries. As the pace of temple construction at Rome quickened, more and more individuals began to make dedications—both inscribed and anepigraphic—at these new temples.

These dedications occurred within a central Italic votive regime nowadays termed the ELC (short for "Etrusco-Latial-Campanian"). While elementary quantification is a staple of published votive deposits, I argue that the application of statistical methods (stochastic and Bayesian modeling) enables us not only to make sense of the scale and extent of this votive habit but to compare the ELC to votive complexes from other periods of Mediterranean history.

To conclude, the paper explores how self-reflexive and self-critical quantitative modeling of temple construction and votive deposition can open the door not only to comparison but to theorizing comparison in the study of ancient religion—provided, of course, one is explicit at every step in the model's formulation about the methodological building blocks and suppositions underpinning quantification and statistical analysis.

Greek Libations from a Visual Perspective

Milette Gaifman, Yale University

The study of Greek religion in its various traditions has been informed by a variety of anthropological theories. For instance, Robert Parker's *Miasma: Pollution and Purification in Early Greek Religion* was inspired by Mary Douglas' seminal book, *Purity and Danger: An Analysis of Concepts of Pollution and Taboo*, or the so-called Paris School's approach to Greek religion (e.g., M. Detienne and J.-P. Vernant, *La cuisine du sacrifice en pays grec*), owes much to French anthropological studies. Using various theoretical models, such studies seek to bring together evidentiary material, whether textual or material, for the study of various aspects of ancient cult practices, myths, and beliefs. At its core however, the scholarly field of Greek religion is, by and large, a text-based field. The standard textbooks that still dominate it (e.g., M.P. Nilsson, *Geschichte der griechischen Religion*; w. Burkert, *Greek Religion: Archaic and Classical*) rely firstly on texts, whereas archaeological finds are usually cited to confirm and illustrate text-based reconstructions and interpretations. This tendency is also seen in treatments of material evidence, for it is typically classified and interpreted in relation to the modern frameworks that are based on the interpretation of texts. Similarly, Greek imagery is taken as illustrative of textual evidence, as can be witnessed, for example, in the various entries of *Thesaurus Cultus et Rituum*. It goes without saying that textual evidence is of prime import in this field of exploration. However, if we seek to understand ancient religious experience, we cannot take images as ancillary to texts, if only because ancient worshipers encountered their gods on a daily basis in various visual representations ranging from large-scale statues to imagery on painted pottery.

This paper proposes that, side-by-side with current methodologies, visual material ought to be used in the study of Greek religion not merely as illustrative, but as an informative source in its own right. It takes the libation as a case in point for such an approach. It offers a close examination of a well-known vase attributed to the Kekrops Painter that is today in Eichenzell, Germany (Museum Schloß Fasanerie inv. no. AV 77) that features Erichthonius and Athena handling libation vessels. Rather than consider how the vase's imagery may illustrate familiar Athenian myths, the paper considers the ideas that the vase may articulate about the libation. Through close visual analysis it shows that the ritual is presented primarily as a way to affirm relations between various parties. It then examines the consequences of this position by considering the possible use of the large krater in the performance of libations. Altogether the paper shows how ancient images not only articulated ideas about the gods and religious practices, but also shaped ancient religious experience.

Cult Dynamics and Information Technologies: The Case of Mithraism

Matthew McCarty, University of British Columbia

The recognition that Roman religious practices were deeply enmeshed in social life has led to a host of recent work on the shifting dynamics of cult practices, places, and images across the Roman world that went hand-in-hand with the changing power structures of the empire. At the same time, greater focus on localized social frameworks has tessellated accounts of cult life, even in cults (like strains of Christianity) explicitly aiming for a sense of universalism. Against such a background, strong continuities through time and space demand even greater explanation, and perhaps no other cult system demonstrates the level of homogeneity in architecture, iconography, and ritual practice as Mithraism. How and why did communities engaged in the worship of Mithras maintain this coherence across the Roman world over several centuries? Using material from the mithraea at Dura-Europos, Mainz, and the new excavations that I codirect at Apulum, I argue that the dynamics of cult change and continuity in the Roman empire need to be considered in terms of information-transfer networks and information technologies, not on the level of esoteric interpretations (long the bugbear of ancient religious studies), but on the level of ritual craft. Focusing on information technologies and mediation allows us to move beyond the false binary inherent in Harvey Whitehouse's "modes of religiosity," the most common contemporary anthropological model used to understand the interplays between cult, knowledge, and mediation in the ancient world. In Mithraism, the particular information redundancies mediated in various ways (through images, through pageantry, through the manipulation of "small finds" objects) as well as the particular practices (including foundation rites, attested in a series of deposits that have never before been linked) that drove the connectivity of local communities created the ideational infrastructure that allowed a coherent and stable "Mithraic package" to move around the empire. Shifting discussion from general models of social embeddedness to the means of knowledge-transfer can also offer a more robust explanatory model not just for Mithraism, but for the dynamics of cult change and continuity across the empire more broadly.

SESSION 3F: Colloquium
Diverging Trajectories: Urbanism and the Roman Conquest of Italy

ORGANIZER: *Myles McCallum*, Saint Mary's University

Colloquium Overview Statement

The period from the Middle to the Late Republic, which coincides with the Roman conquest of Italy, is an extremely important phase in the development of urbanism and the urban form throughout Italy. Some parts of the peninsula, such as Etruria, Latium, Magna Graecia, and Campania, have long histories of well-developed urban centers predating this transitional period. Others, such as Samnium, appear to be lacking a true urban tradition prior to Roman conquest. Others, such as Apulia and Lucania, were in the process of developing their own distinctive higher-order centers when they became part of the Roman system. The impact of Roman conquest and the establishment of a structured system of imperial intercourse between the new dominant center and its network, including communities allied to Rome as well as the recently established Roman and Latin colonies, is a complex and multifaceted issue that cannot be reduced to a single model. Ancient sources frequently see the Roman conquest as a factor of change that introduces urbanitas among "uncivilized" peoples. However, many authors also describe with a good deal of nostalgia ancient and once-famous cities of Etruria, Latium, and Magna Graecia that had declined to the rank of villages or had been abandoned altogether. Modern scholarship, frequently echoing the views of the ancient sources, has argued that historical events during this transitional period sowed the seeds of true urban development in certain areas of the peninsula, while in others indigenous urban centers would atrophy, decay, and disappear. The complex interplay between Roman conquest and urbanism in Middle and Late Republican Italy beyond those opposite and symmetrical literary topoi and the traditional historical narratives is deserving of further, more nuanced research, for which archaeological evidence is key. The widely accepted views on the modes and times of development of the urban phenomenon in Italy are slowly changing and becoming more articulated. There is also increased interest in the post-conquest phases of the centers of central and south Italy, and a more "optimistic" view is emerging where scholars assumed fast and hopeless decline. This panel examines the trajectories of urban development during this important historical period through different case studies from across the peninsula in an effort to explain why certain settlements survived and flourished, why others did not, and why new urban traditions developed in some parts of Italy.

Early Roman Colonization Beyond the Romanizing Agro-Town: Colonial Rationales and Settlement Patterns in Apennine Italy

Tesse Stek, University of Leiden

Roman expansion and colonization has typically been associated with urbanism, especially in previously nonurbanized landscapes. In the context of the early Roman expansion in Italy, the mountainous Apennine area has been viewed as a prime example where the introduction by Rome of the "new wave of the future" in the Samnite "pre city-state stage" world could be witnessed, to paraphrase Toynbee. However, the expected regular Roman landscapes consisting of monumental urbs and divided ager, have, as yet, not been documented in the Apennine colonies. On the contrary, a rereading of epigraphic and archaeological settlement data from various colonial territories points to more organic, nucleated, or clustered settlement patterns, rather than the anticipated neatly divided landscapes. This hypothesis is now being corroborated by our ongoing fieldwork (2011–) in the colonies of Aesernia (263 B.C.E.) and Venusia (291 B.C.E.) (in the context of the Aesernia Colonial Landscape and Landscapes of Early Roman Colonization projects). In this paper, some of the latest results of the fieldwork in these colonies are discussed, which are compared with contemporary developments in noncolonized Italic territories (e.g. from the Tappino Area Archaeology project, 2013–). Finally, the possible rationales behind such diverging settlement strategies in the early Roman colonies in the Apennine areas are discussed. This involves a reconsideration of the historiographical construction of Roman republican colonization and its primary motivations.

A Middle Republican House from Gabii and the Formation of Roman Urbanism

Marcello Mogetta, University of Missouri, *Rachel Opitz*, University of South Florida, and *Nicola Terrenato*, University of Michigan

Roman urbanism has been excavated, written about, depicted, and reconstructed repeatedly, and yet we know surprisingly little about its early stages. The imposing character of the preserved later remains tends to overshadow our considerable ignorance of the processes that led to their design and formation. Most of what we have for the fifth, the fourth, and the third centuries B.C.E. are massive city walls and temple podiums with their architectural terracottas. While there is no doubt that the known remains are impressive, they do not tell us how the public spaces, which later played such a big part in Roman urbanism, developed. Similarly, the early development of templated layouts for domestic space, prior to their diffusion in the Italian peninsula in the course of the first century B.C.E., and their role in signaling and creating and social differences, is poorly understood.

With the notable exception of Pompeii—which is in many ways a unique site—most of the evidence on the Middle to Late Republican transition comes from sites that were founded ex novo as colonies (Cosa, Fregellae, Alba Fucens, and Norba being the most thoroughly researched), while little is known about the ancient towns of Etruria and Latium. Numerous seasons of survey and excavation by the Gabii Project now allow us to paint a nuanced picture of the urban development of Gabii, a Latin site that enjoyed close political and cultural ties with neighboring Rome. Our ongoing large-scale research revealed designated public areas, private homes, and centrally planned infrastructure emerging in the Republican period on the site of a scatter of huts and compounds established in the Iron Age and redeveloped throughout the Archaic period.

The sequence of occupation of a single house within the town—the Tincu House, located just north of the city's trunk road and slightly east of its midpoint—provides us with a small window into the archaeology and history of the town in the period between the fifth–fourth centuries B.C.E. and the first century C.E. Over time, the Tincu House is transformed into the back-rooms annex of a large public complex, and then abandoned and filled with debris from adjacent quarries. Its architectural features are based on specific choices about the design and use of urban space at Gabii, reflecting both local initiatives and the broader influence of the regional context and Mediterranean social milieu during a crucial period for the formation of Roman urbanism.

Post-Conquest Urbanism in Hellenistic Italy: Comparing Regional and Chronological Trajectories

Jamie Sewell, University of Durham

From the results of the author's analytical database of peninsular Italy's urban centers, regional differences and possible supraregional processes are revealed in the development of towns in the postconquest period. Archaeological evidence does not generally reflect Roman interference in the development of noncolonial centers prior to the first century B.C.E. Yet some processes in the postconquest period are remarkable by their absence when compared with the Early Hellenistic period. There appears to have been a dramatic reduction in the number of new urban fortifications constructed, and the non-Roman founding of fortified hilltop centers effectively ceases. From the third century B.C.E. onward, new urban centers are increasingly founded on lower-lying sites, in mountainous as well as nonmountainous regions. The nucleation of large dispersed centers and an increased rate of urban abandonment are other notable peninsular processes.

The Role of Secondary Centers in Middle Republican Roman Colonial Landscapes

Jeremia Pelgrom, Royal Netherlands Institute in Rome

Studies of Roman territorial expansions strategies have mainly focused on the urban centers on the one hand, or on the isolated colonial farms and connected centuration landscapes on the other. This paper argues that this city-farmstead paradigm has blinded scholars to recognizing the important role other settlement realities had in Middle Republican colonial territories. In the context of the Landscape of Early Colonization Projects, a whole series of intermediary agglomerative settlement sites have been (re)analyzed in two South Italian Roman colonial territories. Adopting a multidisciplinary research strategy, the projects study in detail the spatial dimensions, chronology, consumption patterns, and internal organization of these sites. Preliminary results show that some of these sites must have been very significant population centers and were important nodes in regional trade networks.

Republican Urbanism and the Interior of Lucania and Apulia: Recent Archaeological Developments

Myles McCallum, Saint Mary's University

The frontier zone of the Bradano and Basentello Valleys, which separates ancient Lucania from Apulia, shows evidence for the development of protourban nucleated centers at places such as Monte Irsi, Botromagno, Banzi, and Monte Serico starting in the eighth century B.C.E. In the aftermath of the Roman conquest, however, most of these sites go into precipitous decline, with a tiny minority, such as ancient Bantia, making the transition to urban centers. The resulting Late Republican landscape, while hardly deserted, was largely devoid of urbanism. Various historical explanations have been proposed to explain this urban trajectory, most of which link the collapse of the region's protourban centers after the third century B.C.E. to warfare and the active displacement of indigenous peoples by Roman imperialists. Recent archaeological and environmental data is now challenging these historical narratives. This paper presents archaeological data from excavations at the sites of San Felice, Vagnari, Botromagno, and Monte Serico, regional surveys in the Basentello and Bradano Valleys, and environmental data associated with the Basentello Valley Archaeological Research Project (BVARP) to provide an alternate model of urban development, or lack thereof, that more adequately explains the decline of indigenous nucleated centers. This includes a reassessment of the nature of the indigenous urban centers that suggests we have overestimated their importance and scale, and which proposes a unique regional interaction between indigenous cultural groups and foreign invaders. These data also provide insight into previously hidden elements of cultural agency on the part of the conquered.

Beyond Conquest: Southern Etruria in the Middle and Late Republican Period
Fabio Colivicchi, Queen's University

For a long time historical narratives on South Etruria between the late fourth and the second century B.C.E. have focused primarily on the Roman conquest as the great and practically only factor of change. The heavy hand of Rome would have reshaped South Etruria through conquest, confiscation, and colonization, leaving Etruscan communities in the role of passive victims. Regarding the trends of urbanization, there has been little interest in the postconquest phases of the larger Etruscan centers, based on the shared assumption that there was crisis and decline or at least stagnation, the beginning of a downward trend that will make them almost empty shells in the Early Imperial period. It is not by chance that more research exists on small walled settlements, primarily because their fate could be directly linked with the events of Roman military conquest. Scholarly attention has been on Roman colonial foundations, Cosa above all, which has been the paradigm of a long-standing and influential model of Roman colonization. That view of Middle Republican colonization has been recently criticized and radically revised, but the alleged decline of the old Etruscan cities that was an integral part of that same historiographical model has not undergone equally thorough scrutiny. The reexamination of the archaeological record, which is now much more complete and refined than when the traditional view was developed, can help draw a more nuanced picture of what happened in South Etruria in that crucial period, one in which military and political events are not the only driving force, but large-scale trends that transcend ethnical and political boundaries take center stage in determining the trajectories of urbanism in South Etruria.

Of Unpromising Settings: the Latin Colony of Cosa

Andrea U. De Giorgi, Florida State University

Cosa has gone at regular intervals from 1948 nearly to the present with a respectable and ongoing record of publication. The public areas of the town, the forum and the Arx, have been well tested, not only for the seminal period of the town's growth in the course of the second century B.C.E. but for successive eras as well: the early and later Imperial, "Roman Dark Ages" and Medieval periods. Long held as the quintessential miniature copy of Rome, and later hailed as "intermittent town," Cosa is now undergoing new research. From the vantage point of the current excavations and geophysical surveys, more nuanced interpretative frameworks can be advanced with regard to the city's nucleation and evolution, especially in the context of the frenzy of colonial foundations during the third and second centuries B.C.E. In particular, Cosa's very unpromising setting and an almost empty cityscape—at least until a second draft of colonists came along in 197 B.C.E.—call into question the notion that Cosa served as a bulwark to curb remaining Etruscan ambitions and an escalating Punic threat. Cosa's economic outlook and hybrid social fabric are rather suggestive that the city served as a portal for a unique, durable dialogue with the outlying territory and its constituents.

SESSION 3G
Gold Medal Session: Context is Everything

CHAIR: *Penelope Davies*, University of Texas at Austin

Colloquium Overview Statement

During the course of his career, John R. Clarke has pioneered new approaches to Roman visual culture that have been widely acknowledged and deeply influential for ancient art historians and archaeologists alike. Fundamental to his research is the notion that "context is everything"; his work urges an understanding of Roman art and material culture on Roman terms, through Roman eyes. The papers assembled in this panel respond to some of the areas of his research, including the ways Roman saw their houses and domestic decoration, the role and meaning of sexual representations in antiquity, how art functioned in the lives of ordinary Romans, and the dynamics of Roman visual humor. Papers also touch on his most recent archaeological work at Oplontis, and the use of computer modeling in documentation and research.

The Flash of Recognition, the Point of No Return

Bettina Bergman, Mount Holyoke College

Who is looking and at whom is a pervasive theme in John Clarke's scholarship. This talk examines perhaps the most fraught moment of looking in Roman art: recognition. Dramatic turning points in frescoes and sarcophagi share visual schemata for such moments of heightened awareness: pyramidal groupings, dynamic postures, emphatic gestures, and facial expressions are intensified by reactions of encircling onlookers. The vivid tableaux depicting stories of Io, Iphigenia, Ariadne, Achilles, Pentheus, and Ulysses capture a range of mental and emotional states such as blindness, rapture, disguise, mania, lapsed memory, and metamorphosis.

The talk explores the ways in which standard visual schemes are adapted for different narratives, how they relate to theatrical performance, and what they suggest about viewer response. These questions become amplified when multiple moments are coordinated on a single monument or within one space. A focus is the painted rooms in the Casa della Citarista in Pompeii, where seven spectacular mythological panels of the Augustan and Neronian periods were removed from the walls in 1853; newly cleaned and recontextualized in a virtual model, they now can be appreciated as ensembles in reception rooms opening onto light-filled peristyles. A binding theme in these novel groupings is the power of vision; it is through sight that gods and mortals become enlightened or make a transition, and viewers sometimes see more, sometimes less, than the gods themselves.

How might Pompeians have perceived multiple revelations of sight? Attempts to see through "Roman eyes" are inevitably problematic, but need not be abandoned. A dual approach is rewarding. First, identifying the visual vocabulary of figural types and compositional schemes helps explain how observers recognized stories and, when presented with groupings, interpreted similarities and differences. Second, as John Clarke has argued, physical and social context are essential to begin to understand ancient spectators' experiences. The digital model shows the physical space as an immersive environment that linked subject, space, and viewer. Thanks to location, graffiti, and portable finds, this house allows one to speculate about who some of those viewers might have been. The gens Popidii, one of the oldest families in Pompeii, built the house, and in its last years Popidii freedmen, despite downsizing, preserved early portraits and frescoes celebrating Augustan ideology. The goal of this exercise in considering modes of recognition both among mythical characters and ancient Pompeians is to clarify our modern perceptions of Roman looking.

Greek Sex

Jenifer Neils, Case Western Reserve University

While the indebtedness of much of Roman culture—architecture, sculpture, literature—to its Greek predecessors has been examined in detail, this aspect as it pertains to erotic imagery, namely its roots in Greek visual culture, has not been thoroughly investigated. This paper looks at lovemaking, a subject thoroughly explored by John Clarke, from a Greek perspective, and posits the question to what extent Roman sexual practices and imagery are derived from classical and Hellenistic Greece. Two specific case studies are considered: the Roman silver cup formerly in the collection of Edward Warren and now in the British Museum, and the statue of a boy killing a lizard (Sauroktonos), known in numerous Roman copies.

With its scenes of two male couples in symplegmatic poses, the Warren Cup is exceptional in ancient art. However it can be argued that imagery, now lost, which was labeled "obscene" in antiquity by Greek painters such as Pauson (Arist. *Pol.*1340a33) and Parrhasios of Ephesos (Plin. *HN* 35.72) provided prototypes for the couples on the Warren Cup. A new identification of the lovers on side A as Patroklos (as *erastes*) and Achilles (as *eromenos*) is supported both by the subsidiary imagery on the cup (lyre) and by evidence in literature from Homer to Aeschines.

A new reading of a well-known statue, the Sauroktonos, misidentified and misattributed by Pliny as an image of Apollo by Praxiteles (as argued in my AIA paper of 2016), has implications for the subtlety of Roman erotic imagery and its inspiration from Greece.

Based on the epigram of Martial that warns the lizard-slayer, called puer, not to let the creature "die" by his hand, this statue type can be closely related to pederastic poetry where *saura* is is identified with the *membrum virilis* (LSJ). This androgynous statue's popularity in imperial Rome is due to its identity as a "sexy boy," and its subject no doubt carried a specific homoerotic message to both Greek and Roman viewers.

Illustrated Texts and Ancient Sex Manuals

Andrew M. Riggsby, University of Texas at Austin

Ancient erotic handbooks (perhaps anaischytographia, though the form is unattested), are famously preserved only in tiny fragments and testimonia. It appears, however, that at least one of them was illustrated (in the manner of many seeming modern counterparts), though this has been disputed in the modern literature. This paper begins by arguing in favor of the illustrations, based both on close reading of particular source passages (Suet. *Tib.* 43; *Priap.* 4) and by considering the broader context of what kinds of texts were illustrated in antiquity. The déclassé topic and apparent pseudonymity of authorship both correspond to the (low) status associated with illustration. The prescriptive character of the project conforms to a general tendency to use integral illustrations for constitutive projects rather than descriptive ones.

That broader context also raises issues of the nature of the illustrations. By means of a survey of illustrated texts, I argue that for both social and technical reasons, integral classical manuscript illustrations were normally minimal, in the sense that they schematically represent only as much information as is required for their immediate purpose. (Nonauthorial additions and Late Antique practice in general are significantly different.) The level of detail in the illustrations in these manuals would thus be revealing of their "immediate purpose." Schematic illlustrations (as are used in some modern comparanda, typically for reasons of market-oriented modesty) would in the ancient context suggest a genuinely technical purpose, or at least the pose of such. Naturalistic rendering (of the sort studied in *Looking at Lovemaking*) would by contrast be out of place unless additional motives were in play (e.g., desire to arouse, generic elevation). The paper sketches a couple of possible scenarios and considers whether there is adequate evidence to decide among them.

Frolicking Fullers

Sandra R. Joshel, University of Washington, and *Lauren Hackworth Petersen*, University of Delaware

"Frolicking Fullers" focuses on a fresco that decorated the entire wall of a peristyle in a Pompeian atrium house that had been converted into a fullery—the Fullery of Vesonius Primus (VI.14.22). The painting was located behind several fulling stalls and three large rinsing basins that had been installed on the south wall of the peristyle. It consisted of scenes of workmen with some of the symbols and tools associated with fulling, although the workmen themselves were engaged in various activities that seemingly had nothing to do with fulling—a tribunal, dancing, owl hunting, excreting, etc. The painting was much damaged and faded when Antonio Sogliano uncovered it in 1873 during the excavation of the house. Today, only pieces of its scenes are discernable, but we have Sogliano's description when he excavated the fullery/house and Geremia Discanno's accompanying drawing in *Giornale degli Scavi*. Even a general description of the scenes above the work area of the fullery immediately raises questions about how the painting fits with the pretentions implied by the decoration of other rooms. Did it belong to the owners' strategy—a part of the spectacle of production that gave owners and guests a laugh at the expense of workers? Or were there shared fullers' jokes here that crossed the divide of worker and owner? We argue that the fresco in the context of other material evidence at Pompeii hints at a subculture of fullers, one that perhaps included slave participation. In analyses of particular aspects of the painting and in its more general concerns, our paper addresses the work of John Clarke on Roman popular culture, humor, and painting.

Isolating the Target in Roman Humor

Anthony Corbeill, University of Kansas

In his books on sex and on "ordinary Romans," our honorand consistently encourages us to remember the viewer: who may have stowed their clothes under the frescoed threesomes at the Suburban Baths? How did visitors to the capital react to the Ara Pacis? I would like to invert the question in considering the final book in this trilogy, *Looking at Laughter*. I begin with skepticism: what justifies our claims to know the kinds of visual experience that caused a Roman to laugh? In particular, rather than focus on who found this material funny, I instead delve into how Roman laughter seems to work, and I do so precisely by applying a methodology that these three books consistently warn us not to use—by juxtaposing textual and visual evidence. I begin with a short survey of those written sources that cue the reader into expecting a joke (esp. Cic. *De oratore*) and seek analogous cues in the visual material that Clarke treats. In particular, I compare the audience in written examples of humorous abuse—the hearer who unites with the teller in order to focus derision on the butt of the joke—with the internal viewer that appears in a number of alleged examples of visual humor. The triangulation between speaker, target, and audience that texts stress as a prime characteristic of Roman humor allows us to be more confident about finding laughs in the silent visual material.

RomLab: Interface and Argument

Christopher Johanson, UCLA

This paper responds to a common question about computerized, three-dimensional reconstructions of archaeological sites: once they exist, what can you do with them?

Processions, oratory, and spectacular games form the main elements of a Roman aristocratic funeral. Any examination of this kinetic, multisensory event must attempt to grapple with the surrounding spatial context. At Rome, the Forum Romanum hosted the bulk of the ceremony and without doubt had tremendous influence on the experience and staging of the funerary spectacle.

The Republican Forum, like nearly every known place in antiquity, is now an imagined space. The built environment of the second century B.C.E. will never again be accessible actually or virtually without the aid of reconstruction, modeling, and simulation.

Scholarly arguments about such spaces tend to share an acute deficiency. Since a physical site of the Forum exists, right now, in Italy, it is often tacitly understood that a discussion about the Forum refers to the archaeological site that one can actually visit. Yet scholars who build arguments based on or set within an ancient place create their own invisible, mental construct of the space—a construct that has only a tenuous relationship to the actual extant remains. The level of detail imagined varies greatly between the place envisioned by a scholar with a vivid and active cognitive spatial ability and one whose image of the reconstructed place is little more than a vaguely sketched out plan of the area. Nonetheless, each scholar imagines and inhabits a unique version of the space.

No one would ever discuss Cicero's *Pro Sestio* without first noting the specific text used and then presenting to the reader an exact copy extracted from that version of the text. Should not the same rigor apply to scholarly arguments that reference ancient spaces? What would a spatial citation of an imagined space look like? And how could multiple critical editions of a space be experienced in three dimensions just as versions of a text can be read in two dimensions?

In this paper I present a working, experimental example of how one might build an argument about ancient spaces, set within three-dimensional, digital critical editions. Its exemplar argument centers on the stagecraft of the Roman aristocratic funeral to interrogate the interplay between the Forum of the second century and the procession, eulogy, and subsequent funeral games unfolding within.

Eat, Drink, and Be Impressed: Monumentality, Leisure, and the Evolution of Architectural Design at Oplontis Villa A

Michael L. Thomas, The University of Texas at Austin

Known to many as the Villa of Poppaea, Oplontis Villa A occupied an enviable elevated spot on the Bay of Naples. Sited on cliff at the water's edge, the villa enjoyed views of mountains, sea, and lavish gardens. Originally constructed ca. 50 B.C.E., the villa stood until its destruction by Vesuvius in 79 C.E. Though we cannot identify the owner(s) of the villa, our recent investigations have documented several significant remodels and additions to the villa during its lifetime.

The original manifestation of the villa saw the construction of what are arguably some of the most monumental domestic spaces at that time in Roman Italy. These included the tallest known atrium on the Bay of Naples and several equally impressive entertainment and dining rooms. The first major renovation occurred during the first decade of the first century C.E. and included the addition of a bath complex that must have rivaled the facilities of public baths. Significant changes to the villa's original core and the addition of the massive entertainment area in the east wing occurred at some point after 50 C.E. as part of a remodel that may have more than doubled the size of the original building. What is clear is that the architects of the original villa, as well as those of its subsequent renovations, designed luxurious and often monumental spaces that were meant to impress and entertain.

This paper synthesizes eight years of architectural study as part of the Oplontis Project into a narrative on the evolving design and decoration of such spaces, and the way in which the villa's owners and guests experienced them. Within this evolution of the villa, the combination of scale, views of the natural setting, and spaces for entertainment plays a central role in the architectural design. Following the well-known methodology of John Clarke, we see that architecture joined with decorative ensembles of spaces to manipulate the visual experience and in some cases inform function. The final product can only be defined as a showpiece, the message of which underscored the owner's wealth and his ability to construct private monumental spaces for the enjoyment and experience of the privileged few.

SESSION 3H: Colloquium
Adaptation and Advancement: Investigating Volcanic Landscapes of the Central Mediterranean

ORGANIZER: *Carrie Ann Murray*, Brock University

Colloquium Overview Statement

This session creates a forum for the discussion of archaeological contexts within volcanic landscapes across the central Mediterranean including southern Italy, Sicily, and its islands, and Sardinia over the *longue durée* of human habitation. It is becoming increasing apparent that the role of landscape in volcanic regions plays more than a passive setting. Current methodologies often divide the investigation of volcanic landscapes into categories, such as island archaeology with chronological divisions for prehistoric and classical periods. These divisions mask interdisciplinary and methodological intersections. The presentations here address how different communities utilized and adapted volcanic landscapes for the development of social hierarchies through material culture and cult practices; three of these papers represent international collaborations of scholars.

The first presentation questions the methodological approaches to island archaeology and the volcanic islands of Lipari and Pantelleria in particular, through the concepts of centrality and marginality. He explores why despite their geological similarities and abundance of obsidian, these two islands developed very trajectories from the Neolithic.

Second, the two coauthors deliver the results of a major XRF study of obsidian artifacts from Calabria. The social dynamics behind the widespread and numerous provenances of the obsidian in terms of multidirectional trade networks.

The third presentation discusses the relationships between the volcanic environments of Sicily and Sardinia in terms of their Bronze Age megalithic monuments and explores the advantages of individual examinations of the variability present in the very different funerary traditions.

The fourth paper investigates the *longue durée* of cultural responses to volcanic activity in the Aeolian Islands from the middle Neolithic through the Classical period. Continual reoccupation of the islands even after documented disasters is discussed, as is the use of volcanic material in ceramics.

Next, another coauthored paper exposes the continuity of cult activity at volcanic sites in eastern Sicily from the Neolithic to the Classical periods focused at volcanic crater lakes.

The sixth presentation delves into a cache of votives, each with different provenances, at the volcanic crater lake sanctuary site, Lago di Venere, Pantelleria. The votives, which offer evidence of worship from the Eneolithic through the Roman period, are argued to demonstrate the multicultural importance of the perceived sacred character of this volcanic landscape.

Long-Distance Votives: Evidence of Multicultural Worship at the Lago di Venere Volcanic Crater Lake, Pantelleria, Italy

Carrie Ann Murray, Brock University

A collection of terracotta votives were discovered near the volcanic crater lake, Lago di Venere, by Paolo Orsi at the end of the 19th century. This cache confirmed for many the cult worship of Venus at the proposed sanctuary site. This paper presents a restudy of those votives in connection with the latest findings from the Brock University excavation at the site. I argue that these votives represent evidence of individuals travelling long distances with votives from distant locations for deposition at this sanctuary.

The votives represent dating from the second half of the seventh century to early fifth century B.C.E. The provenances of the figurines indicate manufacture of these individual pieces from East Greek, Sicilian, Carthaginian, and Egyptian origins. The broader context of the site evidences activity from the Eneolithic, Punic, and Roman periods. In particular, the chronological label of Punic, might mask a considerable amount of multiculturalism in visitors to this sanctuary. The site itself contains architectural structures from the Punic period in a confined area, with an elaboration of architecture and increased space during the Roman period, giving insight for the first time into a Punic-Roman transition period in a sacred context.

The remarkable appearance of the volcanic crater lake served as the inspiration for this multicultural worship. The lake itself is characterized by nonpotable water and a location that is difficult to reach by land or sea, and perhaps a perceived chthonic connection. These combined factors caused this site to draw individuals from long distances for sacred purposes.

Two Volcanic Islands, Different Fates: Lipari and Pantelleria, Their Differing Resources, and Place in Central Mediterranean Prehistory

Clive Vella, Joukowsky Institute for Archaeology, Brown University

Islands are widely different within the Mediterranean basin. From almost continental-sized islands to small scattered archipelagoes, archaeologists have long attempted to create comparative methodologies for such circumscribed settings. This interest has led to the burgeoning field of island archaeology, which has grown a great deal since pioneering works in the mid 20th century. Yet there are several issues that remain contested within an island archaeology in a new millennium. Isolation, insularity, connectivity, and risk are keywords often found in the study of islands. However, their use is often rooted in assumptions that islands are either characterized by isolation or else formed intricate parts of wider connectivity.

This presentation makes an alternative proposition: small Mediterranean islands weaved in and out of wider connectivity, finding themselves in positions of centrality or marginality. Inhabitants of these islands did not simply react and adapt to their circumscribed settings. They utilized their island worlds to their own benefit. Despite these conscious actions, wider transformations in the Mediterranean basin also had an echoing effect within such small islands.

Lipari and Pantelleria, both volcanic islands found on opposite sides of Sicily, experienced diverse cultural developments. While these islands are well noted for their obsidian outcrops, Lipari and Pantelleria are similar in their ecological settings. They are semiarid, lacking in perennial water sources, clay, and metallurgical outcrops. They are also diversely located, particularly since Lipari forms part of the Aeolian Islands and is found close to peninsular Italy and Sicily. On the other hand, Pantelleria is situated by itself in the Channel of Sicily between North Africa and Sicily, largely out of sight from these large landmasses.

These differences have led to a varying intellectual focus. Lipari has been well-published and researched, illustrating a long-term human occupation from the sixth millennium B.C.E. On the other hand, Pantelleria has largely featured as an important Neolithic obsidian outcrop that was only permanently inhabited around the mid second millennium B.C.E., with little consideration to its potentially vital role in connecting the Maghrebian coastline to the central Mediterranean.

Therefore, this paper examines these two different islands as examples of differing cultural developments affected by island settings and human decisions. Such islands were locally created but affected by wider transformations. Then, despite their common volcanic geology, Lipari and Pantelleria hold a varying place in the central Mediterranean worth exploring.

Prehistoric Obsidian Use in Calabria, Italy: Identification of Multiple Sources and Subsources Using pXRF Analysis

Robert H. Tykot, University of South Florida, and *Andrea Vianello*, University of Sheffield

Starting in 2014, sourcing of prehistoric obsidian artifacts from archaeological sites in Calabria (Italy), was done for the first time since Ammerman and colleagues' work in Acconia more than 30 years ago. Using a portable XRF spectrometer, nondestructive trace element analyses were conducted on nearly 2,000 obsidian artifacts from 14 sites (Acconia [170], Bova Marina [183], Campolongo [2], Capo Alfiere [150], Casa Trogena [6], Crotone Mandria Vituso [14], Crotone [331], Favella [44], Piani della Corona [141], San Leonardo di Cutro [6], Saracena Cave [385], Serra D'Aiello [130], Sibari [253], Timpone-Steccato Cutro [1]). As with our work on obsidian from sites in Sicily (presented at AIA in 2014), the purpose of our research is to identify the specific obsidian sources and subsources that were utilized, and what this infers about the socioeconomic characteristics of both the local population and those near the sources themselves, the capabilities and perhaps regularity of maritime transport, and whether there were changes over time. Overall, for the Calabria sites tested so far, obsidian from the source islands of Lipari, Palmarola, and Sardinia (Monte Arci) has been identified; the vast majority comes from Lipari, with most artifacts from Gabellotto Gorge, but some from Canneto Dentro are also present. No obsidian from Pantelleria has been found.

The relative proximity of Calabria to Sicily and the Aeolian Islands make the Neolithic-period use of Lipari obsidian unsurprising, following its geological formation in the Mesolithic. Much more work is needed, however, filling geographic and chronological gaps in the obsidian assemblages tested, and especially in incorporating our results with those on lithic production technology and artifact typology, and on wear patterns and residues representing their usage. Furthermore, the documentation of obsidian mobility may reflect parallel and opposite direction movement of other materials such as ceramics, flint, and other lithics, domestic animals and their secondary byproducts, as well as ideas, knowledge, and people.

The identification of some obsidian artifacts from Palmarola and Sardinia was unexpected, although some have previously been found in southern Italy, in the regions of Campania and Puglia. While there are visual (transparency, color, phenocrysts) and physical (sharpness, brittleness) differences between obsidian sources, and apparent selection based on these properties elsewhere, the small quantities found at such great distances from their sources would not have resulted from local preferences but more likely the occasional availability of such unusual lithic material from intermediate communities.

Investigating the Relationship Between Megalithism and Volcanic Environment in Sicilian and Sardinian Bronze Age

Sebastiano Tusa, Soprintendente del Mare, Sicilia, Italy

There is a wide series of megalithic monuments dating to Bronze Age in Sardinia and Sicily that show some peculiarities that could be explained only by taking into account the volcanic environment in which they were built. Volcanic stone is difficult to shape and to work. It was for that reason that, for example, in Pantelleria they built the "sesi" in order to create a place in which it was possible to realize funerary chambers similar to the Sicilian rock-cut graves. On the contrary in the Etna, area burials were placed in typical "lava"-produced long caves because it was impossible to carry on the funerary tradition to cut graves into the rock. Meanwhile in Sardinia we have rock-cut graves as well as dolmenic tombs in an apparently similar volcanic environment. Analyzing case-by-case, it is possible to hypothesize to what extent the cultural tradition was so strong to let people adapt the same funerary typology in a different environment or if environment was strong enough to produce adaptation phenomena.

The Nexus of Geology and Indigenous Culture in Eastern Sicily from Prehistory Through the Early Roman Empire

Laura Maniscalco, Museo Regionale di Aidone, and *Brian E. McConnell*, Florida Atlantic University

Sicily lies at the intersection of the African and the European tectonic plates, and the Margi River valley in eastern Sicily is formed literally by their line of contact. Recent geological study shows that the Hyblaean Plateau on the eastern side of the valley not only offers evidence of igneous intrusion through cracks along the subducted African plate, but also the composition of the waters of the Naphtia Lake (Lago di Naftia), like the several volcanic springs (salinelle) around the base of Mount Etna indicate the presence of direct channels from the deepest levels of the Earth's crust. The nexus of volcanic activity and indigenous culture is evident in archaeological contexts through research by the Soprintendenza per Beni Culturali ed Ambientali di Catania and collaborating institutions since the 1990s at the "Salinelle" of Paternò and Rocchicella di Mineo. At the former, an extensive Neolithic village grew up in the context of the volcanic springs, while at the latter, Sicily's most famous indigenous sanctuary dedicated to the Divine Palikoi developed around the Naphtia Lake, which was described in detail by Diodorus Siculus and other ancient writers for its characteristic "boiling" and for the importance of the phenomenon as a source for oracular judgment. The remarkable continuity in tradition at Palikè from prehistory through the Early Roman empire is enriched by recent study of the site's extensive system of ancient canals that not only controlled the important resource of water, but may even have afforded the manipulation of the geological phenomenon itself.

The 7,500 Years of Living Dangerously: Opportunities and Risks at the Aeolian Islands

Sara T. Levi, Hunter College, The City University of New York, *G. Ayala*, The University of Sheffield, *M. Bettelli*, Istituto di Studi sul Mediterraneo Antico, CNR-Roma, *D. Brunelli*, Università di Modena e Reggio Emilia, *V. Cannavò*, Università di Modena e Reggio Emilia, *A. Di Renzoni*, Istituto di Studi sul Mediterraneo Antico, CNR-Roma, *F. Ferranti*, Istituto di Studi sul Mediterraneo Antico, CNR-Roma, *S. Lugli*, Università di Modena e Reggio Emilia, *M. Martini*, Università di Milano-Bicocca, *F. Maspero*, Università di Milano-Bicocca, *E. Photos-Jones*, Analytical Services for Art and Archaeology (Scotland) Ltd., *A. Renzulli*, Università di Urbino Carlo Bo, *P. Santi*, Università di Urbino Carlo Bo, *F. Speranza*, Istituto Nazionale di Geofisica e Vulcanologia, Roma, and *M. Vidale*, Università di Padova

Human occupation in the seven small Aeolian Islands (southern Tyrrhenian Sea) is a good example of cultural adaptability. Despite intermittent volcanic activity, the archipelago has been occupied for the last 7,500 years (since the Middle Neolithic). The inhabitants benefited from peculiar resources and raw materials (obsidian, pumice, and sulfur) but lacked others (water, clay, and lime). In contrast, this challenging, provocative, and fascinating island-scape is located in a strategic position, playing a fundamental role in Mediterranean trade networks.

This paper focuses on cultural responses to the volcanic landscape, particularly the ongoing interdisciplinary investigation at Stromboli. The earliest occupation at Stromboli is dated ca. 3500 B.C.E. ("Diana-Spatarella"). San Vincenzo is one of the largest plateaus of the island, created by lava flows and scoriae dated by paleoarcheomagnetism at 6.2 kya. A gap in volcanic eruptions matched with the development of the first main and long occupation during the Bronze Age village. Later, eruptions at Stromboli resumed in the Graeco-Roman period (San Bartolo lava flow, dated 100 ±100 C.E.).

Human occupation at Stromboli resumed again during the classical phases, evidenced by the Greek (320–250 B.C.E.) and Roman (second to fourth centuries C.E.) necropoleis. During the Middle Ages, the archipelago was affected by several main volcanic events, such as the famous Monte Pilato eruption, northeast of Lipari (calibrated ^{14}C age of 776 C.E. ±100). After few centuries, a main volcanic episode at Stromboli was mentioned in literature (Tommaso Fazello, 1558 C.E.). Archaeological evidence has been recently discovered with an ash fallout deposit containing green-glazed pottery dating to the 14th to 15th centuries C.E. This chronology is coherent with three ^{14}C dates (1325–1520 C.E., 2 sigma cal. age) from the charcoal within layers immediately below the ash level. Petrographic and volcanological investigations suggest that the ash fallout was the result of a landslide that deeply affected the Sciara del Fuoco landscape and human life.

Finally, in 1930, the most dramatic recent eruption at Stromboli occurred, leading to the overseas emigration of more than 75% of the island's population. Despite this seeming correlation between volcanic activity and abandonment, cultural developments were not always determined by the volcanos. In fact, the abandonment of the villages during the Bronze Age at Stromboli and in other islands of the Aeolian archipelago occurred without any volcanic eruptions.

SESSION 3I
Elites and Civic Life in the Provinces

CHAIR: To be announced

Writing on Temples: Epigraphic Habits of the Hellenistic and Roman Periods
Anna M. Sitz, University of Pennsylvania

Unlike inscriptions on stelae deposited at sanctuaries, inscriptions on the temple itself—on its architrave, antae, walls, and architectural members—could not be easily removed and were visible for the entire lifespan of the building. For example, at Priene, Alexander the Great's dedicatory inscription on the anta coexisted with Hellenistic decrees on the cella walls and finally with a dedication to Augustus on the architrave.

The widespread practice of writing on temples has not received significant study, however. I have therefore collected a catalogue of inscriptions from nearly 60 temples (some with multiple inscriptions) in Greece and Asia Minor, which date primarily from the Hellenistic and Roman periods. This catalogue allows for the identification of several genres of inscriptions, chronological developments, and regional trends. It is therefore of use to both archaeologists and epigraphers.

Scholarship on this topic has focused largely on the origin of temple dedicatory inscriptions as either an eastern innovation or native Greek act (e.g., G. Umholtz, "Architraval Arrogance?" *Hesperia* 71 [2002] 261–93). The general topic of writing on temples is familiar to scholars, but discussions of this phenomenon often lack specificity. For example, van Bremen states that on antae "we often find the earliest texts," but no citations are given. This paper therefore provides clarity and precision on the practice of inscribing temples.

An analysis of the temple inscriptions catalogue reveals that most examples fit into seven categories, classified either by location (e.g., architrave dedication) or by document type (e.g., letters/decrees). I argue that inscriptions should be viewed not as isolated documents but in interaction with other inscriptions on the same building and with the architecture of the temple itself. Certainly not every temple bore inscriptions; regional proclivities for writing on temples can be discerned from this study. The question of who controlled temple wall space is addressed through sites such as Lagina, where generations of priests recorded their names on the walls of the Temple of Hekate, and Aizanoi, where local notable Ulpius Eurykles inscribed letters praising his own political career on the Temple of Zeus.

This paper addresses the motivations behind writing on temples and the wider import of these inscriptions in defining sacred space and the relationship between the civic and the sacred.

Archaism in the Sanctuary of Aphrodite in Aphrodisias

Kenan Eren, Istanbul Mimar Sinan Fine Arts University

The city of Aphrodisias in Caria (modern Turkey) was established around the Sanctuary of Aphrodite, which seems to have a special importance for the entire Carian region during the Roman period. Archaeological investigations show that the history of the sanctuary goes back to the Archaic period. Several life-sized marble lion statue fragments found in the excavations date back to the Archaic period, and were thought to be in relation to the sixth-century B.C.E. phase of the sanctuary. But a more detailed reexamination of the past excavation data shows that these lion statues may not belong to the oldest layers of the sanctuary. Instead, it is more likely that these statues were carried to the sanctuary from elsewhere around the first century C.E.

As a result of the consideration of this material, this paper focuses on the secondary use of the archaic material in the sanctuary and investigates the possible causes of the display of such material in an Early Imperial context. This paper also investigates the existence of similar case studies in western Asia Minor in the same period, and more particularly explores whether a discourse that refers to the ancientness of the city Aphrodisias and its sanctuary existed in the first century C.E. In conclusion, by gathering all the available data, this paper presents different dimensions of creating a visual language that establishes the archaism of the Aphrodite cult in Aphrodisias, which was aimed to increase the prestige of the sanctuary and its city.

Comprehensive and Experiential Benefaction: Festivals, Coins, Statues, and Space
Ann M. Morgan, Trinity University

During the second century C.E., the region of Asia Minor experienced an increase in population, an influx of wealth, and frequent distributions of Roman citizenship. Because of these changes, local elites had to develop innovative tactics to establish themselves within their communities. Earlier scholarship has demonstrated that the boom in festival culture in this period was one such strategy taken up by benefactors. Gifts of this nature allowed a local patron the opportunity to put the social hierarchy, in which he received pride of place, on very public display—the procession of Salutaris in Ephesos being the most famous example.

A similar strategy is found with the mid second century benefactor, Tiberius Claudius Zelos, at Aphrodisias, who took a comprehensive and holistic approach to his euergetism. This paper examines how the specific choices that Zelos made are meaningful because in the execution of generosity, he methodically linked himself to the past of Aphrodisias and continually reiterated those links in a range of media, visually and experientially. Not only did his coins feature the most ancient cults of city, but his choice in renovation reflected his respect for Aphrodisian past. In his theater renovation, he carefully dismantled and then rearticulated the original dedicatory inscription of Aphrodisias' famed first-century B.C.E. benefactor, Gaius Julius Zoilos. Zelos' actions reveal a conscientious effort to preserve the past integrity and memory of the theater as well as one of Aphrodisias' preeminent benefactors. Zelos went a step further and had an honorotifc statue of himself set up in his newly created display space, alongside a statue of Zoilos and others.

These choices, however, were not simply viewed; they were experienced, especially through his sponsorship of the Epinikia. During this festival, Zelos' coins were distributed and Aphrodisians attended events in the very theater he had renovated and where his statue and name were prominently on display. This recursive and reiterative approach to euergetism inundates the Aphrodisian with the name, image, generosity, and importance of Tiberius Claudius Zelos. Such an extensive exposure campaign might stem from Zelos' status within the community. His family name does not appear in the surviving Aphrodisian inscriptions, nor does he include his patronym or genealogy. His benefactions were the appropriate choices for a man who existed outside of the normal social structure and without an impressive local pedigree; they allowed him the opportunity to construct his own place in Aphrodisian history and society.

"Concord Is Impossible for Your Cities": Coinage and Civic Relations in Roman Pamphylia

George C. Watson, Goethe University, Frankfurt am Main

In the speech from which the title of this paper comes (Dio Chrys. *Or*. 38), the orator addresses a crowd of citizens of Nicomedia, for whom goodwill toward the neighboring city of Nicaea is completely inconceivable. Modern historiography follows a similar path, frequently describing the constituent poleis of the Roman empire as rivals or adversaries. Coinage is often used to illustrate this narrative, as cities used their own coins as a medium for self-promotion and aggrandizement. Yet it is often overlooked that coinage also provides a counter-example, since many cities produced their coinage in collaboration with their neighbors, as attested by the occurrence of both the same obverse die and similar engraving styles at multiple cities.

This paper explores how these numismatic features can be used to investigate the relations between cities in the Roman empire. It is based on a die study of more than 6,000 coins from the region of Pamphylia and surrounding areas during the third century C.E., in which many previously unknown shared dies were discovered. I set out the networks created by the sharing of these dies and also expound a new model for the system of coin production, which clarifies the nature of intercity collaboration. I then set these numismatic networks alongside archaeological and epigraphic material to show how the same groupings are reflected in other forms of material culture, thus suggesting that certain groups of cities were collaborating with one another in various different ways. In this way a more nuanced picture of the relations between cities under the Roman empire is offered than one in which neighbors are seen to be eternally in conflict.

Honorary Statues and Cultural Identity in Roman Spain in the Second Century

Rachel L. Meyers, Iowa State University

The type of environment one lives in dramatically shapes his or her cultural identity. How he dresses, how others act, what events take place, and how the environment around him looks—these are all part of the public "fabric" that impacts cultural identity. This paper presents the initial results of a study of Roman Spain during the Antonine period. While the project as a whole aims to investigate aspects of cultural identity in the Spanish provinces during the reigns of the Antonine emperors, this paper focuses on one aspect: the dedications of statues of the imperial family. While it might seem counterintuitive to begin with the rulers when trying to understand local identity, in fact, the emperor and his family were models throughout the empire. Their images were ubiquitous, and they sent powerful messages, whether people reacted positively or negatively to them. Honorary statues were generally placed in public areas that were vital to the functioning of the town. They were dedicated by individuals or groups that not only had the financial resources to commission costly displays but also must have had influence. Thus when we look at where the statues were placed, we can understand what facilities a town had and where people spent time. Analyzing who dedicated the statues informs us about the types of groups or individuals who had the money and influence to make such dedications. Through the name or rank of an individual, aspects of his or her cultural identity are revealed. When groups—such as collegia—dedicate statues, we see what sorts of commercial activities or social groups were active in the town. Thus, a close examination of the inscribed bases and portraits can tell us about significant features about the makeup and functioning of a town.

Inscribed statue bases provide the bulk of evidence for these dedications. Fifty-three inscriptions and 12 portrait heads are analyzed with regard to the dedicator, place of dedication, time period, and impetus for the dedication. While other scholars have focused on the body of statue bases or portrait statues, no one has taken the material as a whole in an effort to document the visual representations of the Antonine family in Roman Spain. Thus this project contextualizes the material evidence within its contemporary visual landscape.

A City Built by Ladies? Exploring Agency and Identity in the Civic Landscape of Thugga in Africa Proconsularis

Allison E. Sterrett-Krause, College of Charleston

In this paper, I argue that elite women in the small city of Thugga in Africa proconsularis explored and directed their town's relationships with its own past, with Carthage, and with Rome through the act of architectural patronage. In the first and second centuries, Licinia Prisca, Maedia Lentula, and Nahania Victoria used public building donations to emphasize their local and global identities as citizens of Thugga, Africa, and Rome. In the early third century, Asicia Victoria sought to change standard patterns of civic behavior with an unusual gift of cash rather than architecture, renegotiating the relationship between the city and its donors. These women expressed their own agency and influenced the town's future choices through their acts of civic patronage.

Thugga's detailed Latin epigraphic record and well-preserved archaeological remains offer insight into the recursive processes of identity formation in the Roman world. The combination of inscriptions and their archaeological contexts provides a diachronic opportunity to examine the choices of individual donors and the ways in which existing urban landscapes and civic responses to previous donations shaped those choices. The elite women of Thugga used architectural and epigraphic clues to point first to Carthage and Rome as appropriate civic models, and then to indicate that the city needed to reconsider its ever-more-extensive practice of public construction.

By employing the established practice of architectural patronage, the elite women of Thugga continually negotiated their city's position in its regional context. Despite standing outside the traditional Roman political hierarchy, they highlighted their own significant contributions to civic life through their building donations and the inscriptions that marked them. The evidence of women's architectural patronage at Thugga suggests that elite women played a crucial and highly visible role in the creation of complex urban landscapes and civic identities in the Roman world.

Embracing Diversity Under the Roman Empire: Architecture and Architectural Ornament in Mauretania Tingitana and North Africa

Niccolò Mugnai, University of Leicester

Architectural styles and decorative motifs traveling across the Mediterranean offer a glimpse of the interconnections between different cultures in the Graeco-Roman world. Also under Roman rule, local traditions and pre-Roman legacies managed to survive and gave birth to hybrid artistic styles, which were often intertwined with the official art diffused by the centers of power. Among the various regions of the Roman empire, North Africa is a context where these phenomena are particularly evident (see N. Mugnai, J. Nikolaus and N. Ray, eds., *De Africa Romaque: Merging Cultures across North Africa* [London 2016]).

In this paper I illustrate the results of recent research on architecture and architectural ornament in the province of Mauretania Tingitana (northern Morocco), with particular focus on four urban sites: Volubilis, Banasa, Sala, and Lixus. This study encompasses a timeframe from the mid first century B.C.E. to third century C.E. The comprehensive analysis of (mostly unpublished) in situ architectural elements shows how different artistic traditions were merged together in this territory during the Roman era: the persistence of pre-Roman features inherited from the Punic, Hellenistic, and Alexandrian world; the influence of Roman official art, architecture, and decoration, which was fostered by the circulation of the so-called Romano-Carthaginian models; and the creation of peculiar, regional motifs and local-style ornament. The study is then extended to a broader extraprovincial level to identify analogous patterns in other areas of North Africa by looking at the architectural decoration of urban centers in Algeria, Tunisia, and Libya, at some monuments of the Libyan pre-desert, and beyond.

The paper also outlines how canonical architectural principles, as effectively recognized by Wilson Jones (*Principles of Roman Architecture* [New Haven and London 2000]), were adapted and altered in this province at the fringes of the Roman empire. The divergences and eccentricities in the design of the Corinthian order, especially at Volubilis, attest to the diverse background and skillsets of the local architects, stonemasons, and artisans.

The approach I adopt in this study echoes the shift in modern scholarship from old-fashioned (biased) paradigms, such as "romanization" or its opposite "resistance," to more dynamic interpretative approaches that take into account the complexity of ancient societies. In this regard, the coexistence of different architectural styles and decorative motifs in both public and private buildings of Tingitana hints toward the identification of equally mixed urban communities. All these elements clearly reveal an unexpected artistic and cultural vitality in a province so far understudied.

SESSION 3J
New Developments in Mycenaean Archaeology

CHAIR: *Joanne Murphy*, University of North Caronlina Greensboro

Mycenaean Northeastern Kopais (MYNEKO) 2016: Report of the Excavations at Aghia Marina Pyrghos, "Aghios Ioannis" and Around Glas

Elena Kountouri, Hellenic Ministry of Culture and Sports, and *Michael F. Lane*, University of Maryland Baltimore County

From 6 June until 15 July 2016, the authors collaborated on archaeological excavations at two satellite settlement sites to the Mycenaean fortress of Glas in the northeastern Kopaic Basin, central mainland Greece, as well as at selected locales in the Late Helladic polder around the fortress. The fieldwork represents the first half of a two-year project titled "MYNEKO" that furthers the aims of both codirector Kountouri's prior investigations of the Mycenaean drainage system in this part of the Kopaïs and codirector Lane's prior geophysical prospection that evidently revealed an irrigation system within the polder (AROURA, 2010–2102). MYNEKO also serves as a bridging project for both investigators better to understand changes in both the settlement pattern and structure and in socioeconomic landscapes of the region before, during, and after the construction of the drainage and irrigation systems.

Discoveries at Aghia Marina Pyrghos included three Middle Helladic infant burials and evidence of a major repurposing of the enclosure within the cyclopean circuit wall at the end of the Late Helladic IIIB, including covering the Middle Helladic cist tombs with a dense fill to create a new construction platform. Discoveries at so-called Aghios Ioannis (the Greek Army Geographical Service's misnomer, in fact Aghios Gheorghios) included looted and unlooted Middle Helladic cist tombs, as well as a Middle Helladic house, and impressive buttressed cyclopean walls internal to the equally impressive circuit wall. Discoveries in the plain around Glas further confirm and lend detail to coauthor Lane's hypothetical reconstruction of a Late Helladic irrigation system fed by gravity from artificially raised river channels, the latter the subject of Kountouri's prior investigations. The codirectors expect the results of relevant radiocarbon and micromorphological analyses in the first quarter of 2017.

The Early Mycenaean Funerary Enclosure at Ancient Eleon in Eastern Boeotia

Brendan Burke, University of Victoria, *Bryan Burns*, Wellesley College, *Alexandra Charami*, Ephorate of Antiquities of Boeotia, *Olga Kyriazi*, Ephorate of Antiquities of Boeotia, and *Nicholas P. Herrmann*, Texas State University

In 2016, the Greek-Canadian Eastern Boeotia Archaeological Project (EBAP) initiated a three-year project at ancient Eleon in central Greece to excavate and study an unusual funerary enclosure that we call the Blue Stone Structure. Excavations since 2011 at Eleon have uncovered extensive remains of a Late Helladic III settlement, a Late Archaic cult deposit, and traces of Ottoman-period occupation. In the midst of these later remains, the funerary complex of the Shaft Grave period stands remarkably well preserved beneath an artificial clay tumulus.

The Blue Stone Structure (BSS) physically separated select burials from a larger cemetery that likely began in the Middle Helladic period. Although the full perimeter is not yet revealed, the exposed walls are consistently capped with pieces of blue limestone. This architecture is currently best seen on the east side, where the building's 17 m length is marked by large orthostates at each corner. Within isolated walls and cobbled surfaces, preserved at several elevations, cover tomb shafts below. To date, we have excavated five tombs in the southern area of the BSS. Although the bone preservation is relatively poor, the tombs were used for multiple interments.

Tomb 5, excavated in 2016, now provides a dramatic example of the trends seen throughout the complex. This tomb was marked by a tall stele, which was later incorporated into the north–south wall that served as part of the structural support for the clay-brick tumulus above. Two broad capstones rested on large cut stones that made the chamber of the tomb. Contained within we found the greatest range of artifactual and osteological evidence thus far at Eleon. Commingled skeletal remains were concentrated in the southwest corner, with well-preserved grave goods. Preliminary analysis suggests the minimum number of individuals interred is more than eight, and the various ceramics primarily date to the early Late Helladic I period. On the tomb floor were the articulated remains of three additional individuals.

Although there are parallels for communal burials during this period, including other rectangular structures in central Greece, several features distinguish the BSS: The burial is monumentalized by markers and tumulus, apparently all dating to the Shaft Grave period. The construction was coordinated for individual tombs, as suggested by the shared walls. The preservation of the tumulus through later periods demonstrated respect through the palatial and postpalatial Mycenaean eras and perhaps into the Archaic period as well.

Use and Reuse in a Mycenaean Tholos: Using Radiocarbon and Bioarchaeology to Reconstruct Burial Practices at Petroto, Mygdalia

Olivia A. Jones, University of Groningen, *Johannes van der Plicht*, University of Groningen, *Lena Papazoglou-Manioudaki*, National Archaeological Museum, Athens, Greece, and *Michalis Petropoulos*, Ephorate of Antiquities of Achaia, Patras, Greece

The reuse of tombs for later burials is a characteristic feature of Mycenaean mortuary practices that has been the subject of much research in past and recent years. Initially, primary burials are often placed on the floor or within pits, while previous burials are piled up along the tomb edges or redeposited in pits. In some tholoi, the reuse was extensive and it produced multiple levels of burials. These levels are often stratigraphically confusing and may lack grave goods, making dating the reuse difficult if not impossible with traditional ceramic chronology. Additionally, the human remains interred within the tholoi are rarely studied by a bioarchaeologist, therefore it is not known if burials in tholoi may have been restricted by biological criteria such as age or sex. In this presentation, I propose to close that gap by employing radiocarbon dating and bioarchaeological analysis in order to reconstruct the burial timing and biological profiles of the individuals buried in a tholos. This data can significantly inform reconstructions of the use and reuse of Mycenaean tholoi.

The tholos of Petroto, located near the current excavation of the Mygdalia settlement in Achaia, contains eight burial levels. Petroto is a prime case study for dating multiple burial levels because the levels of use are all sequential, since later burials did not disturb previous depositions. The floor burial level has been dated by ceramic chronology to the Late Helladic IIB–IIIA1 (ca. 1480–1300 B.C.E.) and represents the initial phase of burial activity. However, the lack of grave goods in the other burial levels necessitated that a fragment of human bone from each burial level be analyzed by radiocarbon dating. Bioarchaeological methodology was employed to estimate the minimum number of individuals (MNI), age, and sex of the deceased persons within the tomb.

This article presents new radiocarbon dates and biological profiles of the human remains in the tholos and employs the results to reconstruct the timing and nature of reuse within the tomb. The results reveal that the tomb was used throughout the Mycenaean period and was the final resting place of males, females, and children of all ages. The demographic composition of the burial sample and the intervals in which Mycenaean people reopened monumental tombs to inter additional burials aids in the interpretation of complex Mycenaean mortuary practices including tomb reuse.

TAPHOS, the Tombs of Aidonia Preservation, Heritage, and Exploration Synergasia: The 2016 Excavation Season

Kim Shelton, University of California, Berkeley, *Konstantinos Kissas*, Korinthian Ephorate of Antiquities, Greek Ministry of Culture, *Lynne A. Kvapil*, Butler University, and *Gypsy C. Price*, University of Florida

We present the preliminary results of the 2016 excavation season at the Late Bronze Age cemetery of Aidonia in the southern Corinthia. These excavations are the first of a five-year systematic program following and expanding on a pilot survey (2014) and rescue excavation (2015) conducted by the TAPHOS project, a cooperative effort between the Corinthian Ephorate of Antiquities and the Nemea Center for Classical Archaeology. TAPHOS was initiated in 2014 due to the resumption and intensification of looting at Aidonia, a cemetery consisting of more than 20 multiburial chamber tombs containing material dating to the 15th to early 13th centuries B.C.E. To date, TAPHOS has revealed three distinct cemeteries (upper, middle, and lower) and looting activity occurring as recently as this past winter. This paper reports on progress toward project goals including: the systematic excavation of tombs in areas where archaeological remains are in danger; the use of artifact and ecofact data, newly recovered and legacy material, to better understand the people who used the cemetery; and the provision of future site security through outreach about the destruction of cultural heritage, and the engagement of the local population in an interactive visitor center.

First we discuss excavations in the middle cemetery with the completion of Tomb 100 (2015) and the excavation of its neighbor, Tomb 101, a Late Helladic III construction containing primary and secondary burials of adults and subadults with pottery and figurine assemblages. We next report the first systematic investigations of the lower cemetery with results from excavations of Tombs 102 and 103. Although both tombs had been previously disturbed, in situ deposits were recovered beneath these levels. Burial features present in Tomb 103 indicate transitions in mortuary practices during Late Helladic II through the combination of shaft grave and chamber tomb characteristics in construction, burial forms, and assemblages. Among the earlier primary burials is an elite group with bronze weapons, implements, and stone seals. Furthermore, our excavation reveals activity at this tomb in the Geometric and Archaic periods, possibly in connection to ancestor or hero veneration. Finally, we report the results of rescue excavations of a Late Roman cemetery, a period previously unattested at Aidonia. Altogether, these investigations add a new depth of chronological and mortuary understanding to a cemetery that has been best known for the loss of knowledge due to illicit excavation.

The Individual, the Body, and Chamber Tombs in Non-Palatial Late Bronze Age Central Greece

Kaitlyn Stiles, University of Tennessee

The concept of the "individual" is often taken for granted in archaeological contexts. In this paper I explore the role of the individual in nonpalatial Mycenaean society through a bioarchaeological study of human remains from two tombs, XVI and XXV, of the Late Bronze Age chamber tomb cemetery of Golemi Agios Georgios in East Lokris, central Greece. The Late Bronze Age individual has been investigated by Nakassis through the Linear B tablets from Pylos (*Individuals and Society in Mycenaean Pylos* [Boston 2013]). Nakassis illustrates that there were nonpalatial and potentially nonelite individuals (e.g., smiths, shepherds) who played crucial roles in the Mycenaean socioeconomic system alongside palatial elites (e.g., *wanax*, *lawagetas*). My analysis employs principles of osteobiography, which has been defined by Robb (2002) as a theoretical perspective in which the body of an individual represents a cultural narrative. The skeleton is considered to embody particular social roles and identities performed throughout life. I assume that the bodies found within each chamber tomb represent a culturally significant unit because of their physical separation from the bodies in other tombs. For practical reasons, the entire tomb group is taken as the unit of analysis because the human remains were commingled and did not allow for the individuation of complete skeletons. I first consider markers of health, activity, and trauma of individual bones that in turn inform personal identity and lived experiences. These aspects are then combined to create a broader narrative of each tomb group in terms of demography, health, and lifestyle. Finally, the two tomb groups are compared based on these biological attributes along with contextual features such as tomb size, grave goods, degree of skeletal articulation, and location of the bones. The lived experiences reflected in the skeletons of specific individuals and the relationships between individuals in the tomb partly define the group's communal identity in death. Therefore, group tomb identity is in some ways reflective of individual identity, which both, in turn, illuminate what it meant to be "Mycenaean," both socially and physically in life and death. Results of this study indicate that Tombs XVI and XXV exhibit distinct differences in terms of the types of bone present, preservation, and position of skeletons within the tomb. Biological features are generally less variable, but differences in specific markers of stress and trauma indicate variation in lifestyles between the two groups. Nonmetric traits and demography provide tentative support for familial relationships within the tombs.

The Palace of Nestor at Pylos, 2015–2016

Sharon R. Stocker, University of Cincinnati, and *Jack L. Davis*, University of Cincinnati

After a lapse of 45 years, excavations at the Palace of Nestor resumed in May 2015, the first of five anticipated campaigns sponsored by the University of Cincinnati. These new excavations followed several years of close collaboration with the Ministry of Culture of Greece, which have resulted in considerable improvements in the infrastructure of the archaeological site, including the erection of a new modern shelter over the remains of the palace itself, inaugurated in June of 2016.

In our first two seasons of excavation, focus has been on expanding our understanding of the site in times earlier than the 13th century B.C.E., particularly for the Middle Helladic and Late Helladic (LH) I–IIIA periods. Excavation on the acropolis, near the Northeast Gateway, has uncovered more of an Early Mycenaean fortification wall. In the so-called Lower Town, between Tholos Tomb IV and the Northeast Gateway, settlement deposits of the Middle Helladic period and of the earlier phases of the Late Bronze Age have been uncovered, as well as an extensive ritual deposit in front of the dromos of Tholos IV. Farther south, there have been found parts of buildings that were apparently destroyed at the same time as the palace, at the transition between LH IIIB and LH IIIC.

But of all finds, the most spectacular and unanticipated was an undisturbed Early Mycenaean built tomb containing the burial of a single male warrior, accompanied by a staggeringly large number of grave goods, manufactured of gold, silver, ivory, bronze, and semiprecious gemstones. The warrior was buried in a wooden coffin at the bottom of a stone-lined shaft cut into the bedrock. To his left lay a sword and a dagger, both with hilts decorated in a rare technique known as gold embroidery. In addition to many stone beads and a bronze mirror with an ivory handle, the grave contained more than 50 hard-stone seals, the largest number yet found associated with a single Mycenaean or Minoan burial, and four gold signet rings with scenes of Minoan cult. The rings will be fully illustrated in this presentation.

A Tale of Two Citadels: A Comparison of Landscape Stability at Postpalatial and Early Iron Age Tiryns and Mycenae, Greece

Daniel J. Fallu, Boston University

Although still debated, and awaiting more precise dating control to understand causation, the sudden accumulation of sediments during the Late Neolithic and Early Bronze Age is often attributed to erosion caused by advances in agricultural technology and the extent of slope exploitation. Contrarily, the so-called Great Flood at Late Helladic Tiryns has been portrayed as a singular event, unique in the alluvial history of the region and contributing to the destruction of the palace. Recent excavations by the German Archaeological Institute; however, suggest that this was not a singular "flash flood," and likely predated the destruction of the palace. Current sedimentological and micromorphological analyses at the lower town excavations at both Tiryns (ca. 20 masl) in the plain and Mycenae (ca. 260 masl, excavated by Dickinson College) in the northern Argolid suggest that the Late Helladic IIIB alluviation over the lower town at Tiryns was not an isolated event, but rather an early event in a period of increased instability across the Agolid.

At Tiryns, micromorphological analysis of the sediments separating the Late Helladic and Early Iron Age remains suggests that the nearby dam did not completely curb accumulation at the site, resulting in 20–40 cm of overbank alluvium. The deposition of these sediments corresponds broadly with the deposition of 1.5–2 m of debris flows over the "Lower Town" of Mycenae (studied 2013–2015). When this is combined with OSL evidence at Mycenae for an Early Holocene disturbance predating the development of the Bronze Age slope soils that bury the Mycenaean remains, a picture of general long-term stability arises, punctuated by slope loss and alluviation after the end of the Palace period. The observation of this punctuated equilibrium suggests that Mycenaean landscape engineering, including the "recently" built dam at Tiryns and presumed soil and water management systems in the area around Mycenae, was not completely effective in curbing soil loss and alluviation. The combination of micromorphological and sedimentological evidence at these two important sites calls into question the timing and causation of such major sedimentary events and suggests that the environment in the Argolid was more complex than previously suggested, likely suffering from increased seasonality and aridity. Continued research into the sedimentary history of this important region is hoped to help understand the interplay of disaster and resilience in the aftermath of the palatial collapse.

Mt. Lykaion Excavation and Survey Project, Summer Season 2016

David Gilman Romano, University of Arizona, *Mary E. Voyatzis*, University of Arizona, and *Anna Karapanagiotou*, Arcadian Ephorate of Antiquities, Tripolis

During the summer of 2016 renewed excavation at the Sanctuary of Zeus at Mt. Lykaion in Arcadia produced exciting new discoveries. The Mt. Lykaion Excavation and Survey Project is a synergasia between the Arcadian Ephorate of Antiquities of the Ministry of Culture and Sport and the University of Arizona, under the auspices of the American School of Classical Studies at Athens. The directors are Anna Karapanagiotou of the Arcadian Ephorate and David Gilman Romano and Mary E. Voyatzis of the University of Arizona.

At the ash altar of Zeus, near the center of the southern peak of the mountain and close to a man-made platform of stones, a stunning discovery was made this season: a simple human burial was uncovered inside the sacrificial altar, within a border of fieldstones on the long sides, and with an east–west orientation. The length of the stones is 1.52 m. Preliminary analysis of the burial indicates that it is of an adolescent male. Associated ceramics found with the skeleton suggest a date of the 11th century B.C.E., after the collapse of the Mycenaean palaces at the time of transition from the end of the Late Bronze Age to the Early Iron Age. Scientific analyses of the bones will begin immediately. Although it is premature to speculate on the nature of the death, the prominent location of the burial within the sacrificial altar and its east–west orientation indicate its significance. Several ancient literary sources mention rumors that human sacrifice took place at the altar, but up until now there has been no trace whatsoever of human bones discovered at the site.

New discoveries were also made in the lower sanctuary. Some of the highlights include an impressive stone staircase at the top of the fourth-century B.C.E. corridor, and a large stone archway at the other end, presumably through which athletes would have descended toward the hippodrome and stadium. In the Administrative Building, a large, decorated terracotta sima block was uncovered. In addition, within a large circular depression visible from Google Earth, excavations revealed two well-preserved water channels, a stone water basin, and the beginning of a stone wall, perhaps to be associated with the Sanctuary of Pan. Within the hippodrome, the only visible example in the Greek world, a section of the racecourse floor was exposed. Excavations in the area of the fourth-century bath facility has also revealed walls from earlier phases.

SESSION 3K: Workshop
Balancing Archaeological Fieldwork and Family Life

MODERATORS: *Gretchen E. Meyers*, Franklin & Marshall College

Workshop Overview Statement

Fieldwork and field-based research are integral components of an archaeologist's scholarship and academic program. It is not uncommon for archaeologists to spend many weeks each year at sites and museums far from home. While certainly rewarding, this type of research travel, which is often necessary for the advancement of academic careers in archaeology, can also pose significant challenges for an archaeologist's home life and parenting. Despite an increase of overall attention in the academy to issues of work-life balance, this particular professional concern does not generate much public discussion. For early-career archaeologists it can be daunting to even find examples of how peers manage to arrange fieldwork around family and parenting commitments. This workshop is a forum for scholars at all stages of an archaeological career to discuss and share experiences and strategies for the management of family life while maintaining an active archaeological research agenda in the field.

The workshop's moderator has recently completed an interdisciplinary study that surveyed more than 500 respondents in more than 15 academic fields about balancing an active field research program with family and parenting commitments. A short summary of data from this study serves as the workshop's starting point. A multigenerational panel of male and female archaeologists—all of whom have worked during their careers at sites throughout the Mediterranean while simultaneously balancing family commitments—will respond to the data and offer their own diverse perspectives. Particular topics to be discussed include making the decision about leaving children and family members at home or bringing them into the field, the challenges and rewards of both of these options, childcare options at home and abroad, safety, financial implications, and potential impacts on both one's scholarly productivity and family decisions. Significant time will be allotted to engage audience members as participants in a wider discussion in order to enhance the views presented and highlight additional issues. A final goal of the workshop is to foster networks of professional and peer support and formulate methods for professional organizations and home campuses to serve scholars grappling with this type of work-life balance.

PANELISTS: *Rebecca Ammerman*, Colgate University, *Sarah Costello*, University of Houston-Clear Lake, *Kevin Daly*, Bucknell University, *Stephanie Larson*, Bucknell University, *Molly Swetnam-Burland*, College of William and Mary, *Anthony Tuck*, University of Massachusetts-Amherst, and *Mary E. Voyatzis*, University of Arizona

SESSION 4A
Ceramics

CHAIR: *Kathleen M. Lynch*, University of Cincinnati

Did Mycenaeans Wash Their Hands? A Functional Analysis of Late Helladic IIIC Kalathoi

Trevor Van Damme, Cotsen Institute of Archaeology, UCLA, and *Bartłomiej Lis*, Polish Academy of Sciences

The Mycenaean kalathos (Furumark shape 291) is a rare Late Helladic (LH) IIIC vessel type. It constitutes only a very minor part of household assemblages at that time—British excavations at Xeropolis (Lefkandi) during the 1960s yielded only two mendable examples. The shape appears to have been more popular in funerary contexts, however, and the Perati cemetery produced 46 examples. The discovery of numerous examples in LH IIIC settlement levels at ancient Eleon therefore came as a surprise and still constitutes an intriguing puzzle. To date, 18 kalathoi preserving more than a single sherd have been inventoried, and this number grows with each season. On account of the abundance of the shape at Eleon, we realized that the function of kalathoi has never been properly addressed, despite its clearly specialized shape and often elaborate internal decoration.

In order to shed more light on that aspect, we consider the origins and development of the shape from metal prototypes, traces of use visible on the surfaces of the vessels, and the contexts of their discovery. Our analysis focuses on the catalogued vessels from ancient Eleon, but we extend our discussion to consider kalathoi from contemporary settlements, such as Xeropolis (Lefkandi), Mycenae, Tiryns, and Athens, as well as the cemetery at Perati. We also consider the evidence of contemporary Cretan kalathoi and their better established function as braziers, possibly for the burning of incense in cult spaces.

The results from our initial study are telling. The earliest LH IIIC kalathoi display distinct use-wear marks indicative of scooping action, but later kalathoi, with larger rim diameters, elaborate decoration, and increasingly concave profiles preserve no evidence for such use-wear or any internal marks common on shapes used as vessels for dining or mixing that sustained regular abrasion from utensils used in stirring, cutting, or ladling. While the lack of abrasion suggests a liquid storage function, the tendency of kalathoi to feature pictorial decoration on their interiors adds a second layer of complexity to their function and limits the possibilities for what liquid this could be. Based on a careful analysis of all available sources of evidence, we argue that the most likely use of kalathoi in the Postpalatial period was as a vessel for water, in particular, wash water used for cleansing the hands and, in the case of funerary contexts, very likely the cleansing of the corpse as well.

New Pottery Assemblage from a Late Archaic Fill from Thasos

Martin Perron, Maison de l'Orient et de la Méditerranée, Lyon, and *Anne Tichit*, Université Paris Sorbonne

From 2010 to 2013, the French School at Athens has undertaken excavations in Thasos in an area located north of the Sanctuary of Artemis at the hearth of the ancient Parian colony. Located a few dozen meters west of the 1960s Paul Bernard survey, the excavations have delivered the remains of the last occupation phase of a large tripartite building of pastas type and a thick fill overlaying its destruction level dated to the last quarter of the sixth century B.C.E. This fill, whose most recent artifacts can be dated to the end of the first quarter of the fifth century B.C.E., has delivered more than 1,000 kg of archaic pottery, among which can be counted local productions, imports from the main production centers of the Aegean world as well as north Aegean imitations of Attic, Cycladic, Corinthian, and East Greek vessels. The unusual aspect about this fill is the striking chronological homogeneity of the assemblage, which dates exclusively from the turn of the sixth and fifth centuries B.C.E. to ca. 480 B.C.E. This narrow chronological span provides an unusual opportunity to date more accurately some of the coarse, domestic, and cooking ware, transport amphoras, loomweights and other finds not so well documented in Thasos and the north Aegean, and to become a reference tool for the identification of Late Archaic pottery found on the north Aegean coast. The publication of this assemblage will also provide an opportunity to enhance our knowledge on the trading networks in which Thasos participated and on the influences exerted by the main Aegean workshops on the local Thasian pottery production.

Ceramic Types and Wealth Distributions in the Classical Greek House

Grace Erny, Stanford University

Archaeological approaches to the Greek house have a long and complex history. As Nevett observes, Greek archaeologists of the 19th and early 20th centuries were often more interested in finding connections between the archaeological remains of houses and ancient literary references than in using the archaeological material to understand broader economic and social questions. Although the field of Greek domestic archaeology has now expanded considerably, quantitative approaches to data from Greek houses have not yet been widely adopted. In this paper, I compile and analyze ceramic data from the site of Olynthus in northern Greece, where more than 100 classical houses were excavated in the 1920s and 1930s. Like many classical cities, Olynthus was founded on an orthogonal plan, an arrangement that tends to result in similar house sizes. Such similarities have often been interpreted as a physical manifestation of ideas of citizenship in the Classical period. I explore how the outward appearance of equality projected by grid-planned houses accords with the ceramic finds from the houses at Olynthus. In particular, I investigate how the diversity of ceramic types within houses can be used to assess distribution of wealth and economic inequality in the Olynthian community.

Although Olynthus provides a large sample size of houses to work with, only complete or nearly complete ceramic vessels were included in the final publications. To address this issue, I use comparative evidence from six houses excavated at the Hellenistic city of New Halos, where domestic ceramic assemblages were recorded more comprehensively. I then test whether the frequency distribution of number of ceramic types per house at Olynthus fits a log-normal distribution, a common shape for frequency distributions of economic variables (including individual wealth and income). Finally, I examine whether houses at Olynthus with androns, or rooms for sympotic activity, have a significantly higher diversity of ceramic types than houses without androns. I demonstrate that such statistical methods are valuable tools for evaluating wealth distributions at ancient sites and can be productively applied even to data that were not collected in accordance with modern archaeological standards.

The Hellenistic "Koine" as a Linguistic, Cultural, and Ceramic Concept
Alexandros Laftsidis, University of Cincinnati

The conquests of Alexander created an expanded, politically unified space, where the movement of people, products, and ideas took place much more easily than before. To facilitate governance of the vast and ethnically diversified Hellenistic kingdoms, a linguistic device was introduced in the beginning of the Hellenistic period, the so-called Koine Greek dialect. In form, this language was nothing more than a simplification of the Attic dialect including elements from the rest of the major Greek dialects. Common cultural elements among the Hellenistic world, however, were not confined only to language. In fact, several scholars, including Stella Drougou and Konstantina Gravani, have argued for a "koine" ceramic language characterized by the common appearance of pottery shapes, production methods, and decorative techniques throughout the Hellenistic world. In this paper I argue that language Koine and ceramic "koine" are not parallel phenomena, even though they arise from similar political and cultural developments.

The paper examines the linguistic and ceramic koinai as they developed over time in order to understand better their origins and cultural relevance. Koine Greek, in particular, was used in new and different contexts than existing dialects and was originally imposed from the political administration on the people living in the Hellenistic world, since it comprised the official language of the newly formed kingdoms. In contrast, the ceramic "koine" represents a more or less bottom-to-top process, reflecting an active and unconstrained engagement of common people sharing a global cultural identity, often infused with local traits. This element distinguishes these two phenomena and obliges us to look for an alternative term to describe this common ceramic language. Similar concerns are raised by the ancient commentator on Dionysius the Thrax; speaking of Koine Greek, he argues that it should be better described as "μικτή" (= mixed) rather than "koine," since it shared elements from four separate dialects, including Attic. Hence, "common, mixed ceramic language" might describe more efficiently the phenomenon, since it connotes a process of cultural exchange with all parts contributing.

Understanding Ancient Trade, Agency, and Social Change: An Examination of Thracian Encounters with "Greek Colonists"

Ashlee Hart, University at Buffalo

Trade across the Mediterranean is well documented in the archaeological record throughout the Iron Age. The examination of these trade relationships effects on indigenous identity is less understood than the mere existence of trade between foreign lands. The establishment of Greek trading centers called *emporia* in Thrace between the seventh and second centuries B.C.E. has traditionally been evidence for colonialism during that time. Several archaeological excavations in Thrace present a unique colonial perspective and allow an analysis of indigenous social change and agency. On a large scale, the examination of inscriptions, architecture, and cult practices across the region of ancient Thrace show a unique colonial interaction that involved a two-way exchange of ideas, cultures, objects, and people. On a smaller scale, at the inland *emporion* called Pistiros, archaeological analysis of technological choice in ceramics over time reveals that agency was present at the site and that social identity changed based on Greek interactions. I present the preliminary results from a study of ceramics that were collected over the past three years, which show the changing identity and social associations of people living at the inland emporia. I conclude that the Thracian indigenous population had agency in their decision to exchange goods with the Greeks as well as in their ceramic technological choice. For the lack of a better word, "colonialism" creates interactions between individuals, material objects, and ideas. The collision of such things may lead to conflict, resistance, or cohesion in all aspects of human life. Colonial imperialism did not impact Thracian culture, but the movement of Greek-speaking people into Thrace did impact elements of Thracian culture.

Portuguese Coarse Ware in North Atlantic (16th– to 18th-Centuries)

Tania Manuel Casimiro, NOVA University of Lisbon, and *Sarah Newstead*, University of Leicester

The project is the first analysis of Portuguese coarse ware ceramics exported around the North Atlantic. This ceramic type was produced in Portugal and exported in large quantities to England, Ireland, and the English colonies. There is a serious paucity of research addressing production, export, consumption, and identification characteristics. The project records the occurrence of Portuguese coarse ware on archaeological sites, tracing these ceramics back to Portugal through the study of coarse ware production zones in the country by ICP (inductively coupled plasma mass spectrometry) elemental analysis and visual analysis. Through the incorporation of documentary research, important information is revealed about the role of Portuguese commodities in early modern Anglo households and the dynamic socioeconomic relationships between Portugal, the British Isles, and North America during this period of global expansion.

SESSION 4B
Trade, Movement, and Connectivity in the Roman World

CHAIR: To be announced

Theoretical Approaches to the Terra Sigillata at Gabii: Evidence of the Augustan Period

Matthew Harder, University of Missouri

Recently scholars have afforded more attention to theoretical frameworks and their capacity to analyze or clarify archaeological and historical processes. Specifically, as proposed by Van Oyen the actor-network theory (ANT), agency theory, and an agglutinative economic model can provide a theoretical platform for the posing of hypotheses about production and consumption patterns. This paper argues that the above three concepts constitute a conceptual tool for the analysis and contextualization of the terra sigillata assemblage at Gabii. Terra Sigillata production began ca. 30 B.C.E., with production peaking from ca. 20 B.C.E. to 15 C.E. Literary and archaeological sources attest to a city at Gabii by at least the sixth century B.C.E. Around the second century B.C.E. the city boasted a theater-temple complex as well as a large public building near the Via Praenestina. While the information collected thus far from the Gabii Project suggests that Gabii did not simply collapse after the alleged Tarquinian maneuvering, information gleaned from proper analysis of the terra sigillata assemblage may indicate that the city underwent a more gradual decline into the Imperial period. Furthermore, the information from Oxé, Comfort, and Kenrick poses the questions: Where did the Gabines acquire their terra sigillata? What transport networks did the Gabines tap into to acquire their terra sigillata? It is proposed here that through application of the aforementioned concepts (ANT, agency theory) with the associated production contexts derived from the terra sigillata stamps, a more nuanced picture of Late Republican/Early Imperial Gabii, and perhaps even Latium, may emerge.

Roman Brickstamps in the Carthage National Museum, Tunisia

Jeremy Rossiter, University of Alberta

The store-rooms of the Carthage National Museum in Tunisia contain a collection of almost 100 Roman brickstamps recovered during the last century and a half from sites in and around Carthage. The only systematic publication of these was done in 1904 by Schmidt, Cagnat, and Dessau in *CIL* (Corpus Inscriptionum Latinarum), now available online at Arachne. During three recent visits to Tunisia, the latest in May 2016, I had the opportunity to reexamine this collection of brickstamps in the Carthage National Museum, and this paper offers a preliminary report on my findings. The collection in its current form contains many of the brickstamps recorded in *CIL* but also a number of brickstamps that are not included in that earlier publication. The paper comments on the variety and origin of the Roman brickstamps found at Carthage, many of which indicate manufacture at brickyards in Italy, and discusses their value as evidence for the Mediterranean trade in ceramic building materials during the Early Roman empire. It questions the argument made recently by Philip Mills (*The Ancient Mediterranean Trade in Ceramic Building Materials* [Oxford 2013]) that bricks were shipped into Roman Africa as a regular traded cargo rather than as ballast in returning grain ships.

Meat Merchants of the Roman Mediterranean: Considering Faunal Evidence from Shipwrecks

Carrie A. Fulton, University of Toronto

During the excavation of a first-century B.C.E. shipwreck in the Bay of Cavalière, France, researchers uncovered wine-filled amphoras, several pieces of Campanian ceramics, ballast stones, and more than 10 kg of pig bones. Lacking bones of the vertebrae and feet, these remains indicated the pigs had been systematically butchered, quartered, and packed for transport. While this shipwreck at Cavalière is remarkable in the quantity of butchered pork it was carrying, it is not the only ship that was transporting meat. Using evidence from first-century B.C.E. and first-century C.E. shipwrecks in the western Mediterranean alongside literary and epigraphic attestations of merchants, I argue that meat was traded over long distances and was also a component of a sailor's diet, not just reserved for elite consumption.

In prior research, the trade of meat over long distances has been unnoticed, focusing on the acquisition of meat and animals in local markets. For example, epigraphic and iconographic evidence attests to the butchers (*lanii*) and traders in meat (*macellarii*) who would be found in local markets. While scholars use this to argue for a local and regional supply of meat, the Roman author Varro and the Greek geographer Strabo mention that pork was also imported from Gaul and Hispania. Indeed, three shipwrecks from the first century B.C.E. and first century C.E. have preserved evidence for long-distance trade; the butchered remains of pigs, sheep, and cattle were shipped alongside wine- and olive-filled amphoras, Campanian pottery, and various other sundries. These ships were likely headed to ports along the Mediterranean coastline of modern-day Spain, France, and Italy.

In addition to long-distance trade in meat, faunal remains from five additional shipwrecks attest to the consumption of meat by sailors. Recent zooarchaeological and osteological analyses have highlighted that meat was consumed as part of the Roman diet more frequently than previously thought. Considering evidence from shipwrecks presents us with a glimpse into the consumption practices of a specific group of individuals: sailors. For example, pig bones with incised markings found among a first-century B.C.E. shipwreck at Fourmigue, France, show that meat was consumed aboard by sailors, a group of individuals who are often stereotyped as occupying the lower echelons of society. Consequently, faunal evidence from shipwrecks provides a slightly different view of meat consumption in the western part of the Roman Mediterranean; it showcases dietary practices for nonelite and illuminates an area of trade that has previously been ignored.

Roman Imperial Maritime Connectivity in Central Dalmatia

Nicholas Bartos, AIA Member at Large

Maritime networks defined the socioeconomic interactions of Roman Imperial coastal communities in central Dalmatia. Located in the center of the Mediterranean basin, central Dalmatia was at the confluence of numerous multidirectional regional and interregional maritime routes. The unique coastal geography of the region with its many islands and narrow channels created a dynamic ancient sailing environment that both reinforced and complicated maritime connectivity. Little scholarly attention has been paid to exactly how these ancient sailing conditions influenced central Dalmatian maritime networks and contributed to the sociopolitical makeup of the area during the Roman Imperial period, particularly on a local level.

Incorporating a wide range of sources including modern and historical nautical pilot guides and charts, interviews with local sailors, as well as firsthand sailing and archaeological fieldwork, archaeological reports, and ancient sources, this paper presents a model for central Dalmatian maritime interaction. It suggests that the natural geography and Roman Imperial sailing environment contributed to the formation of discrete coastscapes, constrained maritime spaces containing port and anchorage sites of various sizes. Multiscalar networks overlapped across these coastscapes, and connectivity was structured by relations within and between them. The case study illustrates the utility of a seaman's perspective to understanding socioeconomic interaction and serves as an example of the complexity of the maritime cultural landscape of the Roman Imperial Mediterranean.

No City Is an Island: The Impact of Natural and Constructed Features on Cities of Late Antique Thracia

M.W. Fraser Reed, University of Edinburgh

Although the study of late antiquity has experienced a great deal of growth in recent years, there is still relatively little attention given to the economically and strategically important provinces of central and southern Thrace. Most previous studies of urbanism in the eastern Balkans have focused on the Danubian frontier area, particularly due to the influence of the excavations at Nicopolis ad Istrum. These studies, however, are inherently shaped by the heavily militarized nature of the *limes* and its direct opposition to external threats to the empire; such factors cannot be assumed for cities located in the non-riparian provinces south of the Stara Planina.

Consequently, this paper analyzes the position of three Thracian cities in the landscape and their integration into established networks. Specifically, it considers the inland cities of Philippopolis, Augusta Traiana/Beroe, and Diocletianopolis and their surrounding territory. This territory, which encompassed most of the Late Antique province of Thracia, included much of the fertile Upper Thracian Plain but was also bounded to the north and west by the Stara Planina and to the south by the Rhodope Mountains. Furthermore, the cities of Thracia were positioned on major roads, such as the Via Militaris, or on rivers, such as the Maritsa—both of which serve as effective transportation vectors. The province was not, however, densely urbanized in the same manner as most other areas in the east, resulting in the prevalence of smaller settlements alongside the major cities. Thus, the cities of Thracia had many factors affecting how they used their surroundings for defense, industry, trade, and communication.

The result of this analysis is a reevaluation of the relationship between the cities of Thracia and the natural and constructed features of their surroundings. It demonstrates that the development of cities was influenced by geography, such as the establishment of Diocletianopolis as a major military center at the east end of the Sredna Gora range. It also reveals how the influence of the urban centers extended far beyond their intramural area. The scarcity of rural monasteries in Thracia, for example, is presented as a result of the prominence and continuity of the urban centers. Finally, this paper also contributes to a better understanding of an underrepresented region of the Late Roman empire, for which many of the previous studies are limited to individual sites.

The Island Landscapes of the Taşucu Gulf (Turkey) and Its Hinterland

Gunder Varinlioglu, Mimar Sinan Fine Arts University

The island landscapes of the Taşucu Gulf in Isauria/Rough Cilicia (southern Turkey) provide unusually rich material evidence to model inhabitation and connectivity in the *longue durée* of antiquity and the Middle Ages. This maritime environment comprises an archipelago of four small islands (0.4–266 ha), which were strategically situated less than 3 km off the topographically rough coastlands. Their architectural and archaeological remains indicate occupation and inhabitation particularly during the Roman, Late Antique, and possibly Medieval periods. Alongside the anchorages and small ports on the opposite mainland, the islands served the maritime traffic by providing repair, lodging, bathing, provisioning, as well as commercial, religious, and numerous other services demanded by marine travelers.

Building activity along these sea routes throughout late antiquity was associated with the successful maritime activity, for which there were two fundamental catalyzing factors in the fourth–ninth centuries C.E.: the foundation of Constantinople as the capital of the Eastern Roman empire, and the increasing popularity of pilgrimage to the Holy Land. The establishment of St. Thecla as a major pilgrimage center, in the outskirts of the Isaurian capital of Seleucia ad Calycadnum, must have led to the formation of a vibrant pilgrimage landscape in the Taşucu Gulf. Indeed, while the islands were sporadically, and perhaps only seasonally, utilized before the fourth century C.E., after this time they were transformed into densely built, permanent settlements and nodes of maritime activity.

Boğsak, the easternmost island of the Taşucu Gulf, has been the main case study of the Boğsak Archaeological Survey (BOGA, 2010–present), under the author's direction. This small (ca. 7 ha), arid, and rocky island was the site of a sizeable Christian settlement in the fourth–eighth centuries C.E. Identified as ancient Asteria by an inscription, it has stone masonry structures with residential, commercial, and utilitarian functions; cisterns and drainage systems; quays and piers for maritime navigation; extensive cemeteries; and seven churches decorated with mosaics and polychrome imported marble.

This paper presents the results of BOGA's investigations in the framework of the vibrant maritime activity facilitated by the inhabitation of the islands in the Taşucu Gulf. In addition, the coastlands, possessing seasonal streams and arable fields, and the mountainous hinterland exploited for oleoculture, viticulture, dry farming, forestry, and pastoralism, set the context for interpreting why and how the previously vacant or underused islands have become attractive sites for habitation in late antiquity and beyond.

SESSION 4C
The Imperial Age of Greece

CHAIR: To be announced

Roman Power, Athenian Past: The Temple of Roma and Augustus on the Athenian Acropolis

Mary-Evelyn Farrior, Columbia University

The Temple of Roma and Augustus was a small, circular temple on the eastern edge of the Athenian Acropolis. Constructed ca. 19 B.C.E., it was the final significant architectural addition to the Acropolis in antiquity, as well as the first and only monument to an imperial cult on the mount. Scholarship on the temple, while noting physical similarities to monuments of the Periclean Acropolis, fails to recognize fully the ideological significance of its design. This paper demonstrates how the architecture and context of this unprecedented temple emphasizes the structure's role as both victory monument and site of ruler and civic cult.

After a brief overview of the historical and archaeological evidence of the monument, the paper proceeds in three parts to analyze the temple's context, architectural layout, and ornamentation. First, I consider the temple's location on the Acropolis and how its positioning in front of the Parthenon gave the small temple religious prominence while also connecting Augustus' Parthian settlement with Athens' success in the Persian Wars. Second, I demonstrate that the temple's circular design, which was uncommon in Athens, evoked the Philippeon at Olympia rather than, as others have argued, the hypothetical temple to Mars Ultor portrayed on coins. Third, I show that the ornamentation of the temple, particularly its Ionic capitals, created a direct association with the Erechtheion. This association extended beyond design and into the function of these structures as centers for the worship of civic and ruler deities on the Acropolis.

By erecting this structure, the Athenians conveyed a commitment to Augustus that they did not share with any other Roman leader of the past. While the Temple of Roma and Augustus had no precedent in Athens, the Athenians looked to their own past to provide it with meaning.

Measuring (Down) the Gods: Scale in Athenian Ideal Statuary of the Roman Period

Brian A. Martens, University of Oxford

The depots of the Athenian Agora hold more than 3,700 marble sculptures, the large majority of which is figural. Most of these pieces were excavated from secondary contexts, and few were displayed in the square, itself, as a long history of post-Antique occupation at this urban site has resulted in the importation of many pieces from elsewhere. Yet, despite the frequent loss of primary contexts, the Agora offers unique opportunities for the study of ancient sculpture. Most notably, the excavations have unearthed a cross-section of Athenian sculptural production from the sixth century B.C.E. to at least the fifth century C.E., not to mention a rich Byzantine and Ottoman inheritance. The Agora is one of only a few sites in the eastern Mediterranean with an assemblage from which we can trace changes and continuities in Greek sculptural habits for over a millennium.

In this paper, I present recent and ongoing research of the Athenian Agora's ideal statuary of the Roman period (ca. first century B.C.E. to fourth century C.E.). Based on general proportions, I have reconstructed original heights for the site's often fragmented freestanding statuary of gods, goddesses, and other mythological figures. Although proportions are not fixed—they vary according to time or workmanship—broad patterns emerge from estimating what is now missing. My research has isolated a discrete class of marble divine images standing about one-third life-size, with a marked preference for statuettes around 20–40 cm in height. Although it appears from the surviving evidence that distinct terms for statues of various sizes were not used in antiquity, close study of the Agora material suggests functional differences for statuettes, a class of portable and highly versatile artworks. Moreover, the diachronic view offered by the Agora assemblage shows that within the wider context of production from the Archaic to Late Roman times, marble divine figures of this size were almost exclusively works of the Roman period. Their numbers are probably too large for the inhabitants of Athens alone and might point, in part, to an export market.

The Trickle-Down Effect: Private Water-Displays of Hadrian and Herodes Atticus

Dylan K. Rogers, American School of Classical Studies at Athens

The relationship between the emperor Hadrian and the Greek sophist, Herodes Atticus, is well known and appreciated in modern scholarship. Both figures were unique for their time, especially forging links between Italy and Greece. While Hadrian was a philhellene, who visited Greece a few times and made benefactions there, Herodes was an individual that crafted for himself, through his own ancestry and that of his Roman-born wife, Regilla, a bicultural identity. In order to explore this relationship further, this paper examines the privately built structures of these two figures: Villa Adriana (Tivoli, Italy) and the Villa of Herodes Atticus at Loukou (Arcadia, Greece), the latter of which was excavated between 1979–2002.

While there are numerous similarities in design, the focus of this paper is the water displays used in both contexts. While Villa Adriana is much studied and visited, the Villa of Herodes Atticus is less known and less understood. There were similarities, however, in the use of fountains among the two villa structures, especially in large, open-air spaces (e.g., courtyards), gardens, and dining spaces. This paper not only illustrates the most important fountains in each setting but also attempts to understand better why Herodes Atticus chose these specific water displays. What becomes clear is the influence of Italian villa architecture at Loukou, and how Herodes promoted his own Roman identity through the villa. The placement of Herodes' villa near the Gulf of Astros, in addition to this well-watered valley of Arcadia, created a villa marittima similar to those of the Italian peninsula. This examination of water displays in two different contexts of two prominent individuals of the second century C.E. allows for a greater understanding of the creation of a bicultural identity, in addition to illustrating the ways in which water was displayed throughout the Roman empire in luxurious private contexts.

Roman Caryatids at Ancient Corinth

Aileen Ajootian, University of Mississippi

More than 100 years of excavation at ancient Corinth have produced quantities of Roman sculpture unusual or unique in the province of Achaia. A group of rare Roman marble capitals spans the gap between architecture and sculpture. Discovered in deposits of broken, burned marbles near the Sacred Spring in the central Forum and in a trench just east of the Theater and Odeion, these capitals were carved in the shape of woven wicker baskets, kalathoi, wider at the top and tapering toward the bottom, bound with braided straps. There are probably four separate examples, perhaps more, in at least two scales, carved by several hands. Deep cuttings for dowels on the top surfaces of two abaci reveal that the capitals supported an epistyle. But no lower ends of the capitals survive.

One basket fragment preserves locks of hair at its broken edge, suggesting that caryatids, not columns, supported the kalathoi. There are few parallels for this format. Two Silenoi bearing baskets set up along the Canopus at Hadrian's Villa are the best-preserved examples. A head of Erechtheum caryatid type supporting a basket was discovered in Rome, but lacks an ancient context. At Corinth, a life-sized female head (S 1887) discovered at the east end of the South Stoa in Byzantine levels preserves anathyrosis and a large dowel cutting on top for the addition of another piece. It is unlikely that this carefully worked surface was prepared just for the missing top of the head. It may instead have received a capital and is all that remains of a Roman caryatid supporting one of the kalathos capitals.

As for dating the head (and the kalathoi), the sharp modeling of the surviving eye and crisp treatment of locks pulled back from a central part places it in the second century C.E. The deposits that produced the capitals also yielded quantities of burned marble female drapery, fragmentary limbs, and faces, so it is possible that additional material from this monument can be identified. Finally, what was the original setting and meaning of these unusual architectural supports? The evidence is slim, but the group of caryatids might have supported the entablature of a propylon somewhere in the central Forum. The kalathoi may refer to a cult or were significant attributes identifying the caryatids as personifications.

The Lechaion Harbor and Settlement Land Project: Season One

Paul D. Scotton, California State University, Long Beach, and *Constantinos Kissas*, Ephorate of Antiquities of Corinth

The first season of the Lechaion Harbor and Settlement Land Project has produced significant results. This synergaseia between the American School of Classical Studies and the Ephorate of Antiquities of Corinth was established to better understand the geomorphological formation of the site, to determine the parameters of the harbor and settlement both spatially and temporally, to excavate three known structures to test whether orientation may be used as a means to determine approximate chronologies, and to try to determine why the site was abandoned in the sixth century C.E.

Preliminary geomorphological studies have found significant deposits of sand and gravel to the south of the entrance channel. The origin of all these deposits is not yet clear. Some are certainly man-made construction fills. But there are others that appear to be wash from a tsunami. Similarly, it has been theorized that the inner harbor was filled by the same tsunami. The surface, however, with visible bank erosion and fallen stone would suggest at least some natural sedimentation. Whether or not this is true for the entire fill requires further studies.

Geoprospection of an area in excess of four hectares has revealed an area dense with structures and roads in the central area, parallel structures to the south of the inner harbor, and a large structure on the west of the inner harbor of a very different orientation, near a long, straight retaining wall of the inner harbor.

The excavation of three structures, all of different orientations, began. Two of the three, A and B, are in use during the same period, fifth century C.E. In A, however, ceramic outliers of Geometric, Protocorinthian, and Archaic periods indicate a much earlier presence at the harbor than historically documented and the likely nearby presence of a much earlier structure. Area B produced in a small area a significant number of coins and an iron lock. These and multiple fragments of storage vessels suggest a commercial structure. Structure C is a basilica. Aerial survey and satellite imagery indicated an apse that was confirmed by geoprospection. As an apsidal basilica, it was assumed to be a Christian basilica, fourth to fifth century in date. Excavation of its foundations indicate, however, that it dates to the first and into the second century C.E. and therefore must be a civic building. Geoprospection reveals another apsidal building below it that cannot be any earlier than first century C.E.

Fishing for Compliments: A Sculpted Base from Omega House above the Athenian Agora

Barbara Tsakirgis, Vanderbilt University

Throughout classical antiquity, fish was a luxury food. Serving both marine and lake fish to guests was a time-honored method of being recognized as a generous and cultured host. The presence of seafood was desirable, and its absence was lamentable; Aristophanes and other playwrights of Old Comedy decry the deprivations wrought by the Peloponnesian Wars, in particular in the diminished supply of fish.

Because of the desirability of fish at dinner, sea creatures not only appeared on the table but also had a starring role in interior domestic decoration. Scenes of fish, fishing, and the sea abound in floor mosaics and vase paintings. While the scenes of many of the mosaics and vases played with the trope of the drinker as sailor and the symposium at sea, the denizens of the sea frequently find themselves in a starring role. This focus on fish was as true in the Roman period as it was in earlier classical and Hellenistic vases and floors.

This paper details and analyzes a sculpted base recovered from the destruction debris of Omega House, a Late Roman residence excavated on the northern slope of the Areopagos in Athens. While numerous pieces of sculpture also found in the house are well known and much discussed, this base has received very little to no attention. Its presence in the house reveals a continuity of the concept of xenia in Athenian domestic settings and the embodiment of that xenia in the form of marine life; evidence of just the same concept is first found on nearly the same spot almost a millennium earlier in a pebble mosaic recovered from a Late Classical house underlying the later Omega House.

The Late Roman Athenian sculpted base reveals subject matter and details that resonate throughout the Roman luxury arts—sea creatures large and small, including fish, crustaceans, and mollusks, as well as details of the human collecting of the bounty of the sea with nets, baskets, and poles. While the original context of the base is not certain, its proximity to the reception rooms of the palatial residence suggest that it may have completed an ensemble decorated to evoke the tastes, sights, and pleasures of the sea. Tasty treats, the generosity of the host in serving them, and the dangers inherent in their capture are messages conveyed by the base.

SESSION 4D: Colloquium
Current Work in the Roman Archaeology of Southeast Europe

Sponsored by the Roman Provincial Archaeology Interest Group

ORGANIZERS: *Anne H. Chen*, Brown University, and *Sarah Craft*, Florida State University

Colloquium Overview Statement

In 2016 the Roman Provincial Archaeology Interest Group (RPAIG) organized the first of a series of "current excavation" sessions, building on those organized in past years by the AIA Program Committee. The session was a success with topical discussion afterward and important connections made between researchers working on Roman provincial sites. We are now focusing on providing a forum to discuss different geographic regions whose ongoing archaeological work is historically not well known among North American scholars in an effort to integrate data with well known provinces (e.g., Britain, Germany). This approach brings a more realistic understanding of the Roman provinces by combining detailed data of regional trends with broader empirewide phenomena. Southeastern Europe has become a superb area for fresh insight on questions of change in settlement, population groups, and power structures in the period of a growing Roman empire, and how those areas reacted and responded to shifting Mediterranean trends. As an area inaccessible for so long because of modern political issues, researchers from North America are now making connections with those in countries such as Serbia, Croatia, Bulgaria, and Romania. This session brings together a diverse group of European and North American researchers in a collaborative, transnational forum to present the work currently taking place in this region.

While the broad theme of the session is on current work being done in southeastern Europe, some trends and themes have emerged through the particular combination of speakers and research presented here. The range of methods and approaches highlights the diverse nature of the region's ongoing archaeological work, including excavation, landscape survey, geophysical survey, underwater archaeology, aerial prospection, archaeozoology, archaeobotany, and sophisticated Geographic Information Systems (GIS) applications, many of them in combination. Additionally, a discernible pattern across several papers is the presentation of data pertaining to sites that received imperial patronage in the middle and late empire, including a monument to Trajan's Dacian victories, imperial palaces at Sirmium, Split, and Felix Romuliana, and a town founded by Justinian. As an important cultural crossroads and in many ways de facto political capital of the Late Roman empire, this session contributes to the growing appreciation and discussion of southeastern Europe's prominence in the archaeology of the Roman world's peripheral—but in no way insignificant—provinces.

DISCUSSANT: *Elizabeth M. Greene*, University of Western Ontario

New Thoughts About Diocletian's Palace and the Gynaeceum Iovense Aspalathos Dalmatiae

Josko Belamaric, Centre Cvito Fiskovic Institute of Art History

Analyzing an almost neglected item of information from Notitia Dignitatum OC XI 48, where there is a mention of the procurator genaecii Iovensis Dalmatiae-Aspalato (warden of the imperial weaving shop for the production of clothing for the army, that worked in Split, under the title of Jupiter), the author proposes an entirely new way of understanding that syntagma. So far, scholars have always thought—on the rare occasions when this fact has been mentioned at all—that this gynaeceum was only "inscribed" into the palace after Diocletian's death in the early fourth century. The palace itself was thought to have been a kind of pensiopolis of dethroned emperors or pretenders to the throne for the whole of the fifth century, and many have long suspected that the northern part of the palace was reserved for the imperial guard, stables, and the like.

On the contrary, the author presents a number of arguments to prove that the northern half of the palace was conceived as an imperial gynaeceum from the very beginning. The construction of the Split Palace, then, was not—as it is often imagined—some kind of Imperial Xanadu. The thesis is gradually gaining acceptance in the scientific community, and this paper offers new and concrete evidence for the hypothesis.

Diachronic Landscape Survey in the Vicinity of Felix Romuliana

Sarah Craft, Florida State University, and *Stefan Pop-Lazic*, Archaeological Institute, Belgrade

This paper presents the fieldwork and preliminary results of a newly initiated research program in eastern Serbia, carried out as a collaborative project between the Archaeological Institute (Belgrade) and Florida State University. The Roman imperial palace "Felix Romuliana" (modern Gamzigrad) in eastern Serbia, attributed to the emperor Galerius, is an impressive example of a tetrarchic building project from Rome's provinces in southeastern Europe. While much study has been dedicated to this UNESCO World Heritage site, much less is understood about how the palace fits into its wider local and regional landscape. Beginning in August 2016, our goal is to establish a detailed understanding of the inhabited landscape outside of the palace walls as it developed over the millennia, from prehistory through the modern period, through survey, feature mapping, ceramic processing, and historical and spatial analysis in a GIS environment. In addition to intensive, systematic surface survey, we will carry out a targeted, extensive survey of potential resource areas in the region. Of particular interest to the project directors is the archaeological identification of Roman travel infrastructure in the region, which at this time is understood only generally.

Community Archaeology: Surveys and Analysis of Roman Water Management Systems in Southeast Romania (Black Sea Region / Scythia Minor) and Their Continuing Impact on Public Health in the 21st Century

Linda Ellis, San Francisco State University

In the ancient world, the understanding of and control over water, as well as easy access to a reliable supply of potable water, were critical to public health, personal hygiene, disease prevention, agriculture, and animal husbandry—as much in antiquity as in the 21st century. The ancient Roman aqueducts were only one aspect of hydraulic engineering, and a diverse panoply of water management systems were constructed throughout the Roman empire—including water cisterns, groundwater and wells, water distribution systems (aqueducts and piping), purgatory structures, sewer and drainage systems, fountains, spas, and bathing structures.

This study contributes new data, collected by the author on archaeological field campaigns at the Roman city of Tropaeum Traiani (second–sixth centuries C.E.) and its territorium (located in the Roman province of Scythia Minor in Dobrudja, southeast Romania). Water samples were collected throughout the catchment zone; chemical analyses were conducted on the subterranean waters, accessible by aqueducts and fountains. Roman engineers planned aqueducts not only for military purposes but also to establish therapeutic landscapes that promoted public health in the numerous provinces across three continents. More importantly, the engineering decisions made in late antiquity still impact the local Romanian populations to this day who are living near, and surviving from, the Roman aqueduct infrastructure. This research on Roman aqueducts quickly evolved into a program of "community archaeology," whereby the archaeologist can advocate for the health of local residents by identifying water sources on the therapeutic landscapes of antiquity, which are far healthier than those established—and contaminated—by the 20th-century totalitarian state.

Caracin Grad (Justiniana Prima): A New Plan for a Late Antique City

Vujadin Ivanisevic, Archaeological Institute, Belgrade

Caricin Grad represents a rare example of a newly founded city in the interior of the Illyricum. The archaeological investigations, lasting more than 100 years, have revealed an important city that can be identified with Justiniana Prima, erected, according to Novella 11, by Justinian I to be the seat of an archbishopric and of the Praetorian prefect of Illyricum. The new research, conducted by a Serbian, French, and German team, made very important discoveries concerning the landscape, the topography of the city, the urbanism, the attribution of buildings, the water supply, and especially the material culture and archaeozoological and archaeobotanical finds.

The discovery of large suburbia defended by newly revealed walls and many new buildings points to residential expansion in the suburbia, as well as in the interior of the defended city. The discovery of five new churches last year, in the city and the immediate vicinity, shows the importance of the city, with 15 basilicas as an archbishopric seat and probably as a pilgrimage center. Some of the newly identified structures next to churches allow us to suppose the existence of monasteries and hospices. The surveys and the use of modern techniques of remote sensing in Caricin Grad have shown that the Justinianic program of restoration of cities included also the construction of a special ring of defense and the restoration of other fortresses in the wider area of the cities. The new program of research in Caricin Grad is furthermore devoted to the study of the subsistence and the economic resources of the city and the numerous workshops that revealed significant production and interregional trade.

Results of the Recent Research in the Northwestern Part of Sirmium Imperial Palace

Stefan Pop-Lazic, Archaeological Institute, Belgrade

Archaeological research in the northwestern part of the Sirmium Imperial Palace has been conducted since 2002. In the course of these excavations, a polygonal (16-sided) structure was found. The excavated part of one-fourth of the building gives us a strong indication that the building originally measured 76 Roman feet (22.5 m).

The building itself consists of a perimeter concrete wall that is 1.80 m (6 ft.) meters wide. It has foundations that run deep into the ground, more than 2 m. Inside the building, remains of four circularly arranged column bases were found. Marble base remains of one of the pillars give a strong indication that column shafts were rather large, around 1.20 in diameter. The marble bases rest on quadrangular platforms. These platforms were constructed in the same way as the perimeter wall, as huge concrete blocks with deep foundations sunk into the existing soil. Their sides measure 1.90 x 1.90 m forming a sort of square. Excavations below the floor surface have shown that one of these platforms was dug more than 2 m deep into the ground.

According to coin finds inside and on the floor made out of a hydrostatic mortar, the building was erected in the first decade of the fourth century. Above the floor, a strong rubble layer of destruction contained dozens of pieces of porphyry sculptures. Their reconstruction has brought to light at least two porphyry busts, and at least three heads, which according to analogies can be identified as Roman imperial statues and busts. Taking into consideration the context of the finds, especially the position of the porphyry fragments, we can assume that they were originally presented in the polygonal building, which may have served as a sort of temple dedicated to the imperial cult. Later, possibly during the third quarter of the fourth century, both imperial sculptures and polygonal temple were destroyed and leveled due to the construction of new structures.

Submarine Evidence of Seafaring and Seaborne Trade in Roman Dalmatia

Katarina Batur, University of Zadar, and *Irena Radic-Rossi*, University of Zadar

The Early Roman presence in the eastern Adriatic during the Illyrian Wars in the third/second century B.C.E. intensified after Octavian's operations in the second half of the following century. After the suppression of the great rebellion of the local population in the sixth–ninth centuries C.E. (Bellum Batonianum), the Romans reorganized the former province of Illyricum and established the provinces of Pannonia and Dalmatia.

The province of Dalmatia became an important part of the Roman empire, connecting the western and central Mediterranean with the area of the Danube and the Pannonian Plain. The period of peace, the intense and well-organized exploitation of the natural resources, and the surveillance over the sea routes caused the intensification of settlement and navigation and left numerous traces along the mainland and insular coasts.

Most of the coastal sites ended up partly submerged, because of the progressive sea-level change. Many of them are provided with simple or more complex port structures, testifying to the exploitation of the maritime routes. Another set of most valuable evidence of seafaring and seaborne trade comprises numerous shipwreck sites, often heavily looted, but sometimes excellently preserved.

The paper aims to present an overview of submarine sites in the area of the present-day Dalmatia, which, although much smaller than its ancient predecessor, conserves the memory of its important past. Through several of the most significant examples, the paper illustrates the ongoing research and the potential for future studies.

SESSION 4E: Joint AIA/APA Colloquium Sovereignty and Money

ORGANIZER: *Lucia Francesca Carbone*, American Numismatic Society

Colloquium Overview Statement

The complex relationship between "state" and monetary systems has been the subject of much important research in the past, and the frequent emergence of new evidence ensures that it will remain a vital topic for historians in the future. Even from early antiquity, the social production of money, and of coinage, seems to be integral to the "economic struggle." The association of money with the nation combines both horizontal and vertical interpretations (i.e., "the formality of the State with the informality of the community"), illuminating not only the conception of state but also social and economic relationships between members of the same community.

Through close analysis of coinages issued around the Mediterranean, this panel explores new heuristic tools for understanding two interconnected questions. First, how were power and state authority conceived? And second, how did money represent an expression of these two topoi?

Martin convincingly stated that evidence fails to support the idea of "a strongly felt connection between an abstract notion of sovereignty and the right of coinage in the Classical World." Le Rider argued, on the other hand, that in the same period the state was the sole issuer, that the general population served as both first and secondary recipient, and that profit was the intent, with guarantee and a touch of coercion as the primary acceptance mechanisms.

What was the classical idea of monetary sovereignty, if it existed at all? How did this idea change over time? Was it possible for an issuing authority to be something other than sovereign? Would it, then, be possible to have an "unofficial coinage"? As several local communities issued coinage in their names while under foreign dominion, could they be defined as "sovereign" qua money-issuer?

This colloquium explores the relationship between sovereignty and money in the ancient Mediterranean, and specifically the question of whether the relationship between money and the state should be regarded as an issue of functional and administrative necessity, or whether historical contingency defines the relationship.

The panel is meant also to act as a methodological bridge between disciplines in order to answer more thoroughly historical questions. We wish to take the evidence that numismatics provides as a starting point and to incorporate the perspectives of epigraphic, textual, archaeological and papyrological specialists in order to see different nuances of the same issue. The question of sovereignty is particularly suited to this interdisciplinary approach because we can "compare" the degree of control the "state" or "authorities" are willing to extend on certain aspects of governance, such as coinage vs. trade, land inheritance, or taxation.

The papers in this panel address these issues from a variety of perspectives encompassing both the eastern and western parts of the Mediterranean, as in Jeremy Simmons' paper on the reuse of Roman coins in ancient India. They also cover a chronological span of nearly a millennium, beginning with Georgios Tsolakis' study of fifth-century B.C.E. Athens and stretching into late antiquity with Irene Soto's research on fouth-century C.E. Egypt. This diversity of time and place will allow us to investigate the issue not only from the perspective of material evidence, but also from a conceptual point of view. In addition, the broad chronology allows us to explore how the relationship between money and sovereignty changed over time, to the point of making coinage "the most deliberate of all symbols of public identity."

Sovereignty and Coinage: The Case of the Late Cistophori of Tralles

Lucia Francesca Carbone, American Numismatic Society

Can the study of a provincial coinage provide useful elements for a better understanding of the Roman idea of sovereignty? Is sovereignty necessarily related to the right to issue coinage?

According to Martin, no direct relationship can be established between sovereignty and coinage in the classical world. On the other hand, Meadows argues that the involvement of Roman authorities in municipal sovereignty in the provinces was more heavy-handed than in previous centuries and that, therefore, we should consider a direct relationship between sovereignty and coinage in the Roman world. This relationship was further examined in 1999 by Burnett, Amandry, and Ripolles through an analysis of the imperial authorization of local coinages.

The Roman Provincia Asia offers a unique perspective on this question. Here, provincial coinages were issued until the time of Septimius Severus, despite the existence of a well-developed Roman provincial administration and the use of the Roman currency as a unit of account. One such local coinage, cistophori even retained its pre-Roman appearance until the time of Marcus Antonius. Originally the Attalid silver standard-reduced currency, cistophori, appear to have served as a provincial coinage right from the establishment of the province, despite the presence of legends naming the cities in which the mints where located and the persistence of local types. Such cistophori demonstrate the ambivalence of the relationship between sovereignty and coinage in Roman provinces.

While the production and circulation patterns of other important cistophoric mints such as Ephesus, Pergamum, Apamea, and Nysa have already been established in important studies, the study of the Trallian cistophoric mint has, until now, been an important lacuna in our understanding of the Asian monetary system in the first century B.C.E.

Based on an original database of 600 Trallian cistophoric tetradrachms and a new die study of the late cistophori of Tralles, this paper offers an important contribution to the study of this intricate relationship. This study enabled the author to establish, on the basis of hoard evidence, that the production of this coinage could not have not started before the last years of the second century B.C.E., and that its production continued even after the city was severely punished by Sulla and lost its independence.

The impact of the Roman imperium on this coinage is made evident by the presence of the Sullan Age as a dating era on these cistophori and by production peaks corresponding to the Mithridatic Wars. These elements, highlighted here for the first time, show a correlation between the cistophoric mints of the Province, which suggests a province-wide monetary policy. At the same time, evidence for the ultimate municipal responsibility for cistophoric production is found in the use of control marks inspired by contemporary Pontic coinage. These control marks are a testament to the famed amicitia between the city of Tralles and Mithridates, which ultimately caused the above-mentioned punishment at the hand of Sulla and Lucullus.

This study of the production and of the circulation patterns of the Trallian late cistophori strongly suggests that there was no univocal relationship between sovereignty and coinage in Roman Asia, at least insofar as concerns cistophoric issues. The research pursued in this paper, therefore, not only is central to the reconstruction of the monetary system of the Provincia Asia in the course of the 1st century BC, but also provides important insights into the relationship between coinage and local sovereignty under Roman imperium.

When Sovereignty is Not Enough: Money Supply and 'Illegal' Coin Production in Fourth-Century C.E. Egypt

Irene Soto, ISAW

The political turmoil that characterized the Roman state during the 3rd century CE strongly affected the economic stability of the empire. The continuous debasement of coinage caused high inflation as commodity prices were adjusted to fit the new value of the minted currency and its diminished precious metal content. Subsequently, trust in imperial currency declined almost completely throughout the provinces. Even in Egypt, a province which had continued to function under a closed currency system since the conquest by Augustus in 30 B.C.E., papyrological evidence from the 260s orders bankers to accept the newly minted imperial coinage instead of the older ones which had a higher precious metal content.

By the end of this tumultuous century, Diocletian, the new emperor, instituted drastic Empire-wide economic and political reforms that were meant to stabilize the economy. One of these major reforms was the institution of new coinage and the introduction of Egypt into the new currency system that the rest of the Empire utilized. The effect that this reform had on the production of the Alexandrian mint, the only "official" mint in Egypt is unclear. Archaeological evidence points to a high number of bronze nummi throughout the province, hinting at a continuous output. However, during the same time period, archaeological and textual evidence point to both an increase in "illegal" coin production, manifested by hundreds of thousands of clay coin molds, and a shortage of precious metal supply, apparent in papyrological evidence. Furthermore, when looking beyond the bronze coinage, the picture changes. The absence of gold hoards or even single coin-finds of solidi in Egypt prior to the 340s further reinforces the view that the imperial authorities were suffering from a deficiency in precious metal. What did this mean for this highly monetized local economy? The fiduciary and quotidian nature of the bronze coinage during this period represented little, if any, importance to the imperial authorities; nonetheless, it was one of the main modes of exchange in market transactions in the Egyptian countryside. In this paper I will argue that the level of interest in minting small value currency by the Roman authorities varied depending on the type of coinage being imitated, since gold and bronze currency played different roles in the economy. This could have led to an underproduction by the Alexandrian mint and forced local authorities to find a way to supply themselves with the means to support daily transactions, which lead to a widespread manufacture of imitation coinages.

The large-scale quantity of these imitation coinages questions their "clandestine nature" as well as the role of the state in both supplying coinage and controlling the purity of the currency in circulation. What can we say about the sovereignty of a state and its monetary system when tolerated imitative coinage of low intrinsic value make a functioning monetary economy possible, in part, by privately minted coinage?

Roman Coins Abroad: Foreign Coinage and Strategies of Sovereignty in Ancient India

Jeremy Simmons, Columbia University

Was the currency of one ancient culture ever utilized to express the sovereignty of another? This paper explores how the relationship between sovereignty and money in the ancient world changes when a currency created by one state travels well beyond the extent of its sovereign control and becomes an integral feature in other monetary systems. I focus on one example in particular, namely the large presence of imperial Roman coinage in India. Attested by ancient literary sources like Strabo, Pliny the Elder, and the so-called Periplus Maris Erythraei, Roman trade with India involved the transport of Roman goods and coins to the western coast of India by sea, where these items were traded for various Indian commodities. Roman critics largely bemoaned the resulting flow of Roman coinage to India, with Pliny the Elder quantifying the losses to India alone at 50 million HS/annum (HN 6.26.101, 12.41.84). Roman authorities (including Tiberius, according to Tac., *Ann.* 3.53) decried the perceived loss of coinage from the Roman money supply to eastern luxuries, but ancient literary sources fail to address the potential for Roman currency to play larger roles abroad.

The enduring presence of Roman coinage in India resulting from this trade, attested in numerous archaeological finds, is paralleled by the minting activities of Indian potentates. While coinage traditions in India were initially shaped by Mauryan precedents and the Hellenistic coinage of Central Asia, the influx of Roman currency via trade catalyzed new types of coin production by Indian rulers. Scholars have largely focused on the role of Indian currencies in facilitating transoceanic trade. This paper, however, addresses the numismatic evidence from a unique perspective. I suggest that Roman coinage—as an abundant, foreign currency in ancient India—featured prominently in various strategies of sovereignty undertaken by territorial states there during the first two centuries C.E.

This paper differentiates between three geographic regions in particular: (1) northern India/Central Asia, under the power of the Kushans; (2) the western Deccan, contested by the Western Kshatrapas and Satavahanas; and (3) southern

India, ruled over by Tamil chiefdoms. In some cases, these cultures adapted or initiated currency production relying on features of Roman money (imperial portraiture, iconography, weight, etc.). In other cases, they treated defaced, imitation, or unaltered Roman coins as currency, as stores of wealth, or even as specialized commodities. Iconographic emulation speaks to a likening between the Roman emperor's authority (as expressed in coin) and that of various Indian dynasts, while the cooption of Roman gold and silver coins as bullion for this purpose—sometimes through deliberate acts of defacement—reflects a conscious attempt to express control over imported metallic resources. The presence of Roman coinage further prompted dramatic structural changes to Indian monetary systems: for instance, as a result of the influx of the aureus to India, the Kushans began to mint a gold coin called the dīnāra (after the denarius), which matches the aureus in weight, thus adding a whole new metal and denomination to the money supply.

These strategies existed side-by-side with other means of expressing authority over contested territory, such as overstriking rival coinage, instituting a standardization of iconography on coinage, and investing in monastic institutions situated along territorial frontiers. In examining Roman currency far beyond the bounds of Roman political control, we can appreciate the interplay between sovereignty and money in a whole new light: such a relationship is dynamic, as Indian rulers willingly adopt features of a foreign currency designed in an entirely different political context as one of many instruments of local authority.

Owing Money to the Athenian State: Epigraphical Evidence for Private Debt in Classical and Hellenistic Athens

Georgios Tsolakis, Institute for the Study of the Ancient World, New York University

This paper aims to provide a comparative approach of the epigraphical evidence for installments and for the repayment of debt to the city of Athens by private individuals in order to understand the question of sovereignty. Hunter initially categorized types of debtors by the apparent relationship of the state to the citizen, as well as different types of penalties placed on them. However, these initial categories need further nuancing so that to grasp the conceptualization of the goals of the economic policy of Athens. In order to begin to understand the operation of the Athenian government as it pertains to debt, and thus questions of the Greek political economy at large, it is imperative to investigate further the way the citizens became indebted to their city. Moreover, as the majority of attested cases are preserved because the individuals failed to repay the debt to the city in a timely manner or at all, the epigraphic evidence illustrates how the debtors were brought to justice and how they were penalized by the city, along with the specified terms of lending instituted.

The "ὀφείλοντες τῶι δημοσίωι τῶν Ἀθηναίων" ("those who owe money to the Athenian state"; *Agora* 26 41.2, 21; *Agora* 29 P26, 468–69; *IG* 2^2 30, lines 21, 45; cf. Andoc. 1.73) could fall into debt in different ways. The following cases are just two characteristic paradigms concerning of the differential treatment of public debtors by the Athenian state. The list of πωληταί ("sellers") of ca. 340 (*Agora* 29 P26, 463–98) records the confiscation and sale of Meixidemos' property, who assumed liability (ἐνεγυήσατο) for three other public debtors. Since all the debtors failed to fulfill their obligations, Meixidemos was condemned to pay their annual instalments. We are informed by an Athenian decree of 324/3 (*IG* 2[2] 1631; cf. *SEG* 39 172), we are informed that a certain Sopolis failed to comply with a previous decision of the court, according to which he had been condemned to return the naval property that his brother Kephisodoros held as a ταμίας of the νεώρια ("treasurer of the dockyards"). The proposer of the decree suggested that all the property of Sopolis should be confiscated (362–64: "ἡ δὲ οὐσία ἡ Σωπόλιδος ἀπογέγ[ρα]πται δημοσία εἶναι ἅπασα") and he should be disfranchised (368: "ἐπιτιμία").

The most important conclusion that could be drawn from the examination of the epigraphical texts, however, is the way in which they portray the sovereign power of the city of Athens—the way that the polis could have potentially utilized debt in order to control its citizens. Smith defines sovereignty as "that dense array of practices that simultaneously authorize the polity as a legitimate association and defend its order through various disciplinary institutions." I examine the political and juridical institutions that ensured the repayment of the public debt, the procedures followed for the policing of loans, and the mechanisms that were put in action for payout the debt. First, I seek a classification of cases that occur in the epigraphical texts and a categorization of the public debt, then I set them in a political and judicial context. Finally, I examine debt as a form of obligation; the regulations imposed by the state so individuals meet and settle that obligations; and the limits of sovereignty as an expression of the Greek polis' apparatus and "a condition of political interactions" in the historical context and within the "actualities of relations" of the Athenian state.

Silver Coinage, Sovereignty, and Symmachia: Byzantion and Athens in the Fourth Century B.C.E.

Nicholas Cross, Baruch College, CUNY

In this paper I reexamine Byzantion's first autonomous issues of coinage in the Classical Greek period and to what extent their dating can have an impact on the interpretation of Byzantion's politico-economic relationship with Athens. This approach broadens the topic of money and sovereignty from a local to an interstate context. By so doing, this case study demonstrates how a city-state could both mint its own coinage and possess a formal political alliance (*symmachia*) with Athens in the Classical period.

The first half of the paper focuses on the numismatic evidence. Though situated at an economically advantageous point on the Bosphorus Strait from its foundation in the seventh century B.C.E., Byzantion did not issue an autonomous coinage until late in the Classical period. When it did, it minted silver drachms and hemidrachms on the Persian standard and other denominations on the Chian standard. The obverse of these issues contains a bull standing on a dolphin accompanied with the legend BΥ; the reverse an incuse square of mill-sail pattern. There is considerable debate over the dating of these coins.

Many scholars, following Schönert-Geiss (*Die Münzprägung von Byzantion I: Autonome Zeit* [Berlin 1970], position these issues in the context of the Peloponnesian War, and specifically when Byzantion seceded from the Athenian empire.

According to that interpretation, the new coinage should be understood as a strong assertion of sovereignty and indicates liberation from the economic domination inherent in an alliance with Athens. I, however, dispute this scenario and posit that the context of alliance renewal with Athens in the fourth century B.C.E. is a more appropriate one than revolt.

As it happens, Le Rider (*Revue numismatique* 13 [1971] 143–53) anticipated this alternative dating for the new coinage but offered no explanation for its inception. My contribution in the second half of the paper is to build on Le Rider's numismatic work by incorporating previously ignored epigraphic and literary evidence for the reestablishment of alliance ties between Byzantion and Athens in 390/389 B.C.E. (*Hell.* 4.8.27), 383 B.C.E. (*IG* 2 2 41; Dem. 20.59–60), and 377 B.C.E. (*IG* 2 2 43, line 83; Diod. Sic. 15.28.3).

The revised historical context that emerges from this interdisciplinary approach depicts a new Byzantian coinage that coincides with the reconstruction of a politico-economic relationship with Athens. This revised dating necessitates a new explanation: if the Byzantian minting a new coinage was not, in fact, an act of rebellion against Athens, what does it mean for our understanding of the role of money in classical Greek interstate alliances as well as the broader question of the relationship between money and sovereignty?

SESSION 4F: Colloquium
Selinunte: Ten Years of Investigations by the Mission of the Institute of Fine Arts–NYU

ORGANIZER: *Clemente Marconi*, Institute of Fine Arts–NYU

In 2006 a mission by the Institute of Fine Arts–NYU initiated a new archaeological investigation of the main urban sanctuary of Selinunte. Research over the first 10 years focused on the southern sector, especially Temple B (ca. 300 B.C.E.) and Temple R (ca. 580 B.C.E.). The discovery in this area of an intact stratigraphic sequence from the Bronze Age through the Hellenistic period has produced groundbreaking results concerning the history of Selinus, the development of its sacred architecture, and local cult practice. The proposed colloquium offers the first systematic discussion of the findings of this interdisciplinary project.

The first paper ("Discovering Selinus' Early Phase") addresses the seventh century evidence, which provides important indications about the Greek settlement's foundation and the development of its material culture during the first generation of occupation, including interaction with the native hinterland. The following paper ("Gifts to the Goddess") discusses the rich votive deposit excavated inside Temple R. Associated with the construction of the building in ca. 580 B.C.E., this context effectively indicates the range of ritual activities performed at the site, especially when compared with similar assemblages from Himera and Naxos.

The analysis of the faunal remains from the southern sector of the main urban sanctuary is the subject of the next paper ("Holy Smoke!"). The findings suggest developments in ritual practice between the initial use of the area as a sacred space in the seventh century and the later Archaic through Hellenistic periods. The next paper ("Architectural Work at Selinunte") discusses the project's architectural study. Experimentation with a variety of methodological approaches in the production of two-dimensional and three-dimensional architectural documentation, used to analyze numerous archaic and classical structures at Selinunte, has clarified questions of construction and design at a site critical for understanding the development of Greek sacred architecture.

The last two papers concern the Hellenistic phase, when Selinus was under Carthaginian hegemony. The first ("Post-409 Selinunte and the Dangers of Cultural Periodization") argues against the prevailing notion that Selinus was an exclusively Punic community during the Hellenistic period and in favor of a more culturally diverse population, based on the evidence from our excavations. The last ("The Early Hellenistic Ceramic Deposits from Temple B") focuses on the rich ceramic deposit from the fill for the construction of Temple B, featuring a large number of amphoras that reveal trade contact with both Carthage and Campania.

Discovering Selinus' Early Phase

Clemente Marconi, Institute of Fine Arts–NYU

Since 2007 the excavations by the Institute of Fine Arts–NYU mission have uncovered significant evidence concerning the early phase of Greek settlement in Selinunte. This material culture includes architectural features such as clay floors, mudbrick walls on foundations made of rubble, remains of a thatch roof, and numerous artifacts including pottery, metalwork, and terracotta figurines. The finds are concentrated in the area of Temple R, and the more likely possibility is that they all relate to a seventh-century predecessor of this building, which was systematically dismantled to make way for the new stone temple. The construction of this early structure (the earliest thus far documented at Selinunte) can be dated archaeologically to after 620. In ca. 590–580 the building was not only dismantled but apparently also ritually buried, including a rich votive deposition. Underneath this early structure a layer was found that corresponds to the first phase of Greek settlement in Selinunte, during which time an open-air cult took place in the area.

This new evidence contributes essential information concerning the early settlement of Selinus. It speaks against the presence of a native village at the site when the Greeks arrived, for which there is no evidence in Selinunte. It corroborates Selinus' foundation date as provided by Thucydides, due to the lack of pottery safely datable to the first half of the seventh century. Further, it supports the theory that the original Greek settlement was located in the southern sector of the acropolis. More importantly, in consideration of recent discussions about the character of early Greek settlement in the West and the degree of preplanning involved in the new foundations, this evidence confirms the theory that the delimitation of sacred areas was one of the constitutive acts of an archaic *apoikia*. The most notable discovery, however, concerns the rich variety of material culture that includes not only pottery from mainland Greece and eastern Sicily but also Phoenician and native pottery. The last find is particularly remarkable, considering the percentage of the native material, which is far greater than the amount documented at the site from the early sixth century onward. This is the first such evidence from Selinunte, suggestive of an intense interaction with the native hinterland at the time of foundation of the Greek settlement.

Gifts to the Goddess: Architecture, Ritual and the Votive Deposit at Temple R

Marya Fisher, Institute of Fine Arts–NYU

Temple R, the oldest known stone temple on the acropolis of ancient Selinus, has long been studied as an example of early monumental Greek architecture in Sicily, with its form interrogated since its discovery in the nineteenth century. Until recent excavations of the temple by the team from the Institute of Fine Arts–NYU, however, the cult and ritual functions of the building remained obscure. Beginning in the 2012 season, a large votive deposit was found under the floor levels of the classical and archaic phases of the temple. Rich and diverse, the deposit can help to elucidate the ritual use of the small temple. The objects, nestled against the interior of the east and south walls, just beside the cella's door, were varied. There were vases (both imported and local), weapons, terracotta figurines, items of personal adornment, and a musical instrument. This deposit also included the bones from pigs, fish, sheep, and goats.

This paper examines the votive deposit found within Temple R through the lens of ritual. It argues that the deposition and nature of this deposit can grant insight into the cult use of this essential sacred space on the acropolis of Selinus. In particular, this diverse collection of votive offerings are considered as the possible remains of a large-scale ritual action that took place in association with the dedication of the temple. The offerings indicate a series of rituals including animal sacrifice, feasting, libation, and hymns with musical accompaniment, which culminated in the deposition of sacred objects along the interior walls of the temple, adorning and consecrating the new temple for its goddess.

Temple R's votive deposit and its ritual implications are also considered in light of other such discoveries in Sicily. Of special interest is the comparison of the Temple R deposit with those found within temples at the sites of Himera, Naxos, and Gela, among others. By considering the Temple R votives in the context of similar depositions, we may begin to understand the temple and its ritual use as examples of larger trends in the practice of Greek religion in Sicily in the sixth century B.C.E.

Architectural Work at Selinunte

David Scahill, American School of Classical Studies at Athens

Architectural work for the Institute of Fine Arts–NYU mission on the acropolis at Selinunte has concentrated on documenting and clarifying Temple B, the South Building, Temple R, and the monumental altar to the east of Temple B, within an area to the south of Temple C and north of the east–west avenue flanking the temenos. The chronological range of architecture in this area spans from the Early Archaic period to the Medieval period.

First, I present a brief summary of previous architectural studies in this area, before focusing primarily on work carried out over the past six seasons, beginning with an overview of the methodological approaches being used to document the architecture on the site. This new phase of work involves integration of block drawing, total station surveying, CAD mapping and drawing, digital photogrammetry, and aerial drone photography to produce two-dimensional and three-dimensional documentation of architecture on the acropolis. The integration of these methods facilitates comprehensive documentation of all the architectural material on the site for research, presentation and archival retrieval.

Second, I present some preliminary findings from my research on four main structures within our excavation area, focusing on aspects of design, construction, and chronological phases of Temple R, the monumental altar foundations to the east, the South Building and its relation to both Temple R and the altar, and finally Temple B. Within the scope of our architectural work on the acropolis, I also present some observations on Temples A, O, and P and the well-preserved temples at Triolo Nord and in the Demeter Malophoros sanctuary. New understanding of the design, construction, and phasing of the buildings from our work is allowing us to more precisely reconstruct a picture of architectural development on the acropolis from the Early Archaic period up to and including the Punic period; to the destruction and reuse of architectural material in the Medieval period, until final abandonment of the site.

Holy Smoke! Zooarchaeological Analysis from the Southern Sector of the Main Urban Sanctuary of Selinunte

Roberto Miccichè, Università degli Studi di Palermo

Here I present the first results of the zooarchaeological analysis of the faunal remains excavated in the southern sector of the main urban sanctuary of Selinunte by the Institute of Fine Arts–NYU mission. This research involved a large sample of more than 25,000 osteological remains. Coming from contexts covering a wide chronological span, from the Archaic to the Hellenistic period, this evidence for animal sacrifice allows for a diachronic approach to the study of local ritual practice. This study constitutes also the first zooarchaeological analysis concerning the main urban sanctuary of Selinunte.

Our record, excluding malacofauna, comprises at least 22 different species. Despite the rich biodiversity recorded, the most abundant species belongs to domestic animals, which represents 95% of the whole faunal assemblage. The most common taxa recorded are pigs, with a marked predominance of immature individuals, and the sheep/goat group. The prevalence of piglet's remains could be indicative of a connection with the cult of Demeter.

The taxa ratios maintain a certain degree of homogeneity throughout the different periods. However, there is a slight difference in the faunal assemblage associated with the earliest phase of Greek occupation of this area. Here the kill-off patterns of pigs involve older individuals, and the sample highlights an increased frequency of cattle remains and wild species. These differences may be indicative of the transition from a period of less distinct cultic activity to a more institutionalized and organized scenario, which is in accord with the monumental development of the sanctuary.

Analysis relies on taphonomical aspects affecting the remains, including butchery marks and fire exposure, which are highly informative about sacrificial practice. Charred and calcined bones were nearly 20% of the sample. The cross examination of the body parts' distribution between the burnt and unburnt remains shows a distinct pattern in the processing of the carcass that seems to follow prescription connected with the *thysiai*.

Our results constitute an important source of new data, which significantly contribute to our understanding of religious practice in Selinunte between the Archaic and Classical periods.

Post-409 Selinus and the Dangers of Cultural Periodization

Andrew Ward, Institute of Fine Arts–NYU

In the spring of 409, a force under Hannibal Mago of Carthage sacked Selinus. The destruction layer uncovered by the Institute of Fine Arts–NYU excavations corroborates previous archaeological evidence that gives credence to the accuracy of the Graeco-Roman literary accounts. These same sources go on to describe the reoccupation of Selinus by some of its previous Greek inhabitants. Despite no indication of a further depopulation, Selinunte's archaeological record has been interpreted as demonstrating the existence of a Punic colony on the site either immediately following the conquest or in the later fourth century. These interpretations are underlined by a paradigm of cultural periodization, in which the homogenous Greek colony became a homogenous Punic colony, with heterogeneity impossible or unlikely. While a preponderance of evidence does suggests that the site was the settlement identified in numismatics and epigraphy as Rosh Melqart and had a large Phoenician population, this paper argues strongly against Jacques des Courtils summation that "Sélinonte s'inscrit totalement dans le contexte de la civilisation phénico-punique."

While demographic changes did occur, as evidenced by a proliferation of Sicilian-Punic material culture, it is harmful to understand Selinunte in such a binary narrative. Instead, a reevaluation of masonry styles, architectural forms, and standing stones oft-identified as aniconic baetyls, corroborates the objections already raised by Christian Russenberger and others that many "indicators" of Punic culture are in fact misinterpretations of the archaeological record. The discoveries by the Institute of Fine Arts–NYU excavations at Temple B and R within the main urban sanctuary, as well as the reevaluation of excavations and architectural study on contrada Gaggera and on the acropolis all point to Temple B being far from an anomaly and part of a greater phenomenon of urban and ritual continuity before and after 409. While objects are not people, and hence Greek material culture should not be seen as definitive proof of Greek inhabitants, there is no longer valid evidence for the total dominance of Punic culture in Selinunte. This heterogeneous city, then, while still useful for understanding Punic trends on the island, stands as a warning against equating political dominance with cultural homogeneity.

The Early Hellenistic Ceramic Deposits from Temple B

Babette Bechtold, University of Vienna

The Institute of Fine Arts–NYU excavations in the area of Temple B at Selinunte have yielded an extraordinary stratigraphic sequence of leveling layers associated with the construction of this building ca. 300 B.C.E. or slightly later. The study presented here is based on the detailed examination of all diagnostic elements (a total of 314 pieces) and a supervision of the nondiagnostic materials found in nine different soundings. The absolute dating of the whole assemblage relies mostly on the chronological frame indicated by the classes of transport amphoras and black-glazed wares. The stratigraphic units taken together represent a single closed context with a relative low incidence of residuality. This context is characterized by numerous associations of varying ceramic classes and types in use in Selinus between the very late fourth and the beginning of the third century B.C.E. Its detailed study offers therefore the excellent opportunity for an in-depth analysis of the material culture during the earlier phase of Punic occupation of the town.

The bulk of the diagnostic fragments belongs to locally or regionally produced plain (ca. 30%) and cooking wares (ca. 11.5%). Best represented are black-glazed wares (36%), of local or regional fabric, but in certain cases also from Athens and Tyrrhenian Italy, while lamps appear to be quite rare (1.5%). Because of their diversified provenances, the large group of transport amphoras (21%) is particularly significant for our understanding of both the economic relations and the food supply of the city.

44 percent of all diagnostic fragments refer to Punic amphoras, mostly from the area of Palermo and Solunto (ca. 62%). However, the documentation of a small assemblage of Carthaginian amphorae is highly significant in that they might suggest a physical presence of Carthaginians at Selinus itself. The bulk of the remaining diagnostic amphoras fragments (ca. 53%) belong to MGS III–V amphoras, originating from Velia, Paestum, and the Gulf of Naples. The association, within the closed contexts of Temple B's foundations, of significant quantities of possible fish amphorae from northwestern Sicily with containers, potentially for wine, from the central Tyrrhenian area hints at the arrival of these commodities via the Punic emporia of Palermo and Solunto. In fact, the recent identification at Palermo of Early Hellenistic Campanian and Lucanian amphoras and at Velia of Punic containers from Palermo highlights very clearly this important commercial network responsible for the early circulation of Campanian wine in Carthage's area of influence.

SESSION 4G: Colloquium
Landscape and Society: Diachronic Perspectives on Settlement Patterns in River Valleys in Cyprus

Sponsored by the Near Eastern Archaeology Interest Group

ORGANIZER: *Pamela Gaber*, Lycoming College

Colloquium Overview Statement

Regional differences in ancient Cyprus were heavily impacted by the differences in environment between the mountains and the Mesaoria Plain. Many elements affected these differences: topography, geology, hydrography, and the resultant vegetation and natural resources. How did people choose where to live? What environmental, social, and economic factors went into the decisions to build a settlement, and why were settlements abandoned? As societies changed through time, so did their relationships with the environment and the landscape. The balance between landscape, natural resources, and the needs of social groups resulted in the choice of settlement location, economic, and ritual activities, and was a key factor in establishing territoriality. A diachronic approach is necessary to establish how and why communities chose to live in certain places and engage uncertain economic activities at any given time.

Most regional studies of ancient Cyprus to date have centered on broad regional categories, such as "northwestern Cyprus" or "coastal sites." The organizers of this colloquium have observed that settlements in Cyprus gravitated to river valleys and that those in mountainous regions have different characteristics from those in the lowland plains. We believe that by grouping sites by the river valleys in which they are found, differing relationships between settlements and their environments will be illuminated. Thus the first aim of this colloquium is to illuminate the environmental differences that created differences in settlement patterns, that is, the spatial dimension.

The second aim of this colloquium is to investigate the differences between the patterns of human interaction with their landscape in a mountain valley vs. the patterns of interaction with their landscape in the broad limestone Mesaoria Plain from prehistory into the historic periods. By comparing settlements in the Dhiarizos River valley with settlements in the Yialias River valley, we can test hypotheses about how and why humans chose to settle in particular places and how this affected social change. The organizers are especially interested in studies that show explicit relationships between settlement patterns, uses of the landscape, and environmental factors. The diachronic nature of this colloquium necessitates its division into three broad chronological categories: (1) prehistory, (2) protohistory, and (3) states.

Ayia Varvara Asprokremmos, A Pre-Pottery Neolithic A Taskscape on the Yialias River in Central Cyprus: Implications of Focused Resource Exploitation for Understanding Early Connections Between Cyprus and the Mainland

Carole McCartney, University of Cyprus

Excavations at the late Pre-Pottery Neolithic A site of Ayia Varvara Asprokremmos, in central Cyprus, provide new evidence of resource exploitation framed within a taskscape that is clearly different from the expected Neolithic "village" of Mediterranean islands. Site size, organization, and the episodic character of excavated contexts combine to illustrate a nonpermanent temporality that was focused more on exploiting resources from the surrounding environment than on owning it. Evidence of substantial craft work using chipped-stone and groundstone technologies appear linked less to cultivation than serving other craft activities. One of the most unusual features of the Asprokremmos taskscape is found in the collection and processing of considerable amounts of mineral pigments that are present in a wide array of colors. The practices used in the working of these pigments not only intensify throughout the site's history of occupation but increasingly shape the site's contexts and features. These characteristics of the Asprokremmos site prompt discussions of the roots of specialization and exchange of valued commodities such as ocher in the Yialias Basin. Similarly, the current lack of compelling evidence for the intensive use of pigments elsewhere in Pre-Pottery Neolithic

A Cyprus elicits consideration of mainland Neolithic traders and/or tradesmen who gained access to the island's interior via the Yialias River for reasons not associated with farming.

Marki Alonia: A Long-Lived Early and Middle Bronze Age Settlement in the Alykos Valley

Jennifer Webb, LaTrobe University

The Early and Middle Bronze Age settlement of Marki Alonia was founded beside the Alykos River in ca. 2350 B.C.E., on the interface between the igneous formations of the Troodos Mountain foothills and the sedimentary soils of the Mesaoria Plain. This latter aspect of the site's location, which is common to a number of contemporary settlements, allowed the inhabitants access to copper ore deposits some 10 km distant at Mathiatis, Kambia, and Sha and to the fertile soils of the central plain. Evidence for the casting of copper ingots from the very earliest phase of the settlement leaves no doubt that nearby ore deposits were being exploited at this time and, together with pottery from the north coast, suggests that Marki was producing metal for distribution within an extraregional exchange system. Similarly, the survival and growth of the settlement over some 500 years indicates successful exploitation of the immediate environment. The final abandonment of Marki in ca. 1800 B.C.E. remains unexplained. It was a gradual process accompanied by the progressive closure of individual households and settlement retraction. It is possible that the productivity of the soils surrounding the village declined over time. The increasing importance of copper sources in the northwest Troodos and the contemporary abandonment of nearby Alambra Mouttes suggest, however, that larger forces may have been at work. This paper explores the changing use over time by the inhabitants of Marki of the local environment and corresponding shifts in the site's relationship with settlements and regions within and beyond the wider Yialias River valley.

Inland Sites on Cyprus: The Yialias River and Urbanization in the Mesaoria Plain

Pamela Gaber, Lycoming College

Inland sites on Cyprus, and examinations of river landscapes, indicate a long, slow-growth model for the Bronze Age urbanization of the island. The picture emerging from excavations in the Mesaoria limestone plains of interior Cyprus indicates a profound difference from the historical trajectory of urbanization along the coasts. Coastal regions appear to have suffered near-universal disruptions ca. 1200 B.C.E., while inland sites developed without interruption from the Early/Middle Bronze Age, ca. 2000 B.C.E. through to the Iron Age and beyond. In addition, they clearly developed along the two main rivers of the Mesaoria Plain, the Pedeios and the Yialias, which join one another about 12 km from Salamis Bay on the east coast of Cyprus. The large trading cities located on that bay were the Bronze Age settlement at what is now Enkomi and the Iron Age settlement at what is now Salamis, in conjunction with a path through the hills to the south coast—the location of the Bronze Age city at what is now known as Hala-Sultan-Tekke, later "Kition."

Both archaeology and inscriptions appear to indicate that copper was being exploited and traded off-island by ca. 2000 B.C.E. to Mesopotamia, and to the Levant and Egypt by ca. 1900 B.C.E. Exploitation and trade of copper was facilitated by access to the rivers and their routes to the sea—and to the coastal sites from which copper was presumably traded abroad.

Two of the famous city-kingdoms of Iron Age Cyprus, Idalion and Tamassos, have been excavated for a century. What emerges from examination of the evidence is the picture of growth described above. Idalion was preceded on the Yialias River by a site at Agios Sozomenos. The Medinet Habu inscription names a place, "Ithal." It is argued that this inscription refers to this settlement. By 701 B.C.E. Assyrian inscriptions refer to a city-kingdom as "Id-di-al." These are early names for what later Greek visitors call "Idalion."

It is argued that the city of "Ithal—Id-di-al—Idalion" developed in its known location(s) because of proximity to the Yialias River and its juncture with the least-cost path to the south coast. Such rivers were central to development of inland cities like Idalion.

The "Prehistory" of a Cypriot Monastery: Prasteio Mesorotsos Archaeological Expedition and the Agios Savvas tis Karonos Monastery

Lisa Kennan, Independent Researcher

The multiperiod settlement of Prasteio-Mesorotsos in the Dhiarizos Valley existed for thousands of years before the arrival of Christianity, but it is not until the establishment of the nearby (1 km) 12th-century monastery of Agios Savvas tis Karonos that this specific location appears in written sources, thus entering the "historical" era. Once built, the monastery sat in a rich landscape that probably held the Mesorotsos settlement as the centerpiece of its landholdings and the source of its wealth. Excavations at the Mesorotsos site have revealed layers of residential contexts, agricultural and industrial activities, and a building of some significance situated on the very peak of a prominent rocky outcrop, a strategic topographical feature in the valley. The fact that the village at Mesorotsos predated the monastery by millennia, however, suggests that the choice of location for the monastery was the existence of the settlement, rather than the other way around. Recent work at the site of Prasteio-Mesorotsos from the Late Antique and Medieval periods shows the development of the village community before the appearance of the monastery, as well as the shifts in the use of the landscape that laid the foundation for the establishment of monastic control.

The Middle Cypriot Foundations of Complexity at Prasteio-Mesorotsos

Lisa Graham, University of Edinburgh

The transition from the Chalcolithic to the Bronze Age is typically thought to be the period when major social changes took place that laid the foundations for the complex urban societies of the Late Bronze Age in Cyprus. This Chalcolithic to Early Cypriot transition at Prasteio-Mesorotsos does not seem to signal very great changes, however. On the contrary, the major indication that the social trajectory takes a turn is between the Early and the Middle Cypriot periods, a transition marked by changes in architecture, ceramics, burials, and, inferentially, social stratification. The culmination of this Middle Cypriot sequence sees a monumental wall constructed at the site, built just prior to the site's complete abandonment. This Middle Cypriot abandonment seems to reflect a general population decline in the rural area, coinciding with the coalescence of communities around Palaipaphos on the coast. This paper argues that the Middle Cypriot social trajectory of increasing complexity in the rural village of Prasteio-Mesorotsos led to its eventual abandonment and subsequently the population agglomeration at a new and burgeoning coastal urban center.

Landscape of Ritual Behavior at Neolithic Prasteio-Mesorotsos

Andrew McCartney, Cyprus American Archaeological Research Institute

The Dhiarizos Valley in prehistory was a rich environment that offered a wide range of resources and ideal locations for permanent settlement. The evidence for the first inhabitants at the site of Prasteio-Mesorotsos, however, shows that there were seasonal and mobile behaviors exhibited by the first human inhabitants of this spot. Likewise, there is remarkable evidence in the form of a massive cooking installation that probably served as a focal point for large intercommunity feasts that brought together multiple groups from the region. Repeated use of the site brought with it increasing investment in the location such that ritual behaviors can start to be seen, including a ritual pit complex where discarded special objects were buried, indicating continuity of behavior over a great span of time. This paper discusses the location of the site in the valley and the reasons why it was chosen by the Neolithic inhabitants in terms of resources. It also discusses how this initial choice of site location created increasing engagement with the site as a special ritual place and eventually led to it being permanently inhabited, in spite of having to make compromises in terms of resources.

SESSION 4H
Faces of Power: Roman Imperial Portraits

CHAIR: *Francesco de Angelis*, Columbia University

Ancient or Modern? The Enigmatic Case of the "Group" from Fayum

Alessia Di Santi, Scuola Normale Superiore (Pisa)

At the Ny Carlsberg Glyptotek there are three important marble portraits representing Augustus (I.N. 1443), Livia (I.N. 1444), and Tiberius (I.N. 1445). They are generally considered as the "Group from Fayum," but actually we should wonder whether it is an ancient or a modern group.

These pieces, in fact, come from the antiquities market: Carl Jacobsen, the founder of the Ny Carlsberg Glyptotek, bought them in 1896 from the Greek-Egyptian art dealer Alexander Dingli, about whom we have only few biographical notes.

The purchase was made through the mediation of the Danish orientalist Valdemar Schmidt, to whom Dingli wrote some letters in order to sell the sculptures. These documents, now at the Glyptotek, are very important because they throw light not only on the acquisition of the portraits but also on their find.

The study of the letters, which I present in the first part of my paper, shows that there is not certainty about the fact that the three pieces were found together: so we do not know whether they were set up in the same place in the antiquity, forming in this way an ancient group, or if they were put together in modern times by the dealers.

In the second part of the paper I propose to solve this problem through a stylistic and technical analysis, which consists of the presentation of the results of my autoptic observations on the sculptures, with detailed measurements of them, and of the results of the marble analysis made by Lorenzo Lazzarini for my research project.

The first thing to note is that the head of Livia is smaller than the other two, but the portraits of Livia and Tiberius are very similar from a formal point of view. This affinity is confirmed by the marble analysis, which shows that Livia and Tiberius are made of the same kind of marble, while Augustus is made of a different one.

In conclusion, I think that only the busts of Livia and Tiberius were originally made together, while the portrait of Augustus was added to the group at a later date, probably by the modern dealers.

Trajan with a Dacian: A New Identification of the Cuirassed Emperor with a Barbarian at His Feet in the Villa Poggio Imperiale

Lee Ann Riccardi, The College of New Jersey

Languishing in a little-used courtyard of the lovely Villa Poggio Imperiale (a former Medici villa, now being used as a high school) on the outskirts of Florence, is a life-sized statue of a cuirassed emperor with a small shackled barbarian crouching at his feet. Although precise records of the original context for the statue are lacking, it probably entered into the villa's collection between 1818 and 1837. The head of the statue was at some point reworked and crudely restored. Pieces of marble, now mostly missing, were attached to the face and hair with iron pins and glue. The original appearance of the face is no longer detectable, and the emperor has been identified as Augustus, an Antonine, and as a statue of the emperor Geta. This last appears to be the most accepted and is based on comparisons of his hairstyle to other known portraits of the emperor. A close examination of the statue, however, reveals that the hair was recut along with the face, and therefore it should not be the main basis for its identification.

Without the face or hair as criteria, in order to identify the emperor represented in the statue, it is necessary to turn to other elements. The cuirass is not much help, as it is a very generic type that was used over a long period of time. Neither are there dateable aspects of the workmanship. The little barbarian at the emperor's feet, however, provides the best clues. The motif of the cuirassed emperor with a barbarian at his feet first appears under the Flavians and continues under Trajan, with the most surviving examples occurring under Hadrian. A few Antonine examples are also known, and although the motif continues to appear in coin representations well into late antiquity, there are no examples of it in sculpture after Marcus Aurelius. Furthermore, the costume of the barbarian compares favorably to the costumes of Dacian captives, such as those that decorated the Forum of Trajan in Rome. There is little reason to associate Geta or any of the Severans either with this motif or with the Dacians.

In this paper, therefore, I propose a new identification of the cuirassed statue in the Villa Poggio Imperiale as a portrait of the emperor Trajan.

The Youthful Portrait of Hadrian

Martin Beckmann, McMaster University

A rare portrait type of Hadrian shows the emperor as a young man, with sideburns and wispy moustache instead of a full beard. The portrait appears both in marble and on Hadrian's coinage, where it is used on coins dating roughly to ca. 128–138, when the emperor was in his 50s or early 60s. The dramatic "rejuvenation" seen in this portrait is unparalleled in imperial iconography, and various explanations have been suggested. Schröder argued that it depicted Hadrian as a "new Romulus"; Birley connected it to Hadrian's initiation to the mysteries at Eleusis, which led to the emperor's "rebirth." This paper presents the results of an attempt to solve this problem by the application of die analysis to the gold coinage bearing Hadrian's youthful portrait, with the goal of pinpointing the date of production of these coins. The evidence of die links shows that the youthful portrait of Hadrian was only employed at the very end of that emperor's coinage, in 138. This presents two possibilities: that this portrait was created in the last months of Hadrian's life, or that it was created immediately after his death but before his deification, when he received the title *divus*.

In this paper I argue for the latter. This thesis is supported by the five coin types that are paired with the youthful portrait: Trajan and Plotina, with the legend DIVIS PARENTIBVS ("to the deified parents [of Hadrian]"); Romulus, with the legend ROMVLO CONDITORI ("to Romulus the Founder"); Venus, with the legend VENERI GENETRICI ("to Venus the Bearer"); the emperor on horseback with legend VIRTVTI AVG ("the courage of the emperor"); and Hadrian with three military standards and the simple legend COS III PP. The first three types stress Hadrian's divine ancestry and suggest a connection with the mythical founder of Rome; the last two emphasize his role as military leader and advertise his *virtus*. I suggest that both the coins and the portrait were in fact created after Hadrian's death on the authority of his successor Antoninus, during the period when the senate resisted the deification of the former emperor. The youthfulness of the portrait, only made possible by the fact that the emperor was deceased, was intended to project a new public image of Hadrian, rejuvenating him in the eyes of his contemporaries and presenting him as an ideal candidate for deification.

Antinous and the Hem-hem Crown: Portraits with Egyptian Insignia in Roman Italy

Jessica Powers, San Antonio Museum of Art

The many surviving statues of Antinous, the Bithynian youth beloved and posthumously deified by Hadrian, that depict him with the attributes of various Greek and Roman gods or in the attire of an Egyptian king have been extensively studied. In this paper I examine a less well-known subset of Antinous' portraits that combine the classicizing features of his main portrait type with a separately fashioned attribute affixed above the forehead. Previous scholars have identified this now-missing feature as a hem-hem crown, an elaborate Egyptian crown worn by Osiris and Harpocrates and included on some portraits of Alexander the Great and the Ptolemies. Although these statues have been interpreted as presenting Antinous as Dionysos-Osiris, the broader significance of this particular headgear merits further attention. The recent discovery of a cutting for the attachment of a similar attribute on a portrait of Antinous in the San Antonio Museum of Art has prompted my reexamination of the use of the hem-hem crown on his portraits.

I focus on portraits of Antinous wearing the hem-hem crown that were intended for display in Italy. These include a statue from a villa near Palestrina (now in the Vatican Museums), a portrait head from Puteoli that may have been displayed in the Macellum (now in the Museo Archeologico dei Campi Flegrei, Baia), and a bust in the Palazzo Pitti (Florence). I discuss the differing responses that statues with this insignia may have elicited from viewers in public vs. private settings. This headgear was not part of the vocabulary of divine attributes occasionally employed in portraits of Roman emperors and their family members. I therefore consider the role that the hem-hem crown may have played in presenting the deified Antinous as a recipient of worship. Beyond its more general geographic reference to the location of his death and subsequent deification in Egypt, I also explore whether this crown's association with Osiris and Harpocrates may have linked Antinous to the cult of Isis.

The Paired Marble Portrait Busts of Septimius Severus and Julia Domna in Bloomington: New Research

Mark B. Abbe, University of Georgia, and *Julie Van Voorhis*, Indiana University

Although well known and widely reproduced in handbooks of Roman art, the paired marble portrait busts of Septimius Severus and Julia Domna in the Eskenazi Museum of Art, Indiana University, Bloomington, have received little sustained examination since their acquisition in 1975. This paper presents recent technical and archival investigations on these exceptionally well-preserved and high-quality portraits, focusing on previously unexplored issues: their production techniques, surface finishes, and original coloration; their provenance and its implications for understanding their ancient and post-Antique histories; and their possible display contexts and historically defined meanings in the Severan age.

The busts survive in a remarkable state of preservation, with most of their original marble finish and range of subtly variegated "high-gloss" polishes intact. Detailed examination of these surfaces provides new insights into the little-investigated working methods of *politores* in the High Imperial period and the busts' presumed "metropolitan" workshop techniques. Faint vestiges of ancient coloration on the garments of both busts indicate the intimate relationships between marble, surface finish, and painting in their original aesthetic appearance.

It has often been noted that the portrait busts lack a secure archaeological context. Less well known are unpublished anecdotal accounts of their discovery preserved in the archives of the Eskenazi Museum of Art. These vary in detail but generally adhere to a story that the busts were found together on the Esquiline Hill in Rome shortly after World War II, possibly with other sculptures. The alleged circumstances of their discovery, combined with the visual and technical analysis discussed above, reveal the probable intimate indoor contexts within which the busts were likely displayed in antiquity. Technical similarities with other well-preserved Severan portrait busts highlight possible ancient workshop connections, though in the view of the authors the notional Severan workshops postulated by other scholars may reveal more about modern artistic assumptions than the complex realities of ancient sculptural production in and around Rome. Comparative material, including less well-known paired portrait busts of the imperial couple from Gabii, Veii, and Tivoli, demonstrate the historical importance of such groups of imperial portrait busts and their specific historical messages and intended audiences in the Severan period. Thus, we are able to reconstruct a plausible history for the production, display context, and historical significance of the Eskenazi Museum of Art's portrait busts of Septimius Severus and Julia Domna.

Wives of "Crisis": Portraits of Women in the Third Century C.E.

Helen Ackers, Duke University

The third century C.E. has traditionally been defined as a period of "crisis" within the history of the Roman empire. Imperial power faced serious challenges in this period. However, the impact of these challenges on wider levels of Roman society is much less clear. The characterization of this as a period of "crisis" has consequently resulted in a very specific historical interpretation, which has traditionally privileged the portraits of the "soldier" emperors. This follows the circular logic that militaristic circumstances required masculine virtues and responses, which are accordingly identified in the male portraits, which are in turn utilized to confirm the militaristic ideals and focus of this era. In order to compensate for this bias, a focus on women's portraits is required.

As Schade observes, while the male outlook may have primarily determined the social role of women, women's portraits reveal elements of individuality, which indicated the personal, feminine identity of the subject. Roman women's portraits are a testament to the Roman conception that inner virtue and character could be expressed through physical appearance. Consequently, to deconstruct and understand the virtues, ideals, and roles these portraits present is not only to better understand the position of women in Roman society but also to reveal many of the normative values of the time. In this paper, I consequently draw on a number of case studies from my recently completed and yet to be presented D.Phil. research, on third-century women's portrait busts. Through studying these portraits in their physical, social, and historical context, we can learn a huge amount about third-century elite values and preoccupations. I argue that these portraits actually express the heightened ideological status of certain forms of Roman femininity in this period. In particular, a preoccupation with the private sphere and its incumbent virtues is powerfully testified in these portraits. In this respect, women's portraits tell a vital part of the third-century story. Rather than being expressive of spiritual escapism or emotional turmoil, women's portrait busts functioned as a means of reconfirming the Roman rhetoric of feminine virtue in the third century.

This paper draws on the findings from my recently completed D.Phil. at Oxford University, under the supervision of R.R.R. Smith, "Roman Women's Portrait Busts in the Third Century AD."

SESSION 4I
Imaging from the Air to the Artifact

CHAIR: *James Newhard*, College of Charleston

Heatseeker: Aerial Thermography at Ancient Methone

Hugh P.M. Thomas, University of Sydney, Australia

Infrared thermography, or thermal imaging, has traditionally been used as a remote sensing technique to determine whether subsurface features, such as walls or pits, generate a heat differentiation from the surrounding earth. To date, this form of remote sensing has been notoriously difficult to perform due to cost, low-resolution thermal cameras, and an inability to provide a stable aerial photographic platform. Moreover, thermal fluctuations produced by archaeological remains are highly volatile and are dependent on a multitude of uncontrollable variables including soil moisture, particle size, and the construction materials of archaeological features. These issues have restricted the widespread use of infrared thermography within archaeology; however, with the rapid development and adoption of Unmanned Aerial Vehicles (UAVs) over the last decade and developments in thermographic technology, thermal imaging technology is quickly becoming affordable and usable when attached to a UAV.

In this paper, I present a low-cost method of aerial thermography that was successfully employed at the Ancient Methone Archaeological Project, in Pieria, Greece. Ancient Methone was inhabited from the end of the Neolithic period and prospered as a major harbor and industrial center until it was destroyed in 354 B.C.E. by Philip II of Macedon. The site has been the focus of excavations since 2003 by the 27th Ephorate of Prehistoric and Classical Antiquities of Pieria and more recently as a synergesia with UCLA, under the direction of Manthos Besios, John Papadopoulos, and Sarah Morris. Excavations have recently revealed archaic workshops, an early stoa, and at least two deep Hypogeia, or large storage basements.

By using the latest low-cost, compact thermal cameras (Flir Vue Pro) in conjunction with a DJI Phantom 2, aerial thermography was performed at the site at a cost far below that proposed by previous studies, with results equaling or exceeding traditional methodologies. In combination with high-resolution aerial photogrammetry, this methodology has helped to clarify previous archaeological investigations at the site and revealed significant subsurface remains. Substantial sections of the site were flown on multiple occasions during the day, providing vital evidence in assisting our understanding of thermal fluctuations caused to subsurface remains over the course of the diurnal heating cycle.

Rock-Cut Sanctuaries in the Eastern Rhodope Mountains: Survey of the Gluhite Kamani Cult Complex and Surrounding Region

Lynn E. Roller, University of California, Davis, *Georghi Nehrizov*, Bulgarian National Archaeological Institute and Museums, *Julia Tzvetkova*, University of Sofia, and *Maya Vassileva*, New Bulgarian University

The Rhodope Mountains of southeastern Bulgaria are rich in unusual rock-cut formations that were apparently made for the purposes of cult. One concentration of such formations is found at the site of Gluhite Kamani ("Deaf Stones"), near the town of Lyubimets in Haskovo province. A survey conducted on foot in 2011 recorded more than 450 rock-cut formations, primarily trapezoidal niches. Excavation done together with the survey revealed that the site's principal periods of use were during two discontinuous phases, the Early Iron Age, 10th through sixth centuries B.C.E., and the Medieval period, 11th through 13th centuries C.E. Clay figurines, miniature pottery, and evidence for feasting support the cult-use hypothesis but indicate that human activity was limited to periodic visits. The meaning of these rock-cut niches remains obscure, and their relationship to permanent settlements in the surrounding region is unknown. Further efforts to investigate habitation patterns and routes of access to the monuments have been hampered by the rugged mountainous terrain and dense forest cover, making conventional survey techniques of walking the land impractical. Therefore we opted to arrange for a LiDAR scan by Airborne Technologies to survey the surrounding territory and record unusual features that are not visible due to the dense forest canopy. The scan, done in April 2015, provided a digital terrain model of approximately 20 square km of surface area in the vicinity of the niches. Using the LiDAR data, 153 features were identified and marked by GIS coordinates for further investigation on foot. Surface investigations of these features were carried out by a joint Bulgarian-American team in August 2015. Using the data from the LiDAR scan, the survey team was able to concentrate its efforts on selected targets; as a result, the survey successfully recorded and photographed the majority of the features noted from the LiDAR scan. While some proved to be part of the natural terrain, the team obtained evidence for 13 previously unknown archaeological sites, ranging from the Iron Age through Roman periods, and a medieval church. A large medieval fortress on the mountain summit was mapped, and sherds indicating an Iron Age presence there were collected. The information gathered from the survey will enable further investigations into ancient settlement and transportation patterns in the vicinity of the rock-cut cult features. This in turn will aid the project's long-term goal of obtaining a broad overview of settlement and cult activity in the region.

Multispectral UAVs in Classical Archaeology: The Case of Vulci

Maurizio Forte, Duke University, *N. Danelon*, Duke University, *D. Johnston*, Duke University, *K. McCusker*, Duke University, and *E. Newton*, Duke University

The introduction of UAV in archaeology is revolutionary because of the accuracy and quality of the aerial data sets produced and the implementation of multiple sensors in low-cost systems. High-resolution sensors coupled with novel photogrammetry processing techniques allow for the reconstruction of landscapes in three dimensions and can resolve patterns in living (e.g., vegetation patterns) and non-living components (rock, soil, water) that reflect how humans have interacted with that landscape over time. At the archaeological site of Vulci, we have employed a range of UAV platforms (multirotor and fixed wing) at resolutions ranging from 2 cm per pixel down to millimeter scale. Moreover, the involvement of spectral sensors ranging from visible wavelengths (red, green, and blue at 400 to 700 nm) through Red Edge (RE: 715 nm), near infrared (NIR: 850 nm) and infrared wavelengths (IR: 900 to 1300 nm) achieved very successful results in the interpretation of monumental buildings and urban settings. From these two-dimensional data, three-dimensional point clouds and digital terrain models (by structure from motion techniques) show multistratified archaeological features of the Roman and Etruscan city.

Aerial Archaeology: Digital Curation and Landscape Analysis in the South Caucasus Aerial Photo Archive Project (SCAPA)

Jessie Birkett-Rees, Monash University, *Kristen Hopper*, Durham University, *Giorgi Khaburzania*, National Agency for Cultural Heritage Preservation of Georgia, and *Abby Robinson*, The University of Melbourne

We present research into a unique archive of Soviet-era aerial photographs being applied to record, monitor, and model the archaeological landscapes of the South Caucasus. Aerial photography has long been recognized by archaeologists as a crucial resource for identifying and monitoring sites and landscape features. Historical photographs are especially valuable, because of their scarcity relative to modern imagery and given the potential they offer for monitoring change over time at the scale of site and landscape. An archive of approximately 300,000 images, covering most of Georgia and parts of Armenia and Azerbaijan, is currently housed in the Centre for Archaeological Studies at the Georgian National Museum in Tbilisi. The images date from the 1950s to 1985, a period of profound change in the region. Our analyses of a sample of the images shows their value in three key areas: monitoring the condition of existing sites, identifying previously unrecorded sites, and modeling the historic landscape. The South Caucasus Aerial Photographic Archive permits the identification of previously unrecorded archaeological features, some of which have since been attenuated or destroyed by agricultural practices and other activities. Equally, by comparing the archival images with modern imagery available on Google Earth and data from our field surveys, we can assess rates and types of damage that have had an impact on and may still be affecting archaeological sites. Additionally, the images were taken in stereo and therefore offer the prospect of constructing digital surface models of the historical landscape using photogrammetry. The accuracy and utility of the elevation model extracted from the archival imagery is compared with other commonly used digital elevation source data, creating a useful new resource from the archives. Here we outline the collaborative project to house and conserve the archive, provide examples of the key research potentials, and engage with the broader issue of documenting and disseminating archival data in the digital age.

Creating a Virtual World: Terrestrial Laser Scanning at Abdera

Maria Papaioannou, University of New Brunswick, *Peter Dare*, University of New Brunswick, and *Yong-Won Ahn*, University of New Brunswick

Terrestrial Laser Scanning (TLS) over the past 10 years has become an important tool in archaeological inquiry with numerous applications. It is used for detailed geomorphological and geoarchaeological investigations, stratigraphic analysis, architectural surveys, rescue archaeology, and conservation and documentation of historic sites. More specifically, TLS may be applied to previously excavated monuments, sites, and associated artifacts in order to collect accurate three-dimensional data that can be used to adjust previous data (e.g., historical drawings, photographs, plans, reconstructions) collected through empirical methods; detect structural problems; reveal features missed in previous investigations; assist professionals, museum curators, and conservators in taking appropriate steps to protect the site/monument from future deterioration; and serve as an educational tool, since further processing of the data may be used to create animations (such as fly-throughs) for use online, in museums, and in visitor reception areas.

This paper briefly highlights some key examples of TLS applications to archaeological sites/monuments in Greece while focusing on the results from the recent TLS of the Roman-period "Insula of Houses" at the coastal site of Abdera, in Thrace. As this insula was investigated by the Archaeological Society of Athens and the Greek Archaeological Service periodically over the past 60 years, but never excavated in its entirety, scanning of the site has allowed us to correct, adjust and combine existing plans; provide exact elevations for the surviving walls; study relationships not previously observed between the scattered domestic remains and surrounding roads; and create a virtual model for study and teaching purposes. The results of this study underscore the contributions of TLS to the study of town planning and domestic architecture at Abdera, propose new directions for future research and study, and assess the impact of TLS on future archaeological exploration.

The Asphendou Cave Petroglyphs: A Palimpsest in Stone

Thomas F. Strasser, Providence College, *Alexandra van der Geer*, National and Kapodistrian University of Athens, *Sarah Murray*, University of Nebraska–Lincoln, *Christina Kolb*, Freelance Archaeological Illustrator, and *Louis Ruprecht*, Georgia State University

This paper presents new research and documentation of the petroglyphs at Asphendou Cave (southwest Crete), first published in the early 1970s. The petroglyphs comprise a variety of iconographically non-uniform motifs, including most prominently cupules (often in circular patterns) and quadrupeds, but also a diversity of other enigmatic objects. Determining the absolute chronology of the engravings has proven problematic. While the original publication posited a pre-Neolithic date, some scholars prefer to push the engravings into the Minoan period or even later. The purpose of new research in the cave was twofold: to document these puzzling engravings using up-to-date scientific methods of photography and illustration and to reevaluate the likely date of the engravings.

Using photogrammetry, the project produced a detailed three-dimensional model of the flowstone in which the engravings are carved. Although many of the glyphs are less than a millimeter deep, the model was able to capture the surface with .01 mm accuracy and capture even very subtle details. A metrically accurate orthophoto was generated from the three-dimensional model, and this was used to trace a new drawing of the petroglyphs. This approach was advantageous because it yielded a more accurate and more detailed drawing than could have been achieved in the awkward space of the cave using more traditional methods.

In addition, analysis of the RTI imaging and three-dimensional models of the cave surface reveals subtle differences in the various glyphs (e.g., overlapping lines, variation in tool marks). Thus, we believe that we are in a better position to evaluate the meaning and history of the cave if we set aside the idea that the engravings represent a single episode. Instead, the petroglyphs probably represent a sequence of events, each with its own characteristic features. We argue that the earliest coherent set of engravings present on the cave surface might indeed predate the Minoan period.

Establishing Quantifiable Methodologies to Utilize Fingerprints as Reflections of Ancient Cultural Practices

Julie Hruby, Dartmouth College

Ceramics, lost-wax-cast bronzes, and plaster all preserve fingerprints left by their producers. While fingerprints have been used to approach a range of cultural practices for ancient Aegean and Near Eastern cultures, the methodologies developed to date tend to be labor intensive, statistically unsophisticated, or require large numbers of complete prints. Scholars working with modern populations have long recognized that certain print characteristics correlate with the sex, age, or health status of the person whose hands produce them. For example, men typically have wider ridges than do women, only partially accounted for by differences in hand sizes. A few archaeologists have used distributions of mean ridge breadths to evaluate the sexes or ages of potters. More recently, anthropologists have discovered several other quantitative print attributes that correlate with sex or age. Furthermore, it is probable that yet-unrecognized features correlate with producer attributes.

To find these requires the use of high-resolution three-dimensional imagery. Several methods for producing such images exist, each with costs and benefits. It also requires sophisticated data analysis, and I provide a road map for a project to obtain high-resolution scans from modern potters of known sex, whose prints will form a reference sample. We have access to the collections of museums of traditional ceramics in both Greece and Cyprus, each of which has data on many producers. In addition, potters of both sexes remain employed in both Greece and Cyprus, enabling us to contact and survey potters directly.

A scan of a print provides a high-resolution representation that is akin to a digital elevation map of the topography of the print, including ridge patterns, overall size, shape, and depression depth. Members of the team are exploring a range of avenues for analysis, including using the standard digital elevation modeling capabilities build in ArcGIS software, the development of new techniques that apply three-dimensional wavelet analyses, and neural network analysis. Our goal is to develop informative metrics that show high predictive power for the sex of the imprint maker. We plan to use high dimensional multivariate statistical techniques to evaluate the predictive power of the various print metrics. In the long term, we will use these models to explore questions about the identities of artisans in antiquity and associated social implications, predominantly the extent to which division of labor was gendered.

SESSION 4J
Graeco-Roman Graffiti, Seals, and Crafts

CHAIR: To be announced

Tagging Pompeii: Places of Names in Graffiti in the Roman Streetscape
Eeva-Maria Viitanen, Institutum Romanum Finlandiae

Personal names are the most common recognizable element in graffiti scratched on the walls of Roman-era Pompeii. They occur independently and as parts of a great variety of texts from greetings and insults to declarations of love and lines of poetry. Some 3,000 graffiti texts include at least one name, and some 20% of these texts are located on the facades of Pompeian houses. This paper examines the general distribution and singular findspots of personal names. Writing one's own name was as integral part of an ancient graffito as it is in a modern-day tag. Both writing traditions are ways to communicate with others, probably more importantly the community of taggers/writers and only secondarily the rest of the town's population. Pompeian graffiti in general occur on almost all kinds of houses: private, public, commercial, and even on temples. Poor documentation of graffiti during the earlier periods of Pompeii's excavation history affects the reconstruction and interpretation of their distribution, particularly in the western part of the town, but the more recently excavated eastern Pompeii displays interesting trends. Compared with the distribution of electoral notices, it is clear that graffiti were also intended for audiences who moved frequently on the side streets—for example, clusters of greetings are located in the side streets. But for all of the written communications, the doorways in the facades were an important focal point. Names are present in all the graffiti clusters in different parts of Pompeii and usually at least half of the texts in them contain one or more names. Frequency and visibility are important to modern taggers, but this is difficult to verify in Pompeii—some names are quite common, but it is not possible to know whether all graffiti containing Successus were written by the same person. Aemilius Celer, however, can be traced in probably almost 30 graffiti; most of them are on the facades. In the streetscape, Aemilius wrote on the walls of shops and modest private houses in many parts of the city, whereas his few contributions inside houses are in the very large private homes. Analyzing the locations where names have been written gives invaluable insights into the ancient graffiti habit and perceptions of the streetscape.

Conservation and Documentation Strategies for Preserving Ancient Graffiti on a Sandstone Funerary Temple at El Kurru, Sudan

Suzanne L. Davis, Kelsey Museum of Archaeology, University of Michigan,
Caroline I. Roberts, Kelsey Museum of Archaeology, University of Michigan,
Janelle Batkin-Hall, Kelsey Museum of Archaeology, University of Michigan, and
Geoff Emberling, Kelsey Museum of Archaeology, University of Michigan

This paper describes conservation planning and documentation for the preservation of a rock-cut, sandstone funerary temple at the site of El Kurru in Sudan. El Kurru is the location of a royal burial ground of ancient Kush, and the site encompasses multiple Napatan pyramid burials as well as two rock-cut funerary temples. The temple that is the focus of this project was built during the late Napatan period (ca. 350 B.C.E.), and its walls and columns are heavily inscribed with devotional graffiti from the Meroitic period (ca. 100 B.C.E–100 C.E.). It is an impressive and unique structure, a source of pride for local residents, and an interesting and accessible feature for visitors. The sandstone, however, is soft and crumbly, making conservation of the temple a high priority. Our conservation planning included elemental analysis of the sandstone, consolidant testing, a criterion-anchored rating (CAR) condition survey of the figural and geometric graffiti, and reflectance transformation imaging (RTI) of these graffiti.

We briefly describe elemental analysis of the sandstone, which confirmed that it is a straightforward aluminosilicate-bound, quartz-grained sandstone, without detectable clays, carbonates, or salts. These characteristics make the stone a good candidate for treatment with a silane-based consolidant, and we describe successful laboratory and field tests of the consolidant Conservare-OH 100. Special attention is given to our CAR survey and RTI methodology, however, because these techniques have broad application for archaeologists and conservators working with ancient graffiti and rock art.

CAR condition surveys tie a numeric value to a set of criteria that describe the physical condition of the surveyed object (or graffito). These surveys are simple to write, quick to conduct, and provide useful statistics for conservation planning. Our survey tool and its utility for the archaeological project is discussed in detail.

RTI, an imaging technique often used for visual enhancement purposes, is also an extremely useful technique for documenting poorly preserved surfaces. The Kurru graffiti were documented using highlight image capture, where the camera remains fixed and a portable flash is used to create a dome of light over the surface being photographed. A number of simple but significant modifications were made to the standard RTI protocol to adapt it to field conditions. These included adaptation of equipment, image capture, and processing techniques. We describe our modified protocol as well as our basic, low-tech field kit for RTI, a kit that utilizes a point-and-shoot Canon G16 camera.

Seals from the Hellenistic Archives of Kedesh, Seleucia, Uruk, and Delos

Sharon Herbert, University of Michigan

In 1999 and 2000, a joint University of Michigan and University of Minnesota team recovered more than 2,000 Hellenistic seal impressions from an archive room in a large administrative building built in the Persian era but successively repurposed under the Ptolemies and Seleucids. The archive dates to the Seleucid control of the site, from ca. 200 to 140 B.C.E., and is partially contemporary with archives at Seleucia on the Tigris, Uruk, and Delos. At this time Kedesh lay in the territory of the Phoenician city of Tyre and was inhabited, we think, by a mixed Graeco-Phoenician population.

The seal impressions from Kedesh present a wide spectrum of artistic choices available at this time and place. They reflect in some cases local preferences and in others the official symbolism of the Seleucid monarchy. At one end we have a few impressions that show the Phoenician goddess Tanit with a Semitic inscription—"He who is over the land"—in the middle a bilingual seal dated in both the Seleucid and Tyrian eras, and at the far end hundreds of impressions from seals representing Greek gods with their standard Greek paraphernalia—the most striking examples, copies of the Athena Parthenos. But on closer inspection, not all of the "Greek" images are so straightforward. Many show modifications that reflect local customs. This is especially true of the many Aphrodites and Tyches and a subset of Phoenician funerary masks found among the Greek comic masks.

Now that identification of all the Kedesh sealings is complete, we are able to make statistical comparisons on the choices of subject matter made by the artists and clients of its region with those from the users of other published Seleucid archives, namely Seleucia and Uruk, and also with the more cosmopolitan site of Delos. While some subjects are equally popular at all the sites—Apollo, Tyche, and Eros tending to be favorites—each archive exhibits local tastes and traditions as well.

In the Hellenistic era the art produced and used in the various conquered Seleucid territories runs the gamut from total appropriation and assimilation of Greek styles and themes to a conservative, even confrontational, preservation of past norms. With the variations in the thousands of seals documented from the archives of Seleucia, Uruk, Delos, and Kedesh we can demonstrate some of these in dramatic detail and depth.

Reconstructing Networks from the Archive of Seleukeia on the Tigris: Ruler Portraits on Hellenistic Seals

Laure Marest-Caffey, University of California, Berkeley

A better understanding of the use of ruler portraits in the Hellenistic period requires a study of their deployment as devices on seals. In doing so, we increase significantly the corpus of royal portraits that can be tied to documented archaeological contexts and/or specific functions. But the sphragistic evidence presents its own difficulties. Only a small set of sealed documents and containers, mostly papyri discovered in Egyptian caches, retain both the support and its sealing(s) still attached, thus providing specific information concerning the use of engraved portraits. Furthermore, many of the sealings—small lumps of clay or other malleable material on which seals were pressed—have disintegrated since their discovery or are now lost, since the documents themselves were the primary beneficiaries of conservation efforts. Conversely, several archives discovered around the Mediterranean over the last century offer large troves of relatively well-preserved sealings. Unfortunately, the supports were destroyed in the very event that preserved the clay pellets, usually a fire. But is all information contained in the original documents ineluctably lost?

A benefit of the "big data" provided by sealing archives, such as that discovered at Seleukeia on the Tigris (Iraq) in the 1960s and 1970s by an by an Italian mission from the University of Turin, stems from their nature as closed, largely independent systems, as opposed to the isolated discoveries of Egyptian papyri. This paper demonstrates that by applying modern tools such as "network analysis," we can reconstruct—to some extent—patterns of use of engraved portraits and even deduce the general content of the lost documents. Sealings carry evidence of the social and economic interactions between persons, groups, and administrative offices that originally took place within the archival building.

Comparing Third-Millennium Material Use: Siliceous Paste (Faience) in the Indus Valley, Mesopotamia, and Egypt

Heather M.-L. Miller, University of Toronto

A bewildering assortment of materials using siliceous pastes (also known as faience, frit, or composition) were used to make small objects such as figures, beads, and containers, in ancient Egypt, Mesopotamia, the Indus Valley, the Mediterranean, and regions beyond and between. From very early beginnings in the sixth millennium B.C.E. or earlier in some regions, the assortment of these materials reached a great diversity of production techniques and materials in the third and second millennia B.C.E., with much less diversity of appearance. In places where these materials have seen more analytical study, such as Egypt and the Indus Valley, similarities, but also striking differences, occur in the regional assortments of materials and techniques employed to produce quite similarly appearing materials, used to make objects clearly belonging to the local corpus of style and topic. I suggest multiple mechanisms involved in the spread of these materials and their manufacture. I also discuss the different use and value of these materials in different regions, in the context of the very different data sets available. I address these issues primarily from the perspective of the Indus Valley, my own area of research, but with a focus on how the data from Egypt and Mesopotamia indicate similarities and differences in these answers. With this paper, I particularly hope to reach out to researchers working in the Near East, where aside from Moorey's masterful summary, this material class has seen very little attention in comparison with Egypt and the Indus.

Textile Production and Consumption in Karanis, Egypt

Andrew Cabaniss, University of Michigan, and *Michael Koletsos*, University of Michigan

The recent boom in studies of textile production in the ancient Mediterranean has focused on sites that lack both preserved textiles and production implements. In this paper, we focus on the collection of materials from the Graeco-Roman site of Karanis (modern Kom Aushim), located in the Fayum of Egypt, and currently housed in the Kelsey Museum of Archaeology at the University of Michigan. Since their excavation in the 1920s and 1930s, the textiles have received sporadic treatment and publication, but little attention has been paid to the production implements themselves. Ranging from the wool and flax fibers through the tools for cleaning, spinning, dying, and weaving, the entire process of production is evident from the material under study.

Karanis provides a unique combination of extensive excavation and a representative preserved sample of both textile production implements and the textiles themselves. Using methods developed by the Center for Textile Research in Copenhagen that tie production practices with the morphology of tools, we link the different materials, tools, and manufacturing techniques with the general corpus of textile fragments. By taking a holistic site-wide approach and using more narrow chronological information when possible, we believe we can elucidate a connection between the different modes of production and the use and distribution of these textiles across the site. Not only does this study test a common methodology in current scholarship, but we also examine specialization and diversity within the communities of production in a manner that can be tied to the extensive papyrological sources that mention the production of textiles, enabling further interdisciplinary work on the organization of the economy and society in Graeco-Roman Egypt.

SESSION 5A
Women in Greece and the Near East

CHAIR: *Kathryn Topper*, University of Washington

Solon and the Women of Early Greece

Anne Weis, University of Pittsburgh

In a well-known passage, Plutarch (*Vit. Sol.* 21.4) summarized the laws of Solon as they pertained to the public appearances of women, observing that he "imposed a law on the women's 'appearances' [tais exodois ton gynaikov]—both those for mourning and those for festivals [kai tois penthesi kai tais eortais]" and specifying the limitations that Solon placed on dress, the amounts of food the women carried, and their other accoutrement. The details of this passage are often confused with the restrictions Solon placed on funerals but as J.H. Blok observed, the text distinguishes clearly between the two sets of rules.

Plutarch's use of the word *exodoi* in this context is almost certainly anachronistic: it may appear first in Greek authors of the fourth through the first centuries B.C.E. who characterized the *exodoi* as carefully considered projections of family piety, wealth, and social status (cf. e.g., Phintys apud Stob. 4.23.61 p. 590; Thescliff p. 152; Pl. *Leg*. 784d; Theophr. *Char.* 22.10). The practice is, however, older: images of women in procession appear first on funerary and votive dedications of the seventh century B.C.E. and increased rapidly in number, fabric, and format in the sixth century to include votive pinakes and offering plates, statuettes in terracotta and bronze, and marble statuary. These images are, ostensibly, the feminine counterpart to those of men drinking, arming, hunting, and fighting that emerged in this period as vehicles for the aristocratic male virtues of heroism, status, and wealth.

Processional images were used in different ways in different vase fabrics or in other contexts, but, by the seventh century they were already a topos. They celebrated, variously, the piety of elite women, the achievements of heroes (and by association those of elite males), civic prosperity, and perhaps the friendships that bound individual women together. At base, however, they provide collective evidence for the "public appearances" of elite women as an early polis institution, one that provided a backdrop to and filled the space between the rich female graves of Late Geometric Athens and the showy korai of the later Archaic period. This material has not been systematically collected or analyzed. The talk focuses, therefore, on some of the better-known examples, their context in the archaeological and visual record, and their relationship to the few written sources for women of this period that survive, especially the Laws of Solon.

Engendering Dynasty: Female Bodies and Figural Traditions in Lycian Relief

Patricia E. Kim, University of Pennsylvania

The figural reliefs on the Lycian tombs of Asia Minor have drawn scholarly attention for their fusion of Greek and Near Eastern stylistic techniques and iconography. Lycian pillar tomb monuments in particular are now acknowledged to have adapted specific themes (e.g., wrestling, hunting, banqueting) and compositional strategies (royal audience frieze format) in their sculptural projects as ways to define a new visual language of power and dynastic self-representation. However, this emphasis on the adaptation of attributes related to the "heroic male" takes for granted the social and cultural contexts in which this new visual language of dynasty was created: dynastic and commemorative pillar tombs of the fifth and fourth centuries began to include representations of high-ranking, dynastic female bodies, which was a unique practice within this time period on either side of the Aegean.

After establishing this as an exceptional feature in artistic and sculptural practice, I proceed to draw out its implications for understanding key aspects of visual languages of power. First, my observations expand on the scholarly conversations around "fusion" art by focusing on the models for the representation of female bodies in local Anatolian contexts as well as in artistic practices that constituted a supraregional koinée. Second, I argue that Lycian expansion and consolidation of territory led to the development of a dynastic visual culture grounded in normative notions of the family to validate historical narratives that legitimized political power. Depictions of high-ranking women in particular enforced ideologies of power, authority, and stability. Rather than embodying "otherness" as a category of exclusion and polarity, female bodies were organized into an ideology of difference in which men conferred a hierarchical superiority to themselves over women. In these ways, I argue that the inclusion of female bodies in dynastic monuments bolstered the constructs of heroic masculinity that elite men had traditionally emphasized. Finally, I address how these visual constructs of the dynastic *oikos* continued to shape later figural traditions of imperial desire within the development of Hellenistic royal art.

Imagining Amazons in the Hellenistic World: Outsiders, Opponents, or Champions?

Amanda E. Herring, Loyola Marymount University

From their Greek portrayal as bellicose antagonists to their modern depictions as heroes in Wonder Woman comics, Amazons have been subject to frequent reinvention in myth and image. In archaic and classical Greece, Amazons were constructed both as worthy opponents for great heroes like Herakles and Achilles and as others who transgressed against societal norms and upended gender roles. The Hellenistic period saw a reimagining of Amazons and their manner of representation. While not as ubiquitous as in earlier centuries, Amazons remained popular subjects in art, especially on public monuments and sacred buildings. Their manner of depiction, however, varied greatly.

The Little Attalid Dedication in Athens included an Amazonomachy in tandem with a Gigantomachy, a Persianomachy, and a Galatomachy, expressly evoking the classical Athenian iconography of the Amazon as a stand-in for the barbarian other. The Temple of Artemis Leukophryene at Magnesia's depiction of a Heraklean Amazonomachy again echoed traditional ideas of the Amazon as a worthy opponent for the mighty Greek hero. But, due to the historical role of Amazons as founders of the nearby and closely related cult of Artemis Ephesia, this depiction carried additional significance to the local viewer, who would recognize the Amazons not as barbarian others, but as an integral part of their own history.

The image of the Amazon moves even further away from the standard Amazonomachy on the north frieze of Temple of Hekate at Lagina in Karia. Here, Amazons do not fight, but instead actively participate in a treaty between Karia and Rome. It is the Amazons, not the armed soldiers, who stand in for the people of Karia, and it is the Amazons with whom the audience is supposed to identify.

These artworks raise important questions about Hellenistic depictions of Amazons. Can Hellenistic Amazons be interpreted as representations of the other in a period in which the definition of otherness has shifted dramatically? When the dividing line between Greek and barbarian remained fluid, what purpose did images of Amazons serve? In regions such as the Black Sea or Anatolia that were traditionally viewed as homelands for the Amazons, with whom did the audience identify? The Amazon or her opponent? Through a comparative analysis of sculptural representations within their original historical and cultural contexts, this paper provides a reevaluation of one of the most iconic subjects in Greek art and its reimagining in the Hellenistic world.

SESSION 5B
Archaeological Survey

CHAIR: *Alex R. Knodell*, Carleton College

The Ayios Vasilios Survey Project

Corien Wiersma, University of Groningen

The Ayios Vasilios Survey Project targets the Mycenaean palatial settlement of Ayios Vasilios in Laconia, Greece. The survey forms part of the Ayios Vasilios Project. This consists of externally funded excavations carried out under the auspices of the Archaiologiki Etaireia and a public outreach program financed by the local authorities and a fundraising campaign. The project is supervised by the Laconia Directorate of Antiquities. The aims of the five-year survey project are twofold: to start reconstructing the habitation history of the site and to develop a methodology for the survey of prehistoric urban centers.

A pilot survey has been carried out in the Fall of 2015. Part of the main palatial settlement has been intensively surveyed, but also areas of lower find densities were included. The survey was carried out in a grid with units of 10 x 10 m, while larger units of 20 x 20 m were used in areas of lower find densities. Inside the 10 m grid units a total collection took place in an area of 25 m^2 and a grab sample of potentially diagnostic material in the remaining 75m^2. In the 20 m units, only grab samples were collected from the entire 400 m^2. During the collection of the finds by teams of five walkers, the team leader filled out forms detailing information about the weather and surface conditions.

The survey finds largely corroborate the results from earlier surveys and the current excavations: small numbers of Early Helladic II, Middle Helladic, and Late Helladic I–II sherds were collected from a limited area around the palace, while Late Helladic IIIA material was more widespread. Very few Late Helladic IIIB ceramics were found, and no Protogeometric or Archaic material was found. Some classical–Hellenistic ceramic material was found, as well as a significant amount of painted tiles indicating the presence of a building. Byzantine ceramics were found widespread over the area.

The earlier obtained geophysical data have helped in evaluating our survey data and have confirmed the location of habitation as seen in the survey data. The survey and geophysical data together have provided various locations of interest for further geophysical research and potential digging of test trenches, including a possible location of a classical/Hellenistic building.

The spatial coverage method tested will be retained during the next survey. However, suggestions are made regarding the sampling method.

The Thebes Ismenion Synergasia Project, 2011-2016

Kevin Daly, Bucknell University, *Alexandra Charami*, Ephorate of Boiotian Antiquities, *Nikos Kontoiannis*, Ephorate of Boiotian Antiquities, and *Stephanie Larson*, Bucknell University

We present the main results of six years of exploration on the Ismenion Hill in Thebes, Greece, a synergasia effort between the Ephorate of Antiquities and Boiotia and Bucknell University. The excavation has now begun its first study season and has backfilled all explored areas of the Ismenion Hill. We begin with the results of GPR, electromagnetic, magnetic, and topgraphical surveys, and we compare these results generally with the subsequent findings from the past six years of excavation (2011–2016). The project has revealed numerous phases of activity on the hill, and in this report we highlight the classical temple to Apollo, the Early to Middle Byzantine cemetery, and Late Byzantine habitation on and near the site.

We introduce new fragments of the temple to Ismenion Apollo alongside rediscovered fragments from the sanctuary from the Thebes Museum storerooms, previously excavated by Keramopoullos in the 1910s. We present a new reconstruction of the temple, and we discuss the building's various phases. We also comment on evidence for other structures of the classical sanctuary.

We then detail the results from more than 45 Early and Middle Byzantine graves on the site, all associated with the two nearby funerary churches, both founded in the Early Byzantine period. We present general discoveries from analysis of the skeletal material, and we also introduce evidence for standard burial practices as well as burial practices involved in two Middle Byzantine mass graves.

In the final section of the paper, we offer new thoughts on the Late Byzantine period in Thebes as seen in the evidence from two excavated pits on and near the hill, one which reveals evidence for trade and relationships in pottery export between Thebes and Chalkis, and the other which advances our knowledge of cooking wares and life in general in Catalan Thebes. We briefly compare these findings with Byzantine built structures on the hill and an associated water system, a noteworthy feature of southeast Thebes with very few extant remains.

The paper contributes to knowledge of the classical sanctuary to Ismenian Apollo, the continued use of a large Byzantine cemetery in medieval Thebes, and domestic activity in southeastern Thebes in the heyday of the medieval city. Few results from Byzantine pits or cemeteries in Thebes have been systematically presented, and so with this paper we offer some remedy for this lack of knowledge as well as a contribution to the understanding of the classical site.

When the Goings Gets Rough: Survey in the Lower Göksu Valley, Rough Cilicia

Naoise Mac Sweeney, University of Leicester, and *Tevfik Emre Şerifoğlu*, Bitlis Eren University

The Göksu River valley was a crucial channel of communication during several periods of antiquity, linking the central Anatolian plateau with the Mediterranean Sea. The valley was more than simply a thoroughfare, however, but a dynamic landscape in its own right, with changing patterns of land use and occupation. The Lower Göksu Archaeological Salvage Survey (LGASS) is investigating these local patterns of landscape use, building on the work of previous survey projects in the upper areas of the valley as well as on the results of previous excavations. By adopting an explicitly landscape-focused approach, LGASS is developing a new understanding of the relationship between sites and routes—of both inhabiting and moving through the landscape in different periods from the Early Bronze Age to the Byzantine era. This paper presents the results of our work from 2013 to 2016, highlighting several important new findings. Crucially, we have been able to shed more light on the earliest periods of the valley's occupation, expand our knowledge of the Iron Age, and add nuance to our understanding of Late Antique settlement patterns and religious networks.

In the Mountains, Between Empires: Fieldwork in the Lerik District of Azerbaijan

Lara Fabian, University of Pennsylvania, *Jeyhun Eminli*, Azerbaijan National Academy of Sciences, *Susannah Fishman*, University of Pennsylvania, and *Emil Iskenderov*, Azerbaijan National Academy of Sciences.

The Lerik in Antiquity Archaeological Project (LAAP) considers life at the crossroads of Achaemenid, Seleucid, Roman, Arsacid, and Sarmatian networks of influence in the rugged Talysh Mountains of Azerbaijan. Begun in northern Lerik in 2016, this collaborative Azerbaijani-American project builds on research initiated in 2011 at the Piboz Tepe necropolis, which was conducted under the auspices of the Lerik-Gürdəsər Project of the Institute of Archaeology and Ethnography of the Azerbaijan National Academy of Sciences (ANAS). Since 2011, more than 140 graves have been uncovered at the site, largely corresponding to the fifth century B.C.E.– second century C.E. but continuing into the Islamic period. This paper provides a brief overview of the work of the Lerik-Gürdəsər Project as well as a discussion of the new phase of collaborative research.

The 2016 season, directed jointly by researchers from the ANAS and the University of Pennsylvania, saw the continuation of work at Piboz Tepe, including the osteological examination of burials and petographic analysis of ceramics from the tombs. In conjunction with the work at the necropolis itself, targeted test trenches examined possible settlement locations related to the necropolis. One zone of test excavation uncovered burnt remains of a structural collapse possibly congruent with a period of the necropolis' use, which will be the subject of future research.

The season also included a survey of the valley system surrounding Piboz Tepe and adjacent valleys within a 25 km^2 survey zone. The survey aims to reach a better understanding of land-use patterns across the steep, rugged territory. It included mapping of previously registered archaeological sites and also used extensive and intensive investigative methods as well as remote sensing to identify unrecorded archaeological remains.

Exploration in the zone examines an often-ignored archaeological landscape: a low-density highland region situated at the interstices of empires. We focus on the choices made by these highland dwellers, whose mortuary assemblages indicate interaction with their imperial neighbors, but whose precise place within larger systems of interaction remains unclear. While many archaeological investigations of empires focus the manifestations of imperial power in imperial centers, our research explores "empire" beyond imperial control—arguing that it is impossible to understand the ancient empires without understanding the spaces between them.

Modeling Mortuary Populations Through Systematic Field Survey

Paul R. Duffy, University of Toronto, *László Paja*, University of Szeged, *Györgyi Parditka*, University of Michigan, and *Julia I. Giblin*, Quinnipiac University

Disposal of the dead is a multistep process that often involves a number of people and multiple locations over time. Understanding the size and internal composition of a cemetery generated by these processes is important for estimating the social and chronological patterning of the people buried there. When the number of the dead in a cemetery, the length of time the cemetery was in use, and the life expectancy of the population are known, we can also establish the size and composition of the living community who used it. Although surface collection is increasingly used in characterizing the size and internal organization of settlements, it is infrequently used to model mortuary spaces. This paper addresses the shortfall by combining surface collection and excavation to describe activity areas and population size at a Bronze Age (2300–1100 B.C.E.) cremation cemetery in eastern Hungary. While prehistoric features and activity areas are difficult to identify using surface collection alone, we find that the combination of surface collection and excavation in a GIS setting permits us to estimate of the size of the cemetery, propose plausible extents of activity areas within the cemetery, and model the regional community that produced it.

SESSION 5C
Undergraduate Paper Session

CHAIR: *Ann Olga Koloski-Ostrow*, Brandeis University

Pictorial Graffiti in Context: An Analysis of Drawn Graffiti in Herculaneum

Grace Gibson, Sewanee: The University of the South

Although hundreds of textual graffiti have been documented and published in the *Corpus Inscriptionum Latinarum* and by scholars such as Antonio Varone, pictorial graffiti are often excluded in publication. Martin Langner's work on pictorial graffiti ameliorates this exclusion, but his work omits depictions of *phalloi* and focuses on categories of graffiti rather than their spatial relationships. This artificial division between textual graffiti and pictorial graffiti prevents us from evaluating the relationships between each group and their respective spatial contexts.

Drawing evidence from on-site research with the Herculaneum Graffiti Project as well as the Ancient Graffiti Project's search engine of graffiti from Herculaneum, I discuss the number and content of pictorial graffiti found in Herculaneum. Next, I analyze the subject matter of the graffiti in relation to their placement in domestic spaces. By discussing unique sets of graffiti within their physical context, such as a group of gladiator helmets in the Casa del Gran Portale (V.35), I show how the placement and content of drawn graffiti, especially in high concentrations, challenges our traditional interpretations of Roman house layouts. Furthermore, I discuss how individual graffiti could relate to other graffiti in their respective spaces, providing insight not only into the interaction of pictorial graffiti, but also into the meaning of their nearby textual counterparts.

The Roman Villa at Gerace: African Influence on Sicilian Mosaics in the Fourth Century C.E.

Siena Hutton, The University of British Columbia

During the fourth century C.E., mosaic designs across the Roman empire begin to reflect the African trend of "vegetalization," making use of a range of motifs derived from plant matter, including representations of laurel leaves and rosettes. This paper discusses how the mosaic floor found in the southern corridor at the archaeological site of Gerace, in Enna, Sicily, serves as a prime example of this influence, demonstrating the transference of styles and motifs across the empire. It draws primarily on field observations from the 2015 excavations at Gerace, conducted by Roger Wilson, from the Department of Classical, Near Eastern, and Religious Studies at the University of British Columbia, as well as the works of other scholars. It begins by describing the design motifs, position, and configurations of the mosaics. Next, it offers commentary on their wider significance through comparison to similar designs in Rome, Corinth, Antioch, Sardinia, and Carthage: the hub of the African mosaic industry. Lastly, it describes how the variable quality of the craftsmanship of the Gerace mosaics serves as an example of the way in which trends could spread through the Roman empire. Given their parallels in various other locations, to what extent do the Gerace mosaics demonstrate the spread of vegetal motifs, and how does their quality impact our understanding of how knowledge of such patterns was transmitted?

The Long and Complicated Relationship Between Humans and Infectious Diseases

Sterling Wright, The University of Texas at Austin

The co-evolutionary relationship between humans and infectious diseases dates back to thousands of years. Until the 20th century, scholars could only study the history of infectious diseases through the texts of ancient literary sources. Genetic testing on ancient DNA (aDNA) of infectious diseases, however, has brought forth more information about the impact of infectious diseases in the historic past than could have been imagined. For instance, one type of genetic testing, PCR identification, has aided scholars in diagnosis by providing an alternative method to analyzing a skeleton's morphological traits. Furthermore, PCR identification has helped scholars by confirming that tuberculosis was present in the New World before Columbus. Although PCR identification has aided scholars tremendously in understanding diseases of the ancient past and has been the standard genetic test used for archaeological studies for the past three decades, a new and more advanced form of genetic testing is present and revolutionizing the field of paleopathology. Next-Generation Sequencing (NGS) has not only aided diagnosis but also aided scholars in understanding the evolution of diseases by providing data of the whole genome. NGS, for instance, has provided data to support the claim that Y. pestis persisted throughout Europe for four hundred years after the Black Death. However, although genetics has provided more information about these ancient diseases, the lack of standardization in both fields has caused some scholars to question the veracity of this information. Some scholars have questioned the veracity of genetic testing on aDNA of infectious diseases because of the high risk of contamination not only in the field where the archaeological remains were unearthed, but also in the laboratories where the genetic testing itself occurs. This paper reviews the three case studies presented by Zuckerman and her colleagues in greater detail along with other studies that have shown how the lack of standardization both in the field of excavation and in the laboratory has caused major problems in the field of paleopathology. Furthermore, the author hopes the case studies in this paper urges archaeologists to consider adopting a more uniform protocol when excavating skeletal materials, especially since the cost of NGS methods are decreasing at unprecedented rates. By establishing a protocol, the author believes that scholars will have more confidence when conducting genetic testing on aDNA of infectious diseases.

A Blast from the Past: Digital Antiquity in the Classroom

Jaymie Orchard, University of British Columbia, *Siena Hutton*, University of British Columbia, and *Chloe Martin-Cabanne*, University of British Columbia.

From Stone to Screen (FSTS) is student-run initiative that features an open-access digital database for the artifact collections housed in the Classical, Near Eastern and Religious Studies Department at the University of British Columbia. One challenge associated with the study of the ancient world is the inaccessibility of artifacts due to their age, fragility, and relative rarity. Innovations within the digital humanities have enabled scholars to make traditionally inaccessible materials available online to students and researchers. FSTS's expanding online collections can be accessed by scholars researching material culture, and anyone else who is interested in studying artifacts from the ancient world.

FSTS promotes the use of open-access digital resources by creating teaching modules—developed for students, by students—that are freely available online to a global audience. The modules encourage students and instructors to engage directly with primary source materials that provide context for aspects of religion, society, politics, and economics in the ancient world. Each module integrates objects from the FSTS artifact collection database, ranging from five-minute activities to hour-long lesson plans, complete with information packages, PowerPoint presentations, handouts, worksheets, and answer keys on a wide variety of topics pertaining to antiquity. Students become more engaged with the ancient world when they understand the context of an artifact and how material culture contributes to historical knowledge. Through introductory modules on Roman imperial coinage and ancient pottery, students learn how to read, analyze, and identify different examples of material culture, teaching them the skills required to glean historical significance from artifacts found outside their textbooks. In this paper, we present the Roman Imperial Propaganda module, a lecture demonstrating how coins may be used as tools to understand imperial promotion during the second century C.E.

FSTS aims to make artifacts more approachable for both instructors and students through the development of open-access lecture modules. These modules provide teaching resources for instructors to integrate material culture into the classroom. By teaching students the skills required to engage directly with artifacts from the ancient world, students are offered the opportunity to get their heads out of their textbooks and blast into the past!

SESSION 5D
Sculpture and Greek Sanctuaries

CHAIR: To be announced

To Slay the Slain? (Re)Analyzing a Funerary Scene on an Ivory Plaque from the Sanctuary of Orthia at Sparta

Megan Johanna Daniels, University of Puget Sound

The carved ivory plaques from the Sanctuary of Orthia at Sparta, published in Richard Dawkins' 1929 volume on the excavations, constitute some of the sanctuary's earliest and wealthiest dedications, dating between 800 and 600 B.C.E. As a whole, the ivory plaques have received some attention in scholarly literature, particularly given their Near Eastern associations. Two plaques, however, dating to the mid–late eighth century, have been largely ignored: these plaques are mirror images of one another and show a funerary scene featuring an old man and two young women standing over the body of a youthful male, wrapped in a shroud and lying on a bier.

I argue that these plaques reflect a longstanding, widespread myth of the death of a youthful god, and more specifically are reminiscent of the Ugaritic myth of the death and resurrection of the god Baal, known from the Ugaritic tablets (*Die keilalphabetischen Texte aus Ugarit*, Vol 1, pt. 6). While a gap of around 600 years separates the Ugaritic myth from the ivory plaques, a number of other deities between the Phoenician, Greek, and Italic worlds took on the role of dying god in the first millennium, including Melqart, Herakles, and Adonis. Furthermore, these gods enjoyed worship alongside a powerful female counterpart, who served as their protector and/or lover.

In the first part of this paper, I present the details of the ivory plaques and their associations to the Ugaritic myth of Baal. I then situate these plaques amidst the broader iconographical repertoire from the Sanctuary of Orthia and compare the associations of a dying-and-rising god and powerful female deity within this sanctuary to other archaic religious sites in the Mediterranean, notably the sanctuary at Santa Venera (Pyrgi) in Italy. The results of such comparisons reveal notable parallels in religious symbolism operating between the eastern and western Mediterranean in the Archaic period. Such parallels are especially reflected in (1) textual and iconographic symbolism of deities connected to celestial phenomena and seasonal cycles; and (2) the religious control exercised by elites over worship of these deities, as reflected in wealthy dedications. Finally, I briefly revisit early 20th century conceptions of the dying-and-rising god. I conclude that we can move beyond universalist and ritualist interpretations of this trope, and instead see the worship of a dying god and female counterpart as representative of shared notions of elite sociopolitical power taking form across the Mediterranean in the first millennium B.C.E.

The Most Popular Girl in the Shrine: Reconsidering the Corinthian Standing Female Figurine

Theodora Kopestonsky, University of Tennessee, Knoxville

As a coroplastic leader in the ancient Greek world, Corinthians exported their terracotta figurines alongside their ceramics far and wide. The moldmade standing female figurine holding an attribute in both hands was an especially brilliant creation that survived two centuries (late sixth to late fourth century B.C.E.) virtually unchanged. She became a standard figurine produced, purchased, and dedicated throughout Corinth, the Greek mainland, and beyond. With her *polos* adorned head, rigid frontal stance, simplified outfit, and different attributes, the Corinthian standing female figurine finds stylistic parallels in other poleis. She is not a unique type, but this version is distinctly Corinthian. Due to her pervasiveness in the archaeological record, this figurine type is often overlooked by scholars as too generic or inconsequential. Yet this figurine appears in almost every shrine and sacred context at Corinth during the Classical period and is imported throughout the Greek world. She has an important meaning to the dedicator, and her presence often is the first clue of a ritual deposit. She can be found in the large sanctuaries (Asklepeion, Demeter and Kore on Acrocorinth, and the Sacred Spring) or the small shrines (Kokkinovrysi, Stele Shrine A, Heroon of the Crossroads, Tile Works, and many more) and dedicated to both masculine and feminine deities. Her popularity suggests a modification of ritual practice at Corinth.

During the Classical period, figurines become more standard and mass produced. At this time, the dedicator's intent becomes more important. In truth, the vagueness of this figurine makes her universal. In multiples or in combination with other types, the standing female figurine takes on a new life. She could be anyone. Always appropriate, the Corinthian standing female figurine had consequence due to the antiquity of style and her visibility—she could be seen in sanctuaries for generations. Addressing current research, this paper reconsiders the role of the standing female figurine in dedicatory rites at Corinth and beyond as well as highlighting the importance of the dedicator's narrative.

The Enthroned Archaic, Acrolithic Statues of Demeter and Kore from Morgantina
Laura Maniscalco, Assessorato dei Beni Culturali, Regione Sicilia

The recent restoration of elements from two acrolithic sculptures found at Morgantina in central Sicily, and the identification of more elements that perhaps can be ascribed to the complex, brings together considerable useful information to the study of large-scale cult statuary in the ancient Mediterranean. Traced to the sanctuary in contrada San Francesco Bisconti and returned to the Sicilian region after a landmark judiciary case, the marble faces, hands and feet represent the exposed, fleshy portions of two female figures, most likely Demeter and Kore. A first examination in 2008 by Clemente Marconi, which describes the figures as seated, is now complemented by the careful cleaning of the elements in 2015 by the Centro Regionale per il Restauro at Palermo, which has revealed that holes drilled in the hands continue from one side of the stone to the other, as well as the presence of changes in texture on the side of the faces and clear traces of red paint on the lips, along the edge of the bust line, and on the feet. While the discovery that the holes go through the hands can give us more information on the objects that the female figures were holding, the changes in texture along the side of the faces can give information on the position of a wig or veil. The red lines on the feet clearly indicate sandals. Fragments of terracotta appliques identified among the materials recovered at the site in the past years may have belonged to one or more thrones (other, similar elements of a throne, formerly in Basel, Switzerland, are conserved in the Kunsthistorisches Museum of Vienna), and they seem to confirm the seated composition. A small fragment of a head in terracotta found at the site similar in form to the acrolithic heads suggests that miniature, coroplastic versions of the figures were also being produced. While the importance of statuary to Greek cult is paramount, not many actual cult statues are known. The acrolithic figures from Morgantina join a limited and fragmentary sorority of what were once imposing representations of well-known female Greek divinities.

Idols from the Classical Temple of Hera at the Argive Heraion
Christopher A. Pfaff, Florida State University

In his detailed study of the sculpture of the Argive Heraion, Fritz Eichler (1919) recognized for the first time that there are two representations of archaistic idols clasped by human hands among the fragments of the architectural sculpture of the classical Temple of Hera. On the basis of the testimony of Pausanias (2.17.3), which indicates that the Capture of Troy was depicted "above the columns" of the temple, Eichler assigned both idols to a pedimental composition showing this subject and concluded that one idol was clasped by Kassandra as she was assaulted by the lesser Aias and that the second idol was clasped by Helen as she sought protection from the murderous intentions of her husband Menelaos. Because Kassandra and Helen are often shown with idols in images of the Capture of Troy, Eichler's association of both idols with a pedimental composition showing that subject has seemed until now unobjectionable.

As part of a new comprehensive study of the sculpture of the Temple of Hera, the author reexamined the two idols and discovered that they differ from one another not only in terms of style and scale (which had been known) but also in terms of the type of marble from which they are carved. The more elaborate and larger idol (Athens, NM 3869) is carved from the marble (probably Parian) that was used for the pedimental sculptures, whereas the simpler, small idol (NM 4039) is carved from the marble (almost certainly Pentelic) that was used for the metopes. In light of this discovery, it is now clear that only one idol was included in the Capture of Troy in the pediment; as in the east pediment of the Temple of Asklepios at Epidauros, it was probably Kassandra who was shown clasping this idol, since she is typically shown in vase paintings clutching or embracing an idol, whereas Helen is typically shown merely reaching out to an idol as she runs toward it. Although the other idol can now be assigned with confidence to a metope, it is hard to assign it to its appropriate context. Because the two most securely attested subjects for the metopes (Amazonomachy and Gigantomachy) are not known to include images of idols, the existence of the second idol may provide a clue to a third subject in the sculptural program of the temple.

SESSION 5E: Workshop
Current Events and Heritage Protection: Efforts to Protect Culture at Risk

Sponsored by the Cultural Heritage by Archaeology and Military Panel (CHAMP)

MODERATOR: *Laurie Rush*, U.S. Committee of the Blue Shield

Workshop Overview Statement

This session offers an opportunity to update colleagues on issues related to heritage in crisis areas. Tragically, in today's world, events are overtaking even the most conscientious efforts to keep colleagues informed on critical developments in international efforts to be responsible stewards of global heritage. The AIA Annual Meeting offers a forum for face to face discussion of events as they are unfolding from colleagues with first hand and recent in country experience. Potential topics include updates on conditions of sites and monuments as territory is recovered from DAESH, latest research on the military implications for cultural property protection; implementation of Hague 54 in current conflict zones; disaster response; preservation of collections and institutions under threat; and working with the military and law enforcement to protect cultural property.

PANELISTS: *Suzanne Bott*, Independent Scholar, *Brian Michael Lione*, Irbil Conservation Institute, *Jesse Johnson*, Irbil Conservation Institute, *Brian I. Daniels*, University of Pennsylvania Museum Heritage Center, *Katharyn Hanson*, Smithsonian Institution, *Cori Wegener*, Smithsonian Institution, and *David Selnick*, Tiffin University

SESSION 5F
Ritual and Religion in the Greek World

CHAIR: *Laura Gawlinski*, Loyola University-Chicago

New Patterns in Ritual Animal Sacrifice at Azoria

Flint Dibble, University of Cincinnati

The zooarchaeological evidence from Azoria, Crete, presents a rich record of ancient activity relating to the rearing, processing, and consumption of animals at the Archaic-period settlement. Several hundred burnt bones of sheep, goat, and cattle have been found in six deposits dating from the early seventh century B.C.E. to the early fifth century B.C.E. This material attests to the practice of burnt sacrificial ritual at Azoria. Conclusions are drawn from a detailed taphonomic and anatomical analysis of the burnt zooarchaeological material. The sacrificial assemblages are placed within the context of the Archaic-period settlement at Azoria and within the larger context of Greek ritual sacrifice in the late second and first millennia B.C.E.

Detailed zooarchaeological analyses from a number of sanctuaries in Greece provides a protocol for identifying ritual sacrifice. In all cases, it is possible to determine a pattern in which bones were selected for ritual burning to the gods. The burning of the thighs and/or tails is the most common form of ritual sacrifice extant in both textual sources and from Greek sanctuaries. However, more recent zooarchaeological analyses reveal a wider scope of heterogeneity in sacrificial praxis, with different cults, settlements, and periods revealing a range of patterns in ritually burnt zooarchaeological material.

At Azoria, the lower legs of the victim were typically selected for ritual burning. This pattern of burnt lower limbs has been observed at other Aegean sites, spanning the Late Bronze Age through the Hellenistic period. A reference in the Homeric *Hymn to Hermes* provides an aetiology myth for this specific ritual. The large assemblage of burnt lower leg specimens from Azoria provide additional context and detail to our understanding of this alternative pattern of Greek ritual animal sacrifice.

The burnt sacrificial material from Azoria derives from two different social contexts: near hearths in civic structures and within kitchens from domestic houses. The burnt sacrificial waste was typically found in discrete deposits, with those in civic venues being larger. Similar to most zooarchaeological patterns at the settlement, there are few discernible differences between the praxis of ritual sacrifice in civic vs. domestic contexts. In general, the same animals were consumed and a similar burnt ritual was conducted in both social venues. Despite the similarity in ritual and ingredients, meals in civic venues were frequently prepared from different cuts of meat, potentially showing additional elaboration to civic cuisine.

New Curse Tablets from Classical Attica

Jessica L. Lamont, Yale University

Far from bustling crowds and civic festivals, this paper addresses "private" ritual practices—discrete rites out of view of the public eye, on the margins of "polis religion" itself (as coined by Christiane Sourvinou-Inwood's 1990 article). More specifically, I present a cache of five new curse tablets from classical Athens, four of which are unpublished and appear here for the first time (ΜΠ 11948–11952). All five tablets can be securely dated on archaeological and orthographic grounds to the first quarter of the fourth century, ca. 400–375 B.C.E. Found during rescue excavations in 2003 outside the Athenian Long Walls, all five tablets were pierced with iron nails and deposited together in a pyre-grave of the Classical period (M. Petritaki, "Ανασκαφικές εργασίες: Οδός Πειραιώς 131-133 και 137." Αρχαιολογικόν Δελτίον 56-59 B1 [2010] 449–51). This burnt burial held the remains of a young girl who, according to the excavator, died "either violently or prematurely" (Petritaki 2010). The pyre-grave was part of a much larger classical cemetery located on modern Piraeus Street, likely within the ancient deme of Xypete.

I first offer transcriptions and translations of the four new texts. Then I examine the private act of cursing against the cults of the deme, in order to further illuminate private ritual practices within a local Attic community. Despite the surreptitious nature of such private rituals, the deployment of enchantments, incantations, and especially curse tablets was far from uncommon in classical Athens. In fourth-century Attica, curse tablets were used by and against a wide spectrum of society. The lead tablets, the liminal "impure" setting of the cemetery, the specialized speech—woven together through a ritual act—set this rite apart from the sphere of civic or "polis" religion. The public cults of Xypete and neighboring demes provide a backdrop against which to contextualize the private act of cursing; public rituals within the deme, including the private foundation of public cults, further illuminate personal practices within the local community. In presenting these new inscriptions, this paper reunites the murky ritual of cursing with one of its most popular vehicles, the curse tablet, and contextualizes both within the religious communities of Xypete, an understudied Attic deme. These binding spells aimed to shape and transform the local community in which they circulated; they also reveal one way in which individuals tried to control and manage personal rivalries during the fourth century B.C.E.

Reframing Sacred Space: Ritual Movement in the Sanctuary of Nemean Zeus

Stephanie Kimmey, University of Missouri, Columbia

The Sanctuary of Zeus at Nemea is often overlooked in the study of Greek religion and sanctuaries. As one of the lesser-known Panhellenic sanctuaries, discussion of the site is often incorporated only into larger dialogues of the Panhellenic cycle, assuming that the site functioned in a similar way. Nemea, however, provides an opportunity for a new way of exploring religion and ritual, one that focuses on individuals and their physical relationship with the sacred space. Around 330 B.C.E., Nemea was rebuilt to incorporate both the cult continuity of the site and to reflect deliberate ritual changes, which have not yet been fully explained. In order to do so, I argue that all aspects of the archaeological record must be studied together to reconstruct ritual activity, especially when considering the individual visitor experience.

This approach corresponds with a recent trend in the scholarship of several fields, such as religion, anthropology, and classical archaeology, which calls for new methodologies to study religion and ritual that move beyond the traditional approaches, using only literature and history to acknowledge the importance and place of material culture in the study of religion. Since a visitor's path to the Nemean sanctuary would be determined by the approach through the surrounding landscape and the auxiliary buildings within the site, his movement would be dictated by the spaces left deliberately empty. Thus, expanding the scope of material culture to include the use of landscape and empty spaces allows for a better recreation of ritual movement through a sacred space. This type of spatial analysis builds on the recent work presented by Angelos Chaniotis in *Ritual Dynamics in the Ancient Mediterranean* (Stuttgart 2011), and more specifically, the scholarship of Joan Connelly within the volume on ritual movement and performance.

I argue that ritual movement through a sanctuary can be reconstructed by means of a holistic approach using the objects deposited through human activity and the spaces built to accommodate those activities. Thus this paper, developed from my dissertation research, demonstrates the advantages of a cross-media analysis of built spaces, landscape manipulation, and material culture. By examining the Sanctuary of Zeus at Nemea in the context of the fourth-century reorganization, this paper documents how the changes in the material culture of the site help to reconstruct an individual's experience, which was distinctly different than those of visitors a century prior.

Dance and Music at the Delion on Paros Through Archaeological Considerations

Erica Angliker, University of Zurich, and *Yannos Kourayos*, Paros Museum

Looking at the silent architectural remains of the Delion on Paros today, it is difficult to imagine the music and dance that once animated the space and played a key role in the rituals conducted there. While there is no way of knowing precisely how ancient people engaged in these arts at the site, their importance within the sacred sphere of the sanctuary can be retrieved from a study of the spaces and objects involved in their performance. The present contribution examines the music and dance related to the sanctuary at the Delion on Paros through archaeological evidence, which is particularly abundant at the site. In the first part, I focus on the evidence linked to dance, such as the terrace of the western facade of the Temple of Artemis, which was deemed the site for dance related to the festivals of Delos. In addition, I show that the rock altar dedicated to Apollo could have functioned as a site of ring dance. I show that there are great similarities in function of this altar and the one in Delos (altar of the horns) around which was performed the ritual dance of the *geranos*. I also argue that the performance practiced around the rock altar at the Delion is related to a rare Geometric pendant found on the votive deposits of the sanctuary that according to recent scholarship depicts a labyrinthine floor on one side and the ritual dance of the *geranos* on the other. The iconography of this pendant is compared with a dance scene carved on a seal found on another

Parian sanctuary dedicated to Apollo (Despotiko). This paper also demonstrates that the aryballoi found in votive deposits were prizes granted to dancers, not athletes. In the second part of this paper I analyze objects related to music that have been found among the sanctuary's votive deposits, including figurines with images of musicians that appear to be taking part in the ceremonies. Finally, I discuss in greater depth a rare aulos found among the votive deposits. Its presence at the Delion allows us to explore the relationship between ritual and music, since the aulos was not a mere votive object but also an instrument closely linked to processions and sacrifices to Apollo. All in all, the spaces reserved here for dancing and the objects used to perform music provide a great opportunity for scrutinizing music and dance within cultic practices.

Delos: A Case Study for Examining Household Religion
Catherine W. Person, Kelsey Museum of Archaeology

Household religion was an essential component in both Greek and Roman cultures and vital to the survival of the family unit as well as the community within which the family lived. However, worship in the home was conducted differently by these two cultures and can be distinguished in the archaeological record. The differences lay not only in the deities worshiped but also the location of shrines within the dwelling and the accessibility, both physically and visually, to inhabitants and visitors. Consequently, changes in the location and placement of household shrines, as well as in their form, can in theory be used to trace changes in the cultural identities of the inhabitants. To test this, I have developed a three-fold analysis that examines the physical and visual accessibility of the house, identifies what forms of evidence for household religion are found, and analyzes this evidence within its functional context, taking into account its visibility. This method has been applied to a number of sites throughout the Roman province of Achaia in order to explore the complex issue of cultural identity and cultural interactions within the Roman empire. But the earliest and most complete evidence can be found on Hellenistic Delos, which is the focus of this paper.

Delos, as an important center of trade in the Hellenistic Mediterranean, had the earliest and largest Romano-Italian commercial settlement in this region. This Romano-Italian community is well represented in the epigraphic evidence as well as in a unique religious feature, the shrines to the Lares Compitales. Additionally, the houses on Delos dating from the mid second to early first centuries B.C.E. are well preserved, and the evidence for household religion is one of the largest samples found in Greece. Thus, changes in household accessibility and in household cult practices as related to Roman and Greek cultures can be observed on Delos. Applying this new method to the cultic evidence found within individual households allows a more intimate examination of the nature of household cultural identity on Hellenistic Delos and provides an excellent pre-Roman imperial case study for the dialogue between Roman and Greek cultures with respect to household religion.

SESSION 5G: Colloquium
Vani Regional Survey

ORGANIZER: *Christopher Ratté*, University of Michigan

Colloquium Overview Statement

Vani is one of the principal archaeological sites of Colchis in western Georgia. Occupied throughout the first millennium B.C.E., Vani encompassed an area of 6 ha at its greatest extent. Half a century of scientific excavation has produced a detailed model of the history of the site, and Vani has figured prominently in reconstructions of pre-Roman Colchian society. The excavator Otar Lordkipanidze suggested that Vani was a "temple-city" in its latest phase and that it belonged to a kingdom centered at nearby Kutaisi.

The purpose of the regional survey project begun in 2009 was to assemble a new body of evidence for reconsidering both the local and regional significance of Vani itself and the general nature of the society to which it belonged. The first paper presents a summary of previous research at Vani, concentrating on earlier interpretations of the site in the context of the increasing social complexity of Colchis in the mid and later first millennium B.C.E. The second paper discusses the results of an extensive survey of a 300 km^2 area around Vani, which recorded a total of 95 archaeological points of interest. The third paper concentrates on research at the site of Shuamta 5 km west of Vani, which yielded evidence for occupation from the eighth century B.C.E. through the Hellenistic period. The fourth paper presents the methods and results of an intensive survey of a 56 km^2 area east of Vani, which identified a number of previously unrecorded sites.

None of the sites recorded by the Vani Regional Survey was as large or prosperous as Vani itself, and it is possible that the regional preeminence of Vani was due in part to ritual considerations. In other respects, Vani resembles the center of a local chiefdom, with regional sites such as Shuamta having similar status but more restricted authority. Although all the sites in the region share a common material culture, including the presence of imported objects from both Greece and the Near East, there is no clear indication of the authority of a state-level entity in the evidence recovered by survey and excavation in the area around Vani, and it remains an open question whether Colchis ever attained the level of a state in the pre-Roman period.

Vani and Ancient Colchian Society

Christopher Ratté, University of Michigan

The archaeological site of Vani lies in the territory of ancient Colchis, the triangular area bordered by the Black Sea to the west and by the greater and lesser Caucasus Mountains to the north and south. Vani itself is situated approximately 70 km inland, in the foothills of the lesser Caucasus. Occupied throughout the first millennium B.C.E., Vani encompassed an area of 6 ha at its greatest extent. It is especially famous for its rich sixth–fourth century burials. Archaeological research at Vani has a long history, and major excavations have been carried out at the site since the 1940s, most notably under the direction of Georgian archaeologist Otar Lordkipanidze from 1966 until 2002. Research is continuing under the supervision of Darejan Kacharava.

A regional culture recognizable on the evidence of distinctive traditions of pottery and metalworking had emerged in Colchis by the late second and early first millennia B.C.E. Typical settlement types include mound sites in the plain of the river Phasis (modern Rioni) and hilltop settlements like Vani. Evidence for contact with the Greek and Near Eastern worlds is apparent by the sixth century B.C.E. in the form of imported pottery and precious metal objects; this is also the date of the earliest Colchian coinage. Colchian culture continued to evolve until the late first millennium B.C.E., when Vani and other sites were destroyed. Scholars have traditionally connected the emergence of Colchian culture with processes of state formation that culminated in the establishment of a regional kingdom, possibly centered at Kutaisi near Vani; according to this hypothesis, the kingdom of Colchis ultimately fell victim to the conflicts between Mithridates of Pontus and Rome in the early first century.

The results of archaeological excavation at Vani have been interpreted in the light of this general historical reconstruction, buttressed by the accounts of Greek historians. In particular, Lordkipanidze has suggested that in its latest phase, Vani was the "temple-city" of Leukothea, mentioned by Strabo and supposedly destroyed by Mithridates. The value of the testimony of Strabo and earlier historians is unclear, however, and on the evidence of archaeology alone, it is uncertain whether pre-Roman Colchis ever attained state-level social organization. It may be more useful to consider Vani as the center of one of a number of local "chiefdoms" rather than as a polity subordinate to a unified kingdom.

Extensive Survey in the Region Around Vani

Angela Commito, Union College

The purpose of the Vani Regional Survey project is to integrate existing knowledge about Vani and environs into the kind of technological and conceptual framework characteristic of contemporary survey archaeology in other regions. Of particular importance has been the use of Geographical Information Systems (GIS) as an organizational and analytical tool and geophysical prospection both in the immediate environs of Vani and at regional sites. Like all regional surveys, our project has recorded evidence of all periods, from prehistory to the present day, but we are particularly interested in questions having to do with the increasing social complexity of Colchis in the mid and later first millennium B.C.E.—when Greek explorers began to establish colonies on the Black Sea coast of Colchis, and the Persian empire pushed up against the mountains of the Caucasus.

Between 2009 and 2010, extensive survey in a 300 km^2 area around Vani recorded a total of 95 archaeological points of interest, ranging from isolated graves to substantial villages. Of the sites recorded, Bronze Age occupation was observed at only one, while 11 sites exhibited evidence of Iron Age occupation (eighth–seventh centuries B.C.E.), 27 of occupation in the Classical period (sixth-fourth centuries B.C.E.), 21 of occupation in the Hellenistic period (fourth–first century B.C.E.), and 11 of indeterminate first-millennium B.C.E. occupation. Six sites exhibited evidence of Roman and Late Roman occupation, and 25 sites were occupied in the Medieval and Late Medieval periods. Many sites were of course occupied in multiple periods.

The most prominent archaeological sites in the region occupy locations similar to Vani's—by tributary streams of the Phasis River in the foothills of the lesser Caucasus. Earlier investigations at one of these sites (Dablagomi) had revealed a rich fifth-century grave similar to those at Vani. The results of investigation at another regional site (Shuamta) are discussed in another paper in this session. Although smaller and less prosperous than Vani, these and other sites (Dablagomi, Mtisdziri, Dapnari) appear to have shared a common material culture and similar status with Vani.

Geophysical Prospection and Excavation at Shuamta near Vani

Jana Mokrisova, University of Michigan

The modern village of Shuamta lies 5 km west of Vani on the banks of the Qumuri River, a tributary stream of the Phasis (modern Rioni). The hill of Melashvilebisgora, southwest of the center of the village is crowned by a medieval or early modern watchtower; in the 1980s, artifacts and lumps of burnt daub were observed in a plowed field on the west side of the hill, but the area remained uninvestigated until 2009–2010. In 2009, geophysical prospection (magnetic and resistivity survey) revealed four liner and point anomalies, investigated by excavation in 2010. The anomalies proved to be pits located close to the modern surface and filled with earth and debris, including lumps of burnt daub, pottery, terracotta figurines, and lithics. The pits are all relatively small and irregular in shape, and they exhibit no evidence of postholes or other features. Rather than storage pits or pit houses, they seem to be borrow pits, dug to quarry mud for use in wattle-and-daub structures elsewhere, presumably farther up the hill in the area of the later watchtower. The pottery and other materials from the pits date largely to the eighth and seventh centuries B.C.E. Evidence from surrounding "sheet layers" attests occupation into the Hellenistic period. The site of Shuamta is thus both topographically similar to Vani and occupied during the same period. Perhaps it was the center of a lesser "chiefdom."

The presence of borrow pits in the area of an ancient Iron Age settlement is not surprising, but this is in fact the first time that excavation in the Vani region has succeeded in revealing pit features of this kind, as opposed to graves or simple sheet layers. These results show that geophysical prospection, especially magnetic surveying, is a useful tool in the preliminary exploration and mapping of archaeological sites throughout the region, provided that there is good surface evidence in the form of lumps of burnt daub for architecture of the type detected at Shuamta, and that modern disturbance is not too great.

Intensive Survey in the Region East of Vani

Ryan C. Hughes, AIA Finger Lakes Society

Until recently, research in the region around Vani had been limited to extensive survey, based on local information. In 2011, work was begun on an intensive survey of the region east of Vani (the Eastern Vani Survey), partly because this area was less well known than the area west of Vani, and partly to determine whether intensive survey would yield results different from those of extensive survey.

The subtropical vegetation, varied landscape, and dispersed pattern of modern settlement typical of western Georgia pose special challenges to traditional techniques of intensive archaeological survey. In confronting these challenges, we relied on a combination of techniques of engagement with local stakeholders to access the landscape and digital recording procedures to ensure accurate recovery and analysis of all archaeological materials.

An area of 56 km^2 to the east of Vani was selected for investigation, of which a 25 km^2 portion was intensively surveyed. Over the course of two seasons, 2,375 field plots were examined; 216 of these fields contained material datable to the first millennium B.C.E. Using spatial analytic models, the recorded surface scatters were aggregated into a total of 32 previously unidentified archaeological sites. These sites are predominantly characterized by scatters of the same kinds of common ceramic wares found at Vani. Four areas (Mshvidobis Gora, Gabelauri, Kveda Bzvani, and Kveda Gora), however, showed significant quantities of storage containers, uncommon wares, and evidence of wattle-and-daub architecture in the form of lumps of burnt daub. This evidence suggests these were likely sites of larger-scale private or communal activity. That said, none of the areas identified by the Eastern Vani Survey is comparable with settlements such as those at Vani and points west (Shuamta, Dablagomi, Mtisdziri, and Dapnari). Although more work needs to be done, the evidence suggests that settlement east of Vani was largely dispersed, with a few locations of punctuated activity focused around important geographical features.

SESSION 5H
Art and Architecture of Imperial Ideology

CHAIR: *Ellen Perry,* College of the Holy Cross

Augustan Iconography in Daily Life: The Neighborhood Altars of the Lares Augusti

Amy Russell, Durham University

In this paper I examine the typology and iconography of surviving altars set up in Rome's neighborhoods to the Lares Augusti, including the altar of the *vicus* Aesculetus now in Centrale Montemartini, the altar of the *vicus* Sandaliarius now in the Uffizi, the Soriano altar now in the Palazzo dei Conservatori, and the altar of the Sala delle Muse in the Vatican (collected by M. Hano, "A l'origine du culte impérial: Les autels des Lares Augusti. Recherches sur les thèmes iconographiques et leur signification," *ANRW* 2.16.3 [1978] 2333–81). These small altars, erected by the freedmen and slave *vicomagistri* and *ministri* of each urban neighbourhood, share themes and even specific iconographic elements with contemporary 'state' monuments like the Ara Pacis, but were produced by different patrons and artisans situated well beyond any kind of official circles (see P. Zanker, "Uber die Werkstatten augusteischer Larenaltare und damit zusammenhangende Probleme der Interpretation" *BullCom* 82 [1970–1971] 147–55 for an analysis of the workshops). Their position between central impetus and the free reign given to individual patrons and artisans makes them valuable for the study of image making in the early empire.

I analyze the altars through a series of productive interactions between two modern ways of viewing them. One applies art historical methodologies more typically associated with the study of the higher-status reliefs from which these altars often take their inspiration; the second takes a more traditionally archaeological approach and sees the altars as objects, part of their original audience's daily life. The results open up new avenues for the study of Augustan iconography and how it was created, used, and reused throughout society.

If we compare these altars to higher-status relief sculpture like that of the Ara Pacis, we can see them as documents of reception. The way the altars' patrons and artists reused and remixed visual elements from the great Augustan monuments just a few miles away can help us determine how they understood that ideologically charged iconography. Conversely, if we place the altars in their original audience's world we can see that for the people who used these altars and walked past them every day, they were just as important sources of imagery and ideology as "state" art. The iconography originally created for these altars by trial and error and without central coordination eventually became standardized and spread to other media, from painted lararia in Pompeii to moldmade lamps. My analysis therefore breaks down distinctions between "state" and "vernacular" art, while also emphasizing the particular importance of these altars as key documents of the place of Augustan iconography in everyday life.

Arms, Eagles, and Empire: Roman Swords and their Decoration

Steve Burges, Boston University

The aim of this paper is to evaluate the dynastic imagery of extant Roman armor decoration and to posit that certain examples embody Early Imperial metaphors for apotheosis via eagles in flight. As the excavations of the royal tombs at Vergina have revealed, the rulers of the Hellenistic period often outfitted their graves with full panoplies of richly adorned arms and armor of bronze, gold, and ivory. The elite practice of wearing elaborate cuirasses, phalerae, helmets, and scabbards covered in figural reliefs continued in the Roman Imperial period, and it is attested not only by sculptures of generals but also by the objects themselves, discovered in Roman-era burials from around the empire. The arms entombed with these warriors exemplified their military authority, and many featured individualized repoussé embellishment and divine invocations written in bronze letters. The capture of weapons, armor, or standards by an enemy force represented a major defeat and embarrassment, and self-referential Roman helmets, which include reliefs of captured military equipment or battlefield trophies, appear in several surviving depictions. Two famous sheath decorations from the Early Imperial period, an Augustan plaque in the LandesMuseum in Bonn and the so-called Sword of Tiberius from Mainz in the British Museum, consist of images of Julia with her sons Gaius and Lucius and the enthroned Tiberius (or Augustus) accepting Victoria from a prince, respectively. These suggestions of stable Julio-Claudian dynastic succession, which are similar to the depictions of other propagandistic luxury objects such as cameos, perhaps symbolized the allegiance of powerful Roman generals far from the capital to the sovereignty of the imperial family. They participated in the extension of the imagery of the Pax Augusta to the extremes of the Roman frontier. Other gold ornaments, which have only now been identified as military attire through comprehensive comparative study, also perpetuate these Julio-Claudian themes. A heart-shaped article of metalwork in the Museum of Fine Arts, Boston, for instance, acted as the end tip of a scabbard belt, and it comprises a detailed relief of Jupiter mounted on the back of a flying eagle. This subject is relatively scarce before the principate of Augustus, but afterward it appears more frequently and is associated with the heavenly ascent of a deceased imperial family member. Objects like this minute embellishment thus relate to larger programs of political decoration in private art and establish the eagle as more than a simple legionary emblem.

The Temple of Deified Trajan at Selinus (Cilicia): Cenotaph or Ustrinum

Michael C. Hoff, University of Nebraska

The year 2017 marks the 1,900th anniversary of the death of Trajan, which makes it a timely occasion to look back at the circumstances of his death and, in particular, to reevaluate a monument long associated with his death. In 117, while returning to Rome from Syria, an already enfeebled Trajan became seriously ill and died shortly after his ship made an emergency docking at Selinus in Cilicia (modern Gazipaşa). Early modern travelers visiting the ancient remains at Selinus attributed a structure, reworked in the 13th century by the Seljuks to be a hunting pavilion, as a cenotaph built to honor the memory of Trajan, who died within their community. This building, known locally as the Şekerhane Köşkü, has been recently studied by the German Archaeological Institute. The preliminary report published in 2013 documents that the building was originally temple-like, with all the trappings of a temple, but whether it was indeed a cenotaph, constructed in the manner of a temple-tomb, or an actual temple with all the trappings of cult, could not be determined.

This paper explores the identification of the building as a cenotaph, comparing it with other imperial funerary monuments and known cenotaphs, as well as depictions of the structure on coins minted at Selinus. The paper concludes that the Şekerhane Köşkü was unlikely a cenotaph but served instead as a temple consecrated to the worship of the deified Trajan. Furthermore, based on the circumstances surrounding the emperor's death at Selinus, this papers considers the possibility that the placement of the Şekerhane Köşkü/Trajan temple marks the location of the *ustrinum* where Trajan's body was cremated before the remains were transported to Rome to be interred inside the Column of Trajan in his forum. This theory contradicts the commonly held belief that the emperor's body was transported from Selinus to Syria, where it was cremated, then on to Rome.

Allusions to Imperial Cult in Hadrian's Temple of Venus and Roma
Lillian B. Joyce, University of Alabama in Huntsville

Hadrian's Temple of Venus and Roma was the largest temple in ancient Rome. Despite the emperor Maxentius' reconstruction of it following a fire in the fourth century, evidence remains about the appearance of the original temple and its cult images. Its largely Greek-style peripteral design contrasts with its novel back-to-back cult chambers, a highly unusual organization of interior space. Dio (69.4–5) records the famous observation of the architect Apollodorus that the colossal goddesses would not be able to stand up in their compartments. Scholars have often suggested that the "Greekness" of the temple and its colossal cult images aligned with the Grecophilia of Hadrian. Instead, I propose that these elements express associations with imperial cult.

Roman Tarraco built the first temple in the West to the divine Augustus; it then served as a model for others (Tac. *Ann.* 1.78). Using coins, Mierse argues for a peristyle temple on a three-stepped platform, a decidedly Greek design that recalls temples for imperial cult in the East. Hadrian restored this temple during a visit to the province. Cahill suggests that the back-to-back cellae of the Artemis temple at Sardis may be Julio-Claudian and at that early date planned for imperial cult, which was the eventual use of the space. Found in and around the temple were fragments of six colossi of Antonines, although Hadrian likely began the restorations. In the temple to Augustus and Roma in Lepcis Magna, built in the reign of Tiberius, the cult statues were colossal, intended to convey power—not allusions to classical Greece.

Although the goddess Roma had no temple in Rome prior to that of Hadrian, she appeared on coinage as well as on imperial monuments beginning with the Ara Pacis. In nearby Ostia, Roma was paired with Augustus in a temple that faced the Capitolium. Roma had rich associations with the city of Rome and its people, but she also possessed strong connections to imperial cult. By pairing her with Venus, the goddess linked with Augustus and the divine ancestry of the imperial family, Hadrian created an important ideological, political, and religious tie to the past. Thus, the Greek style of the Hadrianic temple, its unusual interior plan, and the choice of goddesses and their colossal size should not be generically associated with Hadrian's Grecophilia, but should be seen for their strong affinities to imperial cult and the promotion of power.

The Rennes Patera: Content and Context
Robert Cohon, The Nelson-Atkins Museum of Art, University of Missouri–Kansas City

Discovered in 1774 in Rennes, eastern Brittany, a golden bowl—the so-called Rennes Patera—is an outstanding example of the propagandistic imagery of Septimius Severus; it has, however, remained understudied, perhaps because of its location in the infrequently visited Cabinet des Médailles, Paris. The current traveling exhibition of Roman luxury art from the cabinet has brought it to the fore.

The bowl is exceptional: Roman golden vessels are rare, and its imagery is remarkably dense. In the emblema Bacchus outdrinks Hercules, and a Bacchic *thiasos* encircles the scene; 16 aurei with portraits from Hadrian to Septimius Severus and his sons frame the work. The contents of its findspot indicate that an elite family with strong political connections owned the bowl. It probably was used for display purposes rather than banqueting or sacrifice.

Scholars have recognized that the coins are sequenced by the portrayed figure's political rank and that combining second-century and Severan portraits reflects Severus' self-adoption into the Antonines to legitimize his rule. The relationships of the coins are, however, more complex. Coins of Julia Domna and Severus are opposite those of Severus' adopted parents in the prestigious upper half of the bowl, highlighting their relationship. To compensate for his placement in less legible positions, Antoninus Pius, who lent his name to the dynasty, appears more than other emperors and on the ends of the bowl's horizontal axis. Geta appears once and in a tertiary position; Caracalla, twice—once in a primary and once in a secondary position—reflecting their different political advancements.

The bowl evidences the well-known, close relationship between Bacchus and Severus, as on the Leptis Magna Concordia relief. A coin of Severus is directly above Bacchus, who is returning triumphantly from his eastern conquest. Severus' own eastern victories are thereby alluded to. The equation of Severus and Bacchus continues with the emblema's victorious Bacchus.

The bowl's date of 208 C.E. or the first half of 209 C.E. (according to Morelli's numismatic evidence) explains the bowl's extravagance, exceptionality, and imagery. Quite possibly it reflects the impact of the recent completion of the great Temple of Hercules and Bacchus in Rome in 206–207 C.E. Indeed, this bowl may even have been manufactured to celebrate Severus and anticipate his victory when he traveled through northwestern France to invade Scotland in 208 C.E.

The Glass Ball Game Revisited

Garrett G. Fagan, Penn State University, and *Erica Hiddink*, Colgate University

A curious inscription, found at St. Peter's in Rome in the 16th century, has drawn the attention of several scholars from Mommsen in 1872 to Schmidt in 1999. The text (*CIL* 6 9797 = 33815a = *ILS* 5175 = *CLE* 29 = *ML* 124) at first glance appears to commemorate an eccentric old man, Ursus, famed for playing with a glass ball to popular acclaim in the "baths of Trajan, Agrippa and Titus, and frequently in Nero's." But there are strange features, not least the invocation, "if only you believe me," or the call for his fellow ballplayers to celebrate him with perfumes, flowers, and wine—activities appropriate to a funerary setting, even though Ursus is said to be "alive and willing." The text closes with an admission that he has been defeated on multiple occasions by Verus, "my patron, whose exodiarius I am gladly called."

Champlin offered an ingenious interpretation of this text in 1985: Ursus was none other than L. Iulius Ursus Servianus (cols. 90, 102, 134), brother-in-law to Hadrian. For a time Servianus and later his grandson were considered Hadrian's successors, but the emperor had them both executed after he adopted L. Aelius Caesar in 136. By that time, Servianus was about 90 years old. The Verus of the text is certainly M. Annius Verus, thrice consul (97, 121, 126), also a major figure at Hadrian's court, and so Servianus' rival. As Prefect of the City, Verus governed

Rome while Hadrian traveled, and he was father-in-law to Antoninus Pius, Hadrian's successor, and grandfather of M. Aurelius. Verus therefore prevailed mightily over Ursus Servianus in court politics, so that our inscription is a jocular allegory, in which the glass ball represents imperial power, slippery and fragile, and the ballplayers the competing courtiers. Not coincidentally, Verus is known to have been fond of ballgames.

The glass ball as a symbol of power remains central to Champlin's reading. The sensational discovery in December 2005 of imperial scepters, probably belonging to Maxentius and deliberately concealed in a pit in a remote corner of the Palatine, greatly strengthens Champlin's case. In addition to ceremonial lance heads were found three scepters featuring four glass balls, symbols of power. Since emperors would carry these scepters in public appearances, the glass ball would aptly signify political preeminence. Far from being "a fantastic and untenable interpretation," as Courtney dismisses it, Champlin's reading is likely correct.

SESSION 5I
Frontiers and Cultural Contact in the Roman World

CHAIR: To be announced

Colonial Connections and Local Settlement in West-Central Sardinia: Results of the Site-Based Survey at S'Urachi (2015–2016)

Linda Gosner, Clark University, *Alexander Smith*, College at Brockport, SUNY, and *Jessica Nowlin*, University of Texas, San Antonio

The nuraghe of S'Urachi is an imposing Bronze Age stone monument that has served as a central place in the landscape of west-central Sardinia for millennia. While this monumental building was constructed under the indigenous Nuragic culture, the inhabitants of the site came into contact with Phoenician, Punic, and Roman cultural influences over the course of the first millennium B.C.E. Since 2013, the site has been the subject of archaeological excavations jointly carried out by Brown University and the Comune di San Vero Milis. The aim of the project is to shed light on the daily lives of local inhabitants living around the nuraghe from the Bronze Age through the Roman period, when cultural and economic connections between Sardinia and the wider Mediterranean were expanding and often in flux. This project has investigated the immediate surroundings of the nuraghe through microtopographical, soil, and geophysical survey, as well as open excavation immediately adjacent to the nuraghe.

As part of the research program, during the past two seasons we carried out an intensive pedestrian survey and excavated a series of targeted test trenches. Our aim was to investigate long-term trends in the occupation and use of the wider archaeological site and to contextualize the findings of the excavations in the landscape. The unplowed land and heavy vegetation at S'Urachi required an innovative, more intrusive survey approach than is traditionally used in Mediterranean survey: a series of shallow circles excavated on a 20 x 20 m grid. This pedestrian survey conducted in 2015 yielded ceramic and other evidence of habitation that established potential areas of interest, which were further investigated through the excavation of three test trenches during the 2016 season. Our findings illuminated trends in occupation and culture contact from the late Iron Age, Punic, and Early Roman periods as well as patterns of garbage deposition from the early modern period to the present. This paper presents our preliminary results, highlighting the methodology we developed for coping with the various environmental challenges and our future plans for survey both at the site and in the wider landscape of west-central Sardinia.

Reflections on the Emergence of the Lucanian Ethnos: Funerary Evidence from Tricarico-Serra del Cedro (Italy)

Ilaria Battiloro, Mount Allison University, and *Chiara Albanesi*, Scuola di Specializzazione per i Beni Archeologici di Matera

A group of almost 100 tombs excavated at Tricarico-Serra del Cedro, in modern Basilicata (Italy), opens new perspectives in the study of the "ethno-genesis" of the Lucanians. The Lucanians are an Italic group of Samnite origin, which made its appearance in the scenario of Magna Graecia at the end of the fifth century B.C.E., apparently with a hiatus with the preexisting archaic cultures of southern Italy.

The tombs considered in this research cover a timeframe that spans from the sixth century B.C.E. to the fourth century B.C.E., so that they "bridge" the delicate moment that saw the formation of the Lucanian ethnos; in particular, the fourth-century tombs of the Lucanian facies differ from the archaic ones, as the body was deposited in supine—rather than contracted—position.

This paper considers two aspects of the burials of Serra del Cedro: (1) physical location of the graves within the area in which they have been found, with the aim of understanding whether the archaic and the Lucanian tombs are concentrated in two different areas, or the later Lucanian graves are not separated from the more ancient ones; (2) nature of the grave goods sets, in order to identify differences or parallels among the tombs from different cultures. Special attention is paid to the presence of older objects in the fourth-century B.C.E. burials presence that may overshadow some sort of continuity of the Lucanian culture with the preexisting ones.

Ritual Landscapes and Community-Formation on the Frontiers of Roman Britain

Eleri H. Cousins, University of St Andrews

The region centered around Hadrian's Wall, on the edge of the Roman empire, was a complex zone of cultural interaction, with auxiliary soldiers, local peoples, and communities on both sides of the border all coming together in the creation of a frontier society. In particular, the forts that garrisoned the wall and their accompanying civilian settlements, or *vici*, were important foci for interaction between the various groups living in the area.

One of the more significant ways in which the inhabitants of this frontier region constructed individual and group identities was through religious activity. This paper examines the place of religious identities at two neighboring forts,

Housesteads and Vindolanda, and their associated *vici*. At both sites we see the military community reinforcing group cohesion and loyalty to the state through sacrifices to Jupiter Optimus Maximus and the emperor; at the same time, smaller subgroups within the army, many of them from other parts of the Roman empire, used dedications to their ancestral gods to express their ongoing ethnic affiliations with their homelands.

Despite these similarities, however, the two sites demonstrate very different strategies for the ways in which temples, religious epigraphy, and ritual activity were incorporated into the built environments of fort and *vicus*. These differences raise important questions about the intended audiences for religious displays of identity at each fort. For example, epigraphic distributions indicate that military rituals at Vindolanda took place almost exclusively within the fort, in contrast to Housesteads, where the same rituals were performed extramurally, and thus were much more visible to groups outside the army community; this has important implications for the relationship between the fort and *vicus* populations at each site. By looking at the different settings for religious activity at each site, we can begin to understand how the ritual landscapes of forts and *vici* served both to reflect and to structure the social networks of the frontier.

The Nabataean Wheelmade Tubulus: Adoption and Adaptation of a Roman Building Technique

Craig A. Harvey, University of Michigan

Despite being located on the southeast extreme of the Roman empire, the Nabataeans were early adopters of Roman-style bathhouses and heating systems, including the tubulus (a ceramic box-shaped pipe used for wall heating). Numerous excavations in the Nabataean world have uncovered these systems that date to a century before the Roman annexation of Nabataea in 106 C.E. More than just adopting the tubulus, the Nabataeans adapted its manufacture, making the box-shaped tubes on a potter's wheel, thereby straying from previous hand-built techniques. Although excavations at many sites in the region have uncovered examples of these wheelmade tubuli, this innovative fabrication technique has completely escaped scholarly attention. This paper addresses this deficiency by presenting the Nabataean wheelmade tubulus and discussing its manufacture through an examination of pipes found at a number of sites in the Nabataean Kingdom, including Wadi Ramm and Petra. Having made the tubulus their own through wheelmade production, the Nabataeans then employed this Roman technology in all their heated rooms. By the time of the Roman annexation of Nabataea in 106 C.E., this new technique was so well established that the wheelmade tubulus continued to be produced and used after the Roman annexation, even in Roman military bathhouses, such as in the bathhouse at the site of Humayma, Jordan. This sustained use illuminates the nature of the organization of ceramic building material production in Roman Arabia and supports other evidence for the close relationship between indigenous craft production and the new imperial administration. This paper thus brings to light a hitherto unknown method of tubulus production. Furthermore, it reveals how the careful examination of this material provides new insights into both the ingenuity of Nabataean builders and the organization of the construction economy within the Nabataean world, both before and after the Roman annexation.

Excavations at Halmyris: A Field Report of the 2014–2016 Seasons

John Karavas, College Year in Athens, and *Mihail Zahariade*, Institute of Archaeology, Bucharest, Romania

This paper presents the preliminary results of the excavations carried out at the site of Halmyris (Murighiol, Tulcea County, Romania) during the 2014, 2015, and 2016 field seasons, respectively.

Halmyris is located in the Danube Delta, near the confluence point of the Danube River and the Black Sea. Its enviable strategic position is the primary reason behind its long and uninterrupted chronological continuity, ranging from the Late Iron Age through to late antiquity as well as its multifaceted nature and character throughout its occupation: emerging as an Iron Age Geto-Dacian fortified settlement and gradually developing into a Greek emporium, a Roman fort and harbor, and, lastly, into an important Byzantine civilian, naval, and military settlement.

The site has been the subject of systematic archaeological investigations since 1981, under the auspices of the Institute of Archaeology in Bucharest and the Romanian Ministry of Culture. Excavations have thus far primarily focused on the Roman and Byzantine fort and naval installation at the site, revealing substantial traces of its defensive elements, including, among others, the north and west gates and enveloping towers, three Late Roman U-shaped towers and two defensive bastions, and observation posts. However, the most remarkable discovery to date remains that of an early fourth-century C.E. Christian basilica and underground crypt within the interior of the fort, which contained the actual remains of two Early Christian martyrs, St. Epictet and St. Astyon, respectively.

The last three field seasons have focused on the eastern section of the main fort, revealing a very intriguing sequence of military and administrative buildings; in this paper, I provide a detailed presentation and description of the architectural remains and significant material finds unearthed from two additional defensive towers and bastions; two distinct and separate barrack complexes and their adjacent storage facilities/annexes; as well as the presentation of an as yet unidentified large paved building, containing a double-arched entrance and yielding clear traces of occupation dating from the third to the sixth centuries C.E. Last, but not least, I also present the preliminary investigations conducted in the area of the site's harbor installation.

I firmly believe that these discoveries will, at large, substantially contribute to our better understanding of the purpose and function of a Late Roman fortification and site in the area.

SESSION 5J: Colloquium
Coins and Archaeology

Sponsored by the Numismatics Interest Group

ORGANIZER: *Martin Beckmann*, McMaster University

Colloquium Overview Statement

Coins have traditionally been viewed by the archaeologist as handy tools for dating strata. But recently increasing attention has been given to coins as archaeological objects in their own right. This session highlights four examples of modern and innovative archaeological approaches to numismatics. "Coins and Pottery: Tracking the Numismatic Profile of Late Roman Sardis" demonstrates the problems that may be encountered in even the most basic archaeological applications of coin evidence, their use as indicators of date, and shows how these might be solved using archaeological methodology from a neighboring discipline. Jane DeRose Evans investigates a common problem at Late Roman sites in the East, the large numbers of fourth- and fifth-century coins found together in the same contexts. By employing Mean Ceramic Date analysis, Evans shows that in fact, fourth-century coins remained in circulation in the fifth century; this has implications not only for the interpretation of site finds but also for our understanding of the economy of the period. "The Circulation of Nerva's Neptune Coins in Britannia" presents a critique of a recently developed approach to the interpretation of reverse types: their study based on their archaeological find context. This methodology has yielded compelling results on some European sites, but Nathan Elkins argues that care must be taken in its application. By studying the distribution of coin types of Nerva in Britain, Elkins critiques earlier interpretations of one particular type, Neptune, and by considering the broader archaeological context of Nervan coin finds concludes that these were connected to a particular event, the foundation of a new colony at Gloucester. "'Death Coins'" in Roman Corinth" presents a new approach to the study of coins in a site-specific context: graves. By examining the use of coins and coin-like objects in Corinthian graves and considering criteria of date of inhumation, age, sex, and social status, Mary Hoskins Walbank concludes that these objects were not "Charon's obol" as often thought but votive offerings or protective talismans. The final paper, "The Antioch Excavation Coins Reexcavated," is an example of a novel approach to long-ago-excavated numismatic material. The coins from the Princeton Antioch excavations might, because of their thorough publication, be thought not worth revisiting. But Alan Stahl shows how a new study of old coin finds can shed new light on our understanding of the history and development of even a well-known site when the coins are considered in the context of the archaeology of their findspots.

DISCUSSANT: *William Metcalf*, AIA New Haven Society

Coins and Pottery: Tracking the Numismatic Profile of Late Roman Sardis

Jane DeRose Evans, Temple University

Copper-alloy coins of the fourth and fifth centuries litter every site in the Roman East, but the problem of deciding whether these coins are indigenous, residual, or infiltrated has plagued numismatists for years. The composition of the supply pool has been argued to have been compromised by wide-ranging recalls or demonetizations of coins as silver content and size of the flan plunged from 324 to 498 (e.g., Harl, *Coinage in the Roman Economy* [Baltimore 1980]). They would thus argue that the fourth-century coins were not available in the fifth century and thus cannot appear as indigenous in deposits. Some numismatists have ventured into this analysis by comparing pottery and coinage, with results that vary widely (e.g., Poblome at Sagalassos; Moorhead at Butrint; Butcher at Beirut). Modifying a statistical method introduced by ceramologists (Mean Ceramic Date), I look at 10 different Late Roman deposits in Sardis that have been dated by the pottery included in the strata to try and differentiate between indigenous and residual. The results do not give precise indicators of the nature of the deposit, but by checking the p value and comparing the results with fifth-century hoards, they do show that fourth-century coins were indigenous to the strata and thus part of the circulation pool. The results also show a wide variation in the closing date of the coins compared with a closing date of the pottery, a warning to archaeologists that Late Roman coins are not necessarily good chronological marker artifacts. This type of analysis has important ramifications as we try to understand the economy of the eastern empire and the local cities, the distribution of coin, and the imperial control over local markets.

The Circulation of Nerva's Neptune Coins in Britannia

Nathan Elkins, Baylor University

Unlike the mobile silver and gold coinage, Roman imperial bronze coinage tended to stay within the area in which it was introduced into circulation. In recent years, intensive archaeological studies have indicated that, at least in some instances, there was a deliberate supply of base-metal coins bearing images relevant to the target population. One of the most compelling cases is the remarkably high concentration of martially themed images on the coins excavated at the Flavian legionary fortress at Nijmegen when compared with the smaller percentages of such images in nearby settlements and in Rome. Other studies have similarly indicated a differentiated supply of coins, seemingly on iconographic grounds, in the Flavian and Trajanic periods.

A potential danger in the realization of deliberate supply according to iconography is, however, an impulse to read all typologically differentiated supplies of coinage as intentional. One must remain cognizant of the fact that coins were first and foremost economic objects and that their function as bearers of communication was secondary. Recently, it was argued that the Neptune coins of Nerva, which are primarily found in Britannia, were deliberately supplied to the area where the image of Neptune resonated with the population who depended on trade and commerce across the English Channel. This interpretation is rather forced, as the legend on the coins denote games in the Circus Maximus and thus would have meant little to the population of Roman Britain. By attending to the broader phenomenon of coin circulation in Britannia in the reign of Nerva, I demonstrate that the unusual concentration of Neptune coins in this region is part of a broader anomaly. In fact, there is an unusual concentration of Nerva's third-emission coins (January 97) in Britannia. I suggest that the prominence of such coins in Britain may be connected with Nerva's foundation of the colony at Glevum (Gloucester).

"Death Coins" in Roman Corinth

Mary Hoskins Walbank, British School at Athens

The term "death coins" is used here to include actual coins and coin-like objects. The material comes primarily from two carefully excavated, but only partially published, cemeteries dating from the Classical period to the fifth/sixth centuries C.E.; it also includes reference to other burial sites at Corinth. The purpose of this paper is to consider, first, the physical relationship of the death coins with the corpse and what light this might throw on the ritual of primary deposition; whether death coins are associated with a particular social group or sex; and how practices changed over several hundred years as coins became part of the commemorative process.

Coins were rare in Greek graves and by no means ubiquitous in Roman Corinthian burials. The well-known "Charon's fee" should be regarded as a literary topos that has disguised other uses of coins. Most actual coins, as elsewhere, are bronze alloy, low denomination, and worn. A very few silver coins were deposited, perhaps because they had been already been used as grave offerings. Gold foil impressions (bracteates or danakes), familiar in the Greek context, have also been found, sometimes with money, in burials up to the Late Roman period; they should not be regarded as a more valuable substitute for low denomination coins. Tesserae coins (blank on one side) deliberately cut or defaced, and glass discs were also deposited at certain times.

My current, overall conclusion is that Corinthian "death coins" were essentially talismans to protect the dead (the type of metal is important) and are associated particularly with females and children.

The Antioch Excavation Coins Reexcavated

Alan Stahl, Princeton University

About 40,000 coins excavated at Antioch-on-the-Orontes in the 1930s were sent to Princeton University at the outbreak of World War II, where they remain. While exemplary catalogues of these were published in the following decades by Miles and Waagé, there was little or no effort to tie the coinage to the other excavated material or the history of the site. The reexamination of the archaeological archives and artifacts also at Princeton has occasioned a review and recataloguing of the excavated coins, housed in the Princeton University Numismatic Collection in Firestone Library. This analysis has already provided much new information on the chronology and use of the site from Hellenistic through Ottoman times. Special attention is given to changes of site distribution of coin issues over time in Antioch itself, in its port of Seleucia, and in its suburb of Daphne. The relevance of numismatic data for questions of continuity and change in this site that has a continuous coin record for 1,500 years is illustrated through a study of coin finds in an urban complex within Antioch that has been the focus of an interdisciplinary pilot study that seeks to lay the groundwork for a more comprehensive reexamination of the results of the excavation.

SESSION 6A: Workshop
So You've Chosen Your Topic—What Now?: Best Practices in Data Collection, Management, and Analysis

Sponsored by the Student Affairs Interest Group

MODERATORS: *Simeon D. Ehrlich*, Stanford University, and *Rachel G. Dewan*, University of Toronto

Workshop Overview Statement

Archaeologists, art historians, classicists, and anthropologists must collect, manage, and analyze large sets of data in their research—but little instruction is given in how to do so. From launching a database to using informational and analytical software to accessing collections and acquiring permissions, the complexities of data management are a daunting yet unavoidable part of the research process. Students rarely receive training in this crucial aspect of their work, yet research faculty are expected to have strong project management skills. Students and early-career scholars would benefit greatly from the insights, advice, and warnings of researchers who have experience working with large sets of data.

This workshop will cover key issues related to the research process. It will provide students and faculty with the opportunity to hear from established experts about best practices in approaching different classes of data, effective strategies for organizing such data, and methods for using a data set to its full analytic potential. What should be considered when designing a database? To what extent should raw data be made accessible to others? How does one secure permissions for working with restricted-access materials? How can data visualizations be used effectively, and what resources are available to help in doing so? Panelists who have worked in libraries, archives, and museums and who work with digital humanities applications, digital data programs, and image services will bring with them a wealth of knowledge and experience relevant to a wide array of interdisciplinary research subjects.

Research and data management are integral to all stages of an academic career. A thorough consideration of how best to collect, store, organize, and analyze data for research projects is sure to benefit scholars at all stages of their careers—students, young professionals, and even established scholars. An improved understanding of how to work with large data sets will lead to better planning, more focused analysis, and more coherent results. Not only will the experiences and advice offered by the panelists assist those just beginning to collect or organize data, but the discussion will leave participants with valuable lessons they can apply throughout their careers.

PANELISTS: *Steven Ellis*, University of Cincinnati, *Marcel Fortin*, Robarts Library, University of Toronto, *Sascha Priewe*, Royal Ontario Museum, *Walter Scheidel*, Stanford University, and *Edward Triplett*, Duke University

SESSION 6B
New Approaches to Roman Death

CHAIR: *Allison L.C. Emmerson*, Tulane University

An Interdisciplinary Approach to Search for the "Invisible Poor" in Roman Italy

Jonathan Weiland, Stanford University, and *Tracy Prowse*, McMaster University

Among both historians and archaeologists there is a growing desire to know more about the broad category of society known as the nonelite in Roman society, and with good reason—a better understanding of the nonelite would contribute to several important topics and fields in classical scholarship including ancient economics, the lives of children in antiquity, studies of identity and gender, and ancient slavery. Unfortunately, there is a paucity of traditional evidence (i.e., literary sources, archaeological evidence) for the daily lives of the nonelite in Roman society, and in particular for the lowest socioeconomic strata of society, identified in this presentation as "the poor." This hindrance has led some scholars to conclude that the poor of the ancient world are invisible.

In this paper, we argue that an interdisciplinary approach to investigating the past is the best means of increasing visibility of the poor through combining bioarchaeology—the population-based study of skeletons in an archaeological context—with more traditional methods of investigating Romans, such as funerary archaeology, epigraphy, and landscape. This approach shifts the focus to the quality of life and the activities of the non-elite living in the Roman empire.

These methods are not mutually exclusive, and we argue that a more nuanced understanding about life in the past can be obtained by integrating these seemingly disparate lines of evidence. The more traditional forms of investigation allow for the construction of a context, in which the results of assessments of human remains can be interpreted and through which new insights can be gained about how the poor worked and lived. As an example of this approach, this paper focuses on recent research at the rural imperial estate of Vagnari in southern Italy—where a cemetery and *vicus* have recently been investigated. Using bioarchaeological evidence, a comparison can be made among the individuals buried at the site, through the study of burial practices and grave goods that can then be analyzed in association with information on sex, age, geographic origins, diet, health, and trauma. With this same information, a general profile for life in the larger context of rural southern Italy can be compared with other populations elsewhere in Italy, such as around the imperial capital and at other rural locations. Using an interdisciplinary and multiscalar approach, we have the potential to make visible the lives of the nonelites who lived in the ancient Roman world.

Well-Trodden Roads: Skeletal Evidence for Sex-Related Mobility at the Roman Site of Vagnari, Italy

Rebecca J. Gilmour, McMaster University, *Megan Brickley*, McMaster University, *Erik Jurriaans*, Juravinski Hospital, and *Tracy Prowse*, McMaster University

Skeletal trauma and biomechanical adaptations were assessed in the limb bones of 66 first–fourth-century C.E. Roman adults from Vagnari (Italy). Vagnari was an imperial estate with archaeological evidence that agriculture, viticulture, and transhumance were important economic activities. Biomechanical and fracture analyses of the Vagnari sample suggest that this population lived a physically demanding lifestyle and that physical strains and injuries related to mobility were different between males and females.

Biomechanical studies investigate the adaptation of bone shapes and sizes to different mechanical loading environments. In particular, investigations of lower limb bone (tibia) cross-sectional areas provide evidence for physical strains associated with the intensity and type of physical mobility. Males at Vagnari exhibited tibial areas that were larger than other reported tibial cross-sections, indicating that from younger ages, the males at Vagnari engaged in relatively more intense physical mobility than elsewhere in the Roman world. This study also found that, compared with other Roman sites, Vagnari males had a greater prevalence of indirect fractures. Indirect fractures are breaks to bone that occur at a location other than the place of impact; these types of injuries are often produced by slips, trips, falls, jumps, as well as overuse. Indirect fractures to the Vagnari leg bones were especially noteworthy and included an example of a tibial stress fracture usually caused by repetitive strain and overuse. Vagnari females did not exhibit similar biomechanical and fracture patterns; they had no indirect fracture types, and their tibial areas were similar to other sites.

The trends observed in the human remains from Vagnari suggest that males and females experienced physical mobility and ambulatory accidents differently. Vagnari males were evidently more intensely mobile and likely encountered greater fracture hazards associated with movement than the females at this site. Transhumance and shepherding, typically a male occupation in the Roman world, is thought to have been important at Vagnari and may provide one possible explanation for the biomechanical and fracture evidence present among the males in this assemblage.

The Trouble with Tombs and Tabernae

Allison L.C. Emmerson, Tulane University

A series of Latin epitaphs of the first to second centuries C.E. records an odd element of the Roman funerary landscape: each describes a tomb complex that includes a *taberna*. Although once understood as apartments for guards, the funerary *tabernae* have come to be seen as shops, incorporated into the tomb precinct to generate income for maintenance and funerary rites. This idea suggests an intriguing relationship between funerary and commercial space. The problem remains, however, that among the many thousands of known Roman tombs, not a single example includes a structure even resembling a shop, nor is there any support in the literary or artistic records. Have we simply lost the relevant material, or are we continuing to misinterpret these enigmatic inscriptions?

This paper returns to the *tabernae* epitaphs, incorporating a diverse collection of evidence—epigraphic, architectural, art historical, archaeological, literary, and legal. The examination raises as many questions as answers, but I argue that neither the shop nor the guardhouse interpretations are likely. Rather, the tabernae are best seen as multifunctional spaces, used for storage and other purposes related to activities within the tomb. Although such a conclusion might seem dull compared with the earlier ideas, looking beyond the *tabernae* themselves and to the broader context of the inscriptions illuminates far more interesting paths of inquiry into the legal complexities surrounding tomb construction and use, the hopes and fears of tomb builders confronting their role in posterity, and the dynamic use of the busy zone surrounding a Roman city.

Grave Reopening and Reuse in Non-Monumental Roman Cemeteries

Liana Brent, Cornell University

Roman tomb violation has been explored through Latin anecdotal, epigraphic, and juridical evidence, although the archaeological aspects have rarely been addressed. What is conspicuously lacking from studies of Roman tomb violation is the human body—the corporeal remains that constitute the tomb as a *locus religiosus*, and whose presence makes the act of tomb violation both possible and contradictory (*Dig*. 11.7.2.5). Too often disturbed, reopened, and reused graves are glossed over in archaeological site reports, without further attention to the postdepositional and continuing commemorative rituals that dealt with the social death of the individual and the creation of a corpse. Scholars working in various European archaeological traditions have articulated numerous terms and ways of recognizing disturbed, reopened, and robbed graves, which offers promising application in Roman archaeology.

According to the principles of "archaeothanatology," as outlined by Henri Duday, collaborative efforts between field anthropologists and archaeologists with knowledge of human osteology facilitate the interpretation of funerary remains, particularly in cases with multiple individuals and complex sequences of decay. Drawing on methods from anthropological archaeology and burial taphonomy, this paper investigates encounters with disarticulated human skeletal remains in reopened Roman mortuary deposits as well as the types of corporeal connections that grave reuse created. Case studies derive from a variety of published rural Roman cemeteries from the first to fourth centuries C.E. as well as the ongoing bioarchaeological investigation of the Vagnari cemetery in southeast Italy.

This paper incorporates published evidence from non-monumental cemeteries from various regions in Italy (e.g., Lombardia, Marche, Lazio, Puglia) into a broader, multidisciplinary dialogue about why postdepositional mortuary activities are present in Roman cemeteries yet are so rarely addressed as part of a wider discussion about Roman death and burial. By examining the state of decomposition at the time of grave reopening, it is possible to understand the sequence of postmortem graveside rites that the living performed. I argue that the addition of individuals and the manipulation of human skeletal elements was often the product of creating corporeal connections between the deceased and the living, rather than tomb violations, as we might be tempted to understand these phenomena from epigraphic and legal sources.

Deviant Burial in Roman Britain: Instances of Symbolic Replacement of Severed Body Parts with Objects

Simon Mays, Historic England, and *Vicky Crosby*, Historic England

Normative inhumation in Late Romano-British cemeteries was extended supine burial, but sporadically burials are found that deviate from this norm. Occasionally such deviations take the form of burial in the prone position and/or decapitation or other mutilation of the corpse. In a small subset of these latter, the severed head or other missing body parts are replaced in the grave by objects at the appropriate anatomical locations. This paper reviews this practice and describes some new examples from a small rural cemetery at Stanwick, England, where there is a high concentration of these practices. The Stanwick cemetery contains 35 inhumation burials. Preliminary dating evidence suggests a second–fourth-century C.E. date. Five burials were decapitated. In two instances, the severed head was placed in the lower part of the grave and a large stone placed atop the vertebral column in place of the head. A further inhumation at the site was found buried prone with a large flat stone wedged in its mouth. Various interpretations of this last burial are possible. However, analogy with other burials from Stanwick, and from other Romano-British cemeteries where severed body parts are replaced with stones or other objects, suggests one possibility: the stone was a symbolic replacement for a severed body part, in this case the tongue. This interpretation is supported by osteological study: the mandible shows alteration that may be consistent with amputation of the tongue in life. A number of causes of tongue ablation are possible. One is judicial mutilation. The medical literature on tongue amputation suggests further possibilities: although assault or accident are sometimes responsible, more frequently such injuries are self inflicted in patients suffering seizures or mental illness. These possibilities are discussed for the Stanwick burial, and the discussion is framed within the broader context of deviant burial practices in Roman Britain.

Ghazali Cemeteries Project (GCP) Field Report 2015/2016

Robert J. Stark, McMaster University, and *Joanna Ciesielska*, University of Warsaw

The Polish-Sudanese Ghazali Archaeological Site Presentation Project is an ongoing project directed by Artur Obluski of the Polish Centre of Mediterranean Archaeology, in conjunction with the National Corporation for Antiquities and Museums of Sudan. Ghazali is located in northern Sudan approximately 20 km southwest of the modern city of Karima, at the entrance to the Wadi Abu Dom.

Excavations at Ghazali were initiated in the 1950s by Peter Shinnie and colleagues, after which time investigation did not resume until 2012 under the current project.

Ghazali, occupied from ca. 670–1270 C.E. based on ^{14}C dating, comprises a monastic complex, a nearby settlement, and three cemeteries: for the monastic community (Cemetery 2), the settlement (Cemetery 3), and potentially local Christians from the region (Cemetery 1). During 2012–2013, Ghazali was surveyed, and geomagnetic prospection and kite photography was undertaken to assess the breadth of material present.

In 2015/2016, excavation in the monastic cemetery (Cemetery 2) was initiated. Based on aerial photography and the density of burials uncovered, it is estimated that more than 300 burials are present. To date, excavation has focused on the southern and northern limits of Cemetery 2 in an attempt to determine which area was used first. No grave goods have been recovered thus far, though a number of in situ burial stelae with inscriptions in Greek and Coptic but with no dates have been identified, necessitating further ^{14}C dating to delineate temporality. Burial superstructures typically conform to a Christian box-grave type, being oriented northwest–southeast and composed of a rectangular construction of uncut stone (ca. 2.5–3.2 m x 0.6–1.2 m, ca. 50 cm ht.), infilled with earth and gravel. Tombs were mapped, drawn, and measured, and ortophotogrammetry was undertaken to facilitate postexcavation reconstructions. Of the burials examined, 64 out of 66 are male, and two are indeterminate, confirming our belief that Cemetery 2 is the monastic cemetery.

The goal of the Ghazali Cemeteries Project is to document the three cemetery complexes and to provide insights to life at this monastic settlement. Little is known of where these desert dwelling monastic individuals originated. An origin in Egypt has commonly been believed, yet textual and archaeological sources so far cannot confidently confirm this fact. To address this issue, postexcavation research at Ghazali will focus on isotopic examinations of mobility (^{18}O, $^{87}Sr/^{86}Sr$) and diet (^{13}C, ^{15}N) in an attempt to gather insight as to the composition and origins of this monastic community.

SESSION 6C: Colloquium
Collecting and Presenting the Etruscans in North America

ORGANIZER: *Alexandra Carpino*, Northern Arizona University

Colloquium Overview Statement

During the late 19th and early 20th centuries, several major public and university museums in North America acquired significant collections of Etruscan art that represent some of the most important examples of this material outside Europe. The institutions' acquisition strategies, along with the philosophies that governed how the collected works were displayed, are not widely known. In this colloquium, five scholars address these issues using a variety of methodologies. "Collecting at the Museum of Fine Arts, Boston: The Strategies of Edward Robinson and Rodolfo Lanciani" focuses on the correspondence between the Museum of Fine Art's curator of antiquities and a highly placed Italian archaeologist and illustrates one popular late 19th-century approach; namely, purchases that privileged the acquisition of scientifically important objects over those with aesthetic and/or technical merits. "The Metropolitan Museum's Etruscans: Collecting and Presenting from the 1870s to the Present" traces the development of the collection by Luigi Palma di Cesnola, the museum's first director, and discusses the role played by John Marshall, the museum's agent in Rome, in selecting and purchasing major antiquities (including major forgeries) between 1906 and 1928. With "Collecting Etruscans for California," the colloquium transitions to the university museum, specifically the Phoebe Hearst Museum of Anthropology (University of California, Berkeley), which includes a large group of Etruscan artifacts acquired by Alfred Emerson in the early 20th century to rival in quality and quantity collections of similar objects in east coast museums. "Out of Etruria: Italian Artifacts to American Museums" straddles both the public and university museum in its discussion of the collection of Evan Gorga, who amassed more than 150,000 objects in a quest to "collect the world"; these include Etruscan and Italic antiquities now in Tucson, San Francisco, and Malibu that speak to a complex paradoxical chapter in Italian archaeology and the management of that nation's heritage. The colloquium concludes with "The Impact of the 1970 UNESCO Convention on Unprovenanced Etruscan Artifacts in America," which analyzes two university collections (New York University and Fordham University) with significant numbers of unprovenanced artifacts and argues that cultural biography should play an important role in gallery displays. The colloquium is timely in light of renewed interest in the Etruscans and their art in North America, as witnessed by reinstallations of important Etruscan galleries and exhibitions such as *From the Temple to the Tomb* (Meadows Museum, 2009), *The Chimaera of Arezzo* (The Getty Villa, 2009–2010), and *The Etruscans–An Ancient Italian Civilization* (Pointe-à-Callière, 2012).

Collecting at the Museum of Fine Arts, Boston: The Strategies of Edward Robinson and Rodolfo Lanciani

Helen Nagy, University of Puget Sound

The magnificent stone sarcophagi of the Tetnie family from Vulci are probably the most impressive Etruscan objects in the Museum of Fine Arts, Boston (MFA). Bought in 1883 by newspaper editor and art collector James Jackson Jarves and the banker George Disney Maquay of Florence, Italy, they were first displayed at the International Exhibition and then were purchased in 1886 by Mrs. Gardner Brewer, who donated one to the MFA and the other to the Athenaeum, but as a loan to the MFA. The latter was eventually purchased and donated to the MFA by Cornelius Vermeule, as part of the museum's desire to increase its holdings of high-quality Etruscan art.

In contrast are the rather convoluted efforts undertaken in 1888 by the MFA's Curator of Antiquities, Edward Robinson, to obtain a relatively small number of Etruscan terracotta votives (a far cry from the stone sarcophagi) for the museum with the help of Rodolfo Lanciani, a highly placed Italian archaeologist and official. This paper focuses on Robinson's strategies to expand the collection of antiquities at the MFA, particularly with respect to its Etruscan holdings. The museum already possessed a large collection of plaster casts, but Robinson wanted a large number of original pieces. By examining the correspondence between Robinson and Lanciani, a window into the museum world of the late 19th and early 20th centuries in America is revealed. American museums competed with one another for the best works and vied for recognition and wealthy donors. They also needed agents to make the purchases and patrons (and patronesses) to finance the transactions, as well as, at times, somewhat unscrupulous foreign facilitators. The group of Etruscan terracottas whose acquisition Lanciani facilitated illustrates one popular late 19th-century approach; namely, purchases that privileged the procurement of scientifically important objects over those with aesthetic and/or technical merits (e.g., the Vulci sarcophagi) so that a museum could become complete, rich, representative, and a first-class institution.

The Metropolitan Museum's Etruscans: Collecting and Presenting from the 1870s to the Present

Richard D. De Puma, University of Iowa

This paper traces the early development of the Etruscan collection by Luigi Palma di Cesnola (1832-1904), the museum's first director, and considers the significant consequences of Edward Robinson's move from the Museum of Fine Arts, Boston, to the Metropolitan Museum of Art in New York in 1905 as a result of a major disagreement in collecting strategies. John Marshall, the museum's agent in Rome, played an especially significant role in selecting and purchasing major antiquities (and sometimes major forgeries) from 1906 to his death in 1928. The paper explores his expertise and connoisseurship as well as relevant interactions with other important curators, scholars, dealers, and collectors. It concludes with Etruscan antiquities acquired by Gisela Richter as well as more recent curators and pays special attention to the major reinstallation of the Etruscan galleries in 2007 and the collection's definitive publication in 2013. Throughout this history of building an important Etruscan collection, we see the tension between acquiring "archaeological material" versus "artistic masterpieces."

Collecting Etruscans for California

Lisa Pieraccini, University of California, Berkeley

Alfred Emerson (1859–1943) was the liaison for Phoebe A. Hearst's acquisition of a large group of Etruscan artifacts at the turn of the 20th century. He was not only proud of supervising these purchases, but even published an article about them in *Sunset Magazine* in 1905. In it, Emerson describes the importance of establishing a collection in California at the University of California, Berkeley. He knew that east coast museums, such as the Metropolitan Museum of Art in New York and the Museum of Fine Arts, Boston, were acquiring Etruscan artifacts, and he wanted to make sure the west coast could rival them in quantity and quality. Emerson also writes poetically about the Etruscan race and imagines how many of their artifacts were used, inventing at times a person and a story to go with specific objects. He describes Etruscan funerary practices, comparing Etruscans with the Egyptians (not uncommon for the era), and expresses a genuine interest in their art. In addition, he not only acknowledges Hearst's remarkable role as a woman establishing a museum but also demonstrates his admiration for her philanthropic and cultural donations. This paper considers the knowledge that Americans such as Emerson had about the Etruscans in the late 19th and early 20th centuries and how he used this information to formulate an effective acquisition strategy for the collection now housed in the Phoebe A. Hearst Museum of Anthropology. Regardless of what Emerson imagined about Etruscan culture at the turn of last century, the artifacts he acquired make up the largest Etruscan collection in the state of California today, worthy in every way of the title of his 1905 article, "California's Etruscan Museum."

Out of Etruria: Italian Artifacts to American Museums

Claire Lyons, J. Paul Getty Museum

Between the late 19th and the mid 20th century, American museums embarked on a mission to build representative holdings of classical art. Most often they turned to Italy, where both official and private excavations operated under the auspices of state-sponsored archaeology. In tandem with the rise of a middle class interested in origins and the demise of aristocratic collectors, rapid urban and agricultural development fueled the flow of ancient artifacts. Strict patrimony laws and the practice of partage scarcely abated the robust trade in antiquities. Rome was the prime destination for international collectors and their agents in what became the most lucrative art market since 18th-century Naples.

Among the crowded network of antiquarians, dealers, and restorers active on the Roman scene, one remarkable figure stands out—the opera tenor Evan Gorga, who amassed more than 150,000 objects in his quest to "collect the world." Groups of Etruscan and Italic antiquities in Tucson, San Francisco, and other museums can be traced to Gorga's manic efforts. Dispersed around the globe through a progressive policy of cultural exchange, Gorga's artifacts witness a complex, paradoxical chapter in Italian archaeology and the management of the nation's heritage.

The Impact of the 1970 UNESCO Convention on Unprovenanced Etruscan Artifacts in America

Laetitia La Follette, University of Massachusetts–Amherst

The revised guidelines of the Association of Art Museum Directors (AAMD) (2013) not only allow more loopholes for the acquisition of ancient artifacts without complete provenance but also raise questions about when the acquisition of such unprovenanced material is justified. Like the more stringent guidelines laid out in the Code of Ethics of the Alliance of American Museums (AAM) or the earlier 2008 AAMD guidelines that recognized the 1970 UNESCO Convention as the terminus ante quem, current museological practice acknowledges the critical importance of provenance research before—and transparency in the public dissemination of that research after—any acquisition of an object with gaps in its provenance. The AIA's own policy, laid out in its recently revised Code of Ethics (2016), along with its 1973 Resolution on the Acquisition of Antiquities by Museums, also explicitly urges members to "refrain from activities that give sanction, directly or indirectly, to that trade [in undocumented antiquities], and to the valuation of such artifacts through authentication, acquisition, publication, or exhibition" and asks museums to refuse "to acquire through purchase, gift or bequest cultural property exported subsequent to December 1973 . . . and be guided by the policies of the [1970] UNESCO Convention."

In practice, however, transparency about unprovenanced artifacts, even those recently acquired or accepted as gifts, is not universal. This paper examines two such collections in New York City (Fordham University and New York University) published in the last decade. It considers when the publication of unprovenanced material might be justified and what responsibilities museums have to notify their visitors about the path unprovenanced and likely looted objects have taken to them. Given that only AAMD members can post their unprovenanced or poorly provenanced artifacts on the AAMD Object Registry, what alternatives exist for university museums to comply with the need for transparency regarding their own material? The paper concludes by arguing for the importance of the cultural biography of an ancient artifact—its multiple histories, uses, and contexts, both in antiquity and since then, up to today—in gallery displays.

SESSION 6D: Colloquium
Investigating Prehistoric Urbanization in East Crete: New Work at Palaikastro, 2012–2016

ORGANIZER: *Carl Knappett*, University of Toronto

Colloquium Overview Statement

This symposium has as its objective the discussion of Minoan urbanization, as viewed through the lens of research at one particular town, Palaikastro. Here excavations have been conducted across multiple decades (1900s, 1960s, 1980s, 1990s, 2000s), revealing many buildings and town blocks and indicating a settlement of considerable extent, surpassed only by Knossos, Phaistos, and Malia. However, Palaikastro differs markedly from these sites insofar as it has yet to reveal any evidence for a "palace," despite repeated efforts to locate it. The recent five-year project at the site (2012–2016), under the auspices of the British School at Athens, has itself addressed this "palatial" question, excavating an area considered to be a candidate locale, but which has actually emerged as a previously unknown neighborhood on the edge of town, with three main structures occupied on and off through the Middle to Late Bronze Age. This gives us the opportunity to use the latest archaeological techniques to explore various questions concerning urban growth, settlement density, and household specialization. As our five-year project also incorporates an important landscape dimension, with survey carried out in 2012, coupled with paleoenvironmental investigations, we are provided with another angle on such urban questions—namely, the interaction between settlement growth and patterns of change in the wider landscape.

There are many different lines of evidence running across a range of scales: soil micromorphology of house floors and features; the various finds of pottery, metal, and stone, and organic remains of shell, bone, and plants; architectural layout and the built environment; and features and sediments in the surrounding environment. Archaeological techniques of analysis become ever more sophisticated, but this also means increasing specialization, a negative corollary of which can be fragmentation. Archaeological projects of this kind face particular challenges in articulating the various forms of evidence they generate, and without proper dialogue and open interface between all specialists, holistic interpretation is elusive, if not impossible. Therefore, we propose this symposium as an exercise in interpretative integration, exploring how the various strands of evidence and lines of argument might best be brought together. A full range of project members covering all aspects of the project will present papers, with East Cretan Bronze Age specialists from outside the project invited to offer commentaries on both the project's results and the interpretive process.

DISCUSSANT: *Thomas M. Brogan*, INSTAP Study Center for East Crete

Examining the Proto- to Neopalatial Transition through Pottery Production at Palaikastro

John Gait, British School at Athens, *Noémi S. Müller*, British School at Athens, *Evangelia Kiriatzi*, British School at Athens, and *Carl Knappett*, University of Toronto

The paper presents the preliminary results of an ongoing diachronic study of pottery production and use at Bronze Age Palaikastro, East Crete, being undertaken at the Fitch Laboratory of the British School at Athens as part of a wide-ranging, multidisciplinary investigation of the site and its environs. The analysis of the pottery as a whole spans Middle Minoan (MM) IIA through to Late Minoan (LM) IIIA2 (ca. 1800–1330 B.C.E.) and integrates stylistic and macroscopic studies with petrographic and chemical analysis (WD-XRF). In addition, the project has undertaken an investigation of the surrounding landscape to identify potential sources of clay and temper raw materials. Consequently, the project aims to provide an understanding of diachronic changes in local pottery production at Palaikastro, as well as identify the variations in the consumption of imported wares. This paper focuses on the nature of changes in the production of fine and coarse ware vessels during the transition between the Proto- and Neopalatial periods (MM II–MM III); this is a time in which significant political, artistic, and socioeconomic transformations are visible in the archaeology of central Crete. At Palaikastro, this transition appears to have witnessed changes in the layout and planning of the settlement with a shift toward a more urban character, together with changes in material culture, such as the introduction of certain plain wares. Macroscopic, petrographic, and chemical analyses of local pottery appear to indicate that significant changes did occur between the Proto- and Neopalatial periods at Palaikastro, but despite abrupt stylistic innovations, the transition may have been more selective and gradual with regard to fabric composition and production technology. Among the "fine ware" cups and bowls, the semi-fine pale red/orange fabric that dominates in MM IIIA also forms a significant, although secondary, component of MM IIA and MM

IIB assemblages, which are themselves dominated by fine pale yellow calcareous fabrics. This change seems to reflect a use of different raw material sources. Conversely, among the coarse ware jugs, jars, amphoras, pithoi, and cooking vessels, no significant chronological variations are seen, with the characteristic Palaikastro pink to red phyllite-tempered fabric predominating throughout. Pottery from other production centers continues to reach the site, but in consistently small quantities and with no major changes in its sources. These results are considered within the social and economic context of pottery production at Palaikastro and also the wider context of the historical and political forces affecting East Crete.

Architecture and Urbanism at Palaikastro: A New Neighborhood in Perspective

Quentin Letesson, Université Catholique de Louvain, and *Tim Cunningham*, Université Catholique de Louvain

The Palace and Landscape Project at Palaikastro excavations, conducted under the auspices of the British School at Athens from 2013 to 2015, uncovered remains of three buildings in a heretofore unexplored area of the site. These buildings, two of which were completely revealed, show significant differences in construction, plan, and situation in what is essentially a different neighborhood of the Bronze Age town. With preserved floor deposits from Late Minoan IB and Late Minoan IIIB and contexts going back to Middle Minoan II, these newly revealed structures advance our understanding of the layout of the site and have implications for social organisation and chronological developments at Palaikastro and elsewhere on Crete.

At the settlement level, we discuss the integration of this new sector in the overall layout of the town. At the neighbourhood scale, this paper focuses on a description of the three buildings, both in terms of architectural techniques and spatial organization, while drawing comparisons with other buildings from the Roussolakkos area. Finally, we address the functional development of the sector which witnessed important changes when, in Postpalatial times, the domestic nature of the buildings seemed to have dwindled in favor of a clear burst of ritual activities, attested both by various deposits (e.g., cultic material, feasting refuse) and architectural alterations of the preexisting built environment.

The Use of Metals at Minoan Palaikastro: New Finds

Seán Hemingway, Metropolitan Museum of Art

Investigations at Palaikastro, most notably over three excavation campaigns between 1902 and 1906, 1987 and 2003, and recently in 2013–2015, have revealed significant remains of the Minoan settlement, which was one of the largest on Crete during the Late Bronze Age. Since metals have always been valued and metal objects can be recycled even when damaged, they appear much less frequently in the archaeological record than other kinds of objects, such as pottery, and rarely in contexts of use. Nonetheless, a wide range of metal finds have been recovered from the Minoan town and nearby tombs including gold, silver, lead, especially copper alloy, and iron artifacts. Evidence for metalworking has also come to light in the form of crucibles, tuyeres, molds for casting implements and ornamental objects, as well as tools for fashioning and finishing metal objects.

The Palace and Landscape Project at Palaikastro has yielded a small but significant corpus of metal finds that adds to our knowledge of the use of metals at the Minoan settlement in the Bronze Age. This paper presents many of the new metal finds, which include gold jewelry, a circular lead weight, and other lead objects as well as copper alloy implements. The metal finds are considered in light of their archaeological contexts and manufacturing processes as well as in terms of the corpus of metalwork from Palaikastro and more broadly Bronze Age Crete and the neighboring cultures of the Cyclades, mainland Greece, Cyprus, and the Near East.

Phases of Feasting at Palaikastro: Late Minoan III Ceramics From Building AP1

Catherine Pratt, Western University, and *Nicoletta Momigliano*, University of Bristol

During the 2013–2015 excavation seasons of the Palace and Landscape Project at Palaikastro, a large building named AP1 (or the House of the Griffin), was uncovered. AP1 is composed of an imposing rectangular central room with smaller rooms flanking either side. At least three phases of occupation can be identified, spanning the Neopalatial–Postpalatial periods, and possibly going back to Middle Minoan II. The final phase produced the most abundant pottery dating to the Late Minoan IIIA2–B period. Interestingly, while the pottery associated with AP1 was by far the greatest amount recovered from the site, very little was found inside the building itself. Instead, massive quantities of ceramics were found deposited directly outside the front (north), east, and back (south) sides of the building, often abutting the outer walls and spilling out into the adjacent road and open spaces. Although much of this pottery remains to be studied, preliminary results suggest that a considerable amount is not only painted but is of relatively good quality and comprising both open and closed shapes, as well as cooking wares. Moreover, joins from all sides of the building suggest that this pottery could have been deposited during a single event. The impressive nature of the large shapes, such as a highly decorated amphoroid krater, combined with the massive amounts of smaller open shapes, such as cups and bowls, might indicate that this deposit is not the result of daily household activities but of large-scale commensal event(s). This deposit is therefore important for shedding light on consumption practices at Palaikastro and the changing nature of feasting practices after the palatial era. If this deposit does indeed represent a single Late Minoan III event, then its context, located near a Postpalatial ritual area to the east, is especially remarkable.

Building Floors and Activity Areas at Palaikastro: Evidence from Micromorphology

Rachel Kulick, University of Toronto

The geoarchaeological research conducted during the Palace and Landscape Project at Palaikastro 2013–2015 excavations has attempted to serve three agendas: (1) to establish the uses of space in the newly revealed buildings and activity areas;

(2) to connect the town site with activities that may have been occurring around the site, such as agriculture and production activities and other activities potentially impacting the landscape; and (3) to investigate processes of site formation and broader landscape transformation. Toward these goals, in 2013–2015 sediment monolith samples and associated bulk soil samples were collected from the three buildings and associated spaces in the newly excavated town area. This paper discusses the results from the soil thin-section analysis of these samples from the newly revealed building floors and activity areas.

In addition to the use-of-space information provided by this microscale data, the high-resolution record of the depositional processes and anthropogenic inclusions also enables the contextualization of some of the on-site human activities with the natural environmental processes affecting the site's inhabitants. Significantly, it appears that not all of the newly discovered buildings and activity areas were utilized at Palaikastro from the Middle Minoan I/II period through to the Late Minoan III period; rather, some spaces were apparently abandoned while others were reused. This micromorphological research also clarifies the nature and temporal contexts of the processes involved in these different spatial transformations within the town.

Life Beyond the Palace: Managing the Territory of Minoan Palaikastro, Crete

Santiago Riera-Mora, University of Barcelona, *Hector Orengo*, University of Cambridge, *Núria Cañellas*, University of Barcelona, *Alexandra Livarda*, University of Nottingham, *Athanasia Krahtopoulou*, Hellenic Ministry of Culture and Sports, *Rena Veropoulidou*, Museum of Byzantine Culture, Hellenic Ministry of Culture and Sports, *Llorenç Picornell*, Muséum National d'Histoire Naturelle, Paris, and *Vasiliki Tzevelekidi*, Independent Researcher

Theories concerning the emergence of Minoan civilization debate the role of specialized agricultural production and the concentration and redistribution of resources by a centralized proto-state. The arguments, however, are largely based on indirect archaeological evidence recovered from palaces, towns, and other settlements, and little information is available from their territories, where the main productive activities could concentrate. Our study aims to contribute a fresh approach to these debates and is based on the premise that the relevance of on-site discoveries cannot be fully understood and interpreted without complementary landscape research that allows insights into landscape use and the environmental resources available. Landscape analysis is considered here vital to contextualize data gathered during the excavation process within their wider ecological and cultural setting. Focusing on the Bronze Age town of Palaikastro, our study aims to shed new light on how economy and landscape was organized in this east part of Crete. Palaikastro is of particular interest, as to date no central authority/palace has been discovered, and it was possibly organized in different blocks/neighborhoods. The town thrived during a period when other towns were in demise and finally ended in the Late Minoan III period. Combining paleoenvironmental analyses (pollen and NPP, and sedimentology) from closely well-dated organic deltaic sediments, on-site bioarchaeological data (including seeds, charcoal, shells, and bones), and extensive landscape survey and mapping, we provide a new model on how the economy of the town was organized and how its territory was managed.

Minoan Foodways: A Culinary Map of Palaikastro, Crete

Alexandra Livarda, University of Nottingham, *Rena Veropoulidou*, Hellenic Ministry of Culture and Sports, *Vaso Tzevelekidi*, Independent Researcher, *Christina Tsoraki*, Leiden University, *Llorenç Picornell*, Muséum National d'Histoire Naturelle, Paris, *Santiago Riera-Mora*, University of Barcelona, *Núria Cañellas*, University of Barcelona, *Rachel Kulick*, University of Toronto, *Alexandra Kriti*, University of Sheffield, *Mila Andonova*, University of Nottingham, *Michalis Trivizas*, University of Crete, and *Hector Orengo*, University of Cambridge

The selection, production, processing, consumption, and disposal of food are all activities imbued with cultural meaning. The choice of food is, therefore, a matter of sustenance not only for the physical but also the social individual. In Minoan archaeology, the different lines of evidence of food systems, such as bones, seeds, and so on are traditionally treated and reported separately and are often considered to be of secondary importance. Employing data from the Palace and Landscape Project at Palaikastro in East Crete, our aim is to integrate the different proxies together to provide a holistic picture of foodways and place these in the forefront of the Minoan archaeology research agenda as well as at the core of debates on social organization. Systematic bioarchaeological sampling and recovery of animal bones, plant macroremains and shells, stone tool analysis, paleoenvironmental, geoarchaeological, and landscape work were combined to disentangle the reasons why certain resources were selected over others. The various assemblages are first studied through taphonomic filters to provide a solid basis for their interpretation and are then discussed in the framework of Minoan food studies with the ultimate goal of investigating cultural choices and patterns of the period.

SESSION 6E: Colloquium
Pottery from Sanctuaries: What Can it Tell Us?

Sponsored by the Ancient Figure-Decorated Pottery Interest Group

ORGANIZERS: *Mark D. Stansbury-O'Donnell*, University of St. Thomas, and *Thomas H. Carpenter*, Ohio University

Colloquium Overview Statement

Each of the six papers in this session addresses the basic question of what way, if any, fine pottery from sanctuaries can contribute to our understanding of ancient cult practices and beliefs. The sanctuaries considered range from Samothrace to Athens to South Italy to Etruria, and the types of evidence examined include images and inscriptions as well as distinctive shapes from three centuries. Overall, the papers show varying degrees of selectivity for figure-decorated pottery in sanctuaries, whether for its use or absence.

The first paper looks at archaic Attic figure-decorated pottery from the Sanctuary of the Great Gods on Samothrace and argues on the basis of shapes found there that ritual drinking took place in the archaic sanctuary and that Attic figured column kraters may have been the focus during such ritual activity.

The next two papers focus on Athens. "Votive Inscriptions and Figural Pottery on the Athenian Acropolis: A Contextual Approach" surveys the range of painted or inscribed inscriptions on vases from the Acropolis to refine our understanding of cult practices and to disprove some common assumptions about them. The other, "Ex-Voto: Reconsidering a Votive Deposit from the Area of the Hephaisteion in Athens" serves as a corrective by looking at the closed deposit found near the Temple of Hephaistos on Kolonos Agoriaos, often seen as a votive deposit. Through a study of deposition morphology and the character of the pottery assemblage, the paper demonstrates that the assemblage is unlikely to be a votive deposit; rather, it probably originated from a private dining club.

The fourth and fifth papers shift the focus to South Italy. "The Attic Pottery from the Persephoneion of Locri Epizefiri: Between Ritual Practices and Worship" demonstrates that the images on the mostly unpublished vases reflect a close correspondence to the religious and ritual dimensions of the sanctuary. "Hera, Heads, and Hope: South Italian Vases in Paestan Sanctuaries" notes the rarity of South Italian vases in sacral contexts, suggesting that when they do appear they were chosen because they were particularly appropriate for the cult. Possible meanings for isolate female heads on a large number of South Italian vases at two sanctuaries at Paestum are explored.

The final paper, "Women and Drinking Cups in North Etruria: Evidence from Poggio Colla," takes us to Poggio Colla, where excavations have provided extensive evidence for dedications and religious activity. There is almost no figural pottery from the sanctuary, but nearby grave groups show that different black-glazed drinking vessel shapes are strongly correlated to men or women. The occurrence of the same shapes in the sanctuary hints at women's participation in ritual activity along with men at the sanctuary.

Ritual Drinking in Archaic Samothrace: Evidence from the Figure-Decorated Pottery

An Jiang, Emory University

Although archaic Attic figure-decorated pottery has been found in excavations in the Sanctuary of the Great Gods on Samothrace, little attention has hitherto been paid to this group of vases because of their secondary contexts and fragmentary state of preservation. These painted vases have long been assumed to be votive gifts from the initiates who participated the Samothracian Mysteries. However, very little is known about the sanctuary and the ritual taking place there in the Archaic period. Recent excavations have demonstrated that several buildings that were once considered to be archaic sacred architecture must now be dated to the Late Classical and Hellenistic periods. Literary accounts are almost silent about archaic Samothrace, and the epigraphical evidence concerning the worship of the "Theoi Megaloi" and the initiates of the Samothracian Mysteries does not appear until the Late Classical period.

Taking a new approach, this paper argues that this group of imported Attic pottery together with the local wares found inside the sanctuary constitutes our best evidence for understanding the ritual activities taking place in archaic Samothrace. Among the figure-decorated pottery, the predominant shapes are column kraters and drinking vessels. There also seems to be a sequence of figured column kraters that extends from the second quarter of the sixth century B.C.E. down to the end of the Archaic period. The evidence suggests that ritual drinking took place in the archaic sanctuary and that the imported Attic figured column kraters may have been the central focus during such ritual activities. The existence of seventh-century drinking vessels and Hellenistic dining halls also supports the suggestion that drinking wine was an ancient and persistent ritual practice in the history of the sanctuary.

Votive Inscriptions and Figural Pottery on the Athenian Acropolis: A Contextual Approach

Kiki Karoglou, Metropolitan Museum of Art

By using the Athenian Acropolis as a case study, this paper investigates for the first time votive figure-decorated pottery and inscriptions to explore the ritual functions of figural pottery deposited in sanctuaries. After the publication of Graef-Langlotz (1909–1933), vase inscriptions have been largely overlooked, and a comprehensive discussion is still wanting. Regarding inscriptions on votives from the Acropolis, notably statue bases, the focus has been on the socioeconomic status of potters and painters. This paper, instead, surveys the range of painted or inscribed inscriptions on vases from the site (e.g., votive, explanatory, signatures, kalos inscriptions) to examine what types of figured pottery carried inscriptions, the deities to whom they were dedicated, the scenes they depict, and the connection, if any, between the iconography and the inscriptions.

A careful study of the evidence proves common assumptions to be mistaken or in need of further investigation. For instance, the special relationship of potters and craftsmen to Athena Ergane is often considered a reason for the dedication of pottery. In fact, very few Acropolis vases carry inscriptions that manifestly state that they were dedicated by potters and painters. Moreover, the cult epithet Ergane is not attested epigraphically on the Acropolis before the fourth century B.C.E. In a similar fashion, some Acropolis vases with representations of Athena have been widely discussed in relation to contemporary festivals, notably the Panathenaia, or as evidence for the existence of archaic cult statues of Athena, and both the variety of the vase iconography and assortment of Athena's epithets attested in dedicatory inscriptions (i.e., Pallas, Pallas Tritogeneia, Polias, Glaukopis, and Parthenos) deserve closer attention.

This inquiry reveals, for example, that owners' inscriptions appear exclusively on sympotic vases (kylikes and cups; e.g., "Epicharidou eimi kylix"), whereas names of individual dedicators are uncommon on "specialized" votive pottery products such as pinakes and plates. Most vase inscriptions refer to Athena and bear the votive formula "hieros (-a, -on) eimi tes Athenaias" in various combinations and abbreviated forms. Because this formula is interpreted as serving an inventory purpose, it is worthwhile to discuss these specific vase inscriptions in light of relevant evidence such as the later treasuries of Athena. Integrating pottery with other abundant epigraphic evidence will contribute to a broader understanding of cult practices on Acropolis.

Ex-Voto: Reconsidering a Votive Deposit from the area of the Hephaisteion in Athens

Kathleen M. Lynch, University of Cincinnati

In 1936, American excavators discovered a closed deposit of pottery dating ca. 480–450 B.C.E. located 30 m from the Temple of Hephaistos on the Kolonos Agoraios, west of the classical Athenian Agora. The excavators assumed that the deposit's proximity to the later marble temple and high-quality Attic figured pottery indicated a votive origin, despite the lack of evidence for a sanctuary predating the mid fifth-century B.C.E. Hephaisteion. The deposit was never published in full, but recent restudy indicates that contents of the deposit do not support a votive identification. A short digression in the paper discusses methodologies for associating excavated ceramics to original use, including votive and ritual activities, and domestic or civic dining. The deposit lacks key characteristics of a votive deposit, and the quantifiable character of the deposit's pottery does not align with the profile of contemporary domestic deposits. Instead, the large number of drinking cups of uniform shape and size from the deposit signal large-group dining, but the figured pottery points to an elite, private dining establishment rather than civic dining.

There is no evidence for civic dining on top of the Kolonos Agoraios. However, epigraphical and historical evidence documents the presence of a shrine to Eurysakes, the son of Salaminian Aias, on the Kolonos Agoraios, close to the pottery deposit. The Eurysakeion served as the meeting place for the *genos* of the Salaminioi, one of about 100 lineage-based private groups operating in classical Athens. Although there is no written evidence for dining at the shrine of this private group with public functions, archaeological and literary evidence documents that other Athenian *gene* did banquet together as a focus of activity and identity. Thus, it seems possible that the pottery from the ex-Hephaisteion deposit instead represents the contents of the Salaminioi's pantries.

The figured pottery from the deposit includes a few pieces with warriors fighting, with one fragment possibly referencing Aias, but otherwise the figural scenes are typical for the period, although in a greater abundance here than we see in the houses of Athenians.

The Attic Pottery from the Persephoneion of Locri Epizefiri: Between Ritual Practices and Worship

Elvia Giudice, University of Catania, and *Giada Giudice*, University of Catania

Up to the present day not much has been published regarding the pottery of the Persephoneion of Locri Epizefiri. The Attic pottery from the Persephoneion are examined according to two criteria. First on the basis of function: the symposium, perfume containers and vases from the female sphere, plastic vases, skyphoi, and the like. A further distinction is made between those used as anathemata and those, instead, that were essentially instruments for sacrificial and ritual performance.

The second criterion regards the analysis of the painted images on Attic vases, to verify if the iconography can provide support for understanding the dynamics inherent to the sphere of worship. This is far from simple in the case of the Locri material, as the fragmentary nature of the finds first requires reconstruction of the depicted scene.

At the Persephoneion, there is an unusual quantity and variety of Attic pottery when compared with other regional sites such as the necropolis of Lucifero, the city of Croton, and the Temesa shrine. Although the image repertory appears to be aligned with the iconographic range of the period, analysis of the pottery from the Persephoneion demonstrates, in many cases, an iconographic selectivity and specificity linked to the sanctuary and its ritual activity. The presence of chase scenes such as Boreas-Oreithyia are potentially connected to Persephone's abduction, while other scenes such as the rape of the Leukippidae have a close link with the legendary history of the city. Other scenes of the *gynaeceum*, such as women with a kalathos or mirror, are appropriate for young girls who deposited them in the Persephoneion before their wedding, and in some cases these compare with the scenes found on pinakes. Indeed, the selection of images with the Attic repertory does not appear to be the result of a random process and in many cases seems to reflect a close correspondence to the religious and ritual scenario of the sanctuary.

Hera, Heads, and Hope: South Italian Vases in Paestan Sanctuaries

Keely Heuer, State University of New York at New Paltz

South Italian red-figure vases are not found in abundance in the sanctuary deposits of southern Italy and Sicily, unlike moldmade terracottas, which number in the thousands. The rarity of South Italian vases in sacral contexts implies that when they do appear, their shape and iconography was viewed as particularly appropriate for and connected to the respective cult of the site. At Paestum, in the sanctuaries of Hera adjacent to the agora and outside the city walls at Foce del Sele, roughly one-third of the South Italian vases uncovered are decorated with one or more isolated female heads as either the primary or secondary motif, an unsurprising statistic, as such heads are the most frequent theme in South Italian vasepainting, occurring on more than 7,400 pieces. None of the heads is inscribed or has any other attributes to suggest identity, but perhaps in the context of Paestum's sanctuaries, they might have been thought of as representing Hera or the dedicator. However, I propose that the lack of clear indicators of identity may have been intentional, allowing such heads to serve a wholly symbolic function, perhaps as incomplete figures embodying the worshiper's hope for a desired, yet incomplete, future outcome, such as a happy, successful marriage. This interpretation is strengthened by the various types of votive terracottas featuring isolated heads that appear in significant numbers at sanctuaries associated with female coming of age rites in southern Italy and Sicily.

Women and Drinking Cups in North Etruria: Evidence from Poggio Colla

Ann Steiner, Franklin and Marshall College

Greek writers such as Aristotle and Theopompus describe Etruscan women as distinctive because they banquet with men, and Theopompous remarks on both the ease with which they offer toasts and on the quantities they drink. To be sure, images of elite women banqueting with their spouses exist in fourth-century and Hellenistic tomb paintings. Recently excavated material from Poggio Colla in northern Etruria, however, suggests there is also ample evidence for female participation in sanctuary rituals involving commensality as well. The record reveals unexpected corroboration for the extreme picture presented in Greek texts by linking nearly identical evidence from tombs and sanctuaries.

Twenty-one excavation seasons at Poggio Colla (700–200 B.C.E.) have produced extensive evidence for dedications and religious activity, including textile production, dedications of luxury goods including jewelry, and a likely cult focus on a female divinity. In addition, several fourth-century B.C.E. contexts include vessels for drinking and eating in both plain locally made ware, and a smaller percentage of imported black-gloss drinking cups, including *sovradipinti* skyphoi and kylikes with stamped decoration. There is almost no figural pottery preserved at the site.

Material from a substantial cemetery in the same region includes more than 150 tombs, for half of which anthropologists have sexed the human remains. Grave groups reveal that different black-gloss drinking vessel shapes are strongly correlated to women and men. The fact that these same vessels exist in the repertory of commensal shapes excavated at Poggio Colla provides intriguing hints for this facet of women's participation in ritual activity along with men at the sanctuary.

This evidence from pottery at a regional sanctuary helps to develop a more nuanced picture of the roles of women in the religious life of elite Etruscan society, one that complements and corrects the extreme interpretations of their status and behavior as registered by Greek and Roman writers.

SESSION 6F: Colloquium
The Regia Reconsidered: A New Interpretation of the American Excavations Results

ORGANIZERS: *Nicola Terrenato*, University of Michigan, and *Paolo Brocato*, Università della Calabria

Colloquium Overview Statement

The session presents the results of a multiyear research work undertaken on the site of the Regia in the Roman Forum, focusing in particular on the excavations carried out there by the American Academy in Rome. Since 2014, an international team has been working on the archive, the finds, and the remains with the aim of arriving at the publication of a comprehensive final report of the Regia excavations. This involved extensive work of reformatting the data into single-context records in a critical way, recreating a stratigraphic sequence that also included all the structural remains. A three-dimensional digital model representing the complex sequence has been created and will serve as the core of a mixed-media publication. The in-depth reanalysis has also provided crucial new insights into the architectural development of the archaic Regia building, allowing for a radical revision of the phase reconstructions advanced by Frank Brown. A much simpler sequence of buildings can be envisioned, bringing the site much more closely in line with what we now know of archaic central Italian architecture. Introduced by the director of the American Academy in Rome, which sponsors the project, a series of papers by team members and consultants presents an organic view of the new results. A paper by the directors of the project presents an overview of the project. It is followed by four papers that analyze the archaic phases of the Regia in chronological order. A paper then deals with the imperial and Late Roman phases. Three papers follow that deal with materials from the Regia excavation, including the terracottas, the bucchero, and other fine wares. The session thus presents an organic and self-consistent picture of one of the most important sites in Rome.

The Reanalysis of Brown's Excavation at the Regia

Nicola Terrenato, University of Michigan, and *Paolo Brocato*, Università della Calabria

Since 2014, an international team has been working on the archive, the finds, and the remains with the aim of arriving at the publication of a comprehensive final report of the Regia excavations. This involved extensive work of reformatting the data into single-context records in a critical way, recreating a stratigraphic sequence that also included all the structural remains. A three-dimensional digital model representing the complex sequence has been created and will serve as the core of a mixed-media publication. The in-depth reanalysis has also provided crucial new insights into the architectural development of the archaic Regia building, allowing for a radical revision of the phase reconstructions advanced by Frank Brown. A much simpler sequence of buildings can be envisioned, bringing the site much more closely in line with what we now know of archaic central Italian architecture.

In particular, the newly reconstructed sequence shows that there was a very simple rectangular building with stone socles that was created in the late seventh century B.C.E. This finds parallels in similar elite contexts at Tarquinia and elsewhere. This building was succeeded by a much larger one, with an L-shaped plan and rooms on two sides around an enclosed courtyard. Cappellaccio blocks and pavers were employed, as was common in this period in Rome. Again, there are close comparanda for regal construction along these lines, most significantly at Area F of Acquarossa. This imposing building was only modified in a limited way in the course of the sixth century, mostly in relation to its southeastern corner. A complete rebuilding took place only at the end of the century, when the well-known plan with three rooms and a trapezoidal courtyard was arrived at. It is now clear, however, that this plan was the result of the elimination of one wing of the older building, perhaps as a result of the changed political situation. The paper concludes with some observations about the possible function of the complex.

The Prohistoric Huts of the Regia: A Stratigraphic and Functional Analysis of Scompartimento 4

Vincenzo Timpano, Università della Calabria

The Universitá della Calabria and University of Michigan's current reexamination of Frank Brown's excavations at the Regia allows us to present for the first time the stratigraphic sequence of some of his areas, or scompartimenti. Through the study of the stratigraphic and ceramic data and the analysis of the surviving walls, it is possible to make hypotheses regarding the chronology and function of the different areas. In this paper, I reconstruct the phase of the ninth, eighth, and seventh centuries B.C.E.

The earliest archaeological remains that we can relate to an occupation activity consist of a series of postholes. These features belong to small-size huts that we can associate with infant burials located on the south end-western end of the area. These huts and tombs occupy an area of 30 m^2, which corresponds to circa the 3% of the overal surface occupied in the sixth century B.C.E.

Scompartimento 4 features the greatest concentration of this evidence. Small but significant remains are located in scompartiment 3, 6, 7, and 8. The analysis of these data allows us to draw hypothesis on the plans of the protohistoric huts. Therefore, in this paper I present the results of the study of this evidence and I compare it with contemporary evidence from Rome and the Latium Vetus.

A "Regal" Structure in Its Italian Context: The Early Phases of the Roman Regia

J. Troy Samuels, University of Michigan

Since 2014, the University of Michigan and Universitá della Calabria have worked in collaboration with the American Academy in Rome to study, reinterpret, and publish Frank E. Brown's excavations of the Roman Regia. This paper presents one part of this reanalysis and challenges certain aspects of Brown's original phasing and interpretation. This paper specifically focuses on the transition from a series of huts to the first stone buildings, our pre-Regia building and Regia "Phase 1."

Brown's multiple reconstructions of the early Regia argue for a tripartite phasing. A pentagonal building, entered from the east, with two rooms on the western end (Brown's Period 7) expanded to the north while maintaining the same general form (Brown's Period 8). Brown's period 9 saw a radical reorganization, with the entrance shifting from the eastern to the northern side of the building, the creation of a double colonnaded monumental entryway, and a rectangular plan with only a single, offset, western room. This Phase 9 structure is unlike any known contemporaneous central Italian architecture. While the lack of comparanda in and of itself is not grounds for modifying Brown's phasing, I argue that the stratigraphy presents a different picture that is more in line with our growing evidence for Early Iron Age and Archaic-period building practices.

Two of Brown's excavation areas provide the majority of evidence for my argument, the so-called scompartimenti 3 and 6c. Excavated by Brown and his team in 1964 and 1965, scompartimento 3 sits in the southern part of the Regia, while scompartimento 6c sits in the north, fronting the Via Sacra. A restudy of the stratigraphic data at these nodal points using modern digital techniques does not provide evidence for more than one wall phase in scompartimento 3 during Brown's phases 7, 8, and 9 and radically revises the three-phase hypothesis for the northern Regia wall. Instead, we can see a transition from huts, to rectangular stone-footed building, to "monumental regal" structure.

As a wealth of new evidence for Early Iron Age architecture has come to light in the half-century since Brown's excavations at sites such as Gabii, Satricum, Lavinium, and Rome itself, I use the stratigraphic and comparative evidence to place the early Regia phases in dialogue with their architectural contemporaries. This paper synthesizes the various material related to our first Regia phase to present a narrative of development in the area, from hut occupations to a "monumental" stone building.

A Mid-Life Crisis? Architectural Change in the Second Phase of the Roman Regia

Mattew Naglak, University of Michigan

The return to the Regia excavation materials of Frank E. Brown offers a new opportunity to examine this important yet enigmatic structure. Thanks to the thousands of photographs, artifacts, sketches, descriptions, and journal entries left to us by the excavators, a wealth of data remains viable for study and interpretation. Here I wish to look at one important moment in the history of this building: the transition between "Phase 1" and "Phase 2" of Terrenato's and Broccato's recent phasing reevaluation (in this session). At the same time, such an analysis provides the opportunity to present the recent effort to transform the Regia archive into digital data that can be readily accessed by scholars across the world.

Phase 1 reveals a pentagonal structure with the majority of the focus on the eastern end of the building where multiple rooms as well as the entranceway have been discovered. With the construction of the second phase, however, a subtle shift in emphasis can be recognized with the reorientation of the southwesternmost room. Architectural adjustments in this region of the Regia seem to indicate a new importance given to these southern rooms and this corner of the structure in particular. It also foreshadows the future destruction of the western rooms in Phase 3, which may already have been losing their primary functionality. This possibility is enhanced by the expansion of the northern wall of the structure, providing more space for internal activities within the Regia itself while at the same time increasing the overall footprint of the building within the highly desired real estate of the Roman Forum.

While multiple excavation trenches are relevant to the above interpretation, here I focus primarily on scompartimenti 2, 6c, and 6d. Scompartimenti 6c and 6d, lying in the northern portion of the site, offer new evidence for the expansion of the northern wall during this period. Meanwhile, scompirtamento 2, excavated primarily by Mario del'Chiaro in 1964, reveals the important changes occurring in the southwest corner of the Regia over the course of its existence. A new look at these important trenches, using both the original excavation reports and modern techniques in spatial recording and modeling, will prove vital to our new interpretations of the Roman Regia.

The Third Phase of the Regia: An Architectural Revolution?

Arianna Zapelloni Pavia, University of Michigan

The architectural history of the Regia is not as straightforward as it has long been assumed. The Regia Project, led by Terrenato and Broccato, challenges the traditional five different phases of modification and reconstructions of the building between the seventh century B.C.E. and the beginning of the Roman republic. This paper focuses specifically on the last layout that the building received, our Regia "phase 3."

According to Frank E. Brown's reconstruction, the last phase of the Regia represented a clear turning point in the architectural plan of the building. It is in this phase that the three rooms that Brown previously located on the eastern side of the building moved on the southern side of the courtyard, a layout that the Regia retained for all subsequent rebuildings. However, as our new reconstruction shows, this last layout was not innovative as it substantially retraced that of our second phase. Rather than the shift of the rooms to the south, the real architectural innovation of Regia phase 3 was the elimination of the three rooms that lined up on the west side of Regia phases 1 and 2.

Three of Brown's areas, scompartimenti 6, 7, and 8, represent the focus of my investigation. These excavation areas lie on the southwestern side of the building, exactly where the three rooms stood during phases 1 and 2. The reassessment of the excavation data from these sectors demonstrates that these rooms were demolished in the last phase of the Regia. On the other hand, a restudy of the stratigraphic material from sectors 4, 3, and 2, located on the southern side of the Regia, shows that the final layout of the building on this side retraced that of our Regia phases 1 and 2.

This paper presents a different account of the last layout of the Regia. The reevaluation of Brown's excavation data shows that the decisive change in the architectural development of the building does not lie in the shift of the rooms to the south, but rather in the elimination of the second row of rooms located on the western side.

The Life of the Roman Regia After Augustus: A Review of the Available Evidence

Paolo Maranzana, University of Michigan

In 2014, the University of Michigan and the Universitá della Calabria began a new collaborative research project in order to reexamine, reinterpret, and publish the archaeological evidence of the Regia in the Roman Forum. This project developed as a response to the new data made available by the excavation carried out in 1964–1965 by Frank E. Brown. Although this excavation brought to light crucial evidence on the development of the Regia from the Iron Age through the Republican period, little attention has been paid to the development of the building during the post-Republican phases. My paper aims to fill this gap by reviewing all the available evidence of this building during the Imperial and Late Antique periods. Particular emphasis is put on the high and late periods and to the creation of a synthetic narrative of the development of this building in its later phases.

The lack of understanding of the later phases of the Roman Regia is due mostly to the dismantlement of the building carried out in the late 1800s by Boni, who considered most of these phases medieval in origin. Despite this setback, there were other archaeological investigations before and after the dismantling that provide information about the structure in the Late Roman period. My analysis focuses on the archaeological explorations conducted in the late 1800s by Nichols and Hülsen, and by Gjerstad in the mid 20th century. Additionally, it utilizes the investigations of the street system between the Regia and the Atrium Vestae carried out by Middleton, Hülsen, and Lanciani, which aids in the overall understanding of the area. These results, however, have not been comprehensively reanalyzed, and this paper intends to fill this gap in current scholarship.

The Imported Greek Ceramics from the Regia

Carlo Regoli, Università di Roma La Sapienza

Frank E. Brown's mid 20th-century excavations of the Regia in the Forum Romanum recovered a notable and varied assemblage of imported Greek ceramics. These ceramics are mainly Attic in origin, and the forms are primarily related to those used for wine consumption (cups and at least one krater) or oil consumption (lekythoi). Among these ceramics are specimens of high artistic value dated from between the second half of the sixth and first quarter of the fifth century B.C.E. The vessels are decorated in either black-figure, red-figure, or fully painted in black.

Although these vessels are not in the best condition, my first stylistic examination of the pieces has been able to recognize examples of numerous decorative groups. Among the vessels decorated in the black-figure technique, some examples of the Phanyllis, or Leafless Group, can be identified. Among the painters who use the red-figure technique, some examples of early red-figure production, reminiscent of the so-called pioneers can be identified. A nearly complete, ovoid lekythos can be attributed an eastern Greek origin and resembles vessels recently attributed by Dyfri Williams to the "Pontic group." This group could represent Greek immigrant artisans working in southern Etruria.

This paper represents an in-depth study of these imported Greek ceramics, perhaps with the help of targeted archaeometric investigations, and resituates these vessels within their original stratigraphic sequences. In this tumultuous period of transition from monarchy to republic, it is possible to use elements of Brown's old excavation data, the University of Michigan and Universitá della Calabria's new collaborative research, and this ceramic-based study to reconstruct some important aspects of the Regia's original archaeological contexts and associated material culture.

Ceramic Production and the Roman Regia

Mattia D'Acri, Università della Calabria

In recent years the archaeological literature concerning ceramic production in Rome and Latium during the Orientalizing and Archaic periods has flourished, helping to update our knowledge regarding the technical, typological, and chronological aspects of the ceramic repertoire from these periods. This paper, following in this recent tradition, presents a study of the pottery found in the excavations of the Regia in the Roman Forum during the mid 20th century: in particular, attention is focused on impasto production—namely, impasto rosso, impasto rosso-bruno, impasto chiaro-sabbioso, internal/external slip ware—and the production of bucchero, during the chronological span ranging from the Orientalizing period to the Late Archaic.

My paper uses a morphological and chronological approach and defines the formal development of the analyzed ceramics classes; it also proposes a preliminary typology. I furthermore provide references to the distribution of the examined materials within the different areas of the excavation, providing preliminary quantitative estimates for ceramic finds across the site during the relevant periods. All of my findings regarding the ceramics are analyzed in relation to their stratigraphic context and their association with other material classes.

The Architectural Decoration of the Regia

Desiré Di Giuliomaria, Sostituire l'istituzione di appartenenza con Rheinische Friedrich-Wilhelms-Universität Bonn

Frank E. Brown's excavation of the Roman Regia revealed an abundance of architectural material spanning the Archaic to the Augustan periods. Autoptic analysis of the material allows for the creation of a chronology concerning the decorative systems used in each of the different phases of the Regia. These decorative schemes can be connected to their historical and sociopolitical contexts. Grounding my study on the material recovered by Brown, I have identified four main systems of architectonic decoration: the first one belongs to the first phase of the building and is dated around the end of the seventh century B.C.E.; the second, the more complex, is used from the first half of the sixth cenutry B.C.E. until the end of that century. This architectonic decoration shows a complete transformation of the imagery of the building by Etruscan craftsman, perhaps from Caere. While we have enough data to infer the grandeur of the sixth century B.C.E. building, we do not have architectural elements that belong to the initial period of the republic. The next decorative system is dated to the third century B.C.E. and corresponds to the monumental republican phase recognized by Brown. The fourth and last system is dated to the Augustan period and is probably linked to the reconstruction carried out by Domitius Calvinus. It is worth noting that all the republican materials and some of the archaic terracottas are so far unpublished and are presented for the first time at the AIA in Toronto.

My study considers not only the iconographic and stylistic data for each piece of architectonic decoration but also effective methods for their placement in the wooden structure of the Regia. This approach allows us to understand how the decoration of one of the most important buildings of Rome evolved over time.

SESSION 6G: Colloquium
Tell Tayinat (Ancient Kunulua): The Shifting Fortunes of a Bronze and Iron Age Levantine Capital

Sponsored by the Near Eastern Archaeology Interest Group

ORGANIZER: *Stephen Batiuk*, University of Toronto

Colloquium Overview Statement

The proposed session will present the results of a decade of archaeological exploration at the site of Tell Tayinat (ancient Kunulua), in the Hatay province of the Republic of Turkey. Tell Tayinat is located in the North Orontes Valley, at the geographic intersection of the Anatolian Highlands, the inland Syro-Mesopotamian steppe, and the Levantine coast. This strategic position made it a cultural nexus during the Bronze and Iron Ages and an important bellwether of sociocultural change for the broader region. Excavations by the University of Chicago's Syrian-Hittite Expedition in the 1930s revealed occupations from the Early Bronze and Iron Ages, including a Royal Citadel dated to the Iron II–III (ninth to sixth centuries B.C.E.). After a 70-year hiatus, investigations were re-initiated by the University of Toronto's Tayinat Archaeological Project (TAP). Excavations have revealed the well-preserved remains of an Early Bronze Age settlement, a hitherto unknown Iron I occupation (one of the most extensive in the Levant during this period), monumental architecture and sculpture, part of the Neo-Hittite royal citadel in the Iron II, and cuneiform documents and a sacred religious precinct, a product of the Neo-Assyrian imperial transformation of the citadel in the Iron III. This session presents the results of the TAP excavations to date and preliminary syntheses that highlight Tayinat's shifting role as a central settlement in the cultural and political history of the region.

The History of Excavations at Tayinat

Stephen Batiuk, University of Toronto

Investigations in the Amuq Plain began in the 1930s as part of the University of Chicago's Syrian-Hittite Expedition and culminated in the large-scale archaeological excavations of Tell Tayinat from 1935 to 1938. The excavations revealed monumental architecture, including palaces and a temple, dating to the Iron II period (10th–eighth centuries B.C.E.), as well as deep soundings that revealed extensive Early Bronze Age (3100–2000 B.C.E.) remains. After a hiatus of more than 60 years, investigations were reinitialized by the University of Toronto in 1999. Remote sensing and surface survey of the lower town around the site demonstrated that the settlement reached ~40 hectares in size during the Iron II–III period, and paleoenvironmental investigations across the site provide context for the development of the site over time. Full-scale excavations began in 2004, and over the past 12 years a total of 3,500 m^2 have been excavated, revealing substantial remains dating to the Iron II–III, a hitherto unknown Iron I occupation, and extensive and well-preserved Early Bronze Age occupations. The impressive discoveries at Tell

Tayinat have altered our understanding of the history and archaeology of this important region throughout each cultural period.

The Early Bronze Occupation at Tayinat and Ancient Alalahu

Lynn Welton, University of Chicago

Following the excavations conducted in the Amuq Plain in the 1930s by the Oriental Institute of the University of Chicago, Robert Braidwood published the prehistoric material to form one of the most comprehensive archaeological sequences from the northern Levant, spanning the Ceramic Neolithic to the end of the Early Bronze Age. During the Late Chalcolithic and Early Bronze Age (ca. 3500–2000 B.C.E.), settlement in the plain became increasingly centralized, and Tell Tayinat became the primary site in the region. During this period, the site has been linked to the toponym Alalahu, mentioned in archives from the major site of Ebla (Tell Mardikh) in northern Syria (ca. 2400 B.C.E.). This paper reviews the evidence for the Early Bronze Age in the Amuq Plain as a whole, focusing particularly on the growth of the site of Tell Tayinat and its role during this period.

Iron I Tayinat: Sea Peoples and the Land of Palistin

Brian Janeway, University of Toronto, and *Lynn Welton*, University of Chicago

During the 12th century B.C.E., the site of Tell Tayinat was reoccupied after a period of abandonment lasting more than 800 years. The earliest Iron I levels from the site exhibit a variety of cultural influences, including both materials that demonstrate continuity from the Late Bronze Age as well as signs of innovation. Later Iron I levels, beginning in the 11th century B.C.E., provide an assemblage characterized by increasing quantities of Aegeanizing ceramics and other artifact types. These Aegean influences have often been linked to the arrival of the so-called Sea Peoples in the region, a discussion that has been fueled by the recent identification of Tell Tayinat as the capital of a kingdom known from inscriptional evidence as Palistin. However, these Aegeanizing materials exist alongside a variety of historical and archaeological evidence for local continuity. This paper describes the evidence, including architecture and ceramics from the Iron I levels at Tell Tayinat, in order to assess the current state of our understanding of the Aegeanizing influences at Tell Tayinat and to provide a broad outline of the site during this transformative period.

Monumentality and Destruction in Iron II Kunulua

Elif Denel, American Research Institute in Ankara

Monumental architecture and art played a central role in power strategies of the rulers at the Neo-Hittite capital Kunulua. Both construction and destruction of urban centers express the competitive nature of the political dynamics in Iron Age southeast Turkey/northwest Syria. Recent archaeological work in Field 7 at Tell Tayinat strongly suggests that the Neo-Assyrian empire also internalized this trend in the process of establishing military domination over the Amuq region and reducing the kingdom of Patina/Unqi into the Assyrian province of Kinalia. This paper focuses on the recent archaeological work carried out in Field 7 of the Tell Tayinat excavations to discuss the evidence for both local and Neo-Assyrian strategies of sovereignty in a part of the citadel that seemingly carried significant religious and political importance.

Neo-Assyrian Kinalia

J.P. Dessel, University of Tennessee, Knoxville

Tell Tayinat, ancient Kunulua, was the capital city of the Iron Age II state of Patina/Unqi. Throughout the ninth and eighth centuries, the Neo-Assyrians were not only receiving tribute from Patina/Unqi but were actively involved in the local political intrigue. This relationship was radically altered when the site was conquered and destroyed by Tiglath-Pileser III during his second western campaign in 738 B.C.E. He boasts of destroying Kunulua, killing its king, deporting its population, and annexing the region to Assyria as the province of Kinalia. In the late eighth and early seventh centuries, parts of the upper city are then dramatically transformed. Monumental Luwian statuary is removed from the central sacred complex in the core of the upper city, the temples are modified, an Assyrian administrative center is constructed on the southern part of the upper city, and a local administrative center and fortifications are constructed on the eastern side of the tell. The demise of Neo-Assyrian Tayinat is marked by a somewhat enigmatic destruction, after which the site was abandoned.

The Tayinat Lower Town Project

James Osborne, University of Chicago

Although Near Eastern archaeologists have been working extensively on the citadels of Syro-Anatolian cities since the beginning of the discipline, only recently has systematic work commenced in these cities' lower towns, where cities' nonelite residents are presumed to have lived. This paper presents the work of one such initiative, the Tayinat Lower Town Project (TLTP), with two primary research questions beyond simply the exploration of nonelite archaeological contexts. First, TLTP seeks to identify evidence for the production of specialized luxury objects known to have been manufactured in this region and then circulated from northern Mesopotamia to Greece. Second, TLTP hopes to develop an archaeological signature of the Neo-Assyrian forced migration event, distributing people from captured lands to distant parts of the empire, something known to have taken place at Tell Tayinat. These phenomena have been only minimally investigated archaeologically. This paper presents the results of two seasons of intensive surface survey at Tayinat's lower town and the preliminary results of a targeted exploratory excavation.

Tayinat in Time and Space: A Synthesis

Timothy Harrison, University of Toronto

Tell Tayinat's dynamic socioeconomic and political role owes much to its position as a nexus of transit corridors that connected both people and valuable resources from throughout the Near East. In the Early Bronze Age, movements of people into the Amuq from eastern Anatolia and Transcaucasia led to the region's transformation into a dynamic urban landscape with Tayinat the principal settlement. As Tayinat's economic fortunes flourished, the Amuq region was drawn into the greater Syro-Mesopotamian world through its interactions with the kingdom of Ebla during the latter half of the Early Bronze Age. Tayinat was abandoned in the Middle and Late Bronze Ages, corresponding with the rise of neighboring Alalakh. With the collapse of the Late Bronze Age palatial civilizations and the influx of Aegean populations—including the so-called Sea Peoples—Tayinat reemerges as the political center of a "rump" state in the Early Iron I period, maturing into a rich and powerful kingdom during the ensuing Iron II period, with far-reaching economic and political contacts across the Near East and eastern Mediterranean. Tayinat's oscillating relationship with Assyria culminated in its conquest and transformation into a provincial capital annexed into the Neo-Assyrian empire during the Iron III period.

SESSION 6H
A New Look at Old Stones: Reexaminations of Archaeological Projects

CHAIR: To be announced

Retrospective Photogrammetry: Breathing New Life into Archival Imagery

Colin A.B. Wallace, University of Waterloo, and *Dorina Moullou*, Hellenic Ministry of Culture and Sport

This paper documents a project involving the use of archival photographs in combination with modern photogrammetric techniques and other archival data in order to create three-dimensional models of a site as it was when first excavated. Time and the elements as well as backfilling and the removal of features for their own protection often prevent researchers from examining sites as they were initially found. The techniques employed in this project are intended to rectify this impedance by recreating the architectural features of an entire building complex from the archival photographs of an older excavation in Athens, Greece: the Omega House.

The Omega House, also known as House C, is a large Late Roman structure dating from the fourth to sixth centuries C.E. on the slopes of the Areopagus hill in the Athenian Agora. The building's 30 rooms included ornate mosaics, tilework, elaborate water installations, a nymphaeum, and two or three peristyle courtyards, according to some scholars. It is thought to have been one of the last philosophical schools of Athens. Omega House was excavated from 1969 to 1971 and has remained largely exposed to the elements since then, resulting in noticeable natural deterioration.

The goal of this project was to produce three-dimensional models of the house as it is today using contemporary photogrammetry and as it was when initially excavated using retrospective photogrammetry. The contemporary photogrammetric models were produced using terrestrial photographss taken in June 2016. For the retrospective photogrammetry, a novel method using archival photographs, site plans, and drawings was employed. This method relies on the chance that the original photographs are comprehensive and in sufficient numbers as well as on considerable adjustments to them in order to produce acceptable three-dimensional models. Fortunately there is excellent comprehensive photographic documentation of the Omega house as it was when initially excavated, and the photographs in many cases have sufficient overlap to be candidates for retrospective photogrammetric three-dimensional reconstruction. The resulting models can be rotated and manipulated to provide views from angles that were never photographed, thus demonstrating that older documentation is able to retain its validity as new technologies and cross disciplinary innovations repurpose it. In addition, the retrospective models can then be compared with contemporary models to assess damage, measure erosion, and match missing pieces in order to facilitate further preservation and reconstruction efforts of the monument.

Stratigraphical Observations and Considerations at the Sanctuary of Zeus at Olympia in the Late 19th Century

Astrid Lindenlauf, Bryn Mawr College

Stratigraphy is a key concept of archaeology that can be traced back to the late 17th century. It is used today as a fieldwork method to identify, document, and reconstruct cultural layers or human-made deposits. It also serves as an interpretive tool for understanding the relationship between contexts and human interactions with past landscapes. In this paper, I explore the significance of stratigraphy both as a concept and as a practice in Greece during the later 19th century, when large-scale excavations lead to a professionalization of archaeological practice within the discipline of classical archaeology and advanced knowledge of ancient Greece. The German excavations at the sanctuary of Zeus at Olympia, which were carried out between 1875 and 1880/1881, serve as a case study, since their excavation techniques and recording methods were held in high esteem at the time. The following three questions guide my analysis of the notebooks, drawings, and photographs held in the excavation archive of the German Archaeological Institute in Athens and the publications of the finds and findings: (1) What were the goals of this fieldwork project and how did the field directors hope to achieve them? (2) What kind of stratigraphical observations were recorded? (3) What role did stratigraphy play in the interpretive process? A thorough reevaluation of this material suggests that the excavation team reconceptualized the function and meaning of stratigraphy in the course of their campaigns. More specifically, the excavators seem to have developed an early form of artifact stratigraphy and deposit stratigraphy, respectively, elevating stratigraphy from a mere fieldwork technique to an interpretive tool. This transition from soil stratigraphy to deposit stratigraphy is remarkable, as it did not occur in all of the large-scale excavations carried out in Greece at the end of the 19th century.

The Battle of Pydna, 168 B.C.E.: New Methods, New Evidence

Matthew A. Sears, University of New Brunswick, and *C. Jacob Butera*, University of North Carolina at Asheville

The site of the Battle of Pydna of 168 B.C.E., between Rome and Macedon, has never been convincingly located. More than a century of research has led to various reconstructions of the battle that place the events as much as 20 km apart on the Pierian Plain beneath Mount Olympus. At either extreme is Pritchett, who positions the battle in the south of the plain, close to Katerini; and Hammond, who argues for a site to the north, next to Pydna itself. This paper reexamines the evidence, and, based on in-person topographical exploration of the region and satellite imagery, which appears to show the previously unidentified Roman camp, argues for a location in the middle of the plain, south of Kato Ag. Ioannis. If the Roman camp has indeed been found, the location first proposed by Bessios and Krahtopoulou is confirmed.

As opposed to the work of Pritchett, Hammond, and others, who relied mostly on close readings of the ancient literary sources and on-the-ground observations, Bessios and Krahtopoulou made use of geological soundings to determine how the geomorphology of the Pierian Plain has changed since antiquity. Their work radically alters our understanding of the region, particularly how the ancient rivers followed different courses than today. Since rivers play a major role in accounts of the battle, Bessios and Krahtopoulou were able to suggest a new site that takes into account the ancient sources and the ancient topography. Now, a decade-and-a-half after their paper, satellite imagery has emerged as a powerful new tool for investigating the topography of ancient battlefields, shedding even more light on Pydna.

This paper details how satellite imagery complements the work of Bessios and Krahtopoulou. On satellite images of the area south of Kato Ag. Ioannis, three distinct rectangular outlines are visible. The rectangles are each approximately 180 x 85 m and run in a line northwest–southeast for 1 km. These rectangles closely resemble the clearer remains of a Roman camp first identified by Hammond from the Battle of Cynoscephalae, now also visible via satellite imagery. On the ground, however, the markings near Pydna are difficult to make out, obscured by agricultural work and vegetation growth. One long side of the northernmost rectangle, though, appears as a shallow ravine running through an agricultural plot. The discovery of the Roman camp potentially ends more than a century of uncertainty regarding this important battle.

The Challenges of Environmental Studies in Pre-Roman First-Millennium B.C.E. Central Italy: A Methodological Case Study

Meryl Shriver-Rice, University of Miami

Environmental studies such as archaeobotany and zooarchaeology are relatively new to the field of archaeology. Like all methodological shifts, the adoption of these methods has occurred at different rates in different contexts. For pre-Roman central Italy, adoption of these analyses has been somewhat slow and sporadic. In earlier tomb-oriented excavations, the botanical and faunal contents of bowls and food offerings were often discarded as inconsequential. However, in the last 10 years there has been a notable shift both toward investigating nonfunerary contexts such as settlements and sanctuaries and toward the systematic collection of organic remains at projects such as Poggio Colla, Tarquinia, Orvieto, Cetamura del Chianti, the Sant'Omobono Project, and the Gabii Project, among others. The problems that face the incorporation of environmental studies in this region are not entirely unique, and as such, this case study functions as a useful comparison for other archaeological studies in different geographic contexts. In this paper, I trace the historical, technological, theoretical, institutional, and geographic factors driving methodological decisions concerning the study of nonhuman organic remains.

This case study is part of a research project titled "The First Millennium Project: Food and Environment in Pre-Roman Central Italy," which I launched during a fellowship at the American Academy in Rome. This talk presents conclusions I reached through two methods of inquiry. The first involves site visits to excavation projects to interview project directors on the history of their methodological choices concerning the collection of organic material. The second consists of meeting or speaking with current archaeobotanical and zooarchaeological experts working in this time period to discuss their own methodological issues and experiences in central Italy. I argue that these discussions clarified that the accessibility of completed data is the central obstacle faced by archaeologists seeking information on organic remains. Recorded evidence of organic material is currently widely scattered amongst different laboratories, site reports, stored material, and specialist's reports; therefore, the story of where to locate this data aligns with the methodological history of its collection. Tracing this history sheds light on the difficulties of data accessibility and highlights the need for the next step of this project—the creation of an open source digital platform to share environmental data. I posit that improving accessibility and comprehensibility of environmental analyses will enable future researchers to construct a fuller narrative of the relationships between humans and their environment.

Old Dogs, New Tricks: The Pedagogical Value of Old Collections

Christine L. Johnston, Western Washington University

The study of unprovenanced material is highly contentious, as it is intrinsically tied to issues of looting and damage to archaeological heritage. Further implications within the modern climate of regional political instability include the role of looted objects as a lucrative source of income for insurgent and terrorist organizations. Industry and political institutions are increasingly seeking to alleviate threats to cultural and archaeological heritage through both legislation and the adoption of "best practices" policies. While we seek to neutralize new and emerging threats, attention is also deserved for the vast collections of unprovenanced and subsidiary material acquired through the cultural tourism and incipient archaeological exploration of the 19th and 20th centuries. As with artifact and site conservation, we as archaeologists are responsible for the prevention of data degradation resulting from the effects of time and neglect, even for records or materials deemed to be of secondary research value.

Within the "context is king" construct of archaeological inquiry, unprovenanced material traditionally holds little value. While it may be unsuitable for conventional research purposes, there are nonetheless numerous pedagogical applications remaining to which old or unprovenanced material collections may be fruitfully employed. From the opportunity for undergraduates to handle and examine ancient materials in the classroom to the methodological training of graduate students in practical or innovative analytical techniques, the adoption of artifacts in teaching programs creates a vivid learning environment. For young scholars, it also provides an opportunity to develop desirable skills that will increase their marketability in subsequent job searches and prepare them for archaeological employment. This paper presents the results of a recent survey of Canadian and American academic institutions on the prevalence and current pedagogical applications of unprovenanced or old material collections. A sample of successful research and training programs across different disciplines are profiled, including examples from classical and Near Eastern departments. Through the incorporation of old or subsidiary collections into instruction and student training, neglected or underemployed material can thus acquire a new useful life.

Disciplining Schliemann: His Reception and Archaeological Knowledge, 1880–1972

Anne Duray, Stanford University

Heinrich Schliemann has been called a lot of things—from "the most famous archaeologist in the world" to a "pathological liar." Recent studies have brought to the fore issues concerning Schliemann's impact on Aegean prehistory and publication practices. Such analyses invite, but do not directly address, the question: as scholarship on the history of archaeology moves beyond the "great minds" model, how should such a towering bastion of individualism as Schliemann be dealt with in disciplinary historiography?

This paper situates Schliemann within the disciplinary negotiation of Greek archaeology. By "disciplinary negotiation," I refer not only to the formation of the fields we now term classical archaeology and Aegean prehistory but also the "ecology of practices" that make the academic discipline of archaeology what it is—the network of institutions, people, things, and circulations of academic authority that are all active forces in constructing an identifiable community and producing archaeological knowledge. Within this framework, I focus on the reception of Schliemann and his archaeological endeavors through a close examination of how various individuals in the scholarly community discuss Schliemann in a selection of examples, beginning with Virchow's preface in Ilios (1880) and extending to the final publication of the Minnesota Messenia Expedition (1972). Through these, I show that although Schliemann is categorized as an institutional outsider, he nevertheless represents a source of academic authority, despite some critique of his method, for several decades following his excavations as Aegean prehistory came into its own discipline. In the postwar period, rhetoric of Schliemann's monumental discoveries continues, but there is also a shift to a more explicit reflection on his practices.

I then invoke both the chronological range and content of these examples to demonstrate how archaeology is genealogical and self-referential in its articulation and practice—individuals are important in terms of how a community incorporates them within their own disciplinary memory, agendas, and identity. At the same time, this genealogical character means that the development of archaeology cannot necessarily be narrated as merely a progression of increasingly scientific methods or series of paradigm shifts. Furthermore, as I conclude with the case of Schliemann, such a narration can mask alternative discourses. This realization has important repercussions for not only how we produce our own disciplinary historiography but also how we understand what we do as archaeologists.

Unmasked! The Consequences of Emotional Attachment to Neolithic Masks

Morag M. Kersel, DePaul University

Between March and September of 2014 the Israel Museum displayed what was described by curator Debby Hershman as "a small rare group of 9,000 year old masks—the oldest masks known to date." *Face to Face: The Oldest Masks in the World* (Israel Museum, 2014) was the culmination of nearly a decade of research by Israel Museum curators and other archaeologists. The exhibition marked the first time that a group of masks from the Neolithic (7600–6000 B.C.E.) was displayed together and the first time that the majority of them were publicly accessible. Only two of the masks have known archaeological findspots and are part of the permanent collection of the Israel Museum. The Nahal Hemar mask was recovered from controlled scientific excavations by Ofer Bar Yosef, the other purchased by noted military figure Moshe Dayan from a farmer after a chance discovery during agricultural plowing and then donated to the museum. The remaining 10 masks have no known associated archaeological information; all are loaned from the private collection of Michael and Judy Steinhardt, and all are purchased from the antiquities market. The display of these Neolithic masks engendered a complex set of emotions for distinct individual and collective audiences—government employees, museum professionals, collectors, archaeologists, curators, looters, Palestinians, Israelis, and museum visitors. Reverence for a single mask could and did arouse, conjure, crush, and augment sentiments for prehistoric ancestors and ties to contested lands. This paper reflects on the rival passions for 12 ancient masks and the consequences, intended and unintended, of esteem for the ancient.

SESSION 6I: Colloquium
New Research on Roman Sarcophagi: Eastern, Western, Christian

ORGANIZERS: *Sarah Madole*, CUNY–Borough of Manhattan Community College, and *Mont Allen*, Southern Illinois University

Colloquium Overview Statement

These are boom times for sarcophagus studies in the Anglophone world. When we organized our last colloquium session on Roman sarcophagi in 2008, the field was still a Teutonic preserve, a specialist domain where few North American scholars dared to venture. No English-language book had appeared in more than 12 years, and articles were almost as few. Since then, however, the situation has changed dramatically. The last eight years have seen two high-profile international conferences on sarcophagi held on these shores (in Berkeley and New York) and the publication of four major monographs in English, joined by multiple edited volumes, journal articles, and dissertations—all testament to the subject's new vitality.

The time thus seems ripe to revisit this burgeoning field. Our proposed session gathers North America's sarcophagus specialists for a series of papers showcasing their most recent work. The aim is to take stock of what we have learned in the last eight years, present the findings of our ongoing research, and ask what future avenues of research seem most promising.

Our first paper, "Sarcophagus Studies: The State of the Field," provides the opening backdrop. It analyzes what the last few decades of research have yielded, discusses what has proven most fruitful and what less so, and articulates what lacunae remain. With the stage thus set, our papers turn to specific topics, grouped geographically and chronologically. An initial pair cast a critical eye on the much-admired, but little-discussed, sarcophagi from Asia Minor: "Roman Sarcophagi from Dokimeion in Asia Minor: Conceptual Differences Between Rome and Athens" examines how these pieces differ in social function from those carved in the workshops of Rome and Athens, while "A New Mythological Sarcophagus at Aphrodisias" makes sense of a major recent find that forces us to rethink what we thought we knew about Carian production. The following paper, "Beyond Grief: A Mother's Tears and Representations of Semele and Niobe on Roman Sarcophagi," maintains our collective focus on funerary context but redirects our gaze to metropolitan sarcophagi, showing how our default presumption of male viewership at the tomb has blinded us to the particularly gendered appeal of certain classes of imagery. Our final pair, "Strutting Your Stuff: Finger Struts on Roman Sarcophagi" and "Love and Death: The Topos of Jonah-as-Endymion in Early Christian Art," cast new light on the transition from "pagan" to Early Christian sarcophagi by attending to changes in physical manufacture and carving techniques as well as choice of iconography. Concluding connective tissue is provided by our respondents.

DISCUSSANTS: *Christopher Hallett*, University of California, Berkeley, and *Ortwin Dally*, Deutsches Archäologisches Institut

Sarcophagus Studies: The State of the Field (As I See It)

Bjoern C. Ewald, University of Toronto

Sarcophagus studies are no longer a discipline on the margins; over the past decade, they have become a vibrant, even fashionable field of scholarship, attracting an ever increasing number of new voices. My paper critically surveys the state of the field, while highlighting some neglected but potentially fruitful areas for further study.

Recent scholarship has, above all, brought about a welcome expansion of the material basis of study. It is no longer focused on the relatively small number of elaborate frieze sarcophagi, to which the archaeological methodologies have been fine-tuned for more than a century; instead, it now includes sarcophagi of simpler manufacture and reduced decoration, such as the strigillated sarcophagi or those focused on inscriptions. The publication of material from workshops in the provinces (e.g., Aphrodisias, Athens) is progressing rapidly and offers great potential for comparative studies; it also facilitates the examination of local funerary cultures and commemorative environments. The booming study of sarcophagi's display contexts has yielded insight into their interplay with other objects and the modalities of their reception, while sociohistorical approaches, including the study of women, gender, and masculinity on the sarcophagi, are as alive as ever and continue to generate useful insights into the material itself. Finally, questions of raw materials, commerce, and the trade of sarcophagi are receiving renewed and systematic attention.

Lacunae and blind spots remain, however. The language barrier is surprisingly alive and well, ensuring that much fundamental work has, unfortunately, fallen into oblivion. A comprehensive study of the sarcophagus inscriptions continues to be a desideratum. Perhaps more importantly, ambitiously wide-ranging studies that use the sarcophagi to address fundamental questions of the transformation of Roman art from the second to fourth centuries are still largely lacking; this is perhaps the greatest difference between the current situation and that of a century ago, when Riegl drew extensively on the sarcophagi to ground his avant-garde narrative about the transformation of modes of viewing in late antiquity.

Finally, and perhaps inevitably: the different subfields in the study of sarcophagi have begun to drift apart, to the extent that some of them no longer take notice of one another. Put positively, this may be understood as a sign that sarcophagus studies have begun to dissolve into the broader horizon of Roman art history.

Roman Sarcophagi from Dokimeion in Asia Minor: Conceptual Differences from Rome and Athens

Esen Ogus, Ludwig-Maximilians-Universitaet, Munich

Relief-decorated marble sarcophagi were a popular product of the Roman Imperial period, especially the second and third centuries C.E. It has been widely acknowledged that among the many workshops, those of Rome, Athens, and Dokimeion in Asia Minor produced sarcophagi of the highest artistic quality. Previous research has focused relatively more on the iconography of the metropolitan Roman and Attic products, while studies of the Dokimeion sarcophagi have lagged behind. To fill this lacuna, this paper scrutinizes the distinctive form, iconography, and display context of the Dokimeion sarcophagi in certain Turkish museums (Istanbul, Antalya, Hierapolis, Antakya) and compares them with the published sarcophagi of the same period from Rome and Athens.

Close scrutiny of the Dokimeion sarcophagi demonstrates their peculiarity. Firstly, all four sides of the chest receive equal decorative and visual emphasis, in contrast to those from Rome, where the back side of the chest was left rough, and those from Athens, which, while carved on the back, place visual emphasis on the front. Secondly, in terms of subject matter and iconography, Dokimeian sarcophagi drastically differed from the other groups. In Rome, relief decoration in the second century focused on dramatic mythological stories narrated in frieze form. In the third century, these dramatic myths were replaced by scenes such as lion hunts that focus on the qualities of the deceased. In Athens, too, the sarcophagus chests depicted mythological stories, especially those celebrating the heroic Greek past and its culture, as exemplified through the Amazonomachy and Trojan War. By contrast, Dokimeion sarcophagi rarely depicted frieze-type mythological stories: in the second century, hanging garlands were their preferred scheme of decoration; and in the third, most popular were architectural frameworks that served as a background for standing and sometimes seated human figures.

Comparison of the products of these various workshops shows that the Dokimeion sarcophagi were perceived as standalone monuments in their own right, rather than as mere caskets for inhumation. Moreover, they depicted civic, as opposed to private, sensibilities regarding death, reflecting the local funerary culture and historical circumstances in which they were produced. Their iconography is consistent with imperial civic architecture and is closely related to the urban landscape and lifestyle of the elite in the cities of the East. In conclusion, Dokimeion sarcophagi, rather than merely being private memorials of the dead, as they were in the West, were conceived as the medium through which wealthy locals expressed their public and imperial identity and participated in the broader visual and intellectual culture of the Roman empire.

A New Mythological Sarcophagus at Aphrodisias

Heather N. Turnbow, The Catholic University of America

At Aphrodisias in Caria, a Graeco-Roman site in southwest Turkey known for large-scale sculpture production, marble sarcophagi have been found in abundance. Most of them bear sculpted decoration of the well-known "garland" and "columnar" styles, with comparatively few bearing continuous figural friezes, some of which are mythological. Since mythological sarcophagi are in the minority not only at Aphrodisias but across Roman Asia Minor in general, the discovery of a new frieze sarcophagus during the 2007 season of the Aphrodisias Regional Survey was a significant find. This sarcophagus has been treated briefly in my previous studies of the necropoleis of Aphrodisias, but until now has not received in-depth attention with respect to its sculpted imagery.

Drawing on my fieldwork over several seasons of survey and excavation at Aphrodisias, this paper proposes a mythological interpretation of the sarcophagus and explores its possible display context. Found to the southwest of the city, in a necropolis area littered with architectural remains and fragments of additional sarcophagi, it was most likely displayed as part of a monumental tomb complex. The sarcophagus chest is carved on all four sides, the most preserved of which features a large reclining figure in a watery setting, with the prow of a boat visible in the background. Other partial figures are preserved on the adjacent sides and in separate fragments, which together make for a tantalizing iconographic study; no comparable imagery is found on any sarcophagus at Aphrodisias.

Possible identifications of the reclining figure include a river god or other water deity, and Ariadne on Naxos; the latter would suggest that additional episodes of the Theseus narrative are depicted on the other sides of the sarcophagus chest. These mythological subjects are highly unusual on sarcophagi from Asia Minor and may constitute a unique example that promises to expand our understanding of funerary art in this region. Questions related to the social function of the sarcophagus, such as the identity, status, and values of the tomb owner, are also considered in order to place the entire monument into the broader context of funerary culture in Roman Asia Minor.

Beyond Grief: A Mother's Tears and Representations of Semele and Niobe on Roman Sarcophagi

Sarah Madole, CUNY–Borough of Manhattan Community College

This paper addresses two mythological narratives depicted on Roman sarcophagi, the death of Niobe's children and the death of Semele, the mother of Dionysos. I argue that these images in particular were intended to activate a gendered experience of mourning for the female viewer at the tomb. Both Niobe and Semele suffered the pain of childbirth–Semele gave birth concurrent with her death, that is, she died in childbirth, and Niobe survived the birth of 14 children only to suffer the loss of every last one of her brood. The stories of Niobe and Semele obliquely pertain to a female "gaze," and to a specific type of bereavement. The infrequency of these narratives, with less than 15 examples extant among the thousands of second- and third-century mythological sarcophagi, further imply an individualized, "self-exploratory" response by the (female) viewer.

It has been argued that the "emotional work" at the tomb was gendered, an appropriate ritual for Roman women, and as we increasingly are aware, gender is performed. How did these particular narratives engage the performance of gender, grief, and remembrance at the tomb? The two myths in question, one focused on the death of a woman in childbirth, and the other on a mother's loss of her children, bespeak an inquiry that at least begins to acknowledge this gendered alterity at the tomb, a space for performing mourning and memory.

The unusual, violent, and painfully emotional depictions of the Niobids and the laying out of the body of Semele suggest a specialized clientele and stand in stark contrast to the proliferation of sensualized depictions of nudity on High Imperial sarcophagi. Whereas most sarcophagi carried imagery signifying aspects of corporeal pleasure ("wanton" nudity of the female body, e.g., in *thiasos* scenes), or of physical excellence ("heroic" nudity of men, e.g., in Hippolytus narratives that include the laying out of the deceased hero), the overtly consolatory semantic of the narratives of Niobe and Semele specifically embody a female experience of grief. This paper therefore uses these divergent visual narratives as a point of departure from which to explore a gendered "reading" of Semele and the Niobids, a lacuna in sarcophagus studies to date.

Strutting Your Stuff: Finger Struts on Roman Sarcophagi

Mont Allen, Southern Illinois University

Something puzzling begins to creep into the manufacture of Roman sarcophagi during the third century: the inclusion of prominent struts spanning the fingers and thumbs of figures' outstretched hands. The use of struts to lend additional support to relief elements projecting from the surface plane might not, on the face of it, strike one as unexpected. Closer inspection, however, reveals a string of surprises: these struts on late sarcophagi are invariably decorated with eye-catching spiral fluting; they appear only between fingers and thumbs—and nowhere else—no matter how elaborate the scene; and, in many cases, they are structurally unnecessary, "supporting" digits that do not need it.

Taking a cue from the work of Hollinshead, Allen, and others, this paper considers the semantic significance of material facture and technique itself. Culling all known examples of finger struts allows one to trace the development of this strange carving convention and provides critical leverage on what motivated it. It is clear from the earliest third-century examples (such as a strigillated sarcophagus in Rome featuring busts of Helios and Selene) that these struts began as load-bearing structural members intended to add support to vulnerable digits. If they were always spiraled, this must have been a strategy for reducing visual confusion—otherwise a viewer might easily mistake the struts themselves for fingers, especially at a distance. Ornamenting them thus helped to remove them from the domain of representation, a rare example of carvers adding detail to a structural element in order to make it less figural.

Within two generations, however, on Christian sarcophagi of the early fourth century, these struts take on a radically different function. The trend toward flatter carving deprives them of their former load-bearing purpose: the fingers, now typically flush with the body in lower relief, are at little risk of being knocked off. Why, then, keep the struts, let alone expand them? The evidence seems clear: they have come to serve as visual signposts to the fingers, drawing the viewer's attention—through their arrestingly artificial fluting—to the holy hand gestures of central figures, above all, the open-handed gesture of prayer. These struts have, then, been converted: no longer meaningful as supports, their distinctive spirals now serve to enhance crucial (and particularly Christian) figural content, a prime example of a technical device being repurposed to meet the needs of a new visual regime.

Love and Death: Jonah-as-Endymion in Early Christian Art

Robert Couzin, Independent Scholar

Among the most common images on mythological and Christian sarcophagi are Endymion forever asleep before the approaching Selene, and Jonah resting in the shade of a gourd plant. They often appear together on a textbook page or a classroom screen, as if the visual homology spoke for itself. But what does it say? Was the putative connection between these images primarily a matter of workshop practice, based purely on formal similarity? Or was there some particular significance to the story of Endymion that led Christian customers to select Jonah by analogy?

The issue is multifaceted. To gain critical leverage on the problem, this paper focuses on eroticism, a dimension central to figurations of Endymion but absent from, indeed inconsistent with, the Jonah narrative as it is depicted on Christian sarcophagi.

Although still and somnolent, Endymion is typically depicted at a moment of narrative intensity, immediately before his nightly bout of lovemaking. Sexuality is neither hedged here nor hidden: his veil is revealing and inviting, not concealing and protecting; his posture invites the imminent encounter. In short, sensuality is fundamental to the marital meaning and emotional thrust of the scene.

Not so with Jonah, whose canonical narrative—thrown from a ship, swallowed by a sea monster, and disgorged three days later—contains nothing erotic. In his most common pictorial appearance on sarcophagi, the "rest scene," Jonah sleeps alone. His is the nakedness of Adam before the Fall (so we should imagine a Christian audience taking it), his genitalia of aesthetic rather than functional value. No texts, scriptural or patristic, contemplate a sexual Jonah. Nor do the many theories advanced for his popularity: as a type for Christ; an agent of Gentile conversion; a picture of bodily resurrection in Paradise; a parable of salvation; a metaphor of Christian survival in a pagan world.

This dissonance, I argue, militates against projecting on Christian mourners contemplating the figure of Jonah at rest thoughts of the sleeping Endymion. Mere formal convention for depicting sleepers, not any invitation to metaphorical equivalence with Endymion, must have dictated the choice of pose for Jonah on early Christian sarcophagi.

SESSION 6J
New Developments in Minoan Archaeology

CHAIR: *Susan Ferrence*, INSTAP

Intraregional Mobility: Recent Bronze Age Excavations at Mesorachi, Crete

Thomas M. Brogan, INSTAP Study Center for East Crete, *Melissa Eaby*, INSTAP Study Center for East Crete, *Yiannis Papadatos*, University of Athens, and *Chryssa Sofianou*, Lassithi Ephoria of the Greek Ministry of Culture

This paper is an overview of recent excavations at Mesorachi between 2013 and 2015. Geographically, this region of eastern Crete forms a natural boundary on the north coast between the Mirabello and Siteia Bays, which for most of the island's history was a sparsely inhabited periphery. In 2012, a survey of the plateau identified 11 sites. Of these, eight belonged to the Late Final Neolithic and Early Minoan (EM) I periods, including two Late Final Neolithic settlements on the western plateau of Xerokampos. At the beginning of the Bronze Age these sites were abandoned, and six new sites were built on the more protected Mesorachi ridge to the east. Our excavations at Sites 7 and 8 were designed to test the conclusions of this survey that suggested that all six EM I sites were of roughly similar size, function, and date.

The excavated finds revealed a more complex settlement history within an EM I–IIA horizon that serves as a valuable lesson on three levels. First, it demonstrates the need to guard against the potential misinterpretation of survey density maps that span long periods of time (i.e., the hypothesis that all six sites were inhabited continuously during EM I). Next, the new data puts us in a better position to evaluate settlement use at Mesorachi and the possible impact of broader regional developments on these sites, including the appearance of gateway communities at Mochlos, Petras, and Haghia Fotia in EM I.

The paper draws particular attention to Site 7, where excavation revealed an unusual round building with seven rooms measuring 13 x 18 m. This plan contrasts sharply with the rectilinear architecture recovered in EM IA and IIA levels at Site 8 and anticipates the round building at nearby Chamaizi in Middle Minoan I–II. The EM IB finds include a complex set of built furniture in these spaces (i.e., platforms, benches, hearths, and bins) and an impressive assemblage of pottery, stone tools, and bioarchaeological remains that were collected by hand and through an intensive program of soil sampling. This data appears to dovetail nicely with the preliminary results of our phytolith and starch analysis of soil samples and stone tools to illustrate how crops (particularly cereals) were stored, processed, and cooked in the building. One of the questions addressed in the conclusion is whether or not this structure should be interpreted as a house.

Prepalatial Ceramic Production at Priniatikos Pyrgos, Crete

Jo Day, University College Dublin, *Barry Molloy*, University College Dublin, *Matej Pavlacky*, University of Kent, and *Sue Bridgford*, Independent Scholar

Excavations carried out at the multiperiod site of Priniatikos Pyrgos in East Crete have revealed that the headland was the location of extensive activity during the Early Bronze Age (ca. 3200–1900 B.C.E.). In particular, the western slopes of the promontory have yielded large quantities of Early Minoan ceramics. The two pottery kilns excavated thus far from this area of the site (in the 2005–2006 excavations) have been dated to Neopalatial and early Protopalatial periods (B. Hayden and M. Tsipopoulou, *Hesperia* 81 [2012] 507–84), but this paper proposes that ceramic production was occurring here already by the middle of the third millennium B.C.E. Macroscopic and microscopic analysis has established that much of the Early Minoan pottery from the site is local, thanks to the distinct granodiorite fabric of this part of the Bay of Mirabello. Various kinds of production debris, including "firebars" and "firebox fragments" (B. Hayden, "'Firebars' and Other Ceramics of Problematic Function from Priniatikos Pyrgos," in E. Mantzourani and P.P. Betancourt, eds., *Philistor: Studies in Honor of Costis Davaras* [Philadelphia 2012] 59–64) are reevaluated here in the light of results from the 2007–2010 excavations. This material, combined with a reassessment of the smaller kiln, point toward an Early Minoan II ceramic industry. Vasilike Ware in particular dominates the assemblages, and it is suggested that this site was one of the main production centers for this mottled pottery.

The Krasi B Tholos: An Early Minoan I Tomb in Krasi Pediados

Emily Miller Bonney, California State University Fullerton

This paper presents a looted tholos known in the literature as Krasi B and argues that the tomb adds to the evidence for an Early Minoan I presence in the Krasi Pediadha area and enriches our understanding of the tholos type of tombs on Prepalatial Crete. Situated just under four km northeast of the village of Krasi and the more well-known and easily accessible Krasi A, Tholos B was first noted in 1959 by Platon in *Kretika Chronika* (387), who wrote that Alexiou reported finding a tholos tomb in the Krasi region and that the tomb had contained only a figurine, having long since been looted. The only subsequent report by someone who actually had visited the tomb was by Lucy Goodison who with Carlos Guarita examined the tomb in 2000 and again in 2001 and included it in their 2005 catalogue (SMEA 47, 188–189). Otherwise heretofore unpublished, the tomb most recently was identified as dubious by Legarra Herrero in *Mortuary Behaviour and Social Trajectories in Pre- and Protopalatial Crete* ([Philadelphia 2015], 237). However, inspection of the tomb in the summer of 2016 confirms that the structure is an example of the tholos type and that it most likely was constructed during Early Minoan I (3100–2650 B.C.E.), although when during that period is impossible to determine at this time. Despite its unusual but not unique entrance, the tomb's size and mode of construction align with other Early Minoan I tombs. With Krasi A already dated to early in Early Minoan I, this identification of a second Early Minoan I tholos in the area expands the catalogue of Early Minoan I sites and perhaps more importantly increases to four the number of Early Minoan I tholoi outside south-central Crete.

The Chrysolakkos Buildings at Malia (Crete): An Update

Sylvie Muller Celka, Maison de l'Orient, CNRS, Lyon

The large rectangular building at Chrysolakkos (Malia) has been known for nearly a century as one of the earliest examples of ashlar masonry in Crete. It is usually referred to as a "royal ossuary" of Protopalatial date, and it has been classified as a house tomb enlarged to monumental scale.

However, the funerary function of this rectangular building has been challenged during the past few decades on grounds such as the scarcity of human bones and the domestic aspect of both architecture and pottery. Furthermore, the number, function and date of the successive buildings at Chrysolakkos are still a matter for debate; the dating of the rectangular building alone varies strikingly from one handbook to the other between Early Minoan III and Late Minoan I. All scholars in Aegean prehistory nevertheless agree that Chrysolakkos is crucial for understanding the development of the Minoan town at Malia.

This paper aims to tackle these issues by bringing together the evidence available so far. New information is provided by the careful reading of the original reports and publication in French, the detailed examination of the architectural remains in the field, and a new survey of both published and unpublished pottery. In addition, all these data are interpreted in the light of recent advances in Minoan archaeology, in particular burial practices evidenced by the ongoing excavation in the cemetery at Sissi (5 km east of Malia).

As a result, a new picture of the stratigraphy and history of Chrysolakkos emerges, as a consequence of the dismantling of some long-accepted factoids. First, the rectangular ashlar building must date to the Neopalatial period or at the earliest to the end of Middle Minoan IIB. Its function remains unclear, but neither its type nor the associated material support the hypothesis of funerary use. Second, it must be completely dissociated from the underlying remains, apart from foundation walls that cut through previous constructions. These underlying remains feature a large, probably public, building used for ceremonies possibly related to death management but certainly neither a tomb nor an ossuary. Although noticeably larger than the later building, it was constructed of rubble and did not include ashlar masonry. And third, a Prepalatial cemetery of rectangular house tombs preceded this architectural complex, accounting for the presence of scattered human bones and material matching East Crete Prepalatial grave goods.

Memories and Realities in Early Neopalatial Mochlos

Jeffrey S. Soles, University of North Carolina at Greensboro, *Georgios Doudalis*, Karls-Ruprecht Universität Heidelberg, *Luke F. Kaiser*, University of Arizona, and *Jerolyn E. Morrison*, INSTAP Study Center in East Crete

This paper discusses the early phases of the most important building in the Neopalatial settlement at Mochlos. Building B.2 was a three-story ceremonial complex with a paved terrace running along its south side. It is a rare example of an ashlar building used for ritual purposes outside the palaces. All earlier structures on the site were demolished when the building was constructed at the beginning of the Late Minoan (LM) IB period, except for those that remained beneath its south terrace.

The paper asks why these early remains were preserved. We propose that it was an intentional act, since the earlier remains were carefully encased in walls on their north, east, and south, and capped with the paving stones of the south terrace, many of which were marked with kernoi. The terrace opened only to the west, where a series of steps led down to a theatral area used for ritual performances in memory of dead ancestors.

These remains yielded a stratigraphic sequence ranging from LM IA to Middle Minoan (MM) IIIA, during which time the building underwent a series of changes. The analysis of the ceramic material indicates that destructions occurred on three different occasions. Room 1 was abandoned at the end of MM IIIA; Rooms 2, 3, and an open yard along their south were abandoned at the end of MM IIIB; and Room 4 was abandoned at the end of the LM IA period. The best explanation for each abandonment is earthquake destruction, which has been noted in other parts of the Neopalatial town at the same times and at other sites as far away as Knossos and Palaikastro. The study of these remains has also revealed stylistic transitions in early Neopalatial ceramics, during which new shapes entered the repertoire of older shapes and techniques. It also provides us with information about production, consumption, and the use of spaces during the different subphases of the early Neopalatial period.

The paper illustrates the ceramic transitions of the early Neopalatial period at Mochlos, which are not evident elsewhere in the Mirabello area of East Crete, and links these transitions to other sites in Crete. It proposes that the preservation of the early remains below the south terrace was intended to preserve the memory of the past and create a sense of community identity in the aftermath of the LM IA destructions.

The Mouliana Project: Results of the 2016 Season

Andrew J. Koh, Brandeis University, *Miriam G. Clinton*, Rhodes College, and *Georgia Flouda*, Heraklion Archaeological Museum

Scholars have long been aware of Mouliana tombs dating to the end of the Bronze Age situated in the western Siteia foothills between the Mirabello and Siteia bays in East Crete. Among an array of notable finds, they yielded richly decorated pottery and the rare occurrence of both bronze and iron swords along with inhumation and cremation burials in the same tomb. In other words, these tombs straddle the end of the Bronze Age and beginning of the Iron Age on Crete (ca. 1200 B.C.E.).

Controlled studies began in 1903 with the excavation of two Late Minoan IIIC tholos tombs at Mouliana Sellades by Stefanos Xanthoudidis. While these funerary finds have been incorporated into subsequent studies, these investigations have relied primarily on the initial 1904 publication by Xanthoudidis, which depicted only about half of the excavated objects. This publication, while excellent for its time, is insufficient by 21st-century standards. The Mouliana Project (http://moulianaproject.org) aims to publish these important artifacts comprehensively with a full complement of modern scientific analyses (e.g., X-ray fluorescence spectrometry, organic residue analysis, 0.1 mm-accurate three-dimensional scanning, handheld LiDAR, photogrammetry) in order to make them fully accessible to the wider scholarly world.

During the summer of 2016, 46 of 50 recorded Mouliana objects were located in the Heraklion and Sitia Archaeological Museums, a feat in itself after 113 years, two world wars, and multiple upgrades in curatorial facilities. In addition to the aforementioned bronze and iron swords, the metal artifacts include complementary weapons, shield bosses, gold rings, a gold mask, and assorted smaller objects like fibulae. Many of the ceramic objects were moved to Siteia with the notable exceptions of the famous krater with a warrior depicted on horseback, some "Xanthoudidis Master" stirrup jars, and an impressive larnax with checkerboard pattern. Ceramic objects in Siteia include both stirrup jars and bowls. We present here the initial results from our first study season.

The Minoan Past in the Past: Bronze Age Objects in Early Iron Age Burials at Knossos, Crete

Alice M. Crowe, University of Cincinnati

Knossos is one of the few Aegean Bronze Age palatial centers at which occupation continued uninterrupted into the Early Iron Age; as a result, the site, and especially its burial record, provides a unique setting for a study of the use of the Minoan past in general, and of Bronze Age objects in particular, in Early Iron Age society. Thirty Knossian EIA tombs have produced Bronze Age objects, which would have been between 100 and 1,200 years old at the time of their redeposition. Through an analysis of the morphologies and EIA contexts of these reused Bronze Age objects, this paper examines how and for what purposes the Bronze Age past was employed during the Early Iron Age. The study also explores how and from where the Bronze Age objects were acquired, in what periods of the Early Iron Age they were redeposited, and in what kinds of tombs and with what kinds of objects they were placed.

This analysis suggests that Bronze Age objects are unlikely to have been "heirlooms"—objects passed down within a kin group—but rather functioned as "antiques." It also shows that most were probably robbed from Final Palatial–Postpalatial—rather than from earlier Minoan—tombs. Additionally, the analysis reveals a stark difference in the morphologies and functions of Bronze Age objects redeposited during periods in which the Bronze Age was the "recent past" and in periods during which it was the "deep past." In the Subminoan period (11th century)—only ca. 100 years removed from the end of the Bronze Age—the materials and shapes of the antique Bronze Age objects were ones that were no longer able to be produced in the Early Iron Age, and the restricted distribution of these objects indicates that one elite group monopolized this seemingly exotic past. In the Protogeometric "B"—Orientalizing periods (late ninth to seventh centuries), ca. 400 years removed from the end of the Bronze Age—the materials and motifs of the BA objects resembled those of Early Iron Age burial goods and thereby fit within the constructs of Early Iron Age ideologies. The objects were also dispersed within several tombs of moderate wealth, which suggests that the use of past objects was not only more inclusive but also one of several competing means of expressing status.

SESSION 7A: Colloquium
Beyond Reconstruction: New Approaches to Architectural Depictions in Roman Art

ORGANIZER: *Elizabeth Wolfram Thill*, IUPUI

Colloquium Overview Statement

Depictions of architecture are some of the most overscrutinized and underanalyzed elements of Roman art. The material culture of the Roman empire is replete with illustrations of built structures, crossing boundaries of chronology, geography, and media. Yet for centuries scholarship on architectural depictions has focused almost exclusively on particular issues of topography and reconstruction, rarely moving beyond questions such as "which building is depicted?" and "what did Temple X look like?" (see, e.g., P.V. Hill's paradigmatic 1965–1989 series on buildings and monuments on Roman coins). Recent scholars, however, are moving beyond such positivistic concerns to explore broader phenomena, seeking to understand the importance of architecture, both depicted and actual, to Roman society. Such scholarship strives to contextualize the images and take in a broader extent of artistic representations, incorporating not only those depictions that we can identify with the written or archaeological records but also the far more common illustrations of generic buildings that were never meant to depict a historical structure.

This panel will exemplify such new approaches to the study of architectural depictions in Roman art. Our goal is not only to further research into this important cultural phenomenon but also to draw attention to these depictions' pervasiveness and range, as well as their potential significance for research in a variety of fields, from viewer response to identity. Papers for the panel move from the public to private sphere and from the heart of Rome to the edge of the empire. The papers also encompass both identifiable and generic structures, in media ranging from large-scale reliefs to paintings to sarcophagi to enameled trullae (small pans) held as personal souvenirs. The first paper sets the theoretical stage, exploring contemporary responses to the interplay between depicted architecture and its surroundings, in examples from Villa A at Oplontis to the Baths of Caracalla. The second paper demonstrates how a systematic analysis of depicted architectural details can reveal further significance beyond a building's identity, even for such well-known examples as the Valle-Medici Reliefs. The third paper identifies previously unnoticed distinctions between identifiable and generic representations of temples in numismatic sacrifice scenes, revealing connections to the Ludi Saeculares. The fourth paper addresses representations of known public architecture in the private sphere and the social implications thereof. And the fifth paper demonstrates how even the trullae's humble architectural depictions of Hadrian's Wall can reveal much about identity and sense of place for their owners.

DISCUSSANT: *Jennifer Trimble*, Stanford University

Images Within Images: The Function and Reception of Metapictures in Roman Art

Maryl Gensheimer, University of Maryland

Illustrations of the built environment abound in the Roman material record, ranging from images of buildings in sculpted reliefs overhead to those in mosaic pavements underfoot, from the decoration of colossal wall paintings to that of comparatively small coins. Numerous modern studies have employed these representations of buildings as tools with which to address the topography of Rome and/or the reconstruction of its specific monuments. Yet this important idea of engaging with images that appear as metapictures within larger works merits scholarly attention beyond such approaches.

This paper departs from previous scholarship to explore representations of buildings in the art and architecture of ancient Rome, not from the perspective of topography or reconstruction, but rather from the perspective of what they reveal about the contemporary response to these works at a time close to their production. The case studies addressed vary in format. Some, like the famous historical frieze with battle scenes and cityscapes from the Baths of Caracalla, are images of the same kind as their support, presenting the viewer with metapictures of buildings embellishing a building. Other examples, like the virtuoso but fictive architecture found in the Second Style wall paintings of the atrium of Villa A at Oplontis, play with alternative media, such as painting, sculpture, and mosaic. In all cases, although these images within images are not always precise in their details, nonetheless these metapictures can be understood as significant documents. An interdisciplinary approach both to the archaeological data and to the textual and visual sources facilitates an innovative understanding of the complex relationships between the image and the work on which it appears, the underlying intentions of its artists and patrons, and even its contemporary reception.

This reassessment examines the wide variety of functions fulfilled by metapictures to shed new light on their capacity for both realistic documentation and playful adaptation of architecture in ways that were of interest to artists, patrons, and audiences alike. In so doing, this paper situates images within images as an important phenomenon in their own rights as part of a broader Roman visual culture that can and should be considered independent from modern reconstructions or topographical studies.

The Valle-Medici Reliefs and the Visualization of Rome

Elizabeth Wolfram Thill, IUPUI

Some of the most famous architectural depictions in Roman art are the three temples found on a series of reliefs belonging to a Julio-Claudian altar, known collectively as the Ara Pietatis or Valle-Medici reliefs. Despite their renown, analysis of these depictions has rarely moved beyond the historic buildings they represent, with scholarship focused on which buildings are depicted and why those buildings in particular were chosen (without achieving consensus on either question). Notably, scholars have found the depictions and their striking level of detail to be sufficiently explained by a need for topographic specificity for the monument's sacrifice scenes.

The identification of the Valle-Medici depictions, however important, addresses only one aspect of their meaning. Although the depictions' details may have reflected the appearance of actual temples, most of the incorporated features, such as dentil friezes, could do little to clarify the temples' identity and cannot be explained by a need to provide topographic information. Thus, pursuing the representations' connection to historical temples and going no further misses critical aspects of their potential impact.

I take a different approach, conducting a systematic analysis of all details selected for incorporation in each depiction. This demonstrates several interesting patterns. First, the cumulative effect of all these architectural details, including their repetition and variation, appears calculated to recall the extravagant architectural luxury associated strongly with Augustus. This makes the ornate rendering of the depicted temples a Julio-Claudian dynastic statement. Second, given the narrow parameters of Roman temple architecture, the three depictions achieve a surprising amount of variety, including three different columniations and two orders. Significantly, the three depictions of pedimental sculpture are immediately distinguishable in terms of style, and the different cultural spheres evoked—Roman, eastern, and Greek—correspond with three of the empire's main geographic spheres.

Such careful variation is unlikely to be coincidence, and other relief fragments proposed to belong to the same altar reinforce these patterns. I argue that the desire to create a certain visual representation of Julio-Claudian Rome may have been a significant factor behind which historical temples were chosen to be included on the altar. This visualization would contribute strongly to the monument's overall message, glorifying Julio-Claudian connections to the Augustan architectural tradition and emphasizing the geographic, cultural, and religious span of Rome's rule. Systematic analysis of the Valle-Medici reliefs thus can demonstrate how the significance of depicted architecture can extend beyond identification, even for identifiable depictions.

The Generic Temple-Sacrifice Motif and the Ludi Saeculares

Melanie Grunow Sobocinski, AIA Ann Arbor Society

In Roman coins and medallions, the temple-sacrifice motif sometimes occurs with a specific, identifiable temple, and sometimes with a deliberately general temple. How are we to interpret this iconographic choice to downplay or emphasize the location of the action? M.G. Sobocinski (*AJA* 110 [2006] 581 - 602) points out that the first set of coins to deliberately undercut the identity of the depicted temple(s), the Ludi Saeculares coinage of Domitian in 88 C.E., did so because this ritual involved so many locations within the city of Rome. Here, I argue that this extraordinary set of coins established a strong identification between generic temple sacrifice iconography and the Ludi Saeculares that endured for nearly a century. Indeed, no instances of the temple-sacrifice motif appear in Roman coinage between Domitian's issues of 88 C.E. and rare issues of Antoninus Pius in 145 and 148 C.E., which have not been previously linked to the Ludi Saeculares of 147–8 C.E. The generic temple-sacrifice motif appears again in the issues commemorating the Ludi Saeculares of Septimius Severus in 204 C.E. This curious distribution has not been identified in previous scholarship.

By contrast, when the temple-sacrifice motif is used outside of the Ludi Saeculares, the identity of the temple tends to be stressed through redundant means—legends identifying the deity, specific iconography of the cult statue and/or the pediment, or in the case of the round temple to Vesta, unusual characteristics of the *aedes* itself. In these cases, it is clear that the artists are deliberately seeking to avoid misinterpretation.

The Vota Publica temple-sacrifice issues of Marcus Aurelius (166–9 C.E. and 177–8 C.E.) and the Ludi Saeculares temple-sacrifice issues of Philip the Arab in 248 C.E. complicate this picture, combining what seems to be specific sculptural iconography with topographically vague legends. I conclude that in these liminal cases, the artists are instead addressing two audiences simultaneously: the smaller circle of individuals with the specialized knowledge to interpret the more obscure iconography, and the wider circle of individuals lacking, like us, sufficient context for full understanding. Recognizing and analyzing the difference between identifiable and generic buildings within the larger context of sacrificial imagery thus has implications for our understanding of both an important religious ritual in Rome and questions of audience targeting in numismatic imagery.

Privatizing Public Monuments: Framing Public Life in the Roman Household

Allison Kidd, New York University

Upon entering the atrium of the Praedia of Julia Felix, ancient visitors of the privately owned establishment would have found themselves surrounded on all sides by the Forum of Pompeii, or rather, a 30 m long fresco depicting the city's Roman forum. Identified by the forum's two-storied porticoes and architectural orders, the fresco whisks the viewer away from a residential complex to the center of public life: men read notices posted alongside equestrian statues; women haggle over goods for sale; and a beggar receives alms from a matron. Similarly animated and engaging is a fresco from the House of Actius Anicetus, featuring the idiosyncratic amphitheater of Pompeii and the notorious Nucerian riot of 59 C.E. that took place there (Tac. *Ann.* 14.17).

Long valued as simply "documentary" images in the Roman world, the representation of known, archaeologically attested public monuments in private contexts, as seen on marble and terracotta reliefs, sarcophagi, frescoes, mosaics, and glass vessels, has received little analytical attention in modern scholarship. This paper juxtaposes the evolution of such images from the first to fourth centuries C.E. with those of the public sphere, such as on imperial state reliefs and coins. Unlike state commissions, which used architectural representations as an operative device in the ideological projection of the Roman administration, I argue that architectural representations on media commissioned and distributed in a nonofficial capacity are concerned rather with social participation. The built environment and architecture of Rome were consistently portrayed by citizens with an animated immediacy, offering viewers a vivid sense of the ancient city. This paper examines the resulting representational paradox in which the lines between the public and the private sphere are blurred, and where public architecture is not only featured as a backdrop for daily urban life in Rome but is anthropomorphically treated as an integral participant in daily social life. I will present two case studies. The first considers the phenomenon from a localized and chronologically limited archaeological context by examining simulacra from Pompeii that depict the city's forum. The second considers representations of the Circus Maximus from across the ancient Mediterranean world to provide a more universal and global perspective. Together, these two case studies not only highlight a unique representational paradox in which public architecture was 'privatized' in the Roman household, they also reveal important information about ancient social urban behavior and the conceptual nature of construction and architecture in ancient Rome.

Metamorphosis of a Motif: Portraying Hadrian's Wall on Roman "Souvenirs"
Kimberly Cassibry, Wellesley College

Ancient "souvenirs" of Hadrian's Wall present a conundrum. On two nearly identical enameled trullae (small pans), an inscription around the outer rim names forts lining the wall; a turreted wall motif runs continuously beneath the words. The combination suggests that the motif portrays some part of the wall, but specialists have debated which one. The milecastles guarding the wall between forts, the north gates of forts themselves, or even an aerial view of forts jutting out from the rampart's line have all been proposed. This paper argues for a new reading of the artifacts by reconsidering the local significance of the motif, as well as the materiality and provincial context of creation.

Hadrian's Wall (second century C.E.), stretching across Britain, may be the empire's most ambitious architectural project. Yet the rampart seems not to have been commemorated in relief sculptures on state monuments or on coins. The souvenirs thus highlight local reception at odds with the metropole's. They also reveal distinctly local solutions to visualizing its complex form.

Outsiders associated polychrome enameling with this frontier region (Philostr., *Imag.* 1.28.3). The souvenirs' very materiality therefore reinforced a geographic connection. Materiality also constrained design: because the glassy paste had to be held by small cells, grid patterns were a common solution to ornamenting vessels. The turreted wall motif—essentially an irregularly outlined grid—adapts such designs in a way that alludes to ashlar or turf blocks, without replicating their appearance. The cells' alternating blue and turquoise enamel certainly ornaments rather than describes.

The ultimate source of the motif thus translated has proved puzzling. As many have pointed out, fortified walls appear in floor mosaics, including one in Britain. Yet in military contexts such fortifications occurred more commonly on headgear. Goddesses wear mural crowns in votive sculptures from the wall. Roman cavalry helmets from Britain include mural crowns, too. The motif in all these contexts refers to a single, walled settlement, and I propose that it did so on the souvenirs also, as a generic gloss for each fort named in the inscriptions. The motif thus focuses attention on the sites that structured experiences of the wall.

The vessels, found in southern England and northern France, likely mediated memories of former frontier abodes. Reconsidering their iconography, materiality, and provincial context offers new insights into the ancient conceptualization of imperial architecture.

SESSION 7B: Colloquium
Regional Approaches to Identity and Meaning in Greek Landscapes: Current Work of the Canadian Institute in Greece

Sponsored by the Canadian Institute in Greece

ORGANIZERS: *Brendan Burke*, University of Victoria, and *Angus Smith*, Brock University

Colloquium Overview Statement

This colloquium will feature five papers that highlight ongoing projects carried out by the Canadian Institute in Greece (CIG), which celebrated its 40th anniversary in 2016. In particular, these papers will discuss a variety of approaches to the study of landscape and settlement from the Stone Age to the Hellenistic period, in regions as diverse as the Cyclades, the Peloponnese, and central and northern Greece. The value of the CIG projects is that the areas of study are in parts of Greece beyond the traditional regions of prolonged exploration, such as Crete, Athens, and the western Peloponnese. For example, the Stélida Naxos Archaeological Project in the Cyclades investigates important issues related to the earliest peopling of the Mediterranean; the Western Argolid Research Project is a diachronic archaeological survey investigating the shifting relationships between the communities of the western Argolid and the northeastern Peloponnese and beyond; the Eastern Boeotia Archaeological Project is excavating the secondary center of ancient Eleon, which operated within the orbit of Thebes in Boeotia during the Late Bronze Age and Archaic/Classical periods; excavations at ancient Argilos are devoted to the study of an urban center dating from the Archaic through Hellenistic periods, highlighting relations between Greeks and Thracians on the north coast of Aegean; and Kastro Kallithea in Thessaly is a classical/Hellenistic fortified city with an acropolis, agora, and housing district, which provides an excellent opportunity for the study of the spatial organization of an urban center. Current Canadian research in Greece is investigating many unexplored themes and regions that will be highlighted by this session.

DISCUSSANT: *David Rupp*, Canadian Institute in Greece

Recent Fieldwork at Ancient Argilos

Jacques Y. Perreault, University of Montreal, and *Zisis Bonias*, Greek Ministry of Culture

The Greek-Canadian excavations undertaken at the site of ancient Argilos are part of a program devoted to the study of the historical and architectural development of this ancient city. The main objectives are to improve our understanding of the development of colonial establishments along the north Aegean coast and of the relations between Greeks and Thracians.

The literary tradition dates the foundation of the settlement to 655/4 B.C.E., which makes Argilos the earliest Greek colony on the Thracian coast near the mouth of the Strymon River. The area was a rich source of gold and silver, and with port access for shipping, fertile alluvial land for farming, and a vast supply of precious metals to mine and trade, Argilos became one of the wealthiest cities in the region. Excavations on the acropolis and the southeastern slope of the settlement have uncovered houses and public buildings in a rare state of preservation that attest to the richness of the city during the Archaic and Classical periods. In some cases, walls are preserved to a height of 4 m!

The city's prosperity declined, however, once the Athenians founded the city of Amphipolis just a few kilometers away in 437 B.C.E. Like other colonies in the area, the city was conquered by the Macedonian king Philip II in 357 B.C.E. Historians thought that the city was subsequently abandoned, but the excavations have brought to light evidence of agricultural activity on the acropolis, which dates to the years 350 - 200 B.C.E. The main feature of this activity is the presence of a Hellenistic mansion, remarkably well preserved, in which the ground floor was used for the production of olive oil.

Since 2012, the excavation of a new area of the site has uncovered extremely interesting finds that help us better understand the economic development of the city and the emergence in classical Greece of buildings specifically dedicated to commercial activities. A large building, unique in its size and dating to the sixth century B.C.E., consists of a dozen shops and seems to be linked to an even larger complex in what was probably the commercial agora of the city.

Regional Identity and the Ethnos of Achaia Phthiotis

Margriet Haagsma, University of Alberta, *C.M. Chykerda*, University of California, Los Angeles, *S. Karapanou*, Greek Ministry of Culture and Sports, and *L. Surtees*, Bryn Mawr College

The foundation of the Thessalian League in 197 B.C.E. appears to formalize preexisting notions of a regional Thessalian identity. From the onset, this *koinon* bears all the hallmarks of a true *ethnos*: central sanctuaries, a shared mythological ancestry, a collective religious calendar, a common dialect, and a central political authority. However, not all Thessalians subscribed to this blueprint; there are many signs that the formerly semi-autonomous *perioikoi*, often described in earlier sources as *ethne* in their own right in earlier sources, were reluctant to abandon their cultural and perhaps economic and political independence.

The inhabitants of one such *perioikos*, that of Achaia Phthiotis, for example, sought to differentiate themselves from tetradic Thessaly and employed various forms of resistance tactics against the federal program of the Thessalian League. This resistance was expressed, for example, in an adherence to and monumentalization of local religious practices and a reluctance to adopt the new religious calendar of the Thessalian League.

Using archaeological data synthesized with historic, epigraphic, numismatic, and predominantly archaeological sources, we will chart the shifting expressions and perceptions of regional identities of the Phthiotic Achaians throughout the Hellenistic period. The evidence derives from various archaeological contexts, such as Halos, Melitaia, Pharsalos, and foremost the Kastro Kallithea Archaeological Project, which over the past 12 years has focused on the study of that Late

Classical-Hellenistic city in Achaia Phthiotis. We will demonstrate that constructions of identities in peripheral regions such as Achaia Phthiotis were multifarious and were negotiated on different planes simultaneously.

On the Banks of the Ancient Streams of the Inachos: The Western Argolid Regional Project, 2014 - 2016

Dimitri Nakassis, University of Toronto, *Scott Gallimore*, Wilfrid Laurier University, *William Caraher*, University of North Dakota, and *Sarah James*, University of Colorado, Boulder

The relationships between the city-state of Argos, its hinterland, and neighboring communities are significant lacunae in our knowledge of the northeastern Peloponnese. Since 2014, the Western Argolid Regional Project (WARP) has attempted to address this gap through intensive pedestrian survey in combination with geomorphological, historical, and ethnographic studies. In three field seasons (2014–2016), WARP has intensively surveyed some 20 km^2 along the banks of the Inachos River. This includes territory perhaps controlled by Argos for much of its history, near the modern village of Schinochori, along with the river valley overlooked by the ancient polis of Orneai.

The goal of this paper is to provide a synthetic discussion of the results from the project's three field seasons, with particular emphasis on the 2016 field season, which sought to test preliminary conclusions drawn from two previous seasons, such as that the region lacked not only the small classical sites normally interpreted as farmsteads but also the Late Roman "settlement explosion" commonly encountered by intensive surveys. In the southernmost region of our study area, surveyed in 2015, a full spectrum of occupation history (prehistoric to modern) was noted, but this coincides with limited evidence for large-scale, permanent settlement. This region, approximately 2–3 hours north of Argos on foot, may have been exploited primarily by individuals who traveled to their fields but lived in the city. In the Orneai Valley, surveyed in 2014, Classical to Early Hellenistic and early modern material was predominant, with other periods of occupation less commonly encountered. Settlement focused at Orneai, located immediately above the modern village of Lyrkeia.

The project's highly intensive, "siteless" methodology has revealed dynamic, rapidly changing landscapes. Interpretation of these landscapes does not always conform to standard models for rural settlement on the Greek mainland, however, and our results directly challenge narratives derived from the fairly scanty historical evidence. For instance, our sources suggest that Orneai was a peripheral settlement highly dependent on Argos, but the size of the site in the Classical and Early Hellenistic periods suggest that it was prosperous, perhaps because of its strategic and highly networked location along the terrestrial routes that connected the communities of the northeastern Peloponnese.

Reconstructing Early Prehistoric Activity and Pleistocene Land- and Seascapes in the Cyclades: Survey and Excavation at Stélida, Naxos 2013–16

Tristan Carter, McMaster University, *Demetrios Athanasoulis*, Cycladic Ephorate of Antiquities, *Daniel Contreras*, Aix-Marseille Universite, *Justin Holcomb*, Boston University, *Danica Mihailovič*, University of Belgrade, *Kathryn Campeau*, McMaster University, and *James Feathers*, University of Washington

Survey and excavation at the chert source and knapping floors of Stélida (northwest Naxos) are providing key evidence for the long-term early prehistoric use of this tool-making resource from the Lower Paleolithic to Mesolithic, conceivably ≥250,000–9000 BP.

This paper reviews the site-wide nature of activity based on a GIS analysis of more than 30,000 artifacts collected systematically in 2013–14 by the Stélida Naxos Archaeological Project using transect and gridded survey units, and the ongoing results of a detailed characterization study of the raw material outcrops and their use. We critically reflect on the interpretative limitations of survey data with reference to Stélida-specific challenges (a dynamic erosional landscape, significant vegetation cover, and major modern disturbance) and the larger issues surrounding the evidential requirements to substantiate Pleistocene activity in the Aegean Basin. A further issue is raised-namely, how to interpret the quite atypical nature of the earliest material culture from Stélida. Is this distinction a product of chronological or environmental differences, or more related to the fact that we are contrasting a quarry site with habitation sites-that is, due to behavioral differences?

The paper then details the excavation results and absolute dates generated by the 2015–16 seasons and the different challenges faced through this new form of site analysis. Stratified deposits containing artifacts that can be techno-typologically associated with Lower and Upper Paleolithic traditions were exposed in 2015, along with a series of beachside artifact-bearing exposures of silicified sand dunes (aeolianite deposits). Samples for absolute dating were taken from both, with optically stimulated luminescence producing dates of >30,000 BP terminus ante quem for the uppermost strata of one aeolianite sequence, making Stélida the oldest known site in the Cyclades and the only well-dated "island-based" Pleistocene site outside of Crete. The question of Naxos' insularity at this time remains unresolved, a major issue for our appreciating the significance of Stélida's exploitation during the Lower to Middle Paleolithic and the larger role of the Aegean Basin with regard to hominin movement. To that end, a range of geoarchaeological analyses are being undertaken with the aim of reconstructing site-formation processes, vegetation, climate, and local sea levels. One current working hypothesis–based on the fact that our major lithostratigraphic units appear to relate to periods of hill wash–is that Stélida was only ever visited during those major glacial periods where sea levels were low enough to reveal land bridges into the Aegean Basin from surrounding continental landmasses, periods when scrubby tundra-like vegetation on the site may have lacked the root depth and density to enable soil stability.

In sum, new work at Stélida is providing the first clear evidence for early *Homo sapiens*, Neanderthal and early human activity in the Aegean Basin, data that are helping us to reconfigure our view of Greece from being a Pleistocene cul-de-sac, or refugium, to potentially a major route in early hominin dispersal.

Ebb and Flow at Ancient Eleon

Brendan Burke, University of Victoria, *Bryan Burns*, Wellesley College, and *Alexandra Charami*, Ephoreia of Boeotian Antiquities

The Eastern Boeotia Archaeological Project has excavated at the site of ancient Eleon in the village of Arma each summer since 2011. Our work has shown Eleon to be a center of vibrant activity throughout the Late Bronze Age, from a burial complex of the Late Helladic (LH) I period to significant settlement remains of the LH IIIC period. Excavations also reveal intriguing evidence for the site's reuse in historical periods, when the construction of a massive polygonal wall concentration redefined the site's topography and function.

The earliest architecture preserved on the site is a funerary structure of the Early Mycenaean period, which contained individual cist graves inside a perimeter wall that was mounded with a tumulus. The later Mycenaean occupation surrounds this mound, with architectural units that feature large rooms and tiled roofs. Associated deposits dating to the LH IIIB2, IIIC early, and IIIC middle periods show the population of Eleon to be active in agricultural, pastoral, and industrial activities, without the major disruption recorded at many other Mycenaean sites. Highly elaborate forms, such as pictorial pottery and terracotta bull figures, point to ceremonial activity, which may provide cultic context for the more typical Mycenaean figurines also found here. The Bronze Age remains are framed within an elaborate well-built Mycenaean bastion showing several phases of building toward the end of the Late Bronze Age. These constructions form a massive entrance system, which perhaps inspired the builders who returned to the site of Eleon after a hiatus of nearly 500 years.

Eleon's massive polygonal wall was built in the late sixth century, forming an 85m arc between two angular bastions. Our excavations have uncovered lower portions of the wall and substantial foundations, including those of the northern tower that creates the transition to a ramped entryway that incorporated standing remains of the Mycenaean period. Here we have recovered a large deposit of votive pottery and figurines of the sixth through fifth centuries B.C.E., as well as drinking vessels. The focus of this religious activity is not clear, in terms of an identifiable sacred space or the identity of figure(s) worshiped. Given the proximity and conscious preservation of earlier remains, we suggest that cult activity may be related to the Bronze Age tumulus nearby.

SESSION 7C
Architecture and Urbanism

CHAIR: To be announced

Moving the First Stone Blocks of Greek Architecture: A New Interpretation of the Channels in the Blocks of Corinth and Isthmia

Alessandro Pierattini, University of Notre Dame

The first stone-block walls of Greek architecture, those of the mid seventh-century B.C.E. temples of Corinth and Isthmia, pose a problem for understanding the building practices of the transition from perishable to permanent materials.

Their blocks, cut to uniform dimensions and arranged in a single wythe, have a most peculiar trait: the presence of two parallel channels along the bottom and usually continuing up one end. There is no scholarly consensus on the purpose of these channels, which interestingly disappear in later Greek masonry. Presumably used with ropes, these channels may have served to lift the blocks and then let the ropes slip out (Broneer), or to transport the blocks (Roebuck), or even to remove them from the quarry (Rhodes).

This paper reassesses previous scholarship on the basis of a new analysis of the finds from Isthmia and Corinth, with the help of experimental tests performed on replica blocks.

The first point addressed is how and when the channels were cut. The second concentrates on their function, which leads to a discussion of more general aspects of the construction practices used for in the first Greek stone temples.

The factors relevant to the study of the channels include their size and disposition, the weight of the blocks, and the thickness and strength of the ancient ropes hypothetically used. Combined analysis of these factors shows that lifting the blocks by ropes attached to the channels was technically possible, while recent debate on Corinthian Geometric sarcophagi suggests that simple lifting machines may have been used in the area even before the Protoarchaic period. In short, the association of the channels with lifting would seem to be the most plausible hypothesis, while the other two are less convincing.

However, the closest archaic parallels suggest an alternative interpretation, which is confirmed by experimental tests: regardless of how the blocks were lifted, the channels were involved in setting the blocks tight against their neighbors. Once a block had been lifted on its course, in fact, by pulling and releasing the ropes attached to its channels, a block could be easily maneuvered into place, with a dynamic similar to that later obtained with crowbars.

Such a rudimentary method, nonetheless effective with blocks of a modest size, seems thus to mark the initial stage of a technique that, while remaining unchanged in its essence, grew in sophistication along with technical progress.

Urban Density in Classical Greece: An Evaluation of Geostatistical Methods and Publicly Available Data Sets

Daniel Plekhov, Brown University, and *Evan Levine*, Brown University

The settlement structure of classical Greece is characterized by a diversity of settlement hierarchies, territorial sizes, and urban densities. These differences in settlement organization are often characteristic of specific geographic regions, suggesting a relationship between regional environmental variables and local settlement patterns. Settlement hierarchies and territorial sizes remain, however, difficult to study because of their propensity to change, as well as the paucity of archaeological remains that relate to these aspects of settlement pattern. The study of urban densities, in contrast, requires little more than the known location of a settlement and evidence confirming its occupation during a specific time period. Using available and publicly accessible data sets of ancient Greek sites, we focus specifically on addressing the density of those mainland sites occupied during the fifth and fourth centuries B.C.E. through a variety of geostatistical analyses and making use of several environmental data sets. These data sets include indices of agricultural productivity (NPP and NDVI) and measures of proximity to features such as coasts and mountains.

In doing so, we identify those variables that may have been most influential in determining the settlement structure of classical Greece, while also quantifying the scale of regional diversity present on mainland Greece. The results of such exploratory geostatistical analyses serve as important foundations for further studies on settlement pattern in other regions and time periods, allowing for interesting comparisons to be drawn with broader anthropological implications. Additionally, through this analysis we hope to highlight the potential of using publicly accessible "big data" data sets for archaeological analysis and the relative ease with which such broad-scale regional analyses of hundreds of sites can be done without the collection of new data.

Satellites and Signal Towers: New Considerations on the Defense Network of Mantineia

Matthew Maher, Independent Researcher, and *Alistair Mowat*, University of Western Ontario

The ancient city of Mantineia–established and originally fortified sometime in the fifth century B.C.E.–is located approximately in the center of its territory, which comprises the northern part of Arkadia's great eastern plain. In addition to its impressive fortification circuit, the city was further safeguarded by a number of signal towers located along the periphery of its territory. Constructed to house only a few men and no artillery, these towers functioned as part of an "early warning" system, monitoring the main roads through and access points into the *chora* of Mantineia. While the existence of seven of these towers has been noted by other scholars, they have only ever received brief mention and have never been studied collectively.

This paper represents the first detailed architectural study and synthesis of all the documented towers. For the first time, we are able to see the defensive network of the Mantinike in its entirety. By employing a methodology that combines a review of the published literature with Google Earth and pedestrian reconnaissance, by examining the construction of these towers and their location, and by applying viewshed analyses, it is shown how they functioned together as a larger defensive system to protect both the polis and *chora* of Mantineia from all cardinal directions.

This specific methodology and targeted survey has not only led to the discovery of two previously unknown examples of Mantineian signal towers, but it has allowed us to remove one signal tower from the known corpus and reassign another to its rightful place as part of a larger fort complex. It is now clear from the data collected that all the signal towers share common architectural features, including drafted corners, a mudbrick superstructure, foundations of coursed polygonal masonry, the use of bedrock in their construction, and a standard orientation, size, and shape. Based on these collective architectural similarities, historical probability, and the stylistic affinities they share with other nearby examples of Arkadian military architecture, it is argued that all of these signal towers are contemporary and must date to the early fourth century B.C.E. Finally, as the results produced in this study clearly demonstrate the effectiveness of using Google Earth for archaeological and topographic research, it is hoped that the methodology developed for the present study encourages the further use of such satellite reconnaissance in the field of archaeology.

Against Hippodamos of Miletos

Simeon D. Ehrlich, Stanford University

This paper argues that grid planning is not a defining feature of Graeco-Roman urban form. This stands in stark contrast to a scholarly tradition beginning with F. Haverfield's, *Ancient Town-Planning* (Oxford 1913). While R. Laurence, S. Esmonde Cleary, and G. Sears (*The City in the Roman West c.250 BC - c.AD 250* [Cambridge 2011]) have assigned the orthogonal grid plan a diminished significance, I propose that a more complete revaluation of classical urban form is necessary. Three factors serve as motivation. First, the Hippodamian passages of Aristotle (Pol. 1267b - 1269a, 1330b) that have sustained prolonged scholarly interest in grid form are a weak foundation on which to build a model. Second, grid planning of the sort so often deemed emblematic of the classical city is manifest in the settlements of many contemporary and earlier cultures around the globe. Third, cross-cultural comparisons reveal distinctive spatial organizational characteristics of classical cities not contingent on grid forms. From these observations I construct a more robust model of classical urban form.

The Hippodamian passages are the root of the problem; they are vague and offer little of substance as regards urban form. Yet being one of the very few discussions of urban form by a canonical author, they have been afforded an importance far outweighing their utility. Their cardinal achievement has been to perpetuate the notion that the use of the orthogonal grid plan by the Greeks was both innovative and distinctive. I contend it was neither. Orthogonal grid planning is known from settlements in Egypt, Mesopotamia, China, northern Europe, Mesoamerica, and the Indus Valley–and often from sites planned before the eighth century B.C.E. While it is not as prevalent in any of these cultures as it is among Graeco-Roman cities, I propose that the grid plan is best understood as a universal organizational paradigm and not the specific manifestation of Graeco-Roman ideals. Rather, what distinguishes classical cities from other settlements are the openness and connectivity seen in their plans. I posit that form itself is irrelevant. Instead, it is in how the parts of a city are joined and how the city can be transited that we see the reification of uniquely classical ideas of urban form.

This paper represents a departure from conventional thought about classical urban form. It prompts a reconsideration of our understanding of the classical city both on its own and in its global and historical context.

Money, Marbles, and Chalk: The Ancient Quarries of the Mani Peninsula

Chelsea A.M. Gardner, Mount Allison University

In the Mani Peninsula of southern Lakonia, Greece, the single most copious natural resource located is stone: geologically, most of the peninsula is composed of limestone and marble. While these prolific local materials were exploited potentially as early as the Neolithic period, they were certainly capitalized upon at least by the Late Bronze Age and throughout the remainder of antiquity. Initially, modern scholarly interest in Maniate stone focused on the extensive exploitation and widespread dissemination of a specific marble known as *rosso antico*, a true marble with a red to violet hue, which was especially popular from the Bronze Age to the Byzantine period. Since the rediscovery of these ancient marble quarries in 1829, other local marbles, including black, green and white varieties, have received attention from scholars, especially the latter because of the ongoing debate about the sources for the pure white marble used in the fifth-century Temple of Apollo at Bassai.

In recent years, much work has been done on the natural stone resources throughout the peninsula, particularly with the increasing sophistication of isotopic, petrographic, and chemical testing options. However, the current scholarship on Maniate quarries lacks an all-encompassing, comprehensive analysis of all the quarries within the peninsula. Too often, published works on Maniate quarries focus on a single case study or a set of samples for scientific testing, with the result that the current scholarship is divided based on type of marble or date of exploitation. These narrow agendas have produced only isolated accounts that overlook other scholarship concerning Maniate quarries and artifacts.

This paper synthesizes the locations of all confirmed sources of southern Mani marble and limestone, as well as the evidence for the exploitation of these resources in antiquity. Its goal is to present, for the first time, a comprehensive geographic and chronological understanding of exploitation of the ancient marble landscape in Mani from the Bronze Age through the Roman period.

SESSION 7D: Colloquium
Funerary Sculpture in Palmyra: The Palmyra Portrait Project

ORGANIZER: *Rubina Raja*, Aarhus University, Denmark

Colloquium Overview Statement

Since 2012, the Palmyra Portrait Project has worked on creating the most extensive corpus of Palmyrene funerary portraiture. Currently the corpus holds more than 2,900 portraits, which all stems from grave in Palmyra and date to the period between the late first century B.C.E. and late third century C.E. The corpus has given scholars the possibility for the first time to statistically compare these portraits across portrait groups and time, which has given unique insight into the way the portraiture in Palmyra reflected developing societal trends.

Palmyrene funerary portraiture makes up the largest group of representations of individuals from antiquity outside of Rome. Dating to the period between the late first century B.C.E. and the late third century C.E. when Palmyra was sacked by the Romans under the emperor Aurelian, the portraits, of which 3% are dated through their inscriptions, give unique opportunities to explore aspects of self-representation in antiquity. Situated between world empires, Rome and Parthia, Palmyra developed its own unique style, and the art of Palmyra remains underexplored–although it has been addressed by more than a century of scholarship. Through the corpus, it is now clear that some conclusions made earlier on the basis of a much smaller amount of material have to be reconsidered in light of the now very comprehensive corpus. Therefore, this colloquium will include papers, that highlight various central aspects and groups within Palmyrene funerary sculpture.

Researchers within and connected to the project have worked on various aspects, which will be presented in the colloquium session. These include a general introduction to the corpus and the extensive database in which it is compiled as well as a statistical overview of the various groups of funerary sculpture. Furthermore, there will be presentations on the representations of women, children, and priests in Palmyrene funerary sculpture and their development over time. Last but not least, cultural heritage issues due to the destruction and illicit trade of cultural goods will also be considered to show how the corpus may in some cases help monitor the destruction of tombs and portraits in Palmyra.

DISCUSSANT: *Andreas Kropp*, Nottingham University

The Function of Attributes in Palmyrene Portraiture

Maura Heyn, University of North Carolina, Grennsboro, and *Rubina Raja*, Aarhus University

The deceased of Palmyra display a variety of objects in their funerary portraiture in the first three centuries C.E. Women hold items that are associated with the domestic sphere: spindle and distaff, keys, a child, an unusual object that may be a calendar, and occasionally a palm leaf. Most men hold a book roll in their left hand, but a significant minority display items associated with their profession: a jug and incense bowl for priests, and a sword and whip for men associated with the caravan trade. Men also occasionally hold the palm leaf. These items displayed by both men and women were presumably intended to communicate information about the deceased to the community. The character of this information is not straightforward, however, particularly since most of the female attributes drop out of use at the end of the second century. After this time, most women, if they hold anything, grasp a loop of their cloak. The same is true for some of the men. It seems unlikely that this change in fashion correlates with a change of role in the household or community. A more likely explanation rests with the function of these attributes as markers of group identity in Roman Palmyra. In the centuries following Roman conquest of this caravan city, fluctuating priorities were played out in the funerary portraiture, as certain connections were more advantageous for the family. In this paper, we will explore some of these connections as a means of understanding the significance of the attributes.

Portrayal of Women in Palmyrene Sarcophagi and Banquet Reliefs

Signe Krag, Aarhus University

In their chronological works on Palmyrene sculpture, H. Ingholt and M.A.R. Colledge both focused on the loculus reliefs and stelae. Later, scholars such as K. Parlasca and C.K. Makowski included observations on sarcophagi and banquet reliefs. However, still no comprehensive study of sarcophagi and banquet reliefs has been carried out in relation to Palmyrene funerary sculpture. Sarcophagi and banquet reliefs first appear around the end of the first century C.E., and frequently two to five individuals are portrayed in the scenes. During the second and third centuries C.E., the number of individuals increases, and in the third century C.E. up to 13 individuals are included in the sarcophagi. Women are often portrayed in these scenes together with men, but how men and women are depicted and relate to each other changes over time. This paper aims to explore the overall changes in sarcophagi and banquet reliefs from the first to the third centuries C.E. with a main emphasis on the changing portrayals of women. Furthermore, during the third century C.E. a large increase in the production of both sarcophagi and banquet reliefs is observed. Reasons for this increase will be addressed in the paper.

Palmyrene Priests-Positions or Professions?

Rubina Raja, Aarhus University

Through the comprehensive database compiled within the Palmyra Portrait Project, it is now possible to draw up a complete catalogue of the priestly representations in the funerary sculpture from Palmyra. These amount to approximately 300 portraits of Palmyrene priests shown in various constellations over a period of almost 300 years. It is significant that these representations make up about 17% of all male representations and about 10% of all representations in the funerary sculpture. The corpus makes it possible to investigate the development of the priestly representations over time and to examine trends, such as the representations of the so-called former priests, that came into fashion in the late second century C.E and continued into the third century C.E., as well as to analyze the reasons for such developments and trends. Whereas Palmyrene funerary portraiture is by and large void of representations of professions, apart from a few examples, the representations of the Palmyrene priests can be argued to clearly depict men who held a certain office. However, whether this was a position in society or a profession has not been clear in scholarship until now. In this paper, the specific focus will be on the representations of the so-called former priests and contextualization of the development of this specific mode of representation. It is argued that these representations indeed depict former not priests but priests who were still active in their roles. This is done on the basis of the collection of evidence for the structure of Palmyrene priesthoods, including the epigraphic and literary evidence as well as the many representations now accessible to us through the database of the Palmyra Portrait Project. On the basis of these representations, it is argued that the position of a Palmyrene priest should be viewed more as a status position than as a profession.

A Roman Hairstyle at Palmyra

Fred Albertson, University of Memphis

This paper reexamines a small group of female funerary portraits from Palmyra–some 29 known examples-each sharing a distinctive hairstyle known from Roman portraiture as the "tower type." Previous scholarship has linked the appearance of this fashion to portraits of Faustina the Elder, but no imperial intermediary is needed, as the Palmyra form shows direct links to that appearing on late Hadrianic and early Antonine private portraits from metropolitan Rome. However, the Palmyrene arrangement is unique. In its Roman counterparts, the braids are laid in a circular fashion horizontally at the top of the head to create the characteristic "tower." At Palmyra, twisted plaits are instead extended vertically in a conical fashion and tied at the top in the form of a single, halo-like horizontal braid bound by a fillet. Although the hairstyle is Western, it is proposed here that the Palmyrene alteration is regional in its origin; it appears to imitate a tall conical cap worn by women and known from northern Syria through mosaics from Edessa, wall paintings from Dura, and sculpture from Hatra. This headdress is associated with divinities, royalty, and women of high social standing. Although the cap appears to have religious connotations outside of Palmyra, its reflection in the form of a hairstyle at Palmyra seems to be strictly associated with status: the greater height of the tower is associated with a higher standing both within and outside the family. This is evidenced by the fact that a shorter cone is associated with young girls, while mature women usually wear a much higher tower often richly adorned with jewelry. Additional questions to be addressed are why this hairstyle was fashionable at Palmyra, particularly among young girls, and why it remained in vogue for such a lengthy period of time, appearing initially in the 140s and lasting well past the mid third century.

Representations of Palmyrene Children in Funerary Sculpture from the First to Third Century C.E.

Sara Ringsborg, Aarhus University

The study of children in antiquity has in certain research areas been a great topic for some years now, but the focus has not been on the culture of Palmyra, until now. Portraits of children compose about 8% of the overall corpus of Palmyrene funerary sculpture; the significance of children in the funerary sphere is therefore not to be overlooked. The portraits are shown in a great variety of constellations. Children could appear both together with their parents and siblings, but they could also receive their own individual funerary display. Their role and status differs in the funerary art, as they could function as both an attribute and as the main focus of the display. When children were displayed with a female adult, they could, through their presence and gesture, emphasize the woman's identity as a mother, which is shown to be a role of great importance and power in Palmyrene society. Family constellations were important in Palmyrene funerary art, and family ties are expressed in the many preserved inscriptions. The function as an attribute is therefore not less important than the individual displays. Each portrait is unique, but emphasis is not on the sex of the child but on other aspects that will be discussed. This paper is based on my master's thesis, which examines the different categories of child portraits in loculus reliefs from Palmyra. The categories include young children, adolescents, and adult children. On this basis, a discussion of the role and status of children in the Palmyrene funerary sphere and Palmyrene society will be undertaken.

***Ancient Objects,* Modern Contexts: Biographies of Palmyrene Funerary Portraits**

Anne Ditte Kougstrup Høi, Aarhus University

This paper shows how it is possible through the work of the Palmyra Portrait Project to establish modern historiographies for objects that otherwise have none. This will be achieved by recreating the object biography on a Palmyrene portrait that was sold at an auction, which did not include reference to previous owners. The portrait was last registered on the art market in 1982, when it was sold through Sotheby's in London, with no historiography. The central idea of object biographies is to show how and why changes of the values and meanings assigned to objects influence their historiographies. This is important, as it shows that the history of objects is transformed through human interaction with them. A crucial point in the histories of ancient objects is the moment of their rediscovery through excavation. From this point on, their modern histories begin, and they are included in new social processes and contexts such as collecting, sale, exhibitions, research, and so forth. The Palmyra Portrait Project has compiled the most extensive corpus of Palmyrene portraits, including information on modern contexts in public and private collections and on the art market. This allows the confirmation, refutation, or even reestablishment of modern histories on the Palmyrene portraits that appear on the art market.

SESSION 7E
Field Reports from Italy

CHAIR: To be announced

Archaeological Investigation at the "Villa of the Antonines" at Ancient Lanuvium: The 2016 Season

Deborah Chatr Aryamontri, Montclair State University, *Timothy Renner*, Montclair State University, *Carla Mattei*, Independent Researcher, *Alessandro Blanco*, Independent Researcher, and *Carlo Albo*, Independent Researcher

The seventh field season at the "Villa of the Antonines" in Genzano di Roma, conducted in 2016 by Montclair State University, has considerably broadened our knowledge and understanding of this Antonine-era imperial complex at the 18th mile of the Via Appia. Investigations in the two principal sectors currently under study are increasingly corroborating with tantalizing evidence the traditional identification of this site as the residence ad Lanuvium of the Antonine family, where the emperors Antoninus Pius and Commodus were born. This attribution was once based only on the scanty information of the *Historia Augusta* and the poorly documented discovery in 1701, in these surroundings, of the Antonine family marble portraits now in the Capitoline Museums in Rome.

In the Thermae/Amphitheater sector, the investigation continued to concentrate on the amphitheater, which, despite its small dimensions, was provided with a velarium and a series of galleries and rooms beneath the arena. The 2016 explorations have especially shown the complexity of the underground spaces, where the expected mirror image, on the east, of the plan of the western half has failed to emerge. Instead, we have identified new walls with different orientations and a possible gallery that led beneath the arena from an elliptical stairwell located in the northeast part of the cavea.

In the sector higher uphill, where the view down to the amphitheater and baths, with the distant sea as the backdrop would make an ideal setting for the residential quarters of the villa complex, two years of excavation since 2014 have brought to light rooms decorated with black-and-white mosaics. Two of these presented sophisticated geometric patterns with comparanda at Villa Adriana in Tivoli, while a third included the representation of a Medusa placed in a niche in a context with curved walls of difficult interpretation. In 2016, the continuation of the investigation in targeted areas in the surroundings of this niche has confirmed the hypothesis that it is part of a very large circular room (radius of ca. 11 m), surrounded by at least four niches. These latest findings confirm the archaeological importance of this area, close to which it will hopefully be possible to rediscover the original location where the emperors' marble busts were found and therefore prove without further doubt that our site is the long-lost villa of the Antonines where Commodus first indulged his passion for killing animals in front of spectators.

The Upper Sabina Tiberina Project: Fifth Excavation Season at Vacone

Candace Rice, University of Edinburgh, *Dylan M. Bloy*, Rutgers University, *Tyler Franconi*, University of Oxford, *Matthew Notarian*, Hiram College, and *Gary D. Farney*, Rutgers University

The Upper Sabina Tiberina Project's fifth season of excavation at the Roman villa in Vacone, Italy, exposed two important new parts of the villa, a central peristyle and a second cryptoportico, and provided new evidence for phasing and changes to agricultural production over the life of the villa.

Excavation on the main terrace revealed the stylobate and the northern corner column of a peristyle. The black-and-white mosaic pattern that decorated the covered floor of the peristyle, along with its ancient repair in larger red tesserae, was found on three sides of the peristyle. This mosaic and the mortar from the attachment of missing columns along the stylobate allow us to confidently restore a 14.4m^2 peristyle with five columns along each side, enclosing an 8m^2 courtyard. The peristyle now links rooms excavated at the front and back of the site, improving our understanding of the villa's overall layout and plan.

Furthermore, investigation of the northeastern limit of the lower cryptoportico revealed the existence of a second cryptoportico that had been previously obscured by stone collapse. The new cryptoportico measures 21.6 x 3.5 m and joins with the other cryptoportico to form an L-shaped cave type of *basis villae*, confirming our belief that the terrace on which the villa stands was an artificial construction. The far end of this new cryptoportico ends in an arched doorway exiting toward the villa's productive area. Excavation inside this damaged structure was deemed unsafe; thus, we proceeded to fully document it through photogrammetric modeling.

The completed excavation of several reception rooms within the domestic area yielded substantial painted plaster collapse, now under study. A coin of Commodus dating to 184 C.E., the latest coin on the site, was found on the mosaic floor under this collapse, supporting the ceramic data in demonstrating that the villa was inhabited until the end of the second century C.E.

Continued excavation in the productive zone of the villa revealed a large wine production area. A pressing floor was built over the olive oil press in a second imperial phase, indicating a change in productive strategies by the villa's occupants. The floor emptied into a vat with a capacity of about 900 liters.

Lastly, we made advances in site recording techniques through the implementation of photogrammetric orthorectified photographs and three dimensional modeling of all excavation trenches and some of the standing remains.

Four Seasons of Excavation at the Villa del Vergigno (Montelupo Fiorentino, Tuscany)

C. McKenzie Lewis, Concordia College

The Villa del Vergigno is a large *villa rustica* located 20 km west of Florence. The first investigations at the site, conducted between 1989 and 1994, uncovered a 55 x 15 m structure with 16 rooms and a bath complex, four kilns, and a grape/olive press. In 2013, the University of Wyoming, Sistema Museale di Montelupo Fiorentino, and Cooperativa ICHNOS reopened the site to excavate the "agricultural" area adjacent to the Villa and to analyze and catalogue approximately 200 unstudied boxes of materials found in the excavations of the early 1990s.

Our analysis of the materials found during the first excavations, together with data from 2013 to 2016, suggests that the villa's first phase of occupation dates to the last two centuries B.C.E. and first century C.E. It is possible that the site's foundation was part of the episodes of Roman colonization of Fiesole and Florence between 82 and 30 B.C.E., yet ceramics in the foundation trenches of the villa's earliest walls and amphoras suggest an earlier foundation date in the middle or late second century B.C.E. The area for wine production is datable to the site's initial phase.

In the second century C.E., a reworking of the "residential" area occurred that enlarged the bath complex. At this time, the "agricultural" sector saw its peak in production of wine, domestic ceramics, and amphoras. An analysis of the stamped terra sigillata found in the first and second phases indicates that the regional trade network for fine wares here in the mid Arno Valley shifted from Arezzo to Pisa during the middle of the first century C.E., well after the establishment of new workshops at, and despite the villa's proximity to, Pisa.

The 2013-2016 excavations uncovered walls of a rectangular structure most likely built in late antiquity on the edge of a depression 10 m in diameter, probably part of the last phase of the villa. The enormous depression/landfill has remains of building material, charcoal, pottery, animal bones, glass, fragments of iron, lead, and bronze that likely reflect episodes of spoliation. A dolium stamp, not yet identified, was found in this landfill, which can provide additional information about activity during the site's final phase. Amphoras from Empoli and North Africa indicate that the site was economically productive during the early fourth century C.E., and coins suggest activity at the site into the fifth century C.E.

Investing to Innovate: Results of the Marzuolo Archaeological Project, 2016

Astrid Van Oyen, Cornell University, *Rhodora G. Vennarucci*, University of Arkansas, and *Gijs Tol*, University of Melbourne

In July 2016, the Marzuolo Archaeological Project (MAP) in collaboration with the Comune of Cinigiano and under the auspices of the Soprintendenza per i Beni Archeologici della Toscana launched its first of five seasons of excavation at the Roman-period rural site of Podere Marzuolo (Grosseto, Italy), where production of iconic terra sigillata pottery has been attested in both an experimental and a standardized phase. Over the next several years, MAP aims to disentangle the different parameters that together formed the nexus of innovation in the Roman world through an integrated approach, including targeted excavation, archaeometric and spatial analysis, and archaeobotanical and zooarchaeological analysis, focused on generating high-resolution data.

MAP's first season of excavation was undertaken to better understand the spatial and chronological relations within the site, with significant results for our understanding of the innovation process. While previous work conducted by the Roman Peasant Project (2012–13) indicated that the site's most substantial building in *opus reticulatum* masonry style was sunken into a thick, homogeneous leveling layer of brown silty clay, the latest excavations confirmed that a series of open-fronted rooms doubling as commercial and domestic spaces were constructed in the same uniform layer. Based on layout, size, building style, and phasing, the latter structure can now be related to a strip-row building approximately 80 m to the east previously associated with evidence of terra sigillata production in an experimental phase (ca. 30 - 10 B.C.E.). All of this demonstrates that the site was planned as a single deliberate event, paired with considerable investment and foresight, at an early stage in its production history in the Early Imperial period.

On the one hand, this reconstruction demonstrates the need for a more central place for the concept of investment in models of innovation in the Roman world. Investment as a parameter is hard to pinpoint archaeologically and has therefore often escaped serious historical consideration. The site-wide restructuration at the rural production site of Marzuolo offers a rare glimpse of how deliberate acts of investment profoundly affected community dynamics and economic potential. On the other hand, the evidence of Marzuolo cautions against copying neoclassical models relating investment to return and, in the case of craft goods like terra sigillata pottery, to large-scale distribution. Investment at Marzuolo would have driven innovation and rural connectivity, but not necessarily with a view to large-scale trade.

Revisiting Roccagloriosa: 2016 Site Report

Tanya Henderson, University of Alberta, *Stefano Ferrari*, Field Director, *Carlo Rosa*, Geoarchaeologist, and *Francesco Scelza*, Field Archaeologist

Located in the hinterland of the Gulf of Policastro in Western Lucania, the site of Roccagloriosa documents the sociopolitical organization of a Lucanian settlement from the fifth century B.C.E. to the fortification of the settlement in the fourth century B.C.E. and its eventual decline in the later third century B.C.E. Initial investigations of the site began in 1971, focusing on the visible fortifications and exploration of a habitation area outside the fortifications. From 1976 to 1991, further investigations contributed significant evidence on the sociopolitical organization of Lucanian settlements in the fourth century B.C.E. In 2016, the site was revisited to further document the architectural structures on the Central Plateau, an area that has yielded a number of significant finds in previous years, including a fragmentary bronze tabula in the Oscan language describing important institutional developments and an elite residential structure containing a shrine, altar, and large votive deposit. The research program for 2016 included a series of geophysical testing to identify areas for further investigation and test trenches to substantiate prior geophysical testing. This paper presents the results of the 2016 season and contextualizes the evidence into the preexisting framework of the Central Plateau and within the larger historical significance of the site.

British Archaeological Project at Grumentum: A Report on the 2014, 2015, and 2016 Seasons

Taylor Lauritsen, AIA Member at Large, and *Massimo Betello*, State University of New York at Buffalo

Grumentum is a Roman town situated on a low plateau rising above the right bank of the Agri River in western Basilicata. Founded as a *colonia* in the 50s B.C.E., by the second century C.E. it had emerged as one of the most important urban centers in Lucania and was provided with a range of public buildings (forum-basilica, theater, amphitheater, etc.) that reflected this status. These monumental structures were the focus of excavation campaigns throughout the 20th century, and while they provide useful insights into Grumentum's social and political history, many questions regarding the town's economic development and the composition of its peripheral neighborhoods remain unanswered.

The British Archaeological Project at Grumentum (BAPG) was initiated in 2014 in an effort to address some of these questions. The project, which operates under an agreement between Cardiff University, the Soprintendenza Archeologica della Basilicata, and the Comune di Grumento Nova, aims to explore the growth of Grumentum's commercial and industrial economies between the Late Republic and the Early Dominate. For the past three seasons, the BAPG has been excavating a mercantile quarter situated to the east of the forum. During the 2014 campaign, we identified the primary architecture in the area, including a large building positioned parallel to the forum and a wide road flanked by a colonnade immediately to its west. In 2015, we refined the chronology of the High Imperial and Late Antique phases and inserted a new trench to the west of the road. Previous excavations between the road and the forum's eastern wall suggested that glass and metal production were occurring in this area, and this conclusion was supported by the materials that we recovered from the 2015 trench. For the 2016 season, we are expanding the scale of our excavations substantially. New trenches have been established along the facade of the building and the line of the colonnade to test their continuity. Explorations in the building's western rooms are seeking to identify activity areas within the structure, and further work in the zone to the west of the road is shedding more light on industrial production in the neighborhood.

This paper summarizes the results of these three seasons, offering some preliminary thoughts on the nature of Grumentum's urban economy and the town's role within regional and long-distance trade networks during the Imperial period.

Salapia (Trinitapoli, Italy) in Late Antiquity: Interpreting Urban Transformations in Their Broader Apulian Context

Darian Marie Totten, McGill University, *Roberto Goffredo*, University of Foggia, and *Giovanni De Venuto*, University of Foggia

Recent research has focused on how to define and interpret urban change in late antiquity and the implications of such transformations for social, religious, economic, and political life. In the context of southern Italy–specifically Apulia-the ebbs and flows of urban life can also be applied to debates about the standing of the province within the reorganized political landscape of the Diocletianic reforms, and the economic role of the province in internal and transmarine connections. The coastal site of Salapia can contribute an example from the fourth to sixth centuries C.E. to help elaborate models of economic conditions within the town, the province, and the Adriatic Basin that have long been lacking good evidence from coastal contexts. Textual sources have left a mixed impression of Salapia in late antiquity, with some arguing that the ancient itineraries might point to a decline at Salapia starting in the third century, while conversely, three named bishops from the fourth to fifth century offer an impression of continued urban health. Evidence from archaeology is then necessary to flesh out the broader picture of urban life and community. Over three years of excavation, the remains of a domus, adjacent artisanal space, and a shop front speak to the complexity of modifications and reworkings over time. While the fourth century saw the continued maintenance and investment in the remanaging of these spaces, as well as good evidence of continued transmarine contacts at scale, by the fifth century the site experienced progressively radical transformations. Rooms of the domus were occupied by structures supported by wooden posts; the artisanal space was slowly abandoned; and middens filled in once-inhabited spaces. By the sixth century C.E., the break with the previous urban layout was nearly total, with habitation persisting in new forms. Therefore, the material remains speak to the continued community at the site, even if with the passage of time it assumed a less urban and more inward-looking aspect. When contextualized within the broader trends elsewhere in Apulia, Salapia's circumstances were not unique, with the fifth and especially sixth centuries bringing the most noticeable shifts in evidence of economic and social activity. Such changes likely influenced the intensity and character of connections among places within the province, touching sites on both the interior and the coast and providing strong indication of their economic symbiosis and shared trajectory.

SESSION 7F
Domestic Spaces and Their Decoration in the Roman World

CHAIR: *Brenda Longfellow*, University of Iowa

Space and Graffiti in the House of the Gladiators at Pompeii

Jennifer Trimble, Stanford University

The House of the Gladiators (V.5.3) at Pompeii offers extraordinary but neglected evidence of life in a gladiatorial training school (*ludus*). The late 19th-century excavations unearthed architecture, wall paintings, artifacts, and more than 140 graffiti written by and about the gladiators who lived and trained there (*CIL* 4 4280–4427). The House of the Gladiators thus offers the most detailed material evidence we have of life in a *ludus*—far more detailed than what survives at the Quadriporticus at Pompeii (where the gladiators seem to have moved after the earthquake of 62 C.E.), the partially excavated Ludus Magnus in Rome, or the *ludus* at Carnuntum, known only through remote sensing.

In this talk, I analyze the spatial distribution of the graffiti found in the House of the Gladiators, an approach pioneered in recent scholarship. This mapping shows that the graffiti are heavily concentrated in the south wing of the portico surrounding the central training ground. Inter alia, this suggests that the southern entrance into the training ground was the one in daily use by the fighters; the entrance on the northeast had a different purpose. By far the most graffiti were found on the southwest corner column of the peristyle; this column's graffiti are also more interactive and joking than others in the building, and this is also the only place where outsiders' graffiti are attested. I suggest accordingly that the large room directly opposite this column was the refectory and that the gladiators had more time here for socializing and interacting, before and after meals. The outsiders' graffiti can be explained by the custom of the public banquet of the gladiators the night before an arena spectacle; visitors could come and see the gladiators eat what was possibly their last meal, and some of those visitors left their mark here. Finally, while most of the graffiti were written on the columns of the peristyle from the portico side, several were written from inside the peristyle training ground. Those graffiti are also serious in their content and tone; they suggest that the practice of incising graffiti was part of the lived experience of training and of the culture of this community.

These findings amplify our archaeological and social understanding of *ludi*. They provide insight into the daily lives of gladiators in this training school, their preoccupations and hopes, and their interactions with each other.

Toppling a Pompeian Icon: The True Story of the Casa del Chirurgo

Michael A. Anderson, San Francisco State University

Long-venerated as an iconic, early example of the so-called Roman atrium house, the Casa del Chirurgo has been a keystone of Pompeian and Roman domestic architectural history since its discovery in 1770. Its Sarno stone facade, its seemingly canonical layout, and its apparent lack of significant later alterations have been seen by many scholars, from Mau and Nissen to Gros and De Albentiis, as proof of its great antiquity. Similarly, the method of construction in Sarno stone *opus quadratum* and *opus africanum* has made the house a linchpin in the sequence of building materials and techniques that yet influences archaeological research in Pompeii, a role that was strengthened further by excavations conducted by Maiuri in 1929.

Archaeological investigations in the Soprintendenza Archeologica di Pompei, were directed specifically to reassess the dating of this house and to uncover the actual steps in its developmental history. Through comprehensive stratigraphic excavation and architectural analysis, considerable evidence was produced for the earliest phases of the area and its development over time.

Now, 10 years after the end of excavation and on the verge of final publication, work by a number of specialists on these results, coordinated by the present author, has produced a very different story from that long accepted by scholarship. Far from being an early relic, the Casa del Chirurgo actually dates no earlier than the end of the third to the middle of the second century B.C.E., a fact that is reinforced by new evidence of an earlier structure that preceded it. Nor can the Casa del Chirurgo continue to be seen as a paragon of the atrium-house layout, since it only really became canonical during the Augustan age, apparently during an archaizing "retrofit" so convincing that it has served to deceive modern scholarship.

This paper presents the actual history of this famous house, demonstrating that while the Casa del Chirurgo may no longer be able to retain its traditional role, it nevertheless has a vital contribution to make to Pompeian and Roman archaeology. The true history of the house is one of changing priorities, of builders and responses to earthquake damage, of household identity in Roman Pompeii, of industrialization and commercialization that is ultimately far more valuable than its original role as Pompeii's oldest house.

Competing in Clay: Sacred and Private Uses of Architectural Terracotta at Fregellae

Sophie Crawford Waters, University of Pennsylvania

When Arvid Andrén published his monumental *Architectural Terracottas from Etrusco-Italic Temples* in 1940, terracotta decoration was generally thought to have been limited to religious structures. Excavations over the last several decades have now overturned this notion, and architectural terracottas continue to be uncovered in both public and domestic contexts from the Late Orientalizing period into the Early Empire. More than 70 years after its publication, however, Andrén's work still has not been superseded, and the private usage of architectural terracottas in the Mid to Late Republic has never been systematically examined. This paper takes a first step by considering the case study of Fregellae—one of the few Mediterranean sites to preserve architectural terracottas from contemporaneous domestic and religious structures.

The Latin colony of Fregellae was founded in 328 B.C.E. on the banks of the Liris River, about 100 km southeast of Rome. Excavations beginning in 1978 revealed a number of significant structures, including the forum, comitium, aqueduct, and Sanctuary of Asclepius. Fragments of a remarkable series of terracotta friezes, approximately 0.185 m high, were found in several elite houses in the city center. These appear to be linked thematically and include depictions of ships, soldiers in Roman and Hellenistic armor, trophies flanked by Victories, tripods topped by an omphalos, and even an elephant. Filippo Coarelli has argued that they reference the First Syrian War and can be dated just after 190 B.C.E.

Despite their rarity and inherent interest, the Fregellae friezes have received relatively little scholarly attention. When they are discussed, it is typically in the context of a historical argument. This paper takes a new approach by examining the friezes within the broader framework of architectural terracotta decoration at Fregellae: What do they reflect and signify within their community? How do they speak in dialogue with other terracotta representations in the city? Using comparative evidence from sites like Civitalba, Pompeii, Cosa, and Praeneste, I argue for an innovative adaptation of "public" art at Fregellae, which drew from traditions in terracotta and other decorative media to create a new mode of aristocratic display. This approach illuminates the often-slippery boundaries between "domestic" and "religious" spaces within the broader context of competition between elites and even between towns. Fregellae offers the rare opportunity to study private and public terracottas in tandem, greatly enriching our understanding of this popular republican art form and its role in the visual landscape of central Italy.

Keeping Up with the Joneses: Decoration and Renovation in the Houses of Roman Sicily

Nicole Berlin, Johns Hopkins University

Although Sicily had been a Roman province since the third century B.C.E., it was only in the wake of the Emperor Augustus' visit in 21 B.C.E. that the island became culturally integrated into the Roman empire. While the written record for this dynamic period is silent, archaeological material reveals that Sicilians began to draw inspiration from the Italian mainland as opposed to the kingdoms of the Hellenistic East. The houses of Sicily, with their in situ mosaic floors and frescoed walls, provide a fruitful body of evidence to study the island's changing position within the Mediterranean during the early Roman empire.

In this paper, I examine two townhouses on Sicily, one at Tyndaris and the other at Soluntum, that were dramatically altered in the Julio-Claudian period. Based on these case studies, I argue that the Sicilians under the Roman empire actively participated in their own identity formation within the domestic sphere. They accomplished this through the juxtaposition of preexisting or "Hellenistic" decorative elements and newer "Italic" mosaics and frescoes. House B at Tyndaris features both polychrome mosaics from the house's first phase in the second century B.C.E. and black-and-white pavements installed in the mid first century C.E. In the House of Leda at Soluntum, Fourth Style frescoes depicting the Dioscouri and Leda coexisted with much earlier mosaics. One such pavement in the House of Leda is Soluntum's only in situ emblema representing an Alexandrian astronomic instrument from the late second century B.C.E. The comparison of these two residences demonstrates that Sicilians in the Roman period simultaneously embraced new trends from the Italian Peninsula while also deliberately preserving "historical" decorative elements within their houses.

Traditionally, the older and newer features within Sicilian houses have been studied in isolation, with those from the second century B.C.E. labeled "Hellenistic" and those from later periods "Roman." However, for the viewer in the Roman period such elements were encountered as a singular domestic ensemble. I argue that the hybrid effect of adjacent old and new elements within Sicilian domestic space was a deliberate and desired phenomenon at both House B at Tyndaris and the House of Leda at Soluntum. New decorative ensembles and spatial arrangements within preexisting houses, implemented during the early Roman Imperial-period, created a heterogeneous and Sicily-specific experience at the crossroads of the eastern and western Mediterranean.

Pompeii's Iconotextual Wall Paintings: Dialogues of Image, Text, and City

Carolyn MacDonald, University of New Brunswick

This paper examines Pompeii's iconotextual wall paintings, a rich corpus of frescoes intentionally inscribed with texts in Greek or Latin. Recently, individual examples have featured in work on Pompeii's literary landscape; on the interplay of image and text in antiquity; and on the different aesthetic practices of elite and nonelite members of Roman society. However, there is as yet no comprehensive study or even complete list of Pompeian iconotexts, despite their enormous potential to shed new light on how Roman viewers interacted with the artworks and images that filled their public and domestic spaces. This paper takes a first step toward a more comprehensive approach, by investigating the significance of language choice. Do Pompeii's Greek and Latin iconotexts operate in different ways? Do they invite different kinds of response from their viewers? Why, in pairing texts with images, did artists and viewers inscribe certain visual-verbal interactions in Greek, and others in Latin?

To answer these questions, I begin by briefly surveying different types of Pompeian iconotexts, which range from very simple pairings of figures with name-tag inscriptions to far more complex combinations of images and literary texts. I then focus on three particularly revealing case studies: Exedra y of the Casa degli Epigrammi Greci, where five sacro-idyllic scenes were accompanied by Greek epigrams; the Caupona of Salvius, which featured four tavern vignettes animated by Latin inscriptions; and Cubiculum i of the Casa di Marco Lucrezio Frontone, where a pinax of Pero and Micon is paired with a Latin epigram. My analysis draws on W.J.T. Mitchell's insights into the way that images "hail" and so define their viewers, seeking specific forms of response. I argue that, whereas the frescoes of Exedra y invite their viewer to play the learned Greek and enter the world of the epigrammatic garland, the Latin iconotexts create dialogues with other sights and spaces of the city, embedding their viewer in the here and now of Pompeii. Compared in this way, the iconotexts shed new light on the entanglement of viewing with the production and performance of cultural distinction in a Roman city.

New Pavements and New Discoveries in the House of the Large Oecus (Utica, Tunisia)

Nichole Sheldrick, University of Oxford

Between 2010 and 2016, the Tunisian-British Utica Project, a joint effort between the University of Oxford and the Institut National du Patrimoine (INP) of Tunisia, has conducted excavations at the Roman city of Utica. One of several areas investigated by the project was the House of the Large Oecus, which is the largest known from Roman-period Utica. The house was partially excavated in the 1950s and investigated again in the 1970s, at which time a number of impressive mosaic and marble pavements were fully or partially uncovered and subsequently published in the *Corpus des Mosaïques de Tunisie*. Vol.1.2 *Utique* (Tunis 1974). The primary aims of the Tunisian-British Utica Project in this area were therefore to complete the previous excavations that had been left unfinished and to reassess the state of the pavements, many of which had degraded significantly since they were first uncovered.

Over several seasons of excavation in the house, the Tunisian-British Utica Project has uncovered and reexamined several of the previously published pavements, and four previously unseen pavements have been revealed. In this paper, I present the preliminary results of these investigations, which have added significantly to what was already known about the décor of the house and potentially also the functions of the rooms in which they were installed. Of particular significance was the discovery of an upper-story mosaic that had collapsed in large fragments into the room below. A digital reconstruction of this pavement from the fragments has provided useful insight into the appearance of an upper-story room, an aspect of Roman houses that is often missing from the archaeological record.

Our investigations have also revealed new information about the life of these pavements and the house subsequent to its primary occupation. Visible repairs to some of these pavements and later, intrusive features that have disturbed them, including a possible mill and a number of later silos, give us clues as to the long occupation of the house and its reuse in later periods. Finally, an important part of the project was the consolidation and conservation of many of the pavements in order to ensure their long-term preservation, and many have now been reburied for their protection.

A Consideration of Late-Mythological Statuary in Villas of the Iberian Peninsula

Sarah E. Beckmann, University of Pennsylvania

Late-mythological statuettes produced in the workshops of Asia Minor have been found throughout the Roman world and identified as a particular genre of Late Antique sculpture in recent scholarship. In a study of Late Roman villas in Aquitaine, Lea Stirling suggested that *domini* collected these objects and valued them as the insignia of *paideia*, such that the statuettes evince the habit of elite Romans across the empire. In this paper, I examine two Iberian villas with late-mythological statuettes to test previous hypotheses: Quinta das Longas in eastern-central Lusitania (Elvas, Portugal), and Valdetorres de Jarama in the Spanish plateau. My research suggests that these assemblages have much to add to our understanding of the late-mythological statuette genre and to our characterizations of the elite who acquired them.

Both Quinta das Longas and Valdetorres de Jarama were excavated in the modern era and record late occupation phases loosely dated to the fourth century. Sculptural parallels can be found across both sites. Fragments of an anguiped are documented at both, though iconographic disparities signal a giant at Valdetorres and a possible triton at Quinta das Longas. Fragments of a panther at both sites may suggest a Bacchus group, an understudied type know primarily from a statuette base in Maiden Castle. At Valdetorres, fragments of an eagle likely belong to a Ganymede group, but one that varies from the well-known late-mythological statuette at Carthage. Finally, fragments of a griffin at each point to an unidentified late-mythological group, supplementing the hypothetical corpus of late-mythological types in production.

With these parallels, previous scholarship has connected both to the broader phenomenon of Late Antique collecting. I argue, however, that to do so in Iberia is problematic. Statuary finds are infrequent among Iberia's many Late Roman villas; contemporary sculptures are virtually unknown. Although late-mythological statuettes are documented in two assemblages, these two sites do not attest to wide circulation of these objects in Iberia. It is possible that the *domini* of Valdetorres and Quinta das Longas had special access to contemporary statuettes and participated in imperial bureaucracy. Yet this hypothesis must be reconciled with the material assemblage of each villa, which suggests greater participation in local socioeconomic networks than in trans-regional exchange, because statues are virtually the only imports. Thus, I question our understanding of statuary as a tool of a homogenous elite, and the definition of "elite" identity more broadly in the later Roman era.

Architecture and Mosaics at the Late Roman Villa of Santiago da Guarda (Ansião, Portugal): A Promising Case Study

Filomena Limão, Universidade Nova de Lisboa, and *Rodrigo Pereira*, Câmara Municipal de Ansião

The site of Santiago da Guarda, located in the municipality of Ansião, central Portugal, owes its name to the Routes of Santiago de Compostela. Its most appealing attraction is the 16th-century Manueline-style palace. An outstanding set of geometric mosaics belonging to a Late Antique Roman villa was discovered beneath the palace between 2002 and 2005. So, at the so-called Monumental Complex of Santiago da Guarda, three different chronological layers overlap, configuring an original palimpsest.

The architectural design of the *pars urbana* of the villa dated to the turn of the fifth century C.E. evidences the richness and finely detailed tastes of the owners. The extended mosaic pavements visible in situ display lively colorful geometric patterns allowing virtual reconstitutions. A research team composed by the principal archaeologist of the villa and art historians has just started work on the villa's architecture and decoration. The objective of this work is to prepare the corpus of mosaics of the villa of Santiago da Guarda. Consequently, the purposes of this paper are to introduce the main problems concerning the architectural planning of the *pars urbana* of the villa and to describe the mosaics' ornamental motives.

Despite being still in its early stages, the comparative study of architecture and decoration of the villa of Santiago da Guarda will shed new light on the social and economic transactions, artistic trends, and workshops between the *villae* and the cities to which they were politically connected in the western part of the Roman province of Lusitania during antiquity.

SESSION 7G
Bodies, Costumes, and Ideals in the Roman Empire

CHAIR: To be announced

Ethnic Identity, Social Identity, and the Aesthetics of Sameness in the Funerary Monuments of Roman Freedmen

Devon A. Stewart, Angelo State University

The transition from servitude to citizenship was one of the most important transformations in a Roman slave's life. Upon manumission, the slave gained recognition as a social and legal entity and assumed a host of rights and privileges she or he previously had been denied. Yet Roman freedmen occupied an ambiguous position in Roman society, and some indicators of their former servitude could not be set aside so easily. Rome's nonelite population was ethnically diverse, and Roman sources reflect attitudes that link slaves and physical alterity, especially non-Italic ethnicity. Yet some slaves eventually earned Roman citizenship, and for these freedmen the association of non-Italic ethnic identity with servile status must have been particularly difficult to reconcile. Although they became Roman at the time of manumission, removing the stigma of otherness at least theoretically, their physical appearance did not change. In the person of the manumitted slave, the relationship between ethnic identity and social identity becomes much more fraught.

This paper explores one strategy by which some Roman freedmen negotiated the transformation from slavery to citizenship, otherness to Romanitas, through their funerary monuments. From the Late Republic through the Augustan period, the group tomb relief was the most popular type of figural tomb monument among freedmen patrons. Scholars have recognized the lack of physiognomic variation among the subjects of these portraits, which usually has been attributed to the direct replication of aristocratic models by non-Roman freedman patrons. However, commissioning a portrait is a potent act of self-definition, especially in a funerary context, where these monuments are meant to act as lasting memorials to an individual or individuals' memories. In this paper, I argue that freedmen patrons and the artists they employed deliberately omitted features that might identify them as ethnically non-Italic to a Roman audience in order to reinforce their assimilation into Roman society. The rejection of non-Italic physiognomic characteristics in favor of more characteristically Roman portrait features visualized the intangible transformations of social and legal status freedmen underwent at the time of manumission. Moreover, it emphasized membership in a closed set of social groups, all closely defined by the particular social and artistic context of the city of Rome.

There and Back Again: Messages of Labor and Leisure Through Mythic Conflation at Villa A of Oplontis

Zoe Jenkins, University of Michigan

The famous Villa A at Oplontis was home to an impressive collection of Roman art. Previous studies have called attention to numerous thematic connections running through its artistic program, such as the possibility that certain sculptures purposefully blur the lines between mortals and immortals. In this paper, I investigate another example of such a conflation, in this case between Bacchus and Hercules, which brings to light a visual commentary on the perceived roles of villas in the Late Republican and Early Imperial periods.

This study focuses on two sets of sculptures uncovered at the villa during the course of excavation. The first group comprises of four centaurs, two males and two females, while the second is two (almost) identical herm busts of Hercules. Through extensive comparanda and analysis, I demonstrate how these sculptures clearly exhibit both Bacchic and Herculean elements. For example, the two male centaurs possess Hercules' archetypal studded club, a lion-skin cape, and the carcass of a boar, while one of the female centaurs carries a lyre. Since centaurs, especially those playing music, were common additions to Bacchic processions, this group recalls both deities simultaneously. The herm busts are identified as Hercules through comparison with other known sculptures (e.g., the Lansdowne Hercules) but are wearing crowns of grape leaves, a common attribute of Bacchus. In addition to this analysis, I use other literary references and visual depictions (sarcophagi, mosaics, etc.) that feature the two deities together to reveal how this was a recognized connection in antiquity. Through such evidence, I demonstrate how this mythic conflation embodies two opposing yet complementary concepts tied to villas: leisure and labor.

During the period of Villa A, elite villas were, among many things, a respite from busy city life for aristocratic Romans. Despite this trend, however, the utilitarian origins of the Roman villa were never forgotten in their construction. As one sees in the works of ancient agronomists such as Varro and Columella, the ideal of the villa always incorporated levels of production. The imagery of Hercules and his labors, therefore, suits this desired perception of the villa while Bacchus, as the god of wine, embodies its luxurious nature. In this study, I present a preliminary analysis into how these sculptures provide insight into the idealized duality of the Roman villa and its perceived role in contemporary society.

The Pygmy Motif as Somatic Spectacle: Somatic Dialogues in the House of the Menander, Pompeii

Evan Jewell, Columbia University

The dwarfed figure of the "pygmy" that features as a motif in the many wall paintings and mosaics of Roman Pompeii (and elsewhere) has not failed to provoke wildly ranging explanations from archaeologists and art historians ever since it came to the attention of 19th-century scholars working at the buried town. The pygmy has been treated most consistently as a figure tied to the geographical region of Egypt and its traditional ethnographic and historical connotations, whether as a post-Actium Other, a symbol of fertility, a facet of Roman Egyptomania, or an Isiac icon. Most recently, the 19th-century notion of the pygmy as an *apotropaion* has been revived, wherein it functioned as an anthropoid *fascinum* that could provoke apotropaic laughter in human and demon viewers alike. Nevertheless, these interpretations have failed to fully appreciate the representational value of the pygmy for Roman viewers at its most basic level: the aberrant, marvelous body.

In this paper, I therefore first reassess the literary representations of dwarfed bodies in ancient Rome as "somatic spectacles," finding that the visual spectacle of the dwarfed body may offer a surer footing for reading the pygmy motif in Roman decorative contexts. Following recent work on the contextualization of Roman wall painting at Pompeii, in terms of both the decorative and spatial relationships in a given *domus*, the House of the Menander (I.10.4) will then provide a pilot for reading the pygmy motif as a somatic spectacle articulated in spatial and decorative contexts that showcased multiple, contrasting body types. Finally, I will focus on an early pygmy frieze in the bath suite of the house, which depicts scenes from Greek myth and is made all the more notable for the Greek *dipinti* identifying figures in the scene. This scene, I suggest, opens a line of conversation between the House of the Menander's aberrant pygmies and the ideal, epic bodies in the contemporaneous Iliac frieze from the House of the Cryptoporticus (I.6.2) across the street. In so doing, I argue that in contrast to previous scholarship, my somatic reading of the House of the Menander offers a more holistic interpretative framework, which can be replicated elsewhere to rearticulate the Roman rendition of the pygmy motif within its web of literary, spatial, and decorative relationships.

What on Earth Is He Wearing? Representing Attis in Second-Century Rome

Krishni Burns, University of Akron

The collection of votives discovered by Pietro Romanèlli's 1950s excavation within the second phase of the Magna Mater's temple on the Palatine is among the largest single collections of representations of the semidivine figure Attis (*Latomus* 70 [1964] 619 - 29). Consequently, the collection represents a substantial slice of the material attesting to Attis' position within Roman republican religion. As a gender-fluid Eastern deity and the foundational figure for the cult's eunuch priesthood, Attis was supposedly the antithesis of republican values and anathema to Roman culture. The disproportionally large presence of Attis in the votive material is usually accounted for by the necessity of following cultic tradition, even if it was distasteful to the cult's Roman followers. However, there is nothing "traditional" about the Attis figures' representation.

In his analysis of the Attis material available in the mid 1960s, Maarten Jozef Vermaseren describes the figurines as wearing oriental dress (*The Legend of Attis in Greek and Roman Art* [Leiden 1966] 14 - 15). "Oriental dress" is the phrase generally used to describe Attis' costume, but the phrase is a misnomer. Although a few of the Attis figures wear the emblematic Phrygian cap, they do not wear the traditional costume of the Phrygians found on Phrygian votives of the goddess' companion figures, nor the orientalizing *anaxyrides* used to depict Persians and Trojans on Greek vases. Most of the Attis figures are exotically dressed in a hooded, jumpsuit-like garment that is pinned together along the legs and often exposes the belly and genitals.

The overall appearance of the Attis figures is certainly orientalizing. Other pseudo eastern deities in later Roman religion, such as Mithras, wear the Phrygian cap. Likewise, the shape of the upper portions of the garment evokes another divine son worshiped in Hellenized Pergamon, the *cucullus*-wearing Telesphoros. However, the most striking features of the Attis votives' iconography, the garment's open front and pinned legs, are outside of the representation of any figure in any iconographic tradition. The votives' presentation is an invention of the minds of local Roman artists in the interest of creating an exoticized figure outside of any known cultural context. Rather than a concession to a newly imported tradition, the Attis votives represent the deliberate incorporation of a new type of pseudo-foreign divinity into Roman religion in the second century B.C.E.

Statues and Mosaics of Satyrs in Theaters During the Roman Empire

George W.M. Harrison, Carleton University

Much has been written about Silenus and satyrs on black-figure, red-figure, and south Italian vases. Discussion by authors such as Krumreich, Pechstein, and Seidensticker, Carpenter, Taplin, and Taplin and Wyles has restricted itself to vase paintings of the Classical and Late Classical periods that seem to represent performance of satyr drama, the lesser-known companion to Attic tragedy. Although the session on pictorial art at the 2016 Patras conference "Greek Satyr Play" comprised five papers on vases, several papers are beginning to show a growing awareness of the importance of satyrs and Silenus in art and literature during the Roman empire. This paper collects the evidence for satyrs in sculpture and mosaics during the Roman empire in theatrical contexts and in public rooms that were part of some theaters, or in dining rooms often adjacent to theaters. It makes the argument that one category of the statuary, especially, might have been used to mask the curtain during performances.

This paper first considers issues related to statuary in theaters during the Roman empire: Sear, for example, has recorded statues of Silenus and/or of satyrs at Este, Verona, Vienna, Baelo, Olisipo, Lyon, Scupi, Caere, Pompeii, Athens, and Amorgos. Although one would expect satyrs in theaters in the Greek East, the majority of surviving sculpture associated with theaters is in the Latin West. It is argued that this indicates that satyrs became "generic" adjuncts to Dionysus, patron of drama, and so ceased to be identified strongly with a specific Greek performative genre. Further, the secure first-century C.E. dates of many of the statues show that the late Julio-Claudians and Flavians were as interested in satyrs and Silenus as the well-documented repairs and elaborations of theaters of the so-called good emperors of the second century C.E.

This paper also considers the implications of why mosaic evidence for satyrs in dining areas adjacent to theaters begins at the moment when evidence for newly commissioned statues of satyrs and Silenus in theaters disappears. Daphne (near Antioch) is important since its mosaic program includes not just "generic" satyrs who merely establish the context but enticingly also some whose dress and companions strongly suggest the continued performance of satyr play and mime at a time when Christian apologists claimed to have closed the theaters.

SESSION 7H
Bronze Age and Iron Age Anatolia

CHAIR: To be announced

Urbanism and Power in Early Bronze Age Western Anatolia: New Evidence from Seyitömer Höyük

Laura K. Harrison, University of South Florida

In the Early Bronze Age III period, a trend toward urbanization crystallized in western Anatolia, leading to the rise of a type of settlement in which tightly packed row houses are arranged around a central open space. These protourban centers display signs of centralized planning and architectural elaboration and suggest the emergence of an elite social class. Although previous studies have successfully documented the distribution of these settlements in time and space and established typologies that highlight key formal and stylistic attributes of their architecture, less is known about the social significance of this type of settlement pattern. This paper introduces new data from the settlement of Seyitömer Höyük, in the Kütahya region of western Anatolia. It also reveals how movement and interaction in public and private spaces affected power relations during a period of incipient urbanization and sociopolitical change.

Lake Places: Hittite Imperial Wetland Projects and the Local Hydrology of Ilgın, Konya

Peri Johnson, University of Illinois Chicago, *Ömür Harmanşah*, University of Illinois Chicago, *Ben Marsh*, Bucknell University, and *Müge Durusu-Tanrıöver*, Bilkent University

One of the most monumental second-millennium earthwork projects in the Mediterranean world is the Köylütolu Dam, which lies in the western borderlands of the Hittite empire. A Hieroglyphic Luwian inscription found at the site in 1884 provisionally dates the monument to the time of Tudhaliya IV (1237 - 1209 B.C.E.). The 750 m long and 18 - 20 m high earthen embankment at Köylütolu spans a local drainage beginning at an abundant spring and has been investigated by the Yalburt Yaylası Archaeological Landscape Research Project since 2010. Fieldwork in 2015 demonstrated numerous problems with the design of the dam, and earlier coring did not encounter any lake sediments. It is clear that the dam never held any water. Fieldwork in 2016 surveyed settlements in the undulating limestone lowlands around the dam and found settlements at sites known as "gölyeri" (literally, "lake place"). These are ubiquitous geological formations where north-flowing groundwater emerges in depressions and creates localized wetlands. The Köylütolu embankment is built of the deep red and gray soils of the slopes and depressions themselves. This paper argues that the embankment, although designed as a dam to hold water as has long been assumed, was intended to create a lake place. The Köylütolu depression is, however, a swallow hole, and a lake place never emerged, nor did a settlement grow up around the depression. This paper situates the Köylütolu embankment within the context of a series of imperial projects in the borderlands of the Hittite empire. The Yalburt Project had previously documented another nearby project, the construction of a monumental fortress and lower walled settlement at Kale Tepesi, 3.5 km northwest of the embankment. In the 2016 season, an associated settlement of the masons of the fortress was surveyed, and the surface ceramics suggest a date a couple of centuries before the construction of the embankment. We thus suggest that the Köylütolu earthworks project must be understood in the light of long-term investments facilitated by empire but imagined according to local hydrological phenomena such as lake places. The fraught relationship between the two produced a monument of much labor but no fruit.

Pointed Headdress in Hittite Iconography

Hae Won Bang, Columbia University

There is general agreement among Hittitologists that the divine headdress in Hittite iconography takes a particular symbolic form, specifically that the pointed hat functions as an "unmistakable symbol of divinity" and a "characteristic of Hittite gods." A corollary to this consensus holds that the number of ornamental details on the pointed headdress is directly correlated with the cultic standing of the deity depicted. Regrettably, no systematic scholarly effort has hitherto been dedicated to a detailed examination of the iconography of the divine headdress in general, or of the various uses and disuses of the pointed hat in particular. Likewise unexamined is the question of what light these variations might shed on the cultic system and political dynamics of the Hittites. This paper will demonstrate that the Hittites deliberately applied the pointed headdress in specific circumstances and forms for the elucidation and assertion of certain political and cultic messages. These messages were conveyed by using the pointed hat strategically in portrayals of rulers, thereby asserting respective degrees of political authority, and by employing different forms of the pointed hat as representations of deities' ranks, identities, and cultural origins.

Active Phrygians and Passive Greeks

Simon Oswald, Notre Dame

A focus on early Phrygian epigraphy, material culture, and trade routes lends further support for the reintegration of this land locked kingdom into the Aegean-Mediterranean milieu and the idea of a significant Phrygian influence on Greek cultural development in Early Iron Age/archaic Greece. Rodney S. Young (*Hesperia* 38.2 [1969] 252 - 96) was an early advocate for this position, and recent work by Claude Brixhe (*CRAI* 148 [2004] 271 – 89) might suggest that the adaption and modification of the Phoenician abjad into an alphabet was a Phrygian, rather than a Greek, invention-the focus of this paper. Problems for such a position are perpetuated by the "single adaptor single time single place" theory of Lilian Jeffery (*Local Scripts of Archaic Greece* Oxford [1990]), which called for a location of Greek-Phoenician interface, excluding Phrygia for this very reason. The relatively recent decipherment of the Karian alphabet and new bastions of early Greek inscriptions, such as Methone, further complicate the picture, leading to an uncertain alphabetic landscape. Yet Phrygia continues to provide the most convincingly dated early alphabetic inscriptions, predating the earliest Greek by perhaps a generation.

Phrygian material culture offers further support in making the Phrygian adaption theory a viable one. The Phrygians emerge from hazy beginnings in the Late Bronze Age to occupy the heart of the old Hittite empire before its mysterious downfall. As well as iconographic borrowings, it is clear that the Phrygians were at least in part influenced by the literate Hittites in architecture and sculpture. Through the Early Iron Age the Phrygians had direct contact with (among others) the Luwian Kingdom(s), the Assyrians, and the Urartians and were thus exposed to a number of advanced, literate civilizations with clear connections in trade and artistic influence that precipitated the acumen of the Phrygian kingdom in the eighth century B.C.E. The orientalizing model traditionally advocates Eastern influence on the Greeks in art, yet there remains no explicit reason why this cannot extend to the most significant "Greek" invention of all: the alphabet.

This paper will illustrate materially three key points: a way by which the new Phrygian alphabet could have traveled to Greece (or at least have developed independently), reasons behind this development, and the evidence for the necessary Phrygian-Phoenician interface that represents an important yet more obscure link in the theory.

Reconstructing Social Stratigraphy and Political Dynamics in Middle Iron Age Anatolia: Evidence from Phrygian Rock-Cut Monuments

Damjan Krsmanovic, University of Leicester

The Early to Middle Iron Age (ca. 1200 - 550 B.C.E.) in Anatolia saw the development of a patchwork of cultural and sociopolitical entities throughout the geography following the end of the Hittite empire in central Anatolia and polities such as Wiluša, Šeha River Land, and Mira in the west. One prominent Iron Age entity was Phrygia, which arose in the Sakarya River region and is thought to have controlled much of central Anatolia in the Middle Iron Age (ca. 950 - 550 B.C.E.).

However, the foundation, nature, extent, and maintenance of Phrygia's political workings in the Early to Middle Iron Age remains a matter of debate, despite more than six decades of sustained archaeological research on the culture. Most of the discourse has been formed on the basis of evidence from a single site–Gordion, the presumed capital–and later Greek and Roman historical writings, rendering our understanding simultaneously illuminating and problematic.

However, some interesting suggestions on the nature of Phrygian political organization come from rock-cut monuments dating between the eighth and mid sixth centuries B.C.E., situated at Midas City-Yazılıkaya and neighboring locales in the Eskişehir, Kütahya, and Afyonkarahisar provinces. The terminology used to denote rulers and officials on rock-cut monuments in these locales provides a picture of the social stratigraphy at the time. Yet most of the discourse has focused on interpreting this terminology in relation to Indo-European linguistic descent, rather than its "real-time" sociopolitical value.

To that end, I shall discuss the sociopolitical implications of the terms of political authority found on the rock-cut monuments, taking into account archaeological evidence and theoretical perspectives on the nature of premodern political authority to generate alternative ideas on political dynamic in the 10th- to sixth century B.C.E. period in central Anatolia. I shall also discuss the spatial dimension of the inscriptions as embedded in the landscape and part of a discourse resulting from specific dynamics in the Middle Iron Age that resulted in the creation of inscribed landscape monuments.

Gold the First Day: Jewelry from Tumulus A at Gordion

Jane Hickman, University of Pennsylvania

On Monday, 27 March 1950, Penn archaeologist Rodney Young began excavations at Gordion in central Turkey. He focused on Tumulus A, because much of the soil on the mound had already been taken away by local villagers to make mudbricks. Young moved quickly; he was concerned that if he waited too long, the villagers would discover the tomb and inadvertently destroy the burial context. His decision to start with Tumulus A proved to be fortunate. In a 1 April 1950 letter to his colleague G. Roger Edwards, Young wrote, "Gold the first day…[from the burial of] a young damsel." By 6 April, the excavation of the tomb was complete, and the documentation of the finds began.

Tumulus A, about 31 m in diameter, contained the cremation burial of a young female and was dated ca. 540–520 B.C.E., the Late Phrygian period. She was buried with a horse-drawn funerary cart and many objects of value, including a religious statuette, a silver mirror, carved ivory inlays (perhaps for boxes), fine pottery, alabaster vases, spindlewhorls, and golden jewelry. Some of the jewelry was in pristine condition. Other pieces were burned black or melted. If the deceased had been wearing all the jewelry during the cremation, it would surely have melted beyond recognition.

Beautiful gold and electrum ornaments were recovered, among them small and large beads, boat-shaped earrings, numerous pendants in various shapes, fragments of loop-in-loop chains, and a perfectly preserved gold bracelet with lion-head finials. A few gold objects from Tumulus A have been referenced briefly in publications about Gordion, but this collection of objects has never been fully published. The writer is working on that study.

This paper describes the types of objects recovered and the specific context of the discoveries. The cremated remains were not studied in detail or retained; the burial is presumed to be female based on associated grave goods. Evidence will be offered that suggests the age, sex, and status of the individual buried in the tomb. Techniques employed in the manufacturing of more than 160 pieces of jewelry and the possibility of multiple workshops and imported objects will be discussed. Comparanda for several classes of distinctive objects—including two unusual pendants with a "double axe" motif—will be provided, attesting to Gordion's connections to southwest Anatolia and Greece.

Thoughts on the Appearance of Carian Social Groups in the Early Iron Age Bodrum Peninsula

J. Tristan Barnes, University of Missouri

The origins of the Carians as an ethnic or sociopolitical group have long been debated. Herodotus (1.171), for example, states that the Carians migrated to the mainland from the islands; on the other hand, the association between the Carians and the Hittite Karkisa in modern scholarship might suggest an autochthonous origin, but the relationship is uncertain. Studies of Carian self-identity have largely focused on later periods when inscriptional evidence and Hekatomnid political rule provide better evidence. Nevertheless, archaeological evidence in and around the Bodrum Peninsula suggests that Carian communities began to coalesce by the end of the Late Protogeometric period.

I propose that the social geography of the southeast Aegean during the Late Helladic IIIB and IIIC periods can shed light on the origins of a Carian socio political group around the Bodrum Peninsula. During this period, activity at Eleona-Langada on eastern Kos increased sharply, while comparable activity nearby on the mainland at Müskebi declined. Earlier studies have suggested that this respective increase and decrease in funerary activity represents a nucleation of social authority around the population at Kos Town at the expense of populations on the adjacent mainland. This trend continued until end of the Bronze Age; however, by the Late Protogeometric period the situation had reversed. During the Late Protogeometric period, less activity can be detected on eastern Kos, while new sites in and around the Bodrum Peninsula mark the appearance of new social elites in those areas. Because the forms of burial are slightly different at each new Carian cemetery, it is unlikely that the increase in funerary activity should be connected to the arrival of a single new population group. Instead, I propose that the weakening of regional authority on Kos at the end of the Bronze Age created a power vacuum in the Carian periphery. In response to this situation, multiple new elite groups arose within disparate mainland communities. I interpret the appearance of these new local elites as the beginning of a new sociopolitical Carian identity. This autochthonous development of local social structures is consistent with the Carians' own account of their origins, while social engagement with communities on Kos might account for the later tradition of immigration from the islands.

SESSION 7I: Workshop
Researching Ownership Histories for Antiquities in Museum Collections

Sponsored by the AIA Museums and Exhibitions Committee

MODERATOR: *David Saunders*, J. Paul Getty Museum, Los Angeles

Workshop Overview Statement

Building on the success of museum-related panels at recent annual meetings, the AIA Museums and Exhibitions Committee has organized a workshop on current approaches to provenance research. In light of numerous high-profile legal cases and repatriations, together with the policies developed by the Association of Art Museum Directors and the American Alliance of Museums, there is a growing expectation that museums should make available the ownership histories of their objects in a full and clear manner. Many institutions are actively engaged in online documentation projects for their antiquities, and this workshop will explore some of the methods and results, as well as challenges and pitfalls. Researching ownership histories for ancient objects has not received the investment seen for the World War II era, and institutions often lack the resources to undertake this work in a sustained fashion. Furthermore, information in museum files is often speculative or unconfirmed, and discussions regarding the best ways of presenting such information are much needed. Through a series of case studies addressing Greek,

Roman, Etruscan, Egyptian, and ancient Near Eastern artifacts, the participants will explore a broad variety of themes: objects for which ownership information has been "lost" and methods and resources for recovering it; the organization of research projects and the development of common standards; the value of terms such as "said to be"; and how the nuances and ambiguities so often inherent in this subject can be presented meaningfully to scholars, students, school groups, and the general public. More broadly, we hope that this workshop will encourage more open conversation among diverse museum professionals, academics, and field archaeologists with a view to developing guidelines and models for this work that can be shared across the community. A series of short papers will be presented from a variety of museum professionals and academics.

PANELISTS: *Judith Barr*, J. Paul Getty Museum, *Amy Brauer*, Harvard Art Museums, *Paul Denis*, Royal Ontario Museum, Toronto, *Carol Ng-He*, Oriental Institute of the University of Chicago, *John Hopkins*, Rice University, *Sarah Costello*, University of Houston, Clear Lake, *Paul Davis*, de Menil Collection, *Seth Pevnick*, Tampa Museum of Art, *Phoebe Segal*, Museum of Fine Arts, Boston, *Caroline Rocheleau*, North Carolina Museum of Art, and *Ann Brownlee*, University of Pennsylvania Museum

SESSION 7J
Interaction and Production in the Aegean

CHAIR: *Natalie Abell*, University of Michigan

Southern Aegean Connectivity and Cultural Dynamics During the Second Millennium B.C.E.: A Network Analysis Approach
Cristina D. Ichim, UCL Institute of Archaeology

During the Middle and Late Bronze Age, particular communities across the southern Aegean exhibit an intensifying convergence of cultural characteristics, marked by the development of a differentially shared vocabulary of material culture and practices-often referred to via the modern terms "Minoanization" and "Mycenaeanization." These cultural and historical processes are generally seen to represent either emigrating Cretans and Greek mainlanders or the active negotiation and adoption of externally derived cultural elements and practices by local communities, at what are consequently to be viewed as Minoanized and Mycenaeanized communities. These two main opposing perspectives–the colonialist and postcolonialist views–fail, however, to account for the role of the "-ized" communities in the formation or transformation of Minoan and Mycenaean cultures and the impact this interaction had on the perceived cultural core communities on Crete and the Greek mainland. The core-periphery model inherent in both these views sees a Minoan and Mycenaean core area as generating the full range of cultural and ethnic markers, circumscribed by concentric zones of decreasing integration; this is problematic, as it has the effect of homogenizing cultural variability and masking the variable processes involved in the creation of cultural and ethnic identities. This talk considers an alternative model–in many ways, both formally and informally, a network model–that has the potential to systematically analyze the extent to which communities across the whole southern Aegean Basin both differentially participate in, and contribute to, the development of a variably shared cultural discourse–what we identify as the Minoan and Mycenaean cultures. Taking the case of funerary practices at various communities across the whole southern Aegean from the Middle Helladic/Middle Minoan III to the Late Helladic/Late Minoan IIIA1 periods (ca. 1750 to 1350 B.C.E.), I both highlight the rich diversity of cultural expressions and eclectic borrowings and suggest a network methodology for unpacking and making sense of the underlying complex processes of cultural affiliation.

New Evidence for Middle Bronze Settlement on Kea

Evi Gorogianni, University of Akron, and *Tania Panagou*, Ephorate of Antiquities of Cyclades

The island of Kea has been of considerable interest in the discussion of the metals' trade and the establishment of connections between the palatial communities of Crete (and beyond) and the metalliferous area of Lavrion during the Middle Bronze Age. The established assumption, that the site of Ayia Irini after its reestablishment in the Middle Bronze II was pivotal in the facilitation of trade connections, was based on the fact that no major settlement had been detected on the northern part of the island or reported from the southern part. However, recently a Middle Bronze Age assemblage was discovered in the process of excavating Karthaia's ancient theater beneath the stone-built *koilon* of the fourth century B.C.E., an unexpected find that challenges the established assumption.

This paper presents the preliminary results of the study of this assemblage and discusses the implications of this discovery. The ceramic assemblage seems to date to Middle Minoan IIA/Middle Helladic II, a period contemporary with the reestablishment of Ayia Irini (Period IVa and b). Moreover, it seems to include a similar, though not identical, range of imports and does not survive, for whatever reason, into the succeeding phases of the Middle and Late Bronze Age. Therefore, this discovery offers an opportunity to reevaluate the evidence supporting the accepted model of settlement patterns during the Middle Bronze Age on Kea, as well as the role of Ayia Irini as the sole actor in the facilitation of trade and exchange between the metal-hungry parties on Crete and the source at Lavrion. Furthermore, it carries the promise of shedding more light on a dynamic period of the Bronze Age Aegean, a period that has been directly linked to intensification of demand in metals and exotic goods on the part of palatial communities on Crete.

A Holistic Approach to the Analysis of Koan Light-on-Dark/Dark-on-Light Pottery During the Late Bronze Age IA Period

Salvatore Vitale, University of Pisa

This paper employs a holistic approach to the analysis of Koan Light-on-Dark/Dark-on-Light pottery, a relatively poorly known class manufactured at the settlement of the "Serraglio" and widely distributed throughout the Aegean during the Late Bronze Age (LBA) IA Mature period. Within this study, I first reconstruct the complete *chaîne opératoire* from clay preparation to pottery consumption patterns. I then discuss the relevant data using different interpretative lenses, including mobility, practice theory, social agency, and cultural entanglement. Finally, I reassess the significance of Koan Light-on-Dark/Dark-on-Light pottery for understanding early Late Bronze Age potting practices and sociocultural developments at the "Serraglio" and in the wider southeast Aegean area.

Until recently, Koan Light-on-Dark/Dark-on-Light pottery was understood as a more or less direct imitation of Minoan ceramics and a uniform class in terms of manufacture, style, and consumption. This study portrays a more complex picture and suggests the occurrence of two distinct stages of production, corresponding respectively to LBA IA Early and LBA IA Mature. Common features within both phases include the exclusive use of Koan local tradition fabric mixes and forming techniques on the one hand and the creation of an entangled style on the other, which merged local with Minoan-type shapes and decorative treatments. During the second stage, besides the continuation of these features, a dramatic increase in the production of Koan Light-on-Dark/Dark-on-Light pottery can be observed together with the appearance of more refined painting techniques and a wider repertoire of shapes and motifs. Additionally, consumption patterns indicate a distinction between a restricted array of transport containers that traveled outside Kos and the majority of the shapes, which continued to be manufactured exclusively for the needs of the Koan community.

The shifts from the first to the second stage suggest an increasingly complex and specialized production system. The refined painting techniques and wider typological range indicate a closer knowledge of contemporary Minoan repertoires. These elements may also imply more direct exposure to potters trained in the Cretan tradition and the integration of a limited number of nonlocal peoples within the Koan community. The increased production of Koan Light-on-Dark/Dark-on-Light pottery suggests the intent of Koan elites to participate in the "new environment" determined by the economic and cultural expansion of Neopalatial Crete. In this respect, Koan Light-on-Dark/Dark-on-Light pottery served the twofold aim of promoting Minoan-type social practices at the "Serraglio" and contributing to the broad distribution of Koan goods along the Aegean maritime trade routes.

Making Sense of Changes in the Ceramic Assemblage at Phylakopi on Melos During the Late Bronze Age

Jason Earle, Institute for Aegean Prehistory

The 1974–1977 excavations at the site of Phylakopi on Melos revealed a lengthy series of stratified deposits spanning the Late Bronze Age. Diachronic study of the pottery from these levels presents a continuous picture of ceramic production and consumption on this Cycladic island, which can then be interpreted in light of the so-called phenomena of Minoanization and Mycenaeanization and used to illustrate the changing social and economic circumstances in the southern Aegean over five centuries.

This paper presents the results of my study of Late Bronze (LB) II–III pottery from trench PLa, located against the inner face of the city wall in the south-central sector of the town. Since Davis and Cherry have already published the LB I material, I follow their methodology and employ the same ware categories (with minor adjustments to facilitate analysis of a somewhat different ceramic assemblage).

After calculating the percentages of wares in each layer and documenting the number and type of decorative motifs, a number of important observations were made: mainland imports increase at the beginning of Late Helladic (LH) III (but still constitute a small percentage of the assemblage); few examples and a limited range of decorative motifs are identifiable; the frequency and range of motifs on local pottery dip notably in Late Cycladic (LC) IIIA–B; there is an increase in the frequency of goblets/kylikes at the transition from LC II to III; and there is a concomitant decrease in the frequency of conical cups over LC II–III.

From these observations we may conclude that the impact of Mycenaean ceramic styles and associated practices was strong but also tempered by the fact that local production of Mycenaean-style decorated wares did not really take root on Melos until the Postpalatial period (LH IIIC). Moreover, age-old potting traditions, including Minoanizing ones, were not discarded. These conclusions show that contrary to common belief, Minoanization and Mycenaeanization on Melos did not result in the complete displacement of local culture. Instead, there existed a dialectic between local potting traditions and foreign ceramic styles.

Cooking Up a New Model: Using Cooking Ware Vessels from Kalamianos to Identify Production and Exchange

Debra Trusty, Florida State University

Cooking ware vessels are widely understudied because of their lack of visual appeal compared with that of decorated fine ware vessels. Currently, no theoretical model exists that considers the potential that cooking ware vessels have for articulating the characteristics of political economies. In this paper, I present a new model that considers specific features of Bronze Age cooking ware assemblages (findspot, fabric qualities, vessels' functions, etc.). This model builds on hypotheses of craft production proposed by Costin, who established the concepts of context, scale, and intensity as characteristics of certain types of workshops, such as attached or independent production facilities. My model is also influenced by ideas of exchange, as outlined in publications by Galaty et al., Nakassis et al., and Parkinson et al., who closely examine issues of redistribution, reciprocity, and market exchange. The goal of my new model is to identify the vessels' mode of production and distribution, thereby enhancing our image of the ancient political economies of Mycenaean Greece and aiding us in recognizing the signs of elite interaction or involvement in craft production and trade.

In order to test this model I employ data from cooking ware vessels recovered from Kalamianos, a site that was discovered and surveyed by the Saronic Harbor Archaeological Research Project between 2007 and 2010. As part of my methodology I conducted morphological, petrographic, and chemical analyses on a substantial number of Late on 170 Late Helladic cooking ware vessels from the site that were found within and around many of the structures at Kalamianos. These data are presented as a part of this paper and then applied to my model to conclude that the Late Helladic cooking vessels from the site were products of part- and full-time individual potters from Aegina who distributed their goods to Kalamianos via market exchange.

Based on these conclusions, this model is informative and beneficial because it establishes a clear method for considering cooking ware vessels as separate objects instead of treating all ware types in the same manner. This model also encourages interdisciplinary research, combining morphological studies with scientific analyses like petrography. Finally, it opens the floor to new discussions about and considerations for the importance of cooking ware vessels to archaeological interpretation.

The Late Helladic Roofing Tiles from Eleon, Greece: Construction and Form
Kyle A. Jazwa, Monmouth College

Excavations at the site of Eleon in Greece revealed 516 fragments of ceramic roofing tiles dating to the Late Helladic IIIB and IIIC periods. This assemblage is larger than any collection of Mycenaean tiles published to date and includes the first securely dated, Postpalatial roofing tiles in Greece. In this paper, I present a preliminary study of the morphology of Eleon's roofing tiles. I also describe the evidence for the construction of both the cover and pan tiles. By comparing the reconstructed production sequences of these contemporary tiles, I reveal patterns of interaction among builders working in different palatial regions. This analysis also demonstrates continuity of local building knowledge at Eleon during the Postpalatial crisis.

Nearly complete cover and pan tiles were recovered in several deposits at Eleon, allowing for a reconstruction of the full dimensions and morphologies of both tile types. Variety among finer aspects of the morphology of Eleon's tiles indicates that there was not complete standardization at the site. All of the characteristic features found at Eleon, however, are also found among the tiles excavated elsewhere in Greece. As a result, variability in the form of the tiles was likely the norm at each settlement, and the noted differences among all the sites are not necessarily due to regional or site-specific peculiarities.

Despite the variability in the outward form of the tiles, there are generally consistent production techniques used for Eleon's tiles. A close examination of the surface treatments, impressions, finger marks, and cut marks reveals much of their *chaîne opératoires*, or construction sequences. In this paper, I also compare these sequences with those of contemporary Mycenaean tiles to consider the dissemination of technical knowledge among individuals living in distinct political entities. Additionally, a diachronic examination of the *chaîne opératoires* of Eleon's tiles illuminates the continuity of this building tradition from the Palatial to the Postpalatial period at the site.

Metal Allotments from the Palace: Tool Sets in Mycenaean Hoards

Nicholas G. Blackwell, North Carolina State University

Tools represent the most common object in metal hoard from the Aegean Bronze Age, yet they have been largely overlooked. Previous studies have focused primarily on the behavior of hoarding rather than the composition of the individual caches. With 22 extant second-millennium examples, Greek mainland hoards are notable for their contents, several of which exhibit a distinct tool pattern. Seven Mycenaean assemblages from diverse palatial contexts contain the same five implements: a double axe, a chisel with a broad cutting edge, a chisel with a narrow cutting edge, a knife, and a sickle. I argue that this is a standardized set of tools distributed by palaces to dependent craftsmen from Mycenae, Athens, Thebes, Orchomenos, and Anthedon.

Until now, the only evidence for the distribution of metal by the Mycenaean palaces has been the Jn and Ja Linear B tablets from Pylos. The Palace of Nestor annually dispersed allotments (*ta-ra-si-ja*) of metal to craftsmen for undetermined work purposes. Scholars have assumed that this *ta-ra-si-ja* metal system referred only to raw and/or scrap material, yet I propose that metal allotments could also include finished objects such as a kit of tools. The hoard data thus provide a window into the kinds of metal distributed by the palace. The Linear B texts from Knossos and Mycenae indeed testify that those palaces distributed non-metallic products (e.g., cloth, wheels) other than raw materials.

Six of the seven aforementioned hoards contain broken double axes, chisels, knives, and sickles in addition to complete examples. These fragmentary pieces retained a specific value related to palatial supervision. Rather than mere recyclable metal, these implements, despite their broken state, remained palatial property and needed to be returned to the palace. Such a system is indicated by one of the Pylian Linear B tablets, specifically Jn 829, which records the palace's retrieval of recyclable scrap. The Palace of Nestor thus chronicled both distribution and recovery of metals. Some of the Mycenaean hoards offer an analogous picture from a material based point of view.

The palatial hoards considered here reflect a system of allocation and collection of metal—including finished and broken tools—by Mycenaean officials. These archaeological data enhance the image presented by the Pylian records of palatial control over metallic objects and recyclable material.